JEWISH WOMEN
in
GRECO-ROMAN
PALESTINE

Jewish Women
in
Greco-Roman
Palestine

Tal Ilan

HENDRICKSON
PUBLISHERS

Hendrickson Publishers, Inc.
P. O. Box 3473
Peabody, Massachusetts 01961-3473

ISBN 1-56563-240-0

First printing — February 1996

Printed in the United States of America

Library of Congress Cataloging-in-Publication Data

Ilan, Tal.
    Jewish women in Greco-Roman Palestine :   an inquiry into image
and status   /   by Tal Ilan.
    Includes bibliographical references and index.
    ISBN 1-56563-240-0 (alk. paper)
    1. Women in Judaism.   2. Women in rabbinical literature.
3. Jewish women—Palestine—History.   4. Judaism—History—Post-
exilic period, 586 B.C.-210 A.D.   I. Title.
BM729.W6I43   1996
305.48'8924033—dc20   96-4367
                                                              CIP

Dedicated
to my teacher and mentor, the late Professor Menahem Stern
and to his widow Chava

Table of Contents

Preface

This book began its career as a Ph.D. dissertation in the Hebrew University of Jerusalem. Although it was written in the late 1980s, when feminism and women studies were making enormous strides in many disciplines the world over, working in Jerusalem was like working on another planet. The works of feminists were both unknown and viewed with suspicion as devoid of sound scientific methodology. The literature on the subject of women in the Greco-Roman period was not systematically collected by any of the libraries. Some of the most important books, such as Elisabeth Schüssler-Fiorenza's classic, *In Memory of Her*, on women in the New Testament, were not found in any library in the country.

I myself, I must admit, was not aware that I was writing feminist history. On the contrary, when accused of doing so, I defended myself, claiming that a history of women is not necessarily feminist history. I was doing *real* scientific work. My supervisors, colleagues and other well-wishers supported me in this claim. They were not about to be caught participating in subversive activity. Only a post-doctoral year at the Harvard Divinity School in the Women Studies in Religion Program, directed by Constance Buchanan, brought home to me the extent to which we were misinformed in Jerusalem about the nature of women studies, and of the use of gender as a category of analysis. It turns out that I had been writing feminist criticism all along.

I shall thus begin my record of thanks and acknowledgments at the end. In the academic year of 1992–3, while this book was in preparation, I spent a memorable year at Harvard exploring its libraries and acquainting myself with women studies. This was made possible by an affiliation with the Women Studies in Religion Program of the Divinity School, which provided both the funds and the facilities to make that year so fruitful. I would like to thank the director of the program Constance Buchanan for this rare opportunity, as well as Professor Bernadette Brooten, who introduced me to the program and to my colleagues Carol Delaney, Hyung-Kyung Chung, Stephanie Jamison and Rosalind Shaw who have helped me rethink my position by refusing to let my ignorance get the better·of me.

I first heard of women studies from Nancy Sinkof, whom I met as a student. She was an American Jew and a young student like me. Very recently we have been reunited, and I take the opportunity here to thank her for unwittingly influencing my life the way she has.

I chose as the supervisor to my Ph.D. the late Professor Menahem Stern, with whom I had worked in the past and admired greatly. I doubt if there is a living scholar of his stature in the field of Jewish history in the Greco-Roman period. However, Professor Stern was much more than a great scholar. He was the easiest-going helpful and friendly supervisor I could have hoped for, and I believe I would have written these words even had he lived to read them. Professor Stern was brutally murdered, an innocent victim of the Arab-Israeli conflict in which we are all involved in this part of the world. There are no words to express the loss which I suffered when he died, days before the first chapter of my Ph.D. was ready. This book is dedicated to him, and to his admirable widow, Chava, who was no doubt the model for the author of Proverbs when he wrote "A woman of courage who can find?"

Stern's place was taken by the important scholar I. Gafni. Gafni has read every word I wrote in this book with a magnifying glass, scrutinized every error and helped me greatly in bringing my work to the state it is now in. Gafni has also kindly written numerous letters of recommendation on my behalf and has spoken my praise often on his own initiative. I am grateful to be able to count him among my friends.

Sections of this book I discussed with various distinguished scholars. These include my friend Birgit Klein of Heidelberg and Professors Daniel Schwartz, Joseph Geiger and Hannah Cotton of Jerusalem. The latter has been particularly kind, reading the entire manuscript and making many useful comments. The final shape of this book and all errors found in it are, however, entirely my own.

As aptly put by Virginia Woolf in her admirable "A Room of One's Own," in order for a woman to be productive she needs both the physical space and the economic means. My Ph.D. dissertation could not have been completed without the help of various grants and awards which were bestowed on me. Twice, both in 1986–7 and in 1989–90, I received aid from the Memorial Foundation for Jewish Culture in New York. In 1987–8 I was fortunate to be nominated the first recipient of the Rosita and Esteban Herceg grant issued by the newly founded department of Gender Studies at the Hebrew University, and again, in 1990–1 I benefited from the Leifer Grant from the endowment of the Mexican women friends of the Hebrew University. I was also fortunate in 1989-90 to be nominated for the important Rachel Yanait Ben-Zvi grant issued by the Yad Ben Zvi center. Last but not least, in 1991 I won the Yaniv prize awarded by Tel Aviv University.

Every book needs a publisher. Most authors can tell long stories about their exasperating search for a publisher. In my case, my publisher found me. I am most deeply grateful to my friend and mentor Professor Martin Hengel of Tübingen University in Germany for this unexpected honor. Hengel has been generously reading my work, both in English and Hebrew, for the last ten years, and he believed in my academic abilities long before anyone else did, least of all me.

His decision to publish my Ph.D. in his TSAJ series is both a compliment and an honor. I also find it a great honor that his co-editor, Prof. Peter Schäfer of the Freie Universität, Berlin, has found my work worthy of publication. I have found the publishing house of J.C.B. Mohr both efficient and congenial and Herr Georg Siebeck with whom I corresponded very easy to get along with.

For a Hebrew Ph.D. to be published outside the borders of Israel it has to be translated into an international language. The translation of my Ph.D. was undertaken by Dr. Jonathan Price, whom I prize both as a great scholar and a great friend. If the English in this book sounds idiomatically correct, this is to be credited to Jonathan's sound no-nonsense style, which I admire in his own work and am proud to have added to mine, although I freely admit it is by far superior to the Hebrew original. For translations of rabbinic texts Jonathan consulted Danby's *Mishnah*, the Soncino *Babylonian Talmud* Neusner's *Tosefta* and *Talmud of the Land of Israel*, Hammar's *Sifre Deuteronomy*, Goldin's *ARNA* and Saldarini's *ARNB*. The final shape and style, however, are his own. He also consulted the RSV for the New Testament and *Apocrypha*. For the *Pseudepigrapha* Charlesworth edition was consulted.

The translation of this book was financed by another person I am proud to count among my friends. Joy Ungerleider-Mayerson, the chairperson of the Dorot Foundation, found time, despite her busy schedule, to invite me to her house, listen to my presentation and read the abstract to my work before recommending that money be appropriated for this purpose. I am exceedingly grateful to her for this. Sadly Joy died untimely before this book was completed.

Although I have extensively edited and also rewritten large section of this work in order to bring it into a book format, the study suffers, nevertheless, from idiosyncrasies inherent to a first book-length study and a Ph.D. thesis. I find it necessary to point out one of them here. I felt, when writing this Ph.D., that it was necessary for the reader to differentiate between works written by women, and others written by men. For this purpose I have devised a simple method, according to which women authors are cited by their full name while men are cited by initials only. This method has been maintained throughout the book, although I realize that it is not what can be described as politically correct.

Abbreviations of rabbinic literature are standard. In addition, *CII* is *Corpus Inscriptionum Iudaicarum* II, ed. J.-B. Frey (Rome 1952), and *CPJ* is *Corpus Papyrorum Judaicarum* I-III, edd. V. Tcherikover, A. Fuks and M. Stern (Cambridge, MA. 1957–64).

Jerusalem, February 1994   Tal Ilan

Introduction

The great interest that has recently developed for the history of women is the direct result of the prominence which feminism has attained in modern western society. There are many social currents in this movement which have turned historical studies into a partisan tool, to be used both as damning testimony of the extent of degradation, suffering and enslavement to which women have been subjected in the past, and as "proof" of women's true abilities, dignity and wisdom, and of their legacy. Pursuits of this nature are most properly termed metahistory, for even though they make use of historical sources and historiography, their main purpose is not actually to write history.

Yet there exists an inherent justification for writing the history of women separately from that of men (but not *vice versa*): much of what has been written as history *per se* is in fact the chronicle of only men's lives. This choice has been neither conscious nor willfully malicious. Normally the historian, when he came upon women in his sources, would document what they did and how they acted, and the mark they left on the historical record, but quite often, even in wide-ranging and comprehensive studies, these matters would occupy no more than one paragraph. The "golden age" of Athens may serve as a case in point. Literature was written during that period – poetry, philosophy and history – whose influence is felt to this day in western society, and fifth-century Athens is considered the only real democracy before the modern period. But in all of this extensive and important intellectual activity women took no part, nor did the vaunted democracy include women (or for that matter slaves or the many resident aliens in Athens). Naturally the historians of that glorious period have not neglected to mention, for example, the critical influence exercised on Pericles by his common-law wife Aspasia, nor have they failed to draw attention to the heroines of Attic tragedy – Antigone, Medea or Phaedra – but it is clear that this does not comprise the history of Athenian women at that time.[1]

One might argue, therefore, that since women's visible contribution in the sources for the period under study is so small, there is essentially no justification

---

[1] The question of the historicity of the portrayal of women in Attic drama stimulated scholarship already in the beginning of the twentieth century. See, e.g. A. W. Gomme, "The Position of Women in Athens in the Fifth and Fourth Centuries," *Classical Philology* 20 (1925), 1–25. For a summary of research: Sarah B. Pomeroy, *Goddesses, Whores, Wives and Slaves: Women in Classical Antiquity* (New York 1975), 58–60. See also Eva C. Keuls, *The Reign of the Phallus: Sexual Politics in Ancient Athens* (New York 1985), 329–48.

for writing their history separately, and we should be satisfied with what is said about them in books on general history. But by the same argument, if there is no justification for writing the history of half the human race, there would be much less justification for trying to compose the history of a people like the Moabites, who left no historical traditions; although no one disparages the attempt to bring to life the annals of this people by rooting around in the writings of other peoples (e.g. the Bible), by deciphering the ancient inscriptions which the Moabites did leave (e.g. the Mesha stele) or by explicating inanimate archaeological finds.[2] The history of Jewish women is certainly no less important an historical inquiry, focusing in identical manner on a group that produced no written sources of its own and must therefore be investigated by searching for and closely examining sources written by others but mentioning them, more often than not incidentally.

The History of Research

The history of Jewish women is not a new topic of study. In fact, it was not long after the publication of Graetz' monumental history of the Jewish people that the first historical survey of Jewish women appeared: *Die jüdischen Frauen in der Geschichte, Literatur und Kunst*, published in Leipzig in 1879. Its author was M. Kayserling, a rabbi who served primarily in Budapest and a Jewish historian whose principal interest was the Jews of Spain. His book covers a wide swath – from the Second Temple period to his own time – as was the custom for comprehensive historical studies in his day. Kayserling's motives for writing the book stemmed from the cultural climate of his own time, which was producing efforts at reform in religion and in the status of women. The proponents of the feminist movement were active already by the mid-nineteenth century, but the book shows no sign of either a pro- or an anti-feminist program.[3] In any event Kayserling's book laid the groundwork for future research on Jewish women. He was the first, for example, to compile a list of *Talmudic* women whose biographies he felt worth setting out (pp. 120–33). Even though this list, like much of the book, is more a paraphrase of material he assembled than a critical source-study, it nonetheless was important as a starting-point for subsequent scholarship which aimed to identify important women in literature.[4] Kayserling was

---

[2] For instance, A. H. van Zyl, *The Moabites=Pretoria Oriental Series* III (Leiden 1960).

[3] Kayserling was followed closely by H. Zirndorf, *Some Jewish Women* (Philadelphia 1892). Zirndorf was a German-born Reform rabbi who immigrated to the United States at the end of the last century.

[4] See the following lists: a) Zirndorf (previous note), 121–252; b) L. J. Swidler, *Women in Judaism: The Status of Women in Formative Judaism* (Metuchen NJ 1976), 105–11; c) S. Ben Chorin, *Mutter Mirjam: Maria in jüdischer Sicht* (München 1982), 98–9.

also the first, and for many years the only scholar to treat the prominent women in the New Testament as Jews.[5]

While Kayserling wrote from no ideological motive that I am able to discover, ideological tendencies do feature quite prominently in various works written immediately after his. Already in 1884, S.-I. Hurwitz published a series of articles on the subject of Jewish women in the journal *Hashahar*, which was edited by the learned intellectual Peretz Smolenskin. Hurwitz was a Jewish publicist, a *talmudist* by training, a great believer in the revival of the Hebrew language and a Zionist after his own fashion, although a stern opponent of Ahad Ha-am. His articles appeared in the context of a controversy over the character of the *Talmud*, stirred up by a book by A. McCaul published in England at the end of the 1830's[6] but not translated into Hebrew, under the title נתיבות עולם, until the 1870's. In his work, McCaul argues that the *Talmud* is an inferior, debased composition which by no means represents the noble character of Judaism. McCaul was a philo-Semitic Christian who held millenarian views, and his book was translated into Hebrew probably because it openly served the purposes of religious reform movements within Judaism. As part of his indictment, McCaul claimed that the *Talmud* places the woman in a position equivalent to that of a slave (pp. 24–9, 494–503). Hurwitz took upon himself the defense of women's status in Judaism against this attack. In his first article, "R. Eliezer ben Hyrcanus and the Education of Women,"[7] Hurwitz maintained that R. Eliezer is the only one in the entire *talmudic* corpus who disapproves of the instruction of *Torah* to women, and that he had a personal reason for this view, namely, his experience with his learned but wicked wife, Imma Shalom, which convinced him that women should be barred from study. Using the same principle, Hurwitz attempted to prove in another article – "R. Aqiba and the Laws of Matrimony in Israel" – that R. Aqiba favored giving women freedom, education and respect because he was married, as is well-known, to an exemplary woman.[8] In 1891, Hurwitz brought his defen-

---

[5] Kayserling, 47–8; perhaps this is why Zirndorf (144) thought Kayserling was a Christian. Since then, additional surveys of Jewish women of all periods have appeared, usually written by women. These treatments are by and large impressionistic and do not pretend to reach the scholarly standard set by Kayserling. See, e.g. Trude Weiss-Rosemarine, *Jewish Women Through the Ages* (New York 1940); Greta Fink, *Great Jewish Women: Profiles of Courageous Women from the Maccabean Period to the Present* (New York 1978); Sondra Henry and Emily Taitz, *Written Out of History: Our Jewish Foremothers* (Fresh Meadows NY 1983).

[6] A. McCaul, *The Old Paths* (London 1837).

[7] *Hashahar* 11 (1884), 437–41 [Hebrew]. The hostile response by the editor, Peretz Smolenskin, appears immediately following this piece (pp. 441–4).

[8] *Hashahar* 12 (1884), 377–84, 423–33 [Hebrew]. But see the response by A. Atlas, *Ha-asif* 2 (1886), 365–7 [Hebrew]. Atlas was a vociferous anti-Zionist who served as deputy to the editor of *Ha-asif*, Nahum Sokolow. Atlas demonstrated that most of Hurwitz's claims are not supported by a critical reading of the sources; he claimed that R. Ishmael, R.

se of the *Talmud*'s treatment of women to a conclusion with the publication of
*The Hebrew Woman and the Jewess: The Status and Condition of Women in Isra-
el in Family and Society during Biblical and Talmudic Times* (Berditchev). In
this work Hurwitz argued that Moses in the *Torah* considerably improved the
status of the Hebrew woman by reducing much of the father's authority as *pater-
familias (sic!)*, and that those aspects of the woman's status not ameliorated by
Moses were improved by the sages of the *Talmud*: thus a woman's status improved continuously from the biblical to the *talmudic* periods. It is worth noting,
especially in the light of the following discussion, that Hurwitz displayed impressive learning in his various writings, which contained references to previous
scholarship such as Kayserling's book. Hurwitz's critical test in every case was
to ask whether a measure was good or bad for women and whether in a given historical period women's status was better or worse than in the previous or following period. This approach is prevalent to this very day in the study of the history
of Jewish women.

Gershon Stern, a German-Jewish author who immigrated to Israel from Berlin
in 1939, published an article in 1913, "Women in the Bible and the *Aggadah*," in
Ha-shiloah – the Zionist journal first edited by Ahad Ha-am.[9] Stern adopted an
approach directly opposed to Hurwitz': like McCaul, he viewed the literature of
the sages as artificial and distorted. At the same time, his approach revealed a
decidedly romantic strain in its treatment of the Bible as an authentic and living
creation. In his article Stern surveyed the development of the status of women
from the biblical to the *talmudic* period as reflected in the *aggadic* traditions and
concluded that, whereas in the Bible women appear to lead liberated and easy
lives, *talmudic* literature conveys a picture of their oppression and humiliation. In
the latter source (according to Stern), the sole purpose of women's existence is to
enable men to fulfill certain commandments, above all the commandment to "be
fruitful and multiply." This change in the picture presented by the sources, Stern
continued, is connected to a transformation of Judaism from a religion which
emphasized belief to one which emphasized active fulfillment of commandments. Stern's article reflects the controversy between Jewish religious reform
movements of the time and the more conservative currents in Judaism which regarded the Bible merely as a prism through which *talmudic* interpretation was

---

Aqiba's rival in *halakhic* matters, deserves the credit, if anyone does, for his teachings regarding women, which are often in direct opposition to those of R. Aqiba. My opinion,
based on a close reading of the *midrashei halakhah* of both schools, is that the school of R.
Ishmael was far more interested in the condition of women, even if one is to judge only
from the sheer bulk of relevant material. The controversy between Hurwitz and Atlas clearly derives from the interpretation of the terms "good" and "bad," and of what is good and
bad for women. See further by Hurwitz, "Maimonides and the Laws of Matrimony in
Israel," *Hashahar* 11 (1883), 659–66; 12 (1884), 577–80 [Hebrew].

[9] When this article was published the journal's editor was J. Klausner.

focused. A decisive answer has not yet been found to the question raised by Hurwitz and Stern – and probably never will be, as I shall now demonstrate.

In his great work, *A Social and Religious History of the Jews* (1952), Salo Baron devoted a chapter to the status of women in the Second Temple, *mishnaic* and *talmudic* periods.[10] Baron agreed that the status of women improved from the biblical to the *talmudic* periods, and he based his argument almost wholly on *halakhic* material, at the expense of the *aggadic*. Yet it was not necessarily the sources which dictated the conclusions, since this had been the practice followed earlier by S. Zucrow in his book, *Women, Slaves and the Ignorant in Rabbinic Literature* (Boston 1932), but Zucrow had reached conclusions which were the polar opposite of Baron's, arguing that the status of women in the *talmudic* period was far worse than in the time of the Bible.

Feminist theological literature burgeoned in the early 1970s when women joined the controversy which Hurwitz had begun. Yet despite the common feminist thread in their various writings, even women scholars could not agree on how to interpret the sources. Judith Hauptman, after a thorough examination of rabbinic law in three areas – the *sotah* or suspected adulteress, inheritance by women and divorce – was able to find a steady improvement in legislation concerning women.[11] On the other side, Léonie Archer took up Stern's thesis and argued, in two articles stemming from her dissertation, that principally *aggadic* sources from the Second Temple period and afterwards, above all the *Apocrypha* and *Pseudepigrapha* indicate on the whole a considerable deterioration in women's status.[12]

Yet this discussion seems to be less a debate than a dialogue of the deaf, for none of the authors seems to have read, or at least has bothered to acknowledge, previous voices in the debate. Consequently one might question whether this entire discussion holds any value for the serious researcher: for a hundred years men and women have investigated the same problem and, basing themselves on the same sources, have reached diametrically opposite conclusions. Furthermore, there is no pattern to serve as a guide: the women do not as a group reach conclusions opposite from the men's, and the sources have not themselves dictated the conclusions of each side; even the periods in which the different adversaries lived did not decisively influence their conclusions. All this goes to

---

[10] S. Baron, *A Social and Religious History of the Jews* II (New York 1952), 235–41.

[11] Judith Hauptman, "Women's Liberation in the *Talmudic* Period: An Assessment," *Conservative Judaism* 26/4 (1971–2), 22–8. Hauptman teaches *Talmud* in the Jewish Theological Seminary in New York, and the editors of the journal noted her political involvement as a feminist. This article, despite its scholarly style and apparatus, nonetheless reveals a clear apologetic purpose in its effort to demonstrate how women's status can be improved within the framework of the *halakhah,* not by rejection of it.

[12] "The Role of Jewish Women in the Religion, Ritual and Cult of Greco-Roman Palestine," in *Images of Women in Antiquity*, edd. Averil Cameron and Amélie Kuhrt (Detroit 1985), 273–87; "The 'Evil Woman' in *Apocryphal* and *Pseudepigraphical* Writings," *Proceedings of the Ninth World Congress of Jewish Studies*, Div. A (Jerusalem 1986), 239–46.

show that the terms "improvement" and "deterioration" are not relevant to the question of women's status and condition. It appears, therefore, that the role of the historian is to describe changes and developments without making value judgments.[13]

But in fact, feminist literature from its inception has been marked by the tendency to praise or upbraid societies and groups solely on the basis of their treatment of women. As the feminist movement gained form and momentum at the end of the nineteenth century, there appeared a book on the status of women in Judaism by Nehida Remy (Ruth Lazarus), a woman of German-Prussian background who had converted to Judaism and married the Jewish thinker Moritz Lazarus.[14] In her book she tried to demonstrate the positive attitude accorded to Jewish women in history and *halakhah*, and, by contrast, the degraded and inferior position of their Christian sisters. The book has no scholarly pretensions, and despite Lazarus' attempt to base her claims on the sources she obviously knew very little about Christianity and even less about the Judaism which she had just adopted. Even so, her book was a pioneering work in the controversy between Judaism and Christianity, a controversy of decisive importance in any study of the status of women in the Second Temple period. The study of this subject, in fact, serves as a kind of special yardstick for religious feminist movements, Christian as well as Jewish, for late antiquity was the formative period when rules and laws were decided which have shaped both Christian and Jewish religious communities to the present day, including also the determination of women's position in church and synagogue. Thus the study of this period can serve (and has served) to defend the current attitude towards women in Jewish and Christian institutions today, or by the same token to overturn the foundations on which those institutions rest.

The Christian feminist theological movement realized its first-fruits in the great work of Elizabeth Cady-Stanton, *The Woman's Bible*, which was published between 1895 and 1898 in the United States. This work, which represented a stage in women's struggle for equal rights, launched a strong attack against both the Jewish and the Christian scriptures, which Cady-Stanton criticized, stating (p. 12): "I do not believe that any man ever saw or talked with God, I do not believe that God inspired the Mosaic code or told the historians what they say he did about women." The work caused a public uproar and did not gain many admirers. Nearly a century had to pass until Christians, men and women alike, dealt seriously again with the problem of the attitude of their own Scriptures towards

---

[13] Pomeroy's formulation stands in no need of improvement (above, n. 1, 229): "To compose a polemic against the men of Greece and Rome and to write a brief in defense of their women are not the proper objectives of an historian. "

[14] *Das jüdische Weib* (Leipzig 1885); Remy's book was translated into English: Nahida Remy, *The Jewish Woman* (Cincinnati 1897).

women, and when this happened the effort arose within the church itself. This long delay[15] can be partially explained by the fact that the modern battle over equal rights for women could be waged in legislative assemblies and decided by majority vote, without recourse to religious texts, especially in light of the separation between church and state recognized in those same legislatures.

In the intervening period, between the appearance of Cady-Stanton's work and the 1970s, early Christianity's attitude toward women attracted the attention of a completely different group of scholars, namely classicists and ancient historians. Their work, in turn, created a new confrontation between feminism and Judaism, as the following two works will illustrate. In 1914, the Harvard professor A. Hecker published *A Short History of Women's Rights* (New York) in order to advance the cause of equal rights for women, of which he was an enthusiastic advocate. In the work he purported to trace a steady advancement within Roman law towards the granting of more freedoms and rights to women,[16] and a sharp reversal in this progress when the Roman Empire became Christian and consequently introduced severe impediments to women. Christianity, he claimed, had learned its antagonistic and degrading attitude towards women from its parent, Judaism with its corrupting oriental character[17] – for in Hecker's eyes the East represented degeneracy and backwardness, both in antiquity and in his own time.

Similarly, in 1956 C. Seltman, an established Classics professor at Cambridge University, published his *Women in Antiquity* (London) with the purpose of extolling the liberties and sexual freedom enjoyed by women in the classical world, especially in Sparta,[18] but even in Athens[19] and by all means in Rome,[20] in contrast to the oppression they suffered under Pauline Christianity, which had perforce adopted the benighted principles of Judaism.[21] Seltman's book was the product of his classical education in the conservative English tradition, and his anti-Christian posture can be explained accordingly. His motives are revealed not only in his open hostility to Christianity, but also in the praises he lavishes on the classical world in matters for which a sober examination of the facts would hardly justify such praise, for instance the Athenian attitude towards women.[22]

---

[15] Particularly conspicuous in the detailed survey of feminist Christian theology in Elisabeth Schüssler-Fiorenza, *In Memory of Her: A Feminist Theological Reconstruction of Christian Origins* (New York 1983), 7–14. Cady-Stanton's work is followed immediately by articles from the 1970s.

[16] Hecker, 1–49.

[17] *Ibid.* 53–7.

[18] Seltman, 55–72.

[19] *Ibid.* 94–101.

[20] *Ibid.* 136–46.

[21] *Ibid.* 149–51.

[22] See Pomeroy (above, n. 1); although Pomeroy's book reflects the growing influence of feminism in the 1970s, she wrote a creditably balanced work; yet her subject was in any

His picture of women in classical Greece resembles rather the fantasy of a modern atheist than the historical reality he purports to describe.

The question of whether Judaism has adversely influenced the Hellenistic gentiles in their attitude to women or vice versa has also been taken up lately by Jewish feminist apologists, who of course make claims exactly the opposite of Seltman's and Hecker's. In 1987 T. Friedman wrote an article asserting, like some of his predecessors, that women's position had indeed deteriorated between the biblical and *talmudic* periods, but that this was the direct result of the arrival of Hellenism in the region.[23] In 1991, another article appeared which made a similar claim with regard to Philo. Philo is universally recognized as holding a very low opinion of women.[24] Judith Wegner approached Philo's attitude by inquiring whether it was to be attributed to his Jewish or his Hellenistic background and decided that it was certainly to be blamed on the latter.[25] However, both Friedman and Wegner seem to be under the impression that Hellenism was monolithic in its attitude to women, which is exemplified by the Athenian model.[26] But it should be remembered that after Alexander the Great conquered the East and Judaism began showing signs of Hellenistic cultural influence, it was not the culture of classical Athens but that of cosmopolitan Hellenistic Macedonian society – which accorded women a completely different status – that was predominant.[27] Hence there is no single answer to the question, whether Judaism via Christianity detrimentally influenced the way women were treated in the classical world, or whether the Hellenism of the classical world detrimentally influenced the treatment of women in Judaism; in fact every proffered answer responds less to a historical problem than to the predisposition of its author.

At the beginning of this century, Christian theologians adopted a different approach to the question of women's status in antiquity. Serious German theologians had long ago noted the prominence of women in the early Christian church.[28] In an attempt to answer the question, why Christianity attracted wo-

---

case less sensitive than the subjects dealt with here. For a discussion centering on Athens, see Keuls (above, n. 1).

[23] "The Shifting Role of Women From Bible to *Talmud*," *Judaism* 36 (1987), 479–87.

[24] See R. A. Baer, *Philo's Use of the Categories Male and Female* (Leiden 1970); Judith R. Wegner, "The Images of Women in Philo," *Society of Biblical Literature Seminar Papers* 16 (1982), 551–63; Dorothy Sly, *Philo's Perception of Women* = *Brown Judaic Studies* CCIX (Atlanta 1990).

[25] Judith R. Wegner, "Philo's Portrayal of Women – Hebraic or Hellenic?" in *'Women Like This': New Perspectives on Jewish Women in the Greco-Roman Period*, ed. Amy-Jill Levine (Atlanta 1991), 41–66.

[26] See above, n. 22.

[27] See Sarah B. Pomeroy, "τεχνικαὶ; καὶ; μουσικαί: The Education of Women in the Fourth Century and the Hellenistic Period," *American Journal of Ancient History* 2 (1977), 51–68; *eadem. Women in Hellenistic Egypt from Alexander to Cleopatra* (New York 1984).

[28] See in particular A. von-Harnack's chapter, "The Spread of Christianity Among

men, they turned to review the position of women in antiquity. The German theologian Joachim Jeremias, in a learned appendix to his book, *Jerusalem zur Zeit Jesu* (Leipzig 1923),[29] painted a gloomy picture of the degradation and oppression which he saw as the lot of Jewish women in Jesus' time. Jesus is presented against this background as one who came to redeem Jewish women from their anguish and suffering.

But Christian theologians began to put their own house in order only when modern feminist theology began to catch hold at the end of the 1960s. In accordance with the general feminist demand for equal rights and opportunities, women struggled within the church, especially the Protestant church in all its forms, to fill offices traditionally held by men. This struggle, however, remained internal and in no way resembled women's battle for political equality which had begun a hundred years earlier, for in the religious arena every new step must be justified, directly or indirectly, through Scripture.[30] The criticism leveled by Hecker and Seltman against the church's treatment of women began to be sounded within the church itself, yet with a major difference: women who had been brought up and trained as Christians and were hoping to win central roles within the church could not indict the founders of Christianity for antagonism towards women; thus they launched a concerted effort to prove that Jesus sympathized with and cherished women and wished to establish equality between the sexes, but that the church as an institution had adopted a mistaken interpretation of Jesus' teachings and above all of Paul's doctrine, which had led to the present inferior status of women within the church.

R. Scroggs in 1972 and W. Meeks in 1974 each wrote an article defending Paul's attitude towards women and trying to absolve him from responsibility for the church's negative treatment of women.[31] For our purposes the value of this debate in its early stages lies in a future development, namely that the effort to

---

Women," in his *The Mission and Expansion of Christianity in the First Three Centuries* (New York 1908), 64–84 (the book was first published in German in 1902).

[29] This appendix (pp. 232–50) is an excellent example of Jeremias' use of Jewish sources. The book has been translated into English (1969), in which edition the appendix is on pp. 359–76.

[30] See, e.g. K. Stendahl, *The Bible and the Role of Women* (Philadelphia 1966), which dealt with this question just when the battle was starting.

[31] R. Scroggs, "Paul and the Eschatological Woman," *Journal of the American Academy of Religion* 40 (1972), 283–303. A response to this article was written by a woman: Elaine H. Pagels, "Paul and Women: A Response to a Recent Discussion," *ibid.* 42 (1974), 538–49. W. Meeks, "The Image of the Androgyne: Some Uses of a Symbol in Earliest Christianity," *History of Religions* 13 (1973–4), 165–208. This article was also answered by a woman: Averil Cameron, "'Neither Male nor Female'," *Greece and Rome* 27 (1980), 60–8. A discussion of the literature on Paul's attitude toward women could fill an entire book. It will suffice here to say that Christians to this day, both men and women, battle constantly over the question of whether Paul was good or bad for women. I shall restrict myself here to mentioning only two quite recent publications on the issue, both written by feminist wo-

clear the founders of Christianity of any hostility towards women meant that the
blame would soon be made to fall on others.

As the debate gathered momentum the number of articles on this subject and
on early Christianity in general grew geometrically. In 1974 a collection of articles was published[32] dealing with women in the early Christian church and Judaism. It is apparent from this volume that the lines sketched out by Jeremias in
his appendix (see above) now supplied the conceptual framework in which
Christian feminist theology, in its search for a new scapegoat, would develop.
One need only compare, for example, the piece in that collection by Constance
Parvey – "The Theology and Leadership of Women in the New Testament" –
which traces an improvement in women's status in early Christianity against the
background of its Jewish origins, with the contribution by Bernard Prusak –
"Women, Seductive Siren and Source of Sin? *Pseudepigraphical* Myth and
Christian Origin" – which explains the image of the evil and dangerous seduc-
tress as the product of the Jewish *Pseudepigrapha* of the Second Temple period.

By the mid-1970s, the battle by Protestant feminist theologians was turning
out well, as they were beginning to join faculties of theology as well as taking
their place in church pulpits. Catholic women had yet to achieve similar success.
In the vanguard of their struggle stood the American Catholic theologian
Leonard J. Swidler, who in 1976 published *Women in Judaism: The Status of
Women in Formative Judaism* (Metuchen NJ), which purports to present serious,
objective historical research on the status of women at the end of the Second
Temple period and in the *mishnaic* and *talmudic* periods. Swidler managed to
create the impression that he was as conversant with the Jewish sources as Jeremias had been, and his thesis was remarkably similar to the one argued by Jeremias fifty years earlier. In fact, however, Swidler seems merely to have stitched
together two previous studies: Meeks' article,[33] on which Swidler relied to des-

---

men, one claiming that Paul was exceptionally good for women, the other claiming just the
opposite: pro-Pauline: Lilian Portefaix, *Sisters Rejoice: Paul's Letter to the Philippians and
Luke-Acts as Seen by First Century Philippian Women = Coniectanea Biblica: New Testament Series* XX (Stockholm 1988). Anti-Pauline: Antoinette C. Wire, *The Corinthian Women Prophets: A Reconstruction through Paul's Rhetoric* (Minneapolis 1990).

[32] Rosemary R. Ruether, ed. *Religion and Sexism: Images of Women in the Jewish and
Christian Traditions* (New York). Several journals also provided a forum for feminist theological discussions. In honor of the Year of the Woman in 1975, *Theological Studies* gave
an entire issue over to feminist scholars. *Evangelische Theologie* did much the same thing
in an issue of 1982, and in that same year *Journal for the Study of the Old Testament* devoted an entire issue to the subject of women in the Bible. Since the early 1980s the field
has grown beyond recognition and it is pointless to attempt to outline a full bibliography. It
will suffice to mention that in 1985, *The Journal of Feminist Studies in Religion* published
its first issue. A glance at the 1992 Abstracts of the Society of Biblical Literature Conference in San Francisco reveals how important the study of women has become in these
fields.

[33] Above, n. 31.

cribe the classical world as the proper setting for "formative Judaism," and the appendix in Jeremias' book, which provided Swidler with source material for his entire book. According to Swidler, in Judaism's formative period it is impossible to find even one bright spot in the status of women, as it is reflected in the *Mishnah* and *Talmud*.

Swidler's second book, *Biblical Affirmations of Women* (Philadelphia 1979), illuminates essentially why the first book was written. This second work surveys the attitudes of the Hebrew Bible and the New Testament towards women, categorizing these attitudes as "positive," "ambivalent" and "negative," and directs the reader to the conclusion that Jesus had a positive attitude toward women whereas that of the Hebrew Bible was negative or at best ambivalent.[34]

Despite the scientific clothing in which Christian feminist works have been robed since the beginning of the 1970s, their basic purpose has been apologetic: Christianity grew up against the background of, and represented a feminist rebellion against, Jewish misogyny; Christianity's every positive or egalitarian attitude toward women is attributable to Jesus himself, and every hostile element has its source in Christianity's natural parent, Judaism.

The Jewish feminist movement did not long remain silent in the face of this attack. In 1980, the American Jewish feminist periodical *Lilith* published articles and interviews by two feminist thinkers, Judith Plaskow and Annette Daum.[35] In her article, Plaskow demonstrated that the Christian feminist movement was using anti-Semitic arguments to further its own cause, and lambasted the bankrupt methods used by feminist historians such as Swidler.[36]

---

[34] Other books on women in the New Testament published since the 1970s include: W. P. Barker, *Women and the Liberator* (Old Tappan NJ 1972); Alicia C. Faxon, *Women and Jesus* (Philadelphia 1973); Lisa Sergio, *Jesus and Woman* (McLean VA 1975); Rachel C. Wahlberg, *Jesus and the Freed Woman* (New York 1978); Evelyn and Frank Stagg, *Women in the World of Jesus* (Philadelphia 1978); Elisabeth Moltmann-Wendel, *The Women Around Jesus* (New York 1982); Shirley Stephens, *A New Testament View of Women* (Nashville 1980); E. Modersohn, *Die Frauen des Neuen Testaments* (Stuttgart 1982); France Quere, *Les Femmes de l'Evangile* (Paris 1982); Faye Field, *Women Who Encountered Jesus* (Nashville 1982); A. F. Ide, *The Teachings of Jesus on Women* (Dallas 1984); T. J. Carlisle, *Beginning with Mary: Women of the Gospel in Portraits* (Grand Rapids 1986); Adrienne von-Speyr, *Three Women and the Lord* (San Francisco 1986); Marla L. Selvidge, *Daughters of Jerusalem* (Scottdale PA 1987); Lesly F. Massey, *Women and the New Testament* (Jefferson NC 1989); W. D. Watley and Suzan D. J. Cook, *Preaching in Two Voices: Sermons on the Women in Jesus' Life* (Valley Forge PA 1992).

[35] Judith Plaskow, "Blaming the Jews for Inventing Patriarchy," *Lilith* 7 (1980), 11–2; Annette Daum, "Blaming the Jews for the Death of the Goddess," *ibid.* 12–3. And see more recently, Susannah Heschel, "Anti-Judaism in Christian Feminist Theology," *Tikkun* 5/3 (1990), 25–8, 92–5.

[36] In her piece, Daum's target was the anti-Christian feminist movement, which she also accused of anti-Semitism in its argument that Judaism, the first truly patriarchal religion, was responsible for the extinction of the polytheistic religions in which female

Plaskow's remarks fell on fertile ground. In the 1980s, Christian feminist literature produced by such women theologians as Elisabeth Schüssler-Fiorenza and Bernadette Brooten blazed new paths for research on Jewish women, professedly avoiding the lines of argument set out by Jeremias and Swidler. Schüssler-Fiorenza, in the fourth chapter of her book *In Memory of Her*, described "The Jesus Movement as a Renewal Movement Within Judaism,"[37] that is (in direct reference to Plaskow), Jesus' movement as essentially Jewish. But it was precisely this claim which led her into the same trap into which others had fallen. For she tries to prove that the Gospels (written by both Jews and Gentiles) took pains to belittle the value of women, purposely presenting in a negative light the positive remarks Jesus made as a Jew because they remained products of the same patriarchal society, which Jesus rejected. Furthermore, she claimed that by close analysis one may strip off the accretions in the Christian Scriptures and lay bare Jesus' actual teachings which, once uncovered, reveal an essential feminism; and this, Jesus' true feminist message, is the only thing that will enable the Christian feminist movement to achieve its ends. Thus it is axiomatic for Schüssler-Fiorenza that the "patriarchal and androcentric" Scriptures have a feminist core which is unique to Jesus and obviously did not come to him through his Jewish heritage. In the end, therefore, Schüssler-Fiorenza makes the same claims as her predecessors, only in a far more sophisticated and learned fashion.[38]

Yet in 1984, right after the appearance of Schüssler-Fiorenza's book, Ben Witherington III published *Women in the Ministry of Jesus* (Cambridge), which demonstrated that even in this feminist age there are still those who believe that Jesus' main message in regard to women was not feminist. Witherington argued that Jesus aspired to teach all humanity to love and respect all creatures, even the humblest, but not to disturb the patriarchal social order.

Brooten published her doctoral dissertation, *Women Leaders in the Ancient Synagogue: Inscriptional Evidence and Background Issues*, in 1982. Without the knowledge that Brooten is Christian, and without acquaintance with Brooten's other feminist studies which reveal a Christian theological back-

---

deities played a central role alongside the male divinities. In this connection it is worth noting two additional debates which were revived by feminists, but remain peripheral to serious historical discussion: 1. The question of prehistoric matriarchy and whether any traces of it remain in Judaism: V. Aptowitzer, "Spuren des Matriarchats in jüdischen Schrifttum," *Hebrew Union College Annual* 4 (1927), 207–40 and 5 (1928), 261–97; M. Kartanger, "Spuren und Reste des Matriarchats in Judentum," *Zeitschrift für Religions- und Geistesgeschichte* 29 (1977), 134–51. 2. A different question is the degree of femininity represented in the image of the Jewish divinity, on which see, R. Patai, *The Hebrew Goddess* (New York 1967); Maryanne Cline-Horowitz, "The Image of God in Man: Is Woman Included?" *Harvard Theological Review* 72 (1979), 175–206.

[37] Above, n. 15, 105–59.

[38] As has already been noted by Ross S. Kraemer in her review of Schüssler-Fiorenza's book: *Religious Studies Review* 11 (1985), 6–9.

ground,[39] one might think that the dissertation was the product of the Jewish feminist movement, struggling to win for women rabbinical positions in the synagogue. And indeed, the effect of Brooten's work has been felt in Jewish feminist circles.

In 1985, Brooten published a programmatic article on the methods for studying the history of women in the ancient world, particularly in early Christianity and in Judaism of the same time.[40] She argued that the Jewish world in the Hellenistic-Roman period was part of the larger classical world, and that the standard question regarding Judaism and Christianity, whether one was a good or bad influence on the other, is not at all relevant. Christianity, she claimed, is not the antithesis of Judaism, but a branch, and every innovation within Christianity regarding the status of women, or any other matter, has Judaism as its source. Brooten's work is a counterweight to the books and articles written by Christian feminists during the 1970s; she initiated the serious attempt, continued by other scholars, to avoid imposing value judgments on ancient sources, and pointed the way to a history of women based on what can actually be found in the sources and on a fresh perspective which the feminist movement would certainly inform but not entirely dictate. Brooten has repeatedly stressed the indispensability of essential skills, such as the ability to read sources in their original language, as well as close acquaintance with the substance and methods of scientific research. At the same time, she has emphatically adhered to feminist interpretations and has openly admitted that she does not purpose to write objective history, which, according to her method, is something which does not exist and never has: not extraterrestrial creatures but human beings have written human history, and by the same token the history of Christianity has been written by Christians, just as Jewish history has been written by Jews. Christians have indeed tried their hand at Jewish history, but their distance from the subject has guaranteed neither a better history nor, certainly, approval by Jews of such attempts.[41] Nevertheless,

---

[39] Bernadette J. Brooten, "Junia ... Outstanding Among the Apostles (*Romans* 16:7)," in *Women Priests: A Catholic Commentary on the Vatican Declaration*, edd. L. J. and Arlene Swidler (New York 1977), 141–4; *eadem.* "Konnten Frauen im alten Judentum die Scheidung betreiben? Überlegung zu *Mk* 10, 11–12 und *1Kor* 7, 10–11," *Evangelische Theologie* 42 (1982), 65–80; *eadem.* "Paul's Views on the Nature of Women and Female Homoeroticism," in *Immaculate and Powerful: The Female in Sacred Image and Social Reality*, edd. Clarissa W. Atkinson, Constance H. Buchanan and Margaret R. Miles (Boston 1985), 61–87; *eadem.* "Paul and the Law: How Complete was the Departure?" *The Princeton Seminary Bulletin Supplementary Issue* 1 (1990), 71–89.

[40] "Early Christian Women and their Cultural Context: Issues of Method in Historical Reconstruction," in *Feminist Perspectives on Biblical Scholarship*, ed. Adela Yarbro Collins (Chico CA 1985), 65–91.

[41] For more on Schüssler-Fiorenza and Brooten and their contribution to feminist research, see Anni L. Millhaven, *13 Valiant Women Challenging the Church* (Mystic CT 1987), 43–63, 173–93.

the debate between Jews and Christians on whether ancient Judaism or early Christianity was better for women has not yet run its course. A new book by Daniel Boyarin, who identifies himself as both a feminist and an orthodox, rabbinic Jew, sets out to demonstrate from rabbinic texts that Judaism on the whole viewed women and womanhood much more favorably than Christianity.[42] Boyarin's book, it is true, incorporates the new sophistication which feminist studies have achieved in the late 1980s and 1990s, centering on complex theoretical issues and extensive interdisciplinary research; but in the final analysis this book has not advanced beyond its predecessors in its assumptions about the objectives of women studies. Furthermore, Boyarin makes the unfortunate mistake of equating a positive attitude to sex in Judaism with a positive attitude to women.

Primarily in America, a Jewish feminist theological movement sprang up in the wake of its Christian predecessor. Just as the latter had previously won pulpits for women in the church, the Jewish movement aimed at winning rabbinical positions for women in the synagogue, but it had first to fight for more basic principles, such as the right to be included in the *minyan* or to be called up to read the *Torah*. Like its Christian counterpart, the Jewish movement sought a religious justification of its goal in a particular reading of the canonical sources – the *Mishnah* and *Talmud* – which, like the New Testament, are used as historical documents in the present study. The struggle began within the Jewish Reform movement, and after success in those quarters it moved on to the Conservative movement, and in America it has reached even Orthodox circles.[43]

The question has existed for some time as an academic issue, for it was debated on a purely theoretical basis by Conservative Jews already in 1922.[44] However, the first work to deal with the question of women's roles in the synagogue in the age of feminism was written in 1966 by an English rabbi, R. Loewe, and was in fact not feminist at all. In response to a request by the Anglican church, which was at that time immersed in its own battle with women over the priesthood, Loewe produced *The Position of Jewish Women in Judaism* (London), in which he maintained that Judaism assigned women certain defined roles which were substantially different from those of men, and that consequently a woman's participation in a *minyan* or her reading from the *Torah*, or most emphatically her ordination as a rabbi, were all inconceivable. Naturally Loewe anchored his views in the rabbinic sources.

---

[42] D. Boyarin, *Carnal Israel: Reading Sex in Talmudic Culture* (Berkeley 1993).

[43] See, e.g. Blu Greenberg, "Will There be Orthodox Women Rabbis?" *Judaism* 33 (1984), 23–33.

[44] See. J. Z. Lauterbach, "Responsum on Question, Shall Women be Ordained Rabbis?" *Central Conference of American Rabbis Year Book* 32 (1922), 156–62, who opposes the idea based on an appeal to Jewish tradition. A negative response to his presentation is found *ibid.* 163–77.

Study of this subject followed pretty much the same path among Jewish authors as it had among Christians. Non-scholarly articles written by both men and women contradicting Loewe's claims began appearing in Jewish periodicals in the 1970s; they tried to show that in almost every instance in which Loewe cited a definitive legal ruling, a minority opinion had ruled the opposite.[45] The debate reached Jewish scholarly circles in 1979, when J.B. Segal published the article, "The Jewish Attitude Towards Women," in the *Journal of Jewish Studies*. This piece, like so many of its scholarly predecessors, evaluated Judaism's attitude to woman as simply "good" or "bad". In 1973 the Jewish periodical *Response* (no. 18) devoted an entire volume to the issue of Jewish women and in 1976, there appeared a Jewish feminist anthology, *The Jewish Woman* (New York), edited by Elizabeth Koltun.[46]

Orthodox Judaism responded in 1978 and 1979 with the publication of two books by American rabbis. Their approaches were different – M. Meiselman, in *Jewish Women in Jewish Law* (New York), took seriously the challenge posed by the articles published earlier in the decade, whereas S. Appleman, in his *The Jewish Woman in Judaism* (Hicksville NY), offered little more than a sermon for a very simple audience – but both authors nonetheless conveyed a message very similar to that which Loewe had advanced in 1966: in Judaism women have a sharply defined status and role which are different from but not necessarily infe-

---

[45] E.g. Rachel Adler, "The Jew Who Wasn't There: *Halacha* and the Jewish Woman," *Davka* 1/4 (1971), 6–11; D. M. Feldman, "Woman's Role and Jewish Law," *Conservative Judaism* 26/4 (1972), 29–39; Paula E. Hyman, "The Other Half: Women in the Jewish Tradition," *ibid.* 26/4 (1972), 14–21; S. Berman, "The Status of Women in *Halakhic* Judaism," *Tradition* 14/2 (1973), 5–28; P. Sigal, "Elements of Male Chauvinism in Classical *Halakhah*," *Judaism* 24 (1975), 226–44.

[46] In 1981 *The Jewish Law Review* brought out a special issue on the subject of a woman's right in Judaism to initiate divorce, and in 1985 *Judaica*, the German-Jewish periodical published in Zurich, devoted all of issue no. 41 to the subject, "Die Frau in Judentum". In addition, since the mid-1970s various articles presuming to survey the status of Jewish women in the Jewish sources have been published by Jewish women in anthologies dealing with the status of women in different world religions or in historical periods for which the sources under study here are relevant: see, e.g. Judith Hauptman, "Images of Women in the *Talmud*," in *Religion and Sexism* (above, n. 32), 184–212; Julia Neuberger, "Women in Judaism: The Fact and the Fiction," in *Women's Religious Experience: Cross-Cultural Perspectives*, ed. Pat Holden (London 1983), 132–42; Judith R. Baskin, "The Separation of Women in Rabbinic Judaism," in *Women, Religion and Social Change*, edd. Yvonne Y. Haddad and Elison B. Findly (Albany 1985), 3–18; Léonie J. Archer, "The Role of Jewish Women," (above, n. 12); Denise L. Carmody, "Judaism," in *Women in World Religions*, ed. A. Sharma (Albany 1987), 183–206. Blu Greenberg, "Female Sexuality and Bodily Functions in the Jewish Tradition," in *Women, Religion and Sexuality*, ed. Jeanne Becher (Philadelphia 1990), 1–44. In 1986–7, the *Encyclopedia Judaica Yearbook* devoted an extended section to women (Alice Shalvi, "Introduction," pp. 12–5; Rachel Biale, "Women and Jewish Law," 16–28; Deborah R. Weissman, "Education of Jewish Women," pp. 29–36; Dafna Izraeli, "Status of Women in Israel," pp. 37–52).

rior to those of men, and this fact cannot be changed by quibbling over or rummaging through the sources.[47]

In all this turmoil, one book, despite its clear feminist aims, stands out as having managed to establish certain unmediated facts about the attitude towards women in the rabbinic sources and later *halakhic* texts. Rachel Biale, in her *Women and the Jewish Law: An Exploration of Women's Issues in Halakhic Sources*, which appeared in 1984, examined the place of women in Jewish law, starting from the Bible and continuing through the *Mishnah* and *Talmud*, Maimonides, the *Posekim* and the *Shulkhan Arukh*; focusing on the very questions which headed the agenda of the Jewish feminist movement, such as: women's participation in fulfilling commandments, studying the *Torah*, and carrying out laws concerning the family such as the commandment to "be fruitful and multiply" and the regulations governing a woman's ritual purity. Biale even investigated the attitude of *halakhah* towards abortion and homosexuality, especially lesbianism.[48] Books of similar scope, dealing with precisely the same subject

---

[47] This is reminiscent of Peretz Smolenskin's answer to Hurwitz, see above, n. 7. This dialogue has been going on ever since. In 1980, Roslyn Lacks published *Women and Judaism: Myth, History and Struggle* (New York), once again representing a feminist perspective. In 1990, E. Berkovitz, a rabbi, published a book with a feminist outlook – *Jewish Women in Time and Torah* (Hoboken NJ 1990) – but in 1992 a woman published an anti-feminist book urging Jewish women to maintain their traditional roles: Lisa Aiken, *To Be a Jewish Woman* (Northvale NJ 1992). The ultimate Jewish feminist manifesto was published in 1990 by the long-standing feminist Judith Plaskow, *Standing Again at Sinai: Judaism from a Feminist Perspective* (San Francisco 1990). A recent Jewish anthology also addresses some of these issues: Susan Grossman and Rivka Haut, edd. *Daughters of the King: Women in the Synagogue* (New York 1992).

[48] It should be noted that these matters were of much more pressing significance to Jews when Biale wrote than in the various periods in which her sources were written. Historians often raise questions arising from their own times but drawing attention to a neglected aspect of the past. For a discussion of the phenomenon and examples see L. I. Levine, "The Zealots at the End of the Second Temple Period as a Historiographical Problem," *Cathedra* 1 (1976), 47–8 [Hebrew]. Also relevant here is S. Safrai, "Was there a Women's Gallery in the Synagogue of Antiquity?" *Tarbiz* 32 (1963), 329–38 [Hebrew]. The pretext for studying this question cannot be found in the sources themselves, which, as Safrai demonstrates, provide only extremely shaky, doubtful evidence for partitions between men and women; Safrai studied the question for more current reasons. The fact is that, until Safrai, all scholars assumed there was a women's section in the ancient synagogue. See, e.g. S. Schechter, "Women in Temple and Synagogue," *Studies in Judaism, First Series* (Philadelphia 1915), 313–25; M. Friedmann, "Mitwirkung von Frauen beim Gottesdienste," *Hebrew Union College Annual* 8–9 (1931–2), 511–23. Unlike these earlier pieces, Safrai's article was written at a time when women's place and responsibilities in Jewish commandments, prayer and the synagogue started to come under intense scrutiny, and this in fact motivated Safrai to write his piece. He anticipated by several years the wave of interest in the subject, but his article nevertheless was used as ammunition by the feminist movement. See: S. J. D. Cohen, "The Women in the Synagogues of Antiquity," *Conservative Judaism* 34/2 (1980–1), 23–9; Bernadette J. Brooten, *Women Leaders in the Ancient*

and using precisely the same sources, had already been written many years before Biale's book. In 1942 and 1948, Louis Epstein published, respectively, *Marriage in the Bible and Talmud* (Cambridge MA) and *Sex Laws and Customs in Judaism* (New York); yet despite the similarity of his subject and frequently similar conclusions, Epstein's main emphasis and focus – *halakhah* – were totally different from Biale's, which were women themselves. Until the modern period and the growth of feminist influence, the only intensive research on the subject of Jewish women could be found in studies of the Jewish family, the history of Jewish law, sex and *halakhah*.[49] Biale's work is refreshingly innovative not only in this respect, but also within feminist literature, in that it does not impose preconceived notions on the sources but tries to let them speak for themselves. Even so, Biale did not write a history of women; at most she studies the history of the relation of *halakhah* to women.

In the 1970s and 1980s Neusner wrote his comprehensive interpretation of the six orders of the *Mishnah*, and he, too, was drawn into the maelstrom surrounding the question of women in the sources. When he arrived at the Order of Women he found occasion to express his opinions regarding the *Mishnah*'s attitude toward the status of women. In 1980, Neusner published his concluding volume which summed up his commentary on the Order of Women: *A History of the Mishnaic Law of Women* V (Leiden) – in which he outlined his views on the proper method for investigating the *Mishnah*'s attitude toward women. This amounted to applying a theory he had already developed, according to which the *Mishnah*'s purpose is to enable every Jew who is not a priest to live a life of holiness comparable to that prescribed for priests, in fulfillment of what is stated, "You shall be for me a kingdom of priests and a holy nation" (*Ex.* 19.15). Furthermore, he stated, the *Mishnah* does not concern itself with everyday life but rather tries to regularize the very marginal situations in which the distinction between purity and impurity is not obvious, in order to preserve the holiness of the Jewish people against any mitigating defect. Accordingly, the tractates of the Order of Women treat those stages in a woman's life – marriage, divorce and levirate marriage – in which, because her personal status is not clearly defined, she endangers the holiness of the men with whom she comes into contact. Neusner's system, by its scientific and analytical approach, raised the subject of Jewish women of rabbinic literature above the political turmoil which had raged until

Synagogue: Inscriptional Evidence and Background Issues = Brown Judaic Studies XXXVI (Chico CA 1982), 103–38; Hannah Safrai, "Women and the Ancient Synagogue," in Grossman and Haut (above, n. 47), 39–49.

[49] See, e.g. the interesting book by D. Mace, *The Hebrew Marriage: A Sociological Study* (New York 1953). Even in the relatively up-to-date collection, *The Jewish People in the First Century = Compendia Rerum Iudaicarum ad Novum Testamentum Section One*, edd. S. Safrai and M. Stern (Assen 1976), discussion of women is confined to the chapter written by Safrai, "Home and Family," 728–92.

then. One can accept or reject his system, but must acknowledge that it did not grow out of a current theological agenda, even if a theological controversy is what spawned the system in the first place.

Neusner also offered his existential justification for studying the Order of Women – or any other work – in isolation, without reference to any other contemporary work, in the case of women or any other matter.[50] Neusner determined that it is in fact impossible to write the true history of women and that all that the historian can do is study the history of a particular source and its attitude towards a particular subject, in this case women. In the end, Neusner neither wrote nor tried to write a history of women, but he did help clarify how the sources relate to them.

Neusner's students followed in his footsteps. An example of an outstanding student is W.C. Trenchard, whose book, *Ben Sira's View on Women: A Literary Analysis*, published in 1982, analyzes the passages dealing with women in *Ben Sira*, as well as *Ben Sira*'s sources. Trenchard concludes that *Ben Sira* was an incorrigible misogynist, although he stresses that this finding does not necessarily represent the period or the environment in which the author lived, for the nature of the research does not permit any conclusions beyond those which relate specifically to the composition being studied. One wonders, then, about the value of such a learned work for the historical study of women, if in the end it can determine only that the book *Ben Sira* was written by a man who hated women. Trenchard's conclusions, however, now serve as a basis for a useful and interesting anthropological analysis of *Ben Sira*'s attitude toward women, placing it against the background of a Mediterranean society.[51] Thus a tension is perceived between scholars who view the text as a means and those who view it as an end in itself. This tension is now quite obvious in the study of women in antiquity. In 1988, Judith Wegner published her *Chattel or Person: The Status of Women in the Mishnah* (Oxford), which expands considerably on Neusner's system. Like

---

[50] Neusner cited Swidler (above, n. 4) as an example of how not to write the history of women. But Neusner chose to attack, not Swidler's conclusions, but his method, i.e. basing an historical study on many diverse sources. According to Neusner, one must study women only from one source or from a homogenous collection of sources which would tend to provide information about one specific group. Neusner's example of this is a Christian publication from Sweden, supposedly dealing with women in the writings of the Qumran sect: A. Isaksson, *Marriage and Ministry in the New Temple: A Study with Special References to Mt. 19:13–22 and 1Cor. 11:3–16 =Acta Seminarii Neotestimentica Upsaliensis XXIV* (Lund 1965). But even from the book's title one can see that the author did not deal particularly with women, and certainly not particularly with the Qumran writings. Nonetheless, Isaksson's careful and thorough source-criticism is apparently what attracted Neusner.

[51] Claudia V. Camp, "Understanding a Patriarchy: Women in Second Century Jerusalem through the Eyes of *Ben Sira*," in *'Women Like This': New Perspectives on Jewish Women in the Greco-Roman Period*, ed. Amy-Jill Levine (Atlanta 1991), 1–40.

her teacher, Wegner shunned all comparisons between the *Mishnah* and even closely related works such as the *Tosefta*. She offered conclusions which are precise, on-target and practically free from any shade of polemic, at least in the book's first part, which is philological rather than synthetic. Yet her work still does not constitute an historical study of the status of women, except insofar as it fulfills its declared purpose of describing the *Mishnah*'s attitude to women. On this question, Wegner concluded that the *Mishnah* relates to women as autonomous personalities with legal integrity in every matter unconnected to their sexuality, whereas their sexual and reproductive systems are always under the ownership of some male – father, husband or levir (deceased husband's brother); the *Mishnah* takes great care and deals in minute detail with those moments in a women's life when the ownership over her sexuality could fall into dispute. It is worth noting that Wegner's conclusion, although based on Neusner's source-critical method and restricted to examination of only the *Mishnah*, is remarkably similar to that put forward 35 years previously by the sociologist David Mace.[52] This may tend to confirm Wegner's conclusions but not her method of source-analysis, for similar conclusions were reached by applying sociological tools to the same sources.[53]

Neusner and his students have made real contributions but their work reveals also the weaknesses of Neusner's system, which can inform directly and in great detail about the treatment of women in each individual source but reveals nothing about the actual condition of women during the period in which the source was written. The historian's purpose is left unsatisfied and unfulfilled. On the other hand, what is of principle importance is not any specific conclusion arising from the feminist debate about Jewish women in the rabbinic sources and other post-biblical Jewish sources, but the raised awareness regarding the value of the whole subject. Many studies have since appeared which treat particular sources, or particular topics within the sources, based on the assumption that there is an intrinsic value in the study of the sources themselves; these studies reach conclusions which are of value for the sociology, psychology and sometimes history of the authors of the texts.[54] There are fewer studies of particular historical pro-

---

[52] Above, n. 49.

[53] Another student of Neusner has recently elaborated further on the theme discussed by Wegner, see P. V. M. Flesher, "Are Women Property in the System of the *Mishnah*?" in *From Ancient Israel to Modern Judaism – Intellect in Quest of Understanding: Essays in Honor of Marvin Fox* I, = *Brown Judaic Studies* CLIX, edd. J. Neusner, E. Frerichs and N. S. Sarna (Atlanta 1989), 219–31.

[54] Several examples: L. H. Feldman, "Josephus' Portrait of Deborah", in *Hellenica et Judaica: Hommage à Valentin Nikiprowetzky*, edd. A. Caquot, M. Hadas-Lebel and J. Riand (Paris 1986), 115–28; J. L. Bailey, "Josephus' Portrayal of the Matriarchs," in *Josephus, Judaism and Christianity*, edd. L. H. Feldman and G. Hata (Detroit 1987), 154–79; Eileen Schuller, "Women of the Exodus in Biblical Retelling in the Second Temple," in *Gender and Difference in Israel*, ed. Peggy L. Day (Minneapolis 1989), 178–94; P. W. van

blems or topics and their results seem to ignore rather than incorporate source-analysis and text criticism.[55]

In this light, we should make special note of three further publications which can be described as history books. The first is Günter Mayer's *Die jüdische Frau in der hellenistisch-römischen Antike*, published in Stuttgart in 1987. This book represents a serious attempt to write a history of women of the period by taking into account all the sources and shunning any ideological or theological point of departure. Mayer seems to be an exemplary product of the classical historical school in Germany, which stresses the use of epigraphic and papyrological material no less than the standard written sources. Yet this emphasis, as well as the book's limited scope, is both its special strength and main weakness. For, first of all, Mayer seems to attach almost mystical importance to historical truth conveyed, for example, by a funerary inscription, despite the fact that such a document reflects nothing more than the mood and taste of the bereaved. Second, Mayer's deliberately very narrow scope and his concentration on epigraphic material naturally reduces the extent to which other sources came into play. Mayer's use of Josephus also reveals his greater facility in Greek than in Hebrew. Moreover, the chronological limits of Mayer's work are slightly wider than those of the present study, and his geographical compass is enormous. One might even say that the book, more than presenting new research, could rather serve as an introduction to the entire field.

The second book, published in 1990, is Léonie Archer's *Her Price is Beyond Rubies: The Jewish Woman in Graeco-Roman Palestine*. This book adopts prac-

---

der Horst, "Images of Women in the Testament of Job," in *Studies on the Testament of Job*, edd. A. Knibb and P. W. van der Horst (Cambridge 1989), 93–116; *idem.* "Portraits of Biblical Women in Pseudo-Philo's Liber Antiquitatum," *Journal for the Study of the Pseudepigrapha* 5 (1989), 29–46; Dorothy Sly (above, n. 24); Leila Bronner, "Biblical Prophetesses through Rabbinic Lenses," *Judaism* 40 (1991), 171–83; Cheryl Anne Brown, *No Longer Be Silent: First Century Jewish Portraits of Biblical Women* (Louisville KY 1992). Note also two collections of articles published recently on similar topics: J. C. Vanderkam, ed. *'No One Spoke Ill of Her': Essays on Judith* (Atlanta 1992) and Amy-Jill Levine, ed. (above, n. 25).

[55] Here are the most prominent examples: D. Daube, "Johanan ben Broqua and Women's Rights," in *Jewish Tradition in the Diaspora: Studies in Memory of Prof. Walter F. Fischel*, ed. M. M. Caspi (Berkeley 1981), 55–60; Ross S. Kraemer, "Non-Literary Evidence for Jewish Women in Rome and Egypt," *Helios* 13 (1987), 85–101; *eadem.* "Hellenistic Jewish Women: the Epigraphical Evidence," *Society of Biblical Literature Seminar Papers* 25 (1986), 183–200; *eadem.* "Monastic Jewish Women in Greco-Roman Egypt: Philo Judaeos on the Therapeutrides," *Signs: Journal of Women in Culture and Society* 14 (1989), 342–59; J. Sievers, "The Role of Women in the Hasmonean Dynasty," in *Josephus, the Bible and History*, edd. L. H. Feldman and G. Hata (Detroit 1989), 132–46; Léonie J. Archer, "'In Thy Blood Live': Gender and Ritual in the Judeo-Christian Tradition," in *Through the Devil's Gateway: Women, Religion and Taboo*, ed. Alison Joseph (London 1990), 22–49; and recently two collections of articles have been published on women's

tically the same chronological limits and uses the same sources and plan as the present study, yet is seriously deficient and flawed. Archer announces that her intention is to describe the condition of the "common," not the aristocratic or the wealthy Jewish woman, in Palestine. For reasons known only to her she decided that it is the *halakhic* rabbinic sources which best document these women, but in her use of this literature she avoids text-criticism entirely and neglects to distinguish sharply between *tannaitic* and *amoraic* sources, to take into account that most of the *tannaitic* sources were written long after the Second Temple period, or to consider the social and economic background of those who composed the *halakhic* collections, as if they represented the "normal" Jews of the Second Temple. Likewise her unexplained acceptance of Philo's writings as a genuine and reliable reflection of the historical reality of the Jews of Palestine: the cautious note sounded in her introduction, that Philo would be treated only as circumstantial evidence, is almost entirely neglected. In sum, Archer's book conveys the impression that Judaism in the Second Temple period functioned according to *tannaitic* norms, and that the status of women in society was similar to the *tannaitic* ideal. The resulting picture is very difficult to accept: women were restricted in every area and situation, without exception. This picture in fact corresponds to Archer's view (see above) that women's status deteriorated considerably from the biblical to the Second Temple periods.

The third publication has appeared very recently in Israel. It was written by Shulamit Valler, a *talmudic* scholar who set out to discuss the position of women as reflected in rabbinic literature.[56] Her initial assumption was that the rabbis could not have really been so negative in their attitude toward women, and she posited, in a review of some of the *aggadic* material in the *Babylonian Talmud*, that the rabbis, after formulating draconic laws to regulate women's lives, did not themselves follow their own dicta. This assumption is reminiscent of the feminist Christian attitude which assumes that despite its later misogynism, Christianity was in its essence an egalitarian, feminist religion.

To sum up this survey. On the one hand, the subject of the Jewish woman in the Hellenistic-Roman period has aroused great interest from the mid-nineteenth century to the present day, but on the other hand there appears to be no historical study which makes use of all the sources and source-critical techniques to describe in a well-balanced and thorough manner the history of Jewish women in Palestine during a period of such great interest and so many vicissitudes. This is the task I have set for myself in this work.

---

historical and social realities: Judith R. Baskin, ed. *Jewish Women in Historical Perspective* (Detroit 1991); P. J. Haas, ed. *Recovering the Role of Women: Power and Authority in Rabbinic Jewish Society* (Atlanta 1992).

[56] Shulamit Valler, *Women and Womanhood in the Stories of the Babylonian Talmud* (Tel Aviv 1993) [Hebrew].

Chronology

Historical research consists of collecting endless detail and drawing conclusions from this detail by way of deduction. Such conclusions are by nature generalizations, to which there are of course always exceptions. A chronological framework should be so designed as to enable the formation of generalizations which are meaningful in as many areas as possible but will neither be exceeded by exceptions to them nor invalidated by anachronism.

The important question is, by what criteria to determine the chronological limits of an historical inquiry on women in Palestine in late antiquity. Three examples from the scholarly literature discussed in the previous section will illustrate possible chronological frameworks. Criticism of them is what will subsequently determine the limits of the present study.

A. The majority of Christian scholars who deal with the history of women started from within faculties of theology, where they study a wide variety of subjects, defined conventionally as poetry, literature, philosophy and history, although the starting point for all these subjects is the Christian Scriptures. The canon includes, naturally, the Hebrew Bible, the New Testament, and for the Catholics also the *Apocrypha*. These writings have accordingly determined the chronological limits of the research of many Christian theologians – that is, from the dawn of history (or at least from the establishment of the Jewish people) to the beginning of the second century CE, when the last books of the New Testament were written.[57] Clearly these criteria were selected for no inherent historical reason but derived rather from the sources with which such scholars were familiar. Their preference for comparing the New Testament with the Hebrew Bible stems from the fact that their education consisted of a broad and detailed study of the latter, but they neither studied nor acquired the critical tools to learn rabbinic literature, and are only slightly better versed in Greek and Latin classics, all of which are closer chronologically to the Christian material than the Hebrew Bible. Naturally such practical circumstances as theological curricula cannot justify the absence of sound historical method. Any student of history knows that biblical Israelite society of the First Temple period suffered punishing blows in the expulsions of Israel and Judah by the Assyrians and Babylonians, and that the Israelites who stayed in Palestine or returned after the Babylonian exile created a society substantially different from the previous one. Add to that the strong influence of Hellenistic culture on Judaism, which began to show

---

[57] So far as the study of women is concerned, this chronological framework was already set out by Elizabeth Cady-Stanton in *The Women's Bible* (New York 1985), even though she did not claim to be writing history. See also, e.g. Swidler, (above, p. 11), and C. Ryder-Smith, *The Biblical Doctrine of Womanhood in its Historical Evolution* (London 1923).

signs already before the conquests of Alexander the Great and only grew after the Roman conquest of Palestine, and one can see clearly that generalizations based on a comparison of events from Jesus' time and the time of the Exodus have value more as a curiosity than as sound historical analysis. One example will suffice. In his article, "Jesus Son of Mary,"[58] H.K. MacArthur asks why, in the Gospel of *Mark*, the Nazarenes call Jesus "son of Mary". To find an answer, MacArthur first scoured the Scriptures he knew for all the examples of males identified by their mother's names. Thus he compares Jesus to the biblical figures Yoav son of Tzeruiah and Adoniah son of Haggit. To be sure, MacArthur himself acknowledges that such comparisons hold little value and teach nothing about Jesus; but if he had instead used Jewish texts of Jesus' time for the comparisons, his results would have had far greater significance.[59]

B. Many Jewish scholars, for their part, also come from backgrounds in which the study and mastery of sacred texts formed the heart of their education; in their case, of course, these texts are the Hebrew Bible and rabbinic literature, primarily the *Mishnah* and *Babylonian Talmud*. As a result, their books on subjects related to women – which I have used extensively in this work – assume a timeframe starting with the Bible and ending with the *Babylonian Talmud*; in other words, from the dawn of history to the Islamic conquest of Babylonia in the seventh century CE. Significantly, Epstein called his book on marriage in Judaism, *Marriage Laws in the Bible and Talmud*. Presumably the chronological range of the book reflects Epstein's ambition to describe the Jewish institution of marriage as it is based on the two canonical Jewish legal texts, and he clearly emphasized the changes and developments that had occurred in marriage laws between the biblical and *talmudic* periods. Yet it nonetheless remains true that the chronological limits of Epstein's book were determined by his sources,[60] and that, just as in the case of the Hebrew Bible and the New Testament, so the Bible and *Talmud* do not fit well into one coherent chronological framework.

C. As if in answer to this criticism, Epstein wrote his second book, *Sex Laws and Customs in Judaism*, which reaches way beyond the *Talmud* to the *Respon-*

---

[58] *Novum Testamentum* 15 (1973), 38–58.

[59] See now my "'Man Born of Woman ...' (*Job* 14. 1): The Phenomenon of Men Bearing Metronymes at the Time of Jesus," *Novum Testamentum* 34 (1992), 23–45.

[60] J. Preuss' monumental work, *Biblische und Talmudische Medizin* (Berlin 1911), now published in English under the title *Biblical and Talmudic Medicine* , translation F. Rosner (New York 1978) which has informed the present study, also encompasses both these sources. Even a fleeting glance at the book shows that a chronological division into two sections – biblical and *talmudic* medicine – would have done the subject greater justice and would have lent Preuss' generalizations greater value. Preuss' work is limited in yet another way by his own limited knowledge of other sources; for while he does cite parallels to the rabbinic sources from Greek and Roman literature, he was far less familiar with Egyptian and Mesopotamian material from the biblical period and thus used the Bible as an exclusive source.

sa, the *Posekim*, Maimonides and the *Shulkhan Arukh,* i.e. from the creation of
the world to Epstein's own period. Biale's book, mentioned above, is marked
by a similar chronological sweep. These two books serve as yet another example of how sources are allowed to dictate chronology: since the topic is, essentially, the history of *halakhah*, which begins with the Bible and continues in
one form or another to the present day, these scholars apparently felt no need to
set real chronological limits to their work. Thus their treatments of changes and
developments are fine but their generalizations are plagued with anachronism.[61]

It is incumbent on the historian to choose a better-defined chronological framework which is not dictated by the sources but, on the contrary, itself determines
which sources are relevant. On the other hand, these two considerations – sources
and chronology – are interdependent and inseparable one from the other.

Choosing the starting-point for the present research is relatively easy. In 332
Alexander the Great conquered Palestine in the course of his conquests throughout the East. This event provides an important chronological boundary for political history. The present study belongs more to social history, but in this area,
too, Alexander's conquests in the East represent a decisive turning-point, marking the beginning of pervasive Hellenistic cultural influence in the region. This
starting-point can also, in fact, be justified by the nature of the sources themselves, for despite what I have argued above, it is practically impossible not at
least to consider sources when trying to find significant chronological divisions.
The sources preceding Alexander's conquests are so sparse and historical traditions so limited, that *Seder Olam Rabbah*, for example, determines that that
entire period lasted only 34 years (30.51), although its true length is almost
200 years. Thus Alexander's conquest serves as a convenient watershed. Admit-
tedly, the sources for Jewish history did not proliferate in Alexander's immediate
wake, but during the first 150 years after him the number of sources grew from a
slow trickle to a substantial stream.

It is more difficult to find an end-date. There are many candidates. The successful Hasmonean revolt in the mid-second century BCE, which ended Hellenistic rule in Palestine, or the Roman conquest, would make good sense in a political history. The destruction of the Second Temple in 70 CE is a favorite date for
those who try to fit Jewish history into coherent periods, and in fact we should
not underestimate the impact of that event on Jewish life in general and on the
lives of Jewish women in particular, as I will demonstrate in the chapters that
follow. The Destruction also serves as an end-date for a number of sources, most
importantly Josephus, the principle source for the pre-Destruction period, and it

---

[61] See my discussion in n. 48 above, on the question of whether a women's section
existed in the ancient synagogue. The assumption by scholars before Safrai, that there had
to have been such a section, rested on anachronistic assumptions about ancient society.

is meaningful, too, for Jewish funerary inscriptions from Jerusalem, which are particularly important for women's history.

Yet I have not used the Destruction as a final *terminus*, for two reasons. First, the destruction of the Temple was not really a beginning for anything other than a contraction and impoverishment of the Jewish population in Palestine, a process which the Bar-Kokhba revolt (132–5 CE) only hastened. The second reason involves sources once again, and in spite of my criticisms above, I do use sources as a chronological criterion, yet in a different way. An indirect result of the Bar-Kokhba revolt was the creation of a whole mine of sources of incomparable value for the history of women in Palestine: refugees from the war deposited many important documents in caves in the Judaean Desert, including marriage contracts, certificates of divorce, deeds of sale and others providing information on women's social and legal status. A history of women from this time cannot be properly written without this new evidence, and ending such a history with the Destruction would have required anachronistic use of the documents.

Thus I could have decided to use the Bar Kokhba revolt as the natural *terminus*, but that event, although marking the end of a period in the history of Jews in Palestine, forms a rather artificial limit with respect to the sources, for it occurred in the middle of the period covered by *tannaitic* literature. It is extremely difficult to divide that *corpus* between the parts which relate to events before and after the rebellion, especially in the case of anonymous *tannaitic* statements pertaining to women. I have decided, therefore, to extend the period under study two generations beyond the Bar Kokhba revolt and include all *tannaitic* sources, which can be separated out with relative ease from the larger *corpus* of rabbinic literature. Thus the period under study ends in approximately the year 200 CE and covers about 500 years.

Geography

Just as valid historical generalizations become difficult if not impossible to make in an over-extended chronological framework, so geographical scope should be controlled and assumptions of continuity among disparate areas avoided. Many historians have failed to do this, and the cause can again be traced to the sources on which they depend. Two main tendencies can be found in research on Jewish women of the Second Temple period:

A. Scholars of early Christianity, using the New Testament as their main source, have jumbled together Jewish women from Palestine with other women, sometimes not even Jewish, from distant places. The source of these errors is to be found in the nature of the New Testament itself. The four Gospels describe events which are supposed to have occurred in Palestine during Jesus' life, events in which many Jewish women took part; the Pauline epistles, on the other hand, were addressed to the first Christian communities in the Mediterranean basin, from Rome to Asia Minor, where the women were not from Palestine and in many cases not even Jewish or only partly Jewish (God-fearers). The lack of other sources compelled scholars of early Christianity to turn their attention, after the death of Jesus, from his women followers in Palestine to other women outside that region. These women participated in a different movement whose connection to the Jesus movement is complex but certainly not a direct continuation of it. An example of this is Schüssler-Fiorenza's *In Memory of Her*, which argues that the four Gospels represent the later Christian missionary movement and actually describe the reality of women only in the later movement. In other words, that the two movements, Jesus' and the first Christians' outside Palestine, do not belong to the same historical context (a claim which I accept). Yet Schüssler-Fiorenza goes further and tries to reconstruct Jesus' movement and women's roles within it from the Gospels, and in doing so links the two in a false sequence. As Brooten noted,[62] this sort of inquiry focuses not on the history of women but on the attitude of the Christian sources to women.

B. Many works on the history of women have uncritically treated the two different compilations of the *Talmud* (the Palestinian and the Babylonian) as one source, which together cover an extremely wide geographical area.[63] Mayer in his *jüdische Frau* was compelled by his chronological framework and his sources to expand his geographical limits even further to incorporate the entire Jewish Diaspora, both within and without the Roman empire. As a result his book is full of groundless generalizations. For example, he claims (p. 33) that the most popular names for women in the Hellenistic-Roman period were Greek, but this is not true for Palestine, where Hebrew names outnumber Greek by three to one.[64] Similarly he claims that the name Mariamme was far more popular than any other for Jewish women in the period, but his sample is heavily biased by the evidence from Palestine, which if excluded would show the name to have been far less popular in different areas of the Diaspora.[65]

Thus the historian must be highly sensitive to the geographical context of each source. Traps are laid for the incautious scholars. An instructive example is Jeremias' unwise reliance on the descriptions in *2* and *3 Maccabees* of the daughters of Jerusalem being secluded in special wings within their houses.[66] The problem is that both these books were composed in Hellenistic Egypt and no Palestinian source describes women living in such conditions. That is, we can assume that *2* and *3 Maccabees* describe the situation of women (including Je-

---

[62] Above, n. 40, 71–2.

[63] See above all Swidler (above, n. 4) and his discussion of his sources, p. 3.

[64] See my "Notes on the Distribution of Women's Names in Palestine in the Second Temple and *Mishnaic* Period," *Journal of Jewish Studies* 40 (1989), 191.

[65] *Ibid.* 191–2.

[66] In his appendix on women in Jesus' day, see Jeremias (above, n. 29), 232–50.

wish women) in Alexandria (see Philo, *Contra Flaccum* 89) and not necessarily the situation in Jerusalem.

Such caution can be taken to extremes, however: sources do not perfectly reflect the location in which they were written, especially when describing the situation in a different geographical area. Authors of Babylonian sources, for example, tend to describe a reality they imagined for Palestine but which was not part of their experience and in fact existed nowhere. The story of Beruriah is a good illustration: as we will see, only Babylonian sources describe her as an outstanding scholar. This point was made by Goodblatt,[67] who thought that a Babylonian reality is reflected in the traditions, i.e. that in Babylonia itself women could reach the same advanced stage of *Torah*-knowledge as Beruriah of the *aggadah*. But Boyarin reached the exact opposite conclusion from the same sources, namely, that the scholar Beruriah would have been possible only in Palestine of the *tannaim* and not in Babylonia of the *amoraim*.[68] The truth is to be found in neither place, but in the realm of the imagination: from Babylonia it was possible to project onto Palestine a reality that did not exist at all in Babylonia – but which did not exist in Palestine, either.[69]

My focus is Jewish women in Palestine. Geographical boundaries do not require exact delineation for they are sufficiently marked off by nature on three sides: desert and sea on the western, desert on the eastern and southern sides. Less clear is the separation from Syria and Phoenicia to the north. For the purpose of this study, I have imagined a line running approximately from Damascus to Sidon; everything north of that line – a region indisputably outside Palestine – I have tried to exclude; southward of that line and north to Akko is arguably Palestine and thus given the benefit of the doubt. In this way I, not my sources, will dictate the geographical limits of this study.[70]

The Sources

After chronology and geography, source methodology. In the following pages I shall outline the sources used in this study together with some comments on the desired methodology in the approach to each of them. I have also tried to evalua-

---

[67] D. Goodblatt, "The Beruriah Traditions," *Journal of Jewish Studies* 26 (1975), 68–85.

[68] Boyarin (above, n. 42), 181–96.

[69] See Rachel Adler, "The Virgin in the Brothel and other Anomalies: Character and Context in the Legend of Beruriah," *Tikkun* 3/6 (1988), 28–32; 102–5.

[70] In the course of this study I will adhere quite strictly to the chronological and geographical limits I have set and will note when a source is marginal in one respect or the other. Occasionally such strictness of method is artificial, but I have preferred artificiality to anachronism and geographical misattribution.

te each source's general attitude toward and characterization of women; this evaluation sometimes allows us to judge the historical reliability and usefulness of
the source.

The *Apocrypha* and *Pseudepigrapha*

This literature comprises a large and diverse group of writings, falling into no
clearly defined literary category or within uniform chronological or geographical limits.[71] The distinction between *Apocrypha* and *Pseudepigrapha* is useful
for the Christian church – the *Apocrypha* form a separate section in the Catholic
Scriptures – but is otherwise irrelevant, in my opinion. Kahana, who published
an edition of these "external books" in Hebrew, judged the distinction between
Apocrypha and *Pseudepigrapha* irrelevant for his Jewish readers and divided his
edition along different lines, *viz.*, between those books related to the Hebrew
Bible and those which are not. But this distinction is literary and no more helpful
for historical research than the standard Christian one. Thus I divide these books
between historiographical and non-historiographical compositions. In the first
category there are only two works, *1* and *2 Maccabees*.[72] It is striking that the
former category shows total lack of interest in women. I do not know of a source
from the Second Temple period that refers less to women than does *1 Maccabees*. On the other hand, in the latter category women figure quite prominently.
In *Jubilees*, Rebecca is more important than in the Bible, in the *Biblical Antiquities* Deborah is perhaps the most important figure, in the *Testament of Job* his
wife and daughters are far more important than in the biblical book and more
prominent than his sons. Two books which were apparently composed in Palestine, *Judith* and *Susanna*, are actually named after women. I can only deduce from
this that in the minds of the ancient historians, real history was enacted in the
male realm, while women were confined to the field of fiction. This attitude is
borne out further in the writings of other predominantly historiographical works
of the period, the books of Josephus. – *V·I·*

Special attention should be paid to the Book of *Ben Sira*. His genre is generally known as "wisdom literature," which is characterized by poignant assertions
regarding many areas of life, although such proclamations are to be found also in

---

[71] Compare the works included by A. Kahana in *The External Books of the Bible* (Jerusalem 1947) [Hebrew], with the works in R. H. Charles, *The Apocrypha and Pseudepigrapha of the Old Testament* (Oxford 1913) and in J. H. Charlesworth, *The Old Testament
Pseudepigrapha* (Garden City NY 1985).

[72] See M. Stern, "Maccabees, Books of the Maccabees," *Encyclopedia Biblica* V (Jerusalem 1978), 287–92 [Hebrew]. *3 Maccabees* and the *Letter of Aristeas* are irrelevant here
because they were both written in Egypt and describe events involving Jews there.

rabbinic literature and even in Josephus and other sources. One of the distinguishing stylistic features of wisdom literature, including the Book of *Ben Sira,* is a
saying in numbers (such as "There are three things which are too wonderful for
me, yea, four which I know not, etc." *Prov.* 30.18–33), which Trenchard dubbed
"Zahlensprüche." [73] *Ben Sira*'s preoccupation with the topic of women makes
him a valuable source of information for the attitudes toward women prevalent
in his day.

Josephus

We possess four works by Josephus, the last, the *Contra Apionem (CA)*, completed apparently in the 90s CE. The *Antiquitates Iudaicae (AJ)* lays out Jewish
history from the Creation to the outbreak of the Great Revolt in 66 CE. The first
eleven books of the *AJ* deal with a period preceding that of the present study and
are important here only for what Josephus reveals about himself and his period
when he departs from his main source, the Hebrew Bible, in his stories about
women and his attitude toward them. The *CA* is not a work of history but of apo-
logy whose purpose is to explain the principles of Judaism in a positive light to
the non-Jewish world. The importance of this source for the present study consists only in Josephus' references to women and their place in Judaism; and it
might be said that such references tell us less about Judaism of the period than
about Josephus himself. In his historical writings – *Bellum Iudaicum (BJ)*,
Jewish Antiquities (AJ) 12–20 and *Vita* – Josephus covers a period stretching
from a point contiguous with the beginning of this study down to the Jewish War,
which ended in 73 with the fall of Masada. From this latter date to the end of the
period covered here, we lack a source the quality of Josephus, which would
provide a continuous narrative particularly of the political history of Jews in
Palestine. Josephus' attitude to women places him in the same historiographical
school as one of his sources, *1 Maccabees*. When women appeared on the scene,
Josephus mentioned them (e.g. Simon Bargiora's wife, *BJ* 4.538–44), but he did
not go out of his way to elaborate their roles, and at times may actually have
downplayed it (e.g. the role of the wise woman from Masada, who was witness to
the fate of the defenders, *BJ* 7.399). However, women do not play minor roles in
all of Josephus' writings on the period, and occasionally they even attain
prominence – yet in these cases, it seems, Josephus is representing not his own
opinion but that of his sources. [74]

---

[73] W. C. Trenchard, *Ben Sira's View on Women: A Literary Analysis = Brown Judaic
Studies* XXXVIII (Chico CA 1982), 175–8.

[74] For a survey of Josephus' attitude to women see: Feldman (above, n. 54), pp. 115–
20.

Josephus' Lost Sources

1. The Tobiad History

Josephus introduces this literary composition (*AJ* 12.154–236) immediately after his narration of the Seleucids' conquest of Palestine from Ptolemaic control
at the beginning of the second century BCE. The passage details the history of
two generations of the Jewish house of Tobias in Transjordan, that of Joseph and
that of his son, Hyrcanus. The nature of this source has been much discussed.
Tcherikover showed already that the story is not in its correct chronological
place and contains many fabulous elements.[75] Now D. Gera has determined that
the entire source should be considered an historical novel in the manner of
another composition contemporary with the Tobiads, the Letter of Aristeas,
which Josephus also treats as a reliable historical source.[76] Gera's conclusion is
adopted in this study. Some women are mentioned in this source, but they are not
prominent enough to draw specific conclusions.

2. Nicolaus of Damascus

Josephus used Nicolaus of Damascus as a source for the period from the death of
Simon the Maccabee to the death of Herod. Unlike Josephus, Nicolaus wrote a
great deal about women and their role in the royal courts. Fully 20 of the 39 Jewish women whom Josephus names from the Second Temple period appear in
passages attributed to Nicolaus, and all but one of these (Acme: *AJ* 17.134; *BJ*
1.641) belong to either the Hasmonean or Herodian court.

Schalit has shown how Nicolaus, a follower of the Aristotelian Peripatetic
school of historical philosophy, emphasized dramatic-psychological elements in
his history.[77] Dramatization was more important than factual accuracy to historians of this school. Schalit demonstrated that when Nicolaus' account can be
compared to his source, Nicolaus himself turns out to be responsible for the drama added to the narrative.[78] Wacholder, in his book on Nicolaus, argued that the
historian tended to favor domestic history – matters internal to the royal courts
and dynasties – at the expense of political and military history.[79] Such a bias perforce enhances the importance of women, as Wacholder demonstrated with se-

---

[75] V. Tcherikover, *Hellenistic Civilization and the Jews*, translation S. Applebaum
(New York 1970), 126–42.
[76] D. Gera, "The Reliability of the Tobiad History," in *Greece and Rome in Eretz-
Israel*, edd. A. Kasher, G. Fuks and U. Rappaport (Jerusalem 1989), 68–84.
[77] A. Schalit, *König Herodes: Der Mann und sein Werk* (Berlin 1969), 577–85.
[78] *Ibid.* 583–4 nn. 38–9.
[79] B. Z. Wacholder, *Nicolaus of Damascus = University of California Publications in
History* LXXV (Berkeley 1962), 57, 80.

veral examples from Nicolaus' writing unconnected to Josephus.[80] Nicolaus' contribution thus makes the work of Josephus much more useful for the study of women.

3. Josephus' Sources for the House of Agrippa

The question of Josephus' sources for the House of Agrippa has been taken up recently by D. R. Schwartz,[81] who demonstrated that Josephus used three principle sources for this period, of which only one paid any attention to or even mentioned the women in Agrippa's court. This particular source Schwartz named "Antip," for the central figure in the composition is the tetrarch Herod Antipas, even though the author was hostile to him and favored King Agrippa I.[82] This source resembles the writings of Nicolaus on women and should probably be assigned to the same historiographical school.

4. The Source for the Conversion of the Royal House of Adiabene

Scholars have identified in *AJ* 20 an Aramaic source[83] which described, among other things, the conversion of the royal house of Adiabene, above all of the queen Helene, the wife of King Monobazus and mother of his heir, Izates. The source is not from Palestine and did not deal principally with events that happened there, but it nevertheless described Queen Helene's visit to Palestine in the 40s CE. Queen Helene, as we learn from rabbinic sources, was an important figure in first-century Judaism and Palestine, and this source is therefore very useful for the study of this woman.

The New Testament

In light of the geographical guidelines I have set, only certain parts of the New Testament will be relevant here, namely, the four Gospels, which narrate Jesus' life and journeys through Palestine as well the activities of his women followers, and the first few chapters of *Acts*, whose setting is also Palestine. It was long ago

---

[80] *Ibid.* 57–8.

[81] D. R. Schwartz, *Agrippa I: The Last King of Judaea* (Tübingen 1990), 1–38.

[82] *Ibid.* 7, 48.

[83] A. Schalit, "Evidence of an Aramaic Source in Josephus' *Antiquities of the Jews*," *Annual of the Swedish Theological Institute* 4 (1975), 171–81; Y. Gafni, "The Conversion of the Adiabene Kings in the Light of *Talmudic* Literature," *Niv Hamidrashia* (Tel Aviv 1971), 208–9 [Hebrew]; L. H. Schiffman, "The Conversion of the Royal House of Adiabene in Josephus and Rabbinic Sources," in *Josephus, Judaism and Christianity*, edd. L. H. Feldman and G. Hata (Detroit 1987), 293–312.

noticed that women play an important, unconventional role in the New Testament.[84] Sixteen women are mentioned by name, and many others who play lesser key roles appear anonymously.

Regarding the text-critical question, I have for the present purpose accepted the theory that *Luke* and *Matthew* made use of two sources, i.e. our *Mark* (or a slightly different version of it) and so-called *Q*, which was composed mostly from a collection of Jesus' sayings. Accordingly, *Luke* and *Matthew* are dependent on *Mark* for every story which appears in all three, and every individual departure in the two later Gospels reflects either an addition or a revision by them.

The Gospel of *John* presents a slightly more difficult problem. Like the three synoptic gospels, *John* was written far away from Palestine, but unlike the other three, it was also written at a time considerably later than the events it describes, and there is no evidence even for reliance on a source written any closer in time or place to Jesus. It has been widely noticed that many descriptions in the fourth gospel reflect the *Johanine* community in Asia Minor and not Judaism in the Palestine of Jesus. I have therefore drawn on this gospel only in support of material found elsewhere.

Rabbinic Literature

The entire corpus of rabbinic literature is of enormous scope and, in contrast to the other sources discussed above, represents not the opinion of just one man but a wide variety of perspectives, opinions and ideas authored by many different people. But two points are in order: a) those who composed rabbinic literature considered themselves to be the spiritual heirs of the Pharisaic sect of the Second Temple period, and their approach to the events from the time of the Temple derives from a Pharisaic world-view, albeit one which reflects changes and developments over time; b) the sages, the authors and the central figures of rabbinic literature belonged to a socially and ideologically uniform group whose fountainhead was *Torah*-study and whose heroes were not politicians or military figures but intellectuals and learned scholars. This gives rise to the question, what women's place was in such a world and to what extent their opinions and viewpoints have been preserved. As to the first part of the question, we may answer that in all the wide range of rabbinic literature which documents the Second Temple and *tannaitic* periods in Palestine, only 25 women are mentioned by name (as opposed to 605 men) and this representation is lower than that in any

---

[84] Above, n. 34; cf. also Luise Schottroff's attempt to establish the social background of Jesus' movement: "Women as Followers of Jesus in New Testament Times: Exercise in Socio-Historical Exegesis of the Bible," in *The Bible and Liberation, Political and Social Hermeneutics*, ed. N. K. Gottwald (Maryknoll NY 1983), 418–27. And see also Schüssler-Fiorenza (above, n. 15), 105–59.

other source from the period. Moreover, even among the women mentioned by name, only one – Beruriah – is connected to the world of religious academies and study-houses. The others are characters mentioned in legal precedents[85] and *aggadot*, whereas most of the 605 men are either sages or their relations. As to the second part of the question, ideas and opinions in *tannaitic* literature are usually cited in the name of the person who said them and thus are attributed to specific men. Naturally, distortions entered through errors in copying and we cannot rely fully on the traditions of transmission, but generally speaking the transmitter of a teaching can sometimes be securely identified from inspection of the manuscripts and the comparison of parallels. In the gigantic rabbinic corpus there are only two laws, each dealing with the impurity of vessels, cited on the authority of a woman: one of Beruriah (*tKel. BM.* 1.6) and the other of the daughter of Hananiah b. Tardion (*tKel. BQ.* 4.17).[86] The fact that these laws do not appear in their name in the *Mishnah*, i.e. the legal corpus which gained canonical status, and that one of the laws is cited there (*mKel.* 11.4) on the authority of a man, suggests that rabbinic sources may contain other laws for which women were the original authority but that this fact was covered up, unintentionally or deliberately, in the course of transmission; yet there are no criteria for identifying such incidents with certainty and thus we are forced to assume that, aside from the two laws mentioned, the rest of the material was taught and transmitted by men.

The historical value of rabbinic sources has been vigorously debated in recent scholarship. Since I am inclined to accept most of the arguments against historical reliability, I have used these sources, with few exceptions, only to identify the attitudes of men toward women. When I used them for other purposes, I have applied various criteria which I shall describe presently. Yet I wish to stress that on the whole, I have maintained throughout my work the chronological framework of rabbinic literature based on the identity of the tradents in it. I am well aware that this method has also recently come under attack. I think, however, that most of this attack is unjustified, and its greatest supporters eventually resort to the same dating techniques. However, this is not the place for a full defense of this method. I might only mention that everyone, even the greatest skeptics, draw the line somewhere. This is where I draw the line.

1. Tannaitic Literature

The chronological limits of this work require inclusion of all *tannaitic* sources: *Mishnah*, *Tosefta* and *midrashei-halakhah*. These works are for the most part *halakhic* but also include legal precedents and *aggadot* in which women are mentioned.

---

[85] I.e. actual cases which served or could serve as the basis for *halakhah*.

[86] The two women are not necessarily the same, see below chapter 7.

Most useful for the present study are legal precedents. These seem to convey reliable historical fact, especially when they are transmitted by someone contemporary with the event or only one generation later. Often precedents are cited against rather than in support of the *halakhah* under discussion. In my opinion, reliable historical material can be found precisely in those stories which do not entirely correspond with the social norm set by the *halakhah*. At the same time, however, we must be careful not to understand past reality only on the basis of serious departures from the norm. As is well known, a society designs its laws as a defense against things which are liable to harm the order to which it aspires. Thus on the one hand, a law often represents not actual but ideal behavior in a society; on the other hand, deviation from behavior prescribed by a law or social norm does not, for its part, necessarily convey an accurate historical picture, either. In the final analysis, if all people were lawbreakers there would be no reason to make laws ("A decree cannot be made for the people unless most of the people can endure it" *bBB* 60b; *bHor*. 3b). It is a safe assumption that the events described in the legal precedents in *halakhic* corpora document exceptional and special cases and not the commonplace. Yet thereby a trap is set which must be avoided: the exceptional, which does in fact fall in the realm of reality, not fable, nonetheless represents only a small part of reality and should not be mistaken for the whole. Thus legal precedents should be treated with extreme caution.

Furthermore, some *halakhic* sources, while propounding a certain *halakhah,* assume but do not elaborate the existence of a situation forbidden by a different *halakhah*. For example, *mNed*. 4.3 allows a man to teach *Torah* to the daughters of a man he had vowed not to receive any benefit from whereas a different *halakhah* forbids teaching *Torah* to girls under any circumstances (*Sifre Deut*. 46, p. 104 ed. Finkelstein). In such cases the situation assumed by the one *halakhah* but proscribed by another is probably an accurate description of reality.

One special element in *tannaitic aggadah* of which I will make considerable use is the parable, particularly those which present relations between men and women in some form. The author of a parable uses examples he perceives as real-life situations in order to illustrate an important idea or message, even if the particular situation described may never have occurred. Thus a parable has the same historical value as an historical novel, such as *Susannah*, *Judith* or *Tobit*.

One further reservation is in order. Although rabbinic literature creates – or tries to create – the impression that it describes the behavior of all Jews, in actuality it describes only the various stages of Pharisaic *halakhah* after the Destruction. Although in the Middle Ages these texts served as the prescriptive norm in large parts of the Jewish world, in the period in which they were composed and to which they refer, the same norm was the actual way of life for only a limited group of men and women.

2. Baraitot

A *bariata* is a *tannaitic* tradition which was not incorporated into the *Mishnah* but was either collected later into various compilations (*Tosefta, midrashei halakhah*) or is quoted in later *amoraic* literature, usually following a fixed formula of introduction such as "our rabbis taught (תנו רבנן)." *Amoraic halakhic* texts (the *Babylonian* and *Palestinian Talmudim*) contain many *baraitot* which do not appear in *tannaitic* literature, as well as interesting variants of *baraitot* which the *tannaim* do mention. The approach to these should be extremely cautious, because the *amoraim* were not above inventing *tannaitic* evidence in support of their opinions.

3. Amoraic Literature

I have scoured *amoraic* literature for *aggadot* and stories involving women of the earlier period as well as stories, related by *tannaitic* authorities, in which women have a part. My approach to these sources is extremely cautious. For each story, I have tried to identify anachronisms which its transmitter introduced from his own time, I have sought out recurrent literary motifs which detract from the story's historical value, and I have tried to understand the setting, the extent to which this influenced the story's content and the reasons for the selection of its central figures, male and female. After all of these considerations, I have tried to extract the historical kernel from the story whenever possible, and have used only such information as remains by the end of the process. *Aggadot* of apparently great historical importance but whose historical kernel could not be identified with certainty have been relegated to the notes.

One of the most important criteria for identifying the historical kernel in an *aggadah* dealing with a woman is the extent to which the woman is integral in the story. An *aggadah* which is pointless without the woman is of less historical value than one whose central figure could just as easily be a male.

When using the *Babylonian Talmud* I have adopted a rigorously skeptical attitude to everything stated therein about the family relations of its central figures, both male and female. Many woman who appear in the Palestinian sources as completely unconnected emerge in the *Babylonian Talmud* as the daughters, wives and sisters of important sages. Thus only in the *Babylonian Talmud* do we find Queen Shelamzion as the sister of Shimeon b. Shetah, R. Aqiba's wife as the daughter of the wealthy Jerusalemite Kalba Sabua, Imma Shalom as the sister of Rabban Gamaliel, and Beruriah as the daughter of Hananiah b. Tardion and the wife of R. Meir.[87] These supposed connections even created contradictions which I have noted whenever relevant.

---

[87] See S. Safrai, "Tales of the Sages in the Palestinian Tradition and the *Babylonian*

4. Midrashim

I have made intensive use of the Palestinian *amoraic midrashim* whose early dates are generally accepted: *Genesis Rabbah, Leviticus Rabbah and Lamentations Rabbah*. These sources have provided *baraitot* and other passages whose central figures lived in the period under investigation. I have also made extensive use of passages in later *midrashic* compilations mentioning *tannaim* and their contemporaries. To these I applied the same methods described above for *amoraic aggadot*.

A few words will be in order regarding the two versions of *Abot de Rabbi Nathan*. This *midrashic* work is composed of *baraitot* and is written entirely in Hebrew, but apparently it was redacted at a late date and Version A seems not only to be familiar with but also to have reworked considerable material from the *Babylonian Talmud*.[88] Since *Abot de Rabbi Nathan* contains a large treasure of valuable material I could not, on the basis of its redaction date, exclude it entirely, but I have exercised special caution, particularly in those instances for which it serves as the primary source. When an earlier parallel existed I have examined the textual variants and have always preferred the earlier version. *Aggadot* for which *Abot de Rabbi Nathan* is the primary source I have used only as supporting evidence for different points based on other sources. Generally speaking I have preferred Version B, which is freer from influences from the *Babylonian Talmud*. In both versions one witnesses a special interest in the story of the creation of woman. This story had far-reaching implications for the attitude to women in all the sources, but the editor of *Abot de Rabbi Nathan*, who exceeded all other sources in the value he placed on the story, was likely to have been influenced by the attitudes of the church fathers on the same subject.

The Dead Sea Scrolls

When women are mentioned in the documents composed by the Dead Sea Sect, it is almost always in *halakhic* contexts. *The Rule of the Community (1QSa)* contains rulings on the marriage of sectarians and the *Damascus Convenant (CD)* contains the laws forbidding multiple marriages (or divorce – the interpretation is controversial) and the marriage of uncles with nieces. *The Temple Scroll* also

---

Talmud," in *Studies in Aggadah and Folk-Literature = Scripta Hierosolymitana* XXII, edd. J. Heinemann and D. Noy (Jerusalem 1971), 229–32.

[88] See Y. L. Zunz, *Die gottesdienstlichen Vorträge der Juden* (Berlin 1832), 108–9. For another view, A. J. Saldarini, *The Fathers According to Rabbi Nathan B* (Leiden 1975), 13–6, who nonetheless agrees that the final redaction was late.

mentions women in this context.[89] One apparently non-sectarian fragment on the evil woman, which is important for the study of the literary attitudes toward women, was discovered at Qumran;[90] it was obviously preserved by the sect because its views of women coincided with theirs. The discovery of women's skeletons in Qumran and the existence in the scrolls of marriage regulations and other laws relating to women have led some scholars to doubt the identification of the authors with Essenes, whom Josephus describes as abstaining from contact with women.[91] Other scholars have tried to resolve this contradiction in various ways.[92] This question is not terribly relevant here, where it will be sufficient to assume that the Dead Sea Sect – as well as the Essenes, the early Christians and the so-called *"hasidim"* of rabbinic literature – belonged to a trend of the time which I will call *"hasidic."* I will use the Dead Sea scrolls to illustrate extremist or *"hasidic" halakhah* in matters regarding women and the relations between men and women.

Funerary Inscriptions

The ossuaries from Jerusalem contain the only funerary inscriptions which can be clearly dated to the Second Temple period (and perhaps down to the time of the Bar Kokhba revolt, but no later than that). These ossuaries are typical of Jewish burial custom around Jerusalem which went out of use when the Jews were forced to leave the area.[93] The funerary inscriptions from outside Jerusalem fall into three categories: a) The inscriptions from Beth She'arim. Given that R. Judah the Patriarch founded this cemetery and that only Caves 14 and 20 seem from the archaeological evidence to be from his time,[94] only the inscriptions from these two caves are relevant to the present study. Other inscriptions from Beth She'arim will be noted only as needed. b) The Jewish cemetery in Jaffa.

---

[89] See L. H. Schiffman, "Laws Pertaining to Women in the Temple Scroll," in *The Dead Sea Scrolls: Forty Years of Research,* edd. Devorah Dimant and U. Rappaport (Leiden 1992), 210–28.

[90] See J. M. Allegro, "The Wiles of the Wicked Woman: A Sapiental Work from Qumran's Fourth Cave," *Palestine Exploration Quarterly* 96 (1964), 53–5.

[91] L. H. Schiffman, *Sectarian Law in the Dead Sea Scrolls: Courts, Testimony and the Penal Code = Brown Judaic Studies* XXXIII (Chico CA 1983), 214–5.

[92] For three different approaches see Isaksson (above, n. 50), 45–65; M. Burrows, *The Dead Sea Scrolls* (New York 1956), 233; J. M. Baumgarten, "The Qumran-Essene Restraints on Marriage," in *Archaeology and History in the Dead Sea Scrolls: The New York University Conference in Memory of Yigael Yadin = Journal for the Study of the Pseudepigrapha Supplement Series* VIII, ed. L. H. Schiffman (Sheffield 1990). 13–24.

[93] L. Y. Rahamani, *The Decoration on the Jewish Ossuaries as Representations of Jerusalem Tombs,* Ph.D. Dissertation (Jerusalem 1977), 22–6 [Hebrew].

[94] N. Avigad, *Beth She'arim* III (New Brunswick NJ 1976), 42–65, 83–115.

The dating of this cemetery is uncertain and will thus be referred to only for comparative purposes or in the notes. c) Other funerary inscriptions, which will be fully presented and discussed in every case.

Ossuary inscriptions from Jerusalem and environs have yielded 153 women's names, compared to 513 names of men; in other words, 23 % of the total. Although this figure seems somewhat unbalanced, it is nonetheless the largest proportion of women in any source. Yet we should not in any case expect to find an equal number of men's and women's names in funerary inscriptions, even in a completely unbiased sample in which women were buried and their burials documented at the same rate as for men, because many women are identified by their full name, that is, their personal name together with the name of their father and even occasionally their grandfather.[95] Frequently, when their patronymics are missing, women are identified by their husbands' names and even sometimes by their sons' names. Therefore, in an ideal situation we would expect 75 % men's names and only 25 % women's names (X daughter of Y for every Y son of Y). This is very close to the figure we have (23 %), but the resemblance is deceptive. For in point of fact most epitaphs were not expertly carved as monumental inscriptions but by unskilled hands for the private use of families. For this reason most women's names appear without the identifying association of a relative, and this would have naturally raised the percentage of women's names, especially since most men's ossuaries bear only one name, that is, the name of the deceased without his patronymic. Thus we would have expected far more than 25 % women's names, whereas the actual figure is lower even than this.

The gap indicates neglect not of women's burial but of the documentation of such burial. Some ossuaries bear inscriptions such as "Eleazar and his wife,"[96] "the wife of Eleazar,"[97] "Shimeon and his wife,"[98] i.e. without any indication of the woman's name. Moreover, we can assume that many men made an effort to ensure that their wives would be buried beside them but failed to indicate even this.[99] Finally, most ossuaries have no inscription whatsoever, and we may assume that women were mostly buried in such anonymous ossuaries.

Hypotheses of this nature could be tested by means of comprehensive examination of the many skeletal remains found in the ossuaries. We would gain a great

---

[95] This situation is particularly common in the case of priests. See *CII*, no. 1352; and D. Barag and D. Flusser, "The Ossuary of Yehohanah Granddaughter of the High-Priest Theophilus," *Israel Exploration Journal* 36 (1986), 39.

[96] *CII*, no. 1247.

[97] *Ibid.* no. 1356.

[98] L. Y. Rahamani, "Jewish Rock-Cut Tombs in Jerusalem," *Atiqot* 3 (1961), 107.

[99] N. Haas, "Anthropological Observations on the Skeletal Remains from Givat Hamivtar," *Israel Exploration Journal* 20 (1970), 39–40 describes the ossuaries of "Simon the Temple-builder" and "Yehonatan the Potter" as each containing the skeletons of both a man and a woman laid side-by-side.

deal of social-anthropological knowledge, such as the distribution of burial between sexes; differences in burial methods for men, women and children; the relation between the deceased and their epitaphs; perhaps even diseases typical to
certain age-groups, and so forth. But anthropological research of this type is still
in its infancy and is presently concentrating not on the above issues but on patho-
logical phenomena (crucifixion, death during childbirth,[100] decapitation,[101] or
abnormal dimensions of the deceased[102]). So far the primary emphasis has been
placed less on the banalities of daily life, the raw material for the kind of statistics which I am suggesting.[103] For example, a good, balanced picture emerges
from three caves whose contents were indeed subjected to skeletal analysis.
Thirty-one skeletons found in a cave in Jericho were examined by Patricia
Smith, who determined that twelve of these were of people who had died before
reaching maturity, seven were of women and eleven of men; the sex of one ske-
leton could not be identified. Thus there was a slight majority of men in this
cave.[104] In another cave, from which the human remains were examined by
Haas, there were found 35 skeletons, of which 12 were of children, 11 of men and
12 of women, a majority of one.[105] In a third cave, excavated by Kloner, from
which the human remains were examined,[106] the sex of only two of the deceased
– one man and one woman – could be determined. These cases provide too small
a sample on which to base any statistical study but they perhaps show the direction in which such research could lead. Thus far we may only guess that the main
difference between women's and men's burial is not in the method of burial but
in documentation of the deceased.

---

[100] Haas, *ibid.* 48, 49–51.

[101] Patricia Smith, "The Human Skeletal Remains from the Abba Cave," *Israel Exploration Journal* 27 (1977), 121–4.

[102] Patricia Smith and Rachel Hachlili, "The Genealogy of the Goliath Family," *Bulletin of the American Schools for Oriental Research* 235 (1979), 67–70.

[103] The problem with this kind of research is rooted in the present time and is unconnected to ancient history *per se*. There is first the fact that most graves have been robbed before
their modern discovery, and skeletons in ossuaries are not whole or *in situ*. Furthermore,
graves were reused already in the ancient period, and ossuaries cannot be assumed to contain their original occupants whose names are inscribed on the outside. It has also been argued that a name on an ossuary could belong to the person who paid for it rather than to the
person buried in it. Naturally, the kind of research I am suggesting involves further problems of a religious, ethnic and political nature.

[104] Rachel Hachlili, "The Goliath Family in Jericho: Funerary Inscriptions from a First
Century A. D. Jewish Monumental Tomb," *Bulletin of the American Schools for Oriental
Research* 235 (1979), 34–5.

[105] Haas (above, n. 99), 39.

[106] A. Kloner, "A Burial-Cave of the Second Temple Period at Giv'at Hamivtar, Jerusalem," in *Jerusalem in the Second Temple Period: Abraham Schalit Memorial Volume*, edd.
A. Oppenheimer, U. Rappaport and M. Stern (Jerusalem 1980), 198–211 [Hebrew].

Papyri and Ostraca from the Judaean Desert

Since the 1950s there have been discovered in the Judaean Desert hoards of papyri deposited in caves of refuge by Jews who were fleeing the Roman legions
during the Bar Kokhba revolt. A French team discovered the first such hoard in
Wadi Muraba'at and published the documents in full.[107] Afterwards an Israeli
team working in the Judaean Desert discovered in Nahal Hever additional documents[108] which have just recently begun to be published.[109] An apparently similar hoard had been found earlier in the same cave and will be published by Jonas
Greenfield and Hannah Cotton. In addition, ostraca have been discovered both in
Masada and in caves in the Judaean Desert.[110]

All this material yields the names of 430 men, as opposed to just 21 women's
names, or 4 % of the total. Moreover, all the women's names appear only in the
legal documents left in the caves by refugees of the Bar Kokhba revolt; none
appear in those texts related to the war itself. This may not be surprising, since
war is and always has been a male domain whereas women were prominently involved, side-by-side with men, in legal issues: women were owners of property
and thus appear in deeds of sale, purchase and gift; they were married and
divorced and thus appear in marriage contracts and writs of divorce. Yet all these
documents reflect a process in which men held the key roles, as judges, witnesses,
clerks and so forth. Thus women are mentioned only in those legal documents
representing matters in which they directly took part. Even the ratio between men
and women in these documents is conspicuously to the detriment of women.

The papyri and ostraca we have been describing have a common denominator.
They all date from the Roman period and have fallen into our hands without the
intervention of a complicated tradition of transmission. The extraordinary experience of handling raw historical material, primary documents for history,
should not cloud the historian's critical eye. Papyri lay traps for the unwary. For
example, the differences in the wording of the *ketubbah* (marriage contract) in
rabbinic sources on the one hand and papyri on the other do not necessarily mean
that only one reflects actual practice. Even an actual *ketubbah* possessed by a

---

[107] R. De Vaux, J. T. Milik and P. Benoit, *Les grottes de Muraba'ât = Discoveries in the
Judaean Desert* II (Oxford 1961).

[108] Y. Yadin, "Expedition D," *Bulletin of the Israel Exploration Society* 25 (1961), 49–
64 [Hebrew]; *idem.* "Expedition D: 'Cave of the Letters'," *ibid.* 26 (1962), 204–36 [He-
brew]; Y. Polotzky, "The Greek Documents from the 'Cave of the Letters'," *ibid.* 237–41
[Hebrew].

[109] N. Lewis, *The Documents from the Bar Kokhba Period from the Cave of Letters* II:
Greek Papyri (Jerusalem 1989).

[110] The papyri and ostraca discovered at Masada have also been published: Y. Yadin
and J. Naveh, *Masada I: The Aramaic and Hebrew Ostraca* (Jerusalem 1989); Hannah M.
Cotton and J. Geiger, *Masada II: The Latin and Greek Documents* (Jerusalem 1989).

woman of the period does not confirm the practice of everything written therein. The only difference between the rabbinic and the documentary *ketubbah* is that the latter was actually written, whereas there is no guarantee that the version in the *Mishnah* was ever used in an actual *ketubbah*. On the other hand, utter incredulity is also out of place. Occasionally something in these documents contradicts our conventional knowledge about the period. For example, in the Qumranic *Rule of the Community* it is ruled that women can serve as witnesses or, according to Milik, an unpublished papyrus was found which is a writ of divorce a woman sent her husband. These texts, which contradict our conventional view of woman's place in Jewish society cannot be solved by merely correcting the text.[111]

The Structure of this Work

In every chapter of this work, an examination of the attitudes towards women in the circles which produced the written sources will precede treatment of our main historical question, namely, the exact social status of Jewish women in Palestine during the Hellenistic-Roman period. This procedure was adopted because in the absence of other evidence, the historian is often liable to mistake the attitudes to women expressed in the sources for the actual history of women. To be sure, such personal expressions occupy quite a significant portion of the literary and documentary evidence relating to women in the period under examination. Moreover, all the sources are associated with more or less the same dominant social strata – the aristocracy and upper middle class – and therefore their opinions are the ones that have survived. Even intellectuals without important social connections (principally *tannaim*) who gained entry into these more prominent circles by virtue of achievement in *Torah* scholarship, adopted the ethical norms of their new social environs. Dominant social status led men in these circles not only to express their opinions regarding women but also to try directly to shape women's social status according to their own evaluation of women's character, abilities and limitations. The literature they left is divided into two parts: general utterances about women in various matters, and legal and *halakhic* material which does not necessarily represent reality but rather indicates an attempt to mold women's social behavior according to prescribed ideas. The degree of success in pressing life into this mold varied; there was constant tension

---

[111] Bernadette Brooten dealt with this matter in her discussion of women who in synagogue inscriptions are called *archisynagoge* or "mother of the synagogue". As she demonstrated, previous scholars had interpreted such titles as purely honorary when borne by women but as reflecting authority and responsibility when attributed to men. See Brooten (above, n. 48), 6–10.

between the literature's ideal woman and the need to apply this ideal in real life, by means of the *halakhah*.

The way the literary sources treat women as a group is reminiscent of the intellectual attitude adopted towards other groups categorized as "outsiders"[112] This can be explained by the obvious fact that all the sources of the period were propounded by and for educated Jewish men.[113] As a result, the way rabbinic literature or other sources regard women obviously cannot be similar to the way those same sources regard the Jewish people as a whole (*Israel*), the Pharisees, the sages or even, in certain cases, the priests, the school of Hillel, or other groups to which the authors belonged or with which they identified. Distance and the lack of personal involvement in a group (in this case women) perforce produce stereotyped generalizations arising both from the desire to see the group as monolithic, its members sharing uniform attributes, and from the lack of identification with the group, even when it is very familiar to a source's author. Moreover, attitudes towards a particular group are influenced also by the extent to which that group can harm or profit the group to which the observer himself belongs. Only on infrequent occasions does the observer's interest in a foreign group extend beyond those areas in which he has direct dealings with it.[114]

The two different questions of the idealized or wished-for and the "actual" social status of women require examination of the same sources; it is incumbent on the researcher to try to sift out the crumbs of incidental information from the subjective or ideal picture of women these sources present, particularly by examining the contradictions between the description of an event or custom and the ideal picture. What remains after such an examination will very likely be an historically accurate picture, whether of a single event or of a permanent situation or condition. Nevertheless, one must always be cognizant of the fact that the everyday and banal occurrence often interested the sources less than the special and the exceptional. It is easy to fall into the trap of assuming that the stories related in the sources, which do indeed sometimes report historically accurate events, reflect the general situation. Social history deals with the banal; historical sources prefer the extraordinary.

---

[112] Terminology varies. Adler uses the expression "peripheral Jews" (above, n. 45), 7. Hyman (above, n. 45), 18, settles on "radical otherness". Neusner terms them "abnormal": J. Neusner, *A History of the Mishnaic Law of Women* V (Leiden 1980) 267.

[113] Cf. e.g. R. Judah's remark: "A person must say three blessings every day: Blessed be He who did not make me a gentile, Blessed be He who did not make me an ignoramus, Blessed be He who did not make me a woman" (*tBer.* 7.18; *yBer.* 9.2, 13b; *bMen.* 43b). "Person" here means a free, educated Jewish male belonging to the same group which produced rabbinic literature. The woman, by contrast, belongs to a foreign group, like gentiles, illiterates and slaves.

[114] Neusner (above, n. 112), 13–4.

I thus recognize that the task I have taken upon myself is formidable, and the nagging question, whether the meager results justify the tremendous effort and the mass of discourse presented in this book, still lingers. The historian can choose his subject-matter and can mold his conclusions to suit his theory. He cannot choose his sources. Thus Palestinian Jewish women of the Hellenistic-Roman period are destined to remain mute. All we can hope for is the discovery of dissident voices and slips of the pen which will reveal to us what our dominant authors preferred to silence. If I have managed to accomplish this to any significant degree, I am gratified.

Chapter 1:

Daughters

The Birth of a Daughter

Various traditions testify to the fact that parents were often disappointed when a daughter was born to them. In *Ben Sira* we read: "It is a disgrace to be the father of an undisciplined son, and the birth of a daughter is a loss" (22.3).[1] The *tannaitic* tradition expresses the same thing in opposite terms: "Anyone who does not have a son is as if dead" (*Gen. R.* 45.2, p. 448 ed. Theodor-Albeck).

Tannaitic tradition counts the sex of an unborn child among the seven secrets concealed from man, along with the day of his death and the date when the Wicked Kingdom (i.e. Rome) will fall (*Gen. R.* 65.12, p. 722–3 ed. Theodor-Albeck). The rabbis discussed what measures could be taken to ensure the birth of sons. R. Joshua gave two different answers: "He shall marry a wife that is worthy of him and conduct himself in modesty [lit., sanctify himself] at the time of marital intercourse" (*bNidd.* 70b–71a); and "He should make his wife glad to perform the commandment (to be fruitful and multiply?)" (*bBB* 10b, where R. Eliezer offers the advice: "he should give generously to the poor"). In both places, R. Joshua's answer provokes the response: "many have done so without results."[2] But the *tannaim* knew enough biology to be aware of the fact that the sex of a child was determined at the time of conception, for they warn: "If a

---

[1] This is based on the Greek. The Hebrew version of this verse has not been preserved. On *Ben Sira* and his attitude towards girls, see W.C. Trenchard, *Ben Sira's View on Women: A Literary Analysis* = *Brown Judaic Studies* XXXVIII (Chico CA 1982), 129–65.

[2] Elsewhere, a *baraita* expresses the opinion, based on what were understood to be biological facts, that "if a woman emits her semen first she bears a male child; if the man emits his semen first she bears a female child" (*bNidd.* 31a). But there and in a parallel at *bBer.* 60a we find the same teaching transmitted by R. Isaac in the name of R. Ammi, and this seems to be the correct version, see *Dikdukei Soferim, ad loc.* Thus the tradition is *amoraic.* A scientific evaluation of this belief can be found in Tirzah Z. Meachem, *Mishnah Tractate Niddah with Introduction: A Critical Edition with Notes on Variants, Commentary, Redaction and Chapters in Legal History and Realia* (Ph.D. diss. The Hebrew University of Jerusalem, 1989), 166–8 [Hebrew]; also Y. Levy, "When a Woman Emits Semen," *Koroth* 5 (1970–2), 716–7. [Hebrew], who claims that the belief does have a scientific basis but argues also that the word we have translated as "emits semen" (מזרעת) actually refers to ovulation and not to orgasm.

man's wife has become pregnant and he says, May it be Thy will that my wife shall bear a male, this prayer is in vain" (*m Ber.* 9.3).

The birth of sons is considered by the rabbis to be a blessing. The passage "she shall be free and conceive children" (*Num.* 5.29), referring to the *sotah* or suspected adulteress, is interpreted by R. Ishmael as follows: "if she used to give birth to females she now gives birth to males" (*Sifre Num.* 19, p. 23 ed. Horovitz; *tSot.* 2.3; *ySot.* 3.4, 18d). In a discussion about the good tidings over which one should say the blessing "Who is good and does good," the *amoraim* cite the *baraita*: "It has been taught: If a man is told that his wife has borne a son, he says: Blessed is He that is good and does good" (*bBer.* 59b).[3] R. Meir taught that Abraham was blessed in the fact that he did *not* have daughters (*tQidd.* 5.17; cf. *Gen. R.* 59.7, p. 635 ed. Theodor-Albeck, where R. Nehemiah says it).[4] Another *baraita* transmitted in the name of Tahlifa declares that in the days of King David, the entire people was blessed in that only males were born to all (*bMQ* 9a).

Further illustrations are found in other *aggadot*. When the wife of R. Shimeon b. Rabbi gave birth to a daughter, R. Hiyya comforted him: "The Holy One, blessed be He, has begun to bless you. What is the proof? he inquired. Because it is written: 'And it came to pass, when man began to multiply and daughters were born to them' (*Gen.* 6.1) " (*Gen. R.* 26.4, p. 246–7 ed. Theodor-Albeck); that is, daughters were considered a sign of fertility and increase, portending the birth of sons. But in the same passage, Rabbi pours cold water on his son's enthusiasm: "He asked him: Did the Babylonian congratulate you? Yes, he answered, and he said thus to me. Nevertheless, he observed, both wine and vinegar are needed, yet wine is more needed than vinegar; both wheat and barley are needed, yet wheat is more needed than barley". In other words, if sons are compared to wine, then daughters are vinegar, and so forth. This story is an important indication of how the rabbis explained the essential need for daughters in the world, as opposed to sons.

Another question which stimulated a debate in that period was why the *Torah* specified that a woman who gave birth to a girl should remain ritually unclean twice as long as a woman who gave birth to a boy (two weeks as opposed to one: *Lev.* 12.1–5). *The Book of Jubilees* found an answer in the story of the Garden of Eden: woman was created in the second week, and thus the period of uncleanness for a female is two weeks; Adam was brought to the Garden of Eden after 40 days, and Eve only after 80 days, thus a woman's period of purification for a son

---

[3] This reading is absent from many MSS, which have an entirely different text; see *Dikdukei Soferim, ad loc.*

[4] S. Lieberman discusses this *midrash* in "Quotations in Light of their Sources," in *Studies in Memory of Moses Shorr*, edd. L. Ginzberg and A. Weiss (New York 1944), 186–8 [Hebrew] emphasizing its connection to Job and the *haftarah* to the weekly *Torah* portion containing the episode of Isaac's birth.

is 40 days and for a daughter 80 (3.8–9). This interpretation does not view the doubly long period for purification after the birth of a daughter as punishment.[5] The sages tried to explain the law in a more scientific way, as it were: a son is formed on the 40th day of pregnancy whereas a daughter is formed only on the 80th (*tNidd.* 4.7; *bNidd.* 30b). The students of R. Ishmael (or alternatively R. Ishmael himself), tried to test this pseudo-scientific explanation by considering the results of an experiment, supposedly carried out in Alexandria, about which they had heard without knowing the full details. "A story is told of Cleopatra the queen of Alexandrus (*scil.* Alexandria) that when her maidservants were sentenced to death by royal decree they were subjected to a test and they found both [a male and a female embryo]" (*bNidd.* 30b); that is, two women who had been condemned to death were sequestered with men who were to impregnate them, and 40 days later, after the women had been executed, the embryos were taken from their wombs, and it was discovered that one was carrying a boy and the other a girl. This is at least one version of the experiment, but there is another version: "A story is told of Cleopatra the Greek queen that when her maidservants were sentenced to death under a government order they were subjected to a test and it was found that a male embryo was fully fashioned on the forty-first day and a female embryo on the eighty-first day" (*ibid.*). This source also does not view a woman's longer period of uncleanness after the birth of a daughter as punishment.

In sum: every source views the birth of a daughter as a disappointment. Yet at the same time, we hear of no practical instruction or theory recommending steps to reduce the number of daughters in a family. In contrast to Hellenistic and Roman sources, which abound with discussions about getting rid of unwanted infants, in particular daughters, the Jewish sources do not even raise this possibility. The only source which even mentions the matter is Josephus (*CA* 2.202), who does so in order to clarify for his non-Jewish readers the extent to which the

---

[5] On this see: G. Anderson, "Celibacy or Consummation in the Garden? Reflections on Early Jewish and Christian Interpretations of the Garden of Eden," *Harvard Theological Review* 82 (1989) 29. In contrast, modern scholarship does view this demand as a punishment to and a degradation of women. See L. J. Swidler , *Women in Judaism: The Status of Women in Formative Judaism* (Metuchen NJ 1976), 132; Rachel Biale, *Women and Jewish Law: An Exploration of Women's Issues in Halakhic Sources* (New York 1984), 152, (who relies on Rachel Adler, "Tumah and Taharah: Ends and Beginnings," in *The Jewish Woman: New Perspectives*, ed. Elizabeth Koltun [New York 1976], 63–71, although Adler does not claim that the doubly long purification period after the birth of a daughter was punishment); Léonie Archer, *Her Price is Beyond Rubies: The Jewish Woman in Graeco-Roman Palestine = Journal for the Study of the Old Testament Supplement Series* LX (Sheffield 1990), 37–8. For a different view, see Meachem (above, n. 2), 168, who suggests that a woman's menstrual blood was considered to be her seed, and the bleeding that accompanies birth was held to impart the same level of impurity as semen; but no support is offered for this opinion.

whole idea is foreign to Judaism. Non-Jewish sources as well confirm that Jews accepted and raised all children born to them, without exception.[6]

Can we examine whether these claims are reliable? Statistical studies have shown that as a rule 105 males are born for every 100 females in human societies, but boys die at a greater rate than girls from childhood diseases. While death in childbirth is a danger to which only women are exposed, war takes its toll primarily on the male population. Generally more females than males survive to old age.[7] In light of this we would expect to find the Jewish population more or less evenly balanced statistically between males and females.

Yet even those statistics which are available to the social historian – namely, personal names – create the mistaken impression that men were far more numerous than women in ancient Jewish society. The number of Jewish women known by name from Palestinian sources is 261,[8] which, given the corresponding sum

---

[6] Cf. Hecataeus of Abdera, in M. Stern, *Greek and Latin Authors on Jews and Judaism* I (Jerusalem 1976), 27, 33. On the custom of exposing infants, especially girls, and their fate, see Sarah B. Pomeroy, *Goddesses, Whores, Wives and Slaves: Women in Classical Antiquity* (New York 1975), 140; and *eadem*. "Infanticide in Hellenistic Greece," in *Images of Women in Antiquity*, edd. Averil Cameron and Amélie Kuhrt (Detroit 1985), 207–22. Also Marcia Guttentag and P. F. Secord, *Too Many Women? The Sex Ratio Question* (London 1985), 49–52. See also: D. Engels, "The Problem of Female Infanticide in the Greco-Roman World," *Classical Philology* 75 (1980), 112–20, who argues that this was rare in Greece as well, and M. Golden, "Demography and the Exposure of Girls at Athens," *Phoenix* 35 (1981) 316–31, who maintains that it was not.

[7] *Encyclopedia Britannica* 25 (1985), 1040; yet according to Guttentag et al. *ibid.* 84–111, statistical studies carried out at the end of the previous century among orthodox Jews in Russia found 130 males born for every 100 females. Guttentag attributed this huge deviation to the Jews' sexual habits, which in her opinion had not changed from *talmudic* times to the modern period, even during assimilation. But since reliable statistics are not available from earlier periods, data from Tsarist Russia can be of little use for the purpose of this study.

[8] These numbers are partly taken from my "Notes on the Distribution of Jewish Women's Names in Palestine in the Second Temple and *Mishnaic* Period," *Journal of Jewish Studies* 40 (1989), 200, but are corrected in accordance with G. Mayer, *Die jüdische Frau in der hellenistisch-römischen Antike* (Stuttgart 1987), 104–27. I am persuaded by Mayer's identification of the name לאותן in a document from the Judaean Desert, since the name appears quite frequently (even if fragmentarily) in her *ketubbah* (P. Benoit, J. T. Milik, and R. de Vaux, *Les grottes de Murabâ'at = Discoveries in the Judaean Desert* II [Oxford 1961], 114–5). I also accept his suggestion that this is an Aramaic name. I am further persuaded that the names Φούλεια Ἀφρεικανά (*CII* 1227), Κοτόλλα (*CII* 1234), Πρωτᾶ (*CII* 1252), Κύθρα (*CII* 1326), Ἀνδρώ (*CII* 1272), and Μόσχα (*CII* 1329), which I originally identified as male names, are female names by virtue of their feminine endings. But I do not accept Mayer's identification of the name Κρόκος and its Hebrew form קרקס ("crocus": *CII* 1212, 1312) as female, since there is at least one clear attribution of this name to a male: see the letter by the apostolic father Ignatius to the Christian community in Rome, § 10. After my article had been sent to the printer, new women's names from Masada were published: Y. Yadin and J. Naveh, *Masada I: The Aramaic and Hebrew Ostraca and Jar Inscriptions from Masada* (Jerusalem 1989), 22: "שלום הגלי[לית]"; Hannah

of about 2300 men's names, amounts to only 11.3 % of the total. This is of course no indication that Jews abandoned daughters immediately after birth,[9] but at least one historian has allowed himself to be fooled by the evidence. Mayer has tabulated the numbers of children in families, based on information from Josephus,[10] and has used it to justify rather strange conclusions. He argues from his tabulations that twice as many boys as girls were raised in Jewish society, and, relying on Pomeroy,[11] he compares this to the similar situation in Rome and implies that Jews, just like non-Jews, disposed of unwanted daughters. Yet it seems to me that until a Jewish source is discovered which deals with this matter, or until it can be proved from existing Jewish sources that Jews did in fact abandon daughters, we have to trust what the sources themselves say and reject Mayer's suggestion as a mistaken interpretation of the evidence.

Relations between Father and Daughter

A girl was brought up in her father's house until she was married. The longest comment on father-daughter relations can be found in *Ben Sira*:

> "Do you have daughters? Be concerned with their chastity / and do not show yourself too indulgent with them. (7.24)
> "A daughter is a snare of falsehood to her father / and worry over her robs him of sleep /
> "When she is young, for fear she may not appeal (to men) / in her virginity, for fear she may be disliked;
> "While a virgin, for fear she may be seduced / or having a husband, for fear she may go astray.
> "When in her father's house, lest she conceive / or when married, for fear she may be barren.
> "My son, keep strict watch over a daughter / or she may make you a laughingstock to your enemies
> "A byword in the city and assembly of the people / and put you to shame in public gatherings.

M. Cotton and J. Geiger, *Masada* II: *The Latin and Greek Documents* (Jerusalem 1989), 118: Σαλώμη; 124: Μαριάμ. And from other Judaean Desert locations N. Lewis, *The Documents from the Bar Kokhba Period in the Cave of Letters: Greek Papyri* (Jerusalem 1989), 67: Θαμαρή; 131: Σαλώμη. Another addition is the name Ψυχή, published a while ago by E. Peuch, "Inscriptions funéraires Palestiniennes: tombeau de Jason et ossuaires," *Revue Biblique* 90 (1983), 524, which I at first understood, following the author, as "funerary monument (נפש)", and only later realized that this was a woman's name just as it was the name of a female figure in Greek mythology. I should also mention in my inventory an unpublished ossuary inscription containing the name "שפירא בת רובנא," which is displayed in the Israel Museum.

[9] On the reasons for the imbalance, see my article, *ibid.* 187–90.

[10] Although he did not exhaust all available material in Josephus and has also included data from the Diaspora, see above (n. 8), 72–3.

[11] Above, n. 6. Mayer referred his reader to p. 251 in Pomeroy (1975); apparently he meant p. 228, since there is no p. 251 in the book.

"See that there is no lattice in her room / no spot that overlooks the approaches to the house." (42.9–11)[12]

Thus in *Ben Sira*'s eyes a daughter is a constant aggravation to her father, especially as a source of sexual temptation. Accordingly he cannot treat her with affection but locks her up behind bars. *Ben Sira*'s continual fears point to a rather impersonal, loveless relationship between father and daughter.

A slightly different picture emerges from parables in rabbinic literature. Clearly the fathers and daughters in these parables are usually allegorical representations of God and Israel, but still the authors were describing reality as they saw it when they depicted mutual feelings of love and respect between father and daughter, the daughter is obligated to obey her father but the father is attached to his daughter by his love for her. The *tannaim* told stories of the king redeeming his daughter from captivity (*Song of Songs R.* 1.9.5); speaking with her in public, in an alleyway and in a courtyard (*ibid.* 3.7.1); proud of her beauty (*ibid.* 3.8.2); recognizing his daughter even when she is dressed in rags (*ibid.* 6.12); and trying to conceal his own suffering from her during her wedding by not stopping the joyous festivities (*Lev. R.* 20.10, p. 468 ed. Margulies).[13] But note that the father's love for his daughter is presented in this last parable as exceptional.

The *halakhah,* too, exhibits a double standard regarding boys and girls, imposing many obligations on a father in connection with his son but awarding rights and benefits in the case of a daughter: "The father has control over his daughter as touching her betrothal ... and he has the right to anything found by her and to the work of her hands" (*mKet.* 4.4).[14] There is economic profit in all these rights. It is true that certain legal restrictions, as we will see, were applied to the profits a man could expect from the betrothal of his daughter, but her handiwork and the things she found could also be valuable.

---

[12] This passage from *Ben Sira* is cited in the *Babylonian Talmud*: "A daughter is a vain treasure to her father; through anxiety on her account he cannot sleep at night. As a minor, lest she be seduced; in her majority, lest she play the harlot; as an adult, lest she not be married; if she marries, lest she bear no children; when she grows old, lest she engage in witchcraft" (*bSanh.* 100b). The fact that this passage from *Ben Sira*, which was not included in the Hebrew Bible, is quoted in the *Talmud* with considerable precision so long afterwards indicates that these opinions were still cherished. And see further, Trenchard (above, n. 1), 146–56. *Ben Sira*'s hostile attitude to daughters has been commented on not only by Trenchard, *ibid.* 163–5, who sees *Ben Sira* as a particularly vociferous enemy of women, but also M. Z. Segal *The Complete Book of Ben Sira* (Jerusalem 1972), 285 [Hebrew].

[13] On wedding parables see Ofra Meir, "The Wedding in Kings' Parables (in the *Aggadah*)," in *Studies in Marriage Customs = Folklore Research Center Studies IV*, edd. D. Noy and I. Ben-Ami (Jerusalem 1974) 9–51 [Hebrew].

[14] On the *Mishnah*'s legal positions regarding women, see Judith R. Wegner, *Chattel or Person: The Status of Women in the Mishnah* (Oxford 1988), 20–39. Wegner demonstrates that the *Mishnah* treats daughters before sexual maturity merely as property with economic value.

A similar picture arises from the *halakhic* discussion of whether a father is required to provide for his daughters: "The father is not liable for his daughter's maintenance. This is the *midrash* R. Eleazar b. Azariah expounded before the Sages in the vineyard at Yavneh: 'The sons inherit and the daughters receive maintenance'[15] – but just as the sons inherit only after the death of their father so the daughters receive maintenance only after the death of their father" (*mKet.* 4.6). We may suppose, as this *baraita* states, that R. Eleazar offered his remarks only as an intellectual exercise and not as a practical teaching, but his view would have gained support as the economic situation deteriorated and it became harder to feed hungry mouths. Thus we find in the reforms of Usha, which generally speaking were promulgated in response to the state of emergency that prevailed after the Bar Kokhba revolt: "In Usha it was ordained that a man must maintain both his sons and his daughters while they are still minors" (*bKet.* 49b, cf. *tKet.* 4.8; *yKet.* 4.8, 28b).[16]

In sum, the various sources treated affection between a father and daughter as exceptional and worthy of note.[17] Even the *halakhah* treated daughters as less valuable than sons. But the propounders of the *halakhah* changed their minds on this matter, at least in one place where it seemed to them that the standard *halakhic* attitude was liable to endanger the lives of daughters.

The Daughter as Only Child

We know of at least seven daughters (and perhaps more) without siblings from the period under study. 1) In the Hasmonean dynasty, Alexandra appears to have been the only child of Hyrcanus II. Four more cases of a daughter as only child are known in the Herodian dynasty: 2) Salome, the daughter of Herodias and her first husband, Herod (son of King Herod and Mariamme the daughter of Boethus). So far as our sources go, no children are known from her mother's second marriage, to Herod Antipas, although Josephus did not pay much attention to Antipas' branch of the family.[18] 3) Cyprus, the granddaughter of Salome,

---

[15] A condition in a *ketubbah*: see *mKet.* 4.10–1.

[16] Archer (above, n. 5), 63 takes R. Eleazar b. Azariah's *midrash* very seriously and claims, using fine *talmudic* reasoning, that a father is not responsible for his daughter's maintenance because, in contrast with a husband, he has no control over her handiwork and the property she finds. But the *halakhah* makes no such point-by-point comparison, nor, therefore, should modern scholars.

[17] Father-daughter relations in Judaism – if our sources present a true picture – are quite the opposite of father-daughter relations pictured by Roman sources of the same period, at least as presented by Judith P. Hallet, *Fathers and Daughters in Roman Society: Women and the Elite Family* (Princeton 1984).

[18] In the New Testament the name of Herodias' daughter who danced her famous dance before the assembled guests is not mentioned. Josephus is the one who names Herodias'

sister of Herod, and daughter of her son, Antipater, is mentioned as an only child (*AJ* 18.138). It is true that women in the Herodian house are often mentioned only by virtue of their having married into the family, but the fact that Cyprus was married to Helkias, a son of Salome's husband, who himself is not known in any other context, suggests that she was not mentioned because of her connection to the Herodian house and that if she had had siblings they would have been mentioned, too. 4) The same considerations hold for Cyprus' daughter, Cyprus (*ibid.*). 5) Jotape, the deaf daughter of Aristobulus, Agrippa's brother, was also an only child (*AJ* 18.135).[19] Other descendants of this Aristobulus, who was the king's brother and the son-in-law of the king of Emesa, would surely have been mentioned.[20]

6) According to Yadin,[21] Babatha, whose archive of documents was found in Nahal Hever, was the only child of her parents, Shimeon and Mariamme, for after their death she inherited all their property. 7) Babatha's second husband, Judah, left an only daughter, Shelamzion, who inherited not only the property of her father but also part of that of her cousins.[22]

---

only child, a daughter from her previous marriage (*AJ* 18.136) - Salome, but scholars have found chronological problems in the information about her life: a) if she was still a child (κοράσιον) when she danced in front of Antipas in the year 30 (the earliest suggested date for the death of John the Baptist), how could she have been married to Philip, her uncle on her father's side, who died in 34 CE? b) If she was married to someone who was old enough to have been her grandfather, how could she then have been married afterwards to her young cousin Aristobulus, who was too young in 49 to inherit the kingdom of Chalcis from his father and became king of Armenia Minor only in 54? Regarding this latter problem, W. Lillie, "Salome or Herodias?" *Expository Times* 65 (1953–4), 251 has claimed, on the basis of manuscript variants, that a certain Herodias, the daughter of Herod Antipas, is the one who did the dance; N. Kokkinos, "Which Salome did Aristobulus Marry?" *Palestine Exploration Quarterly* 118 (1986), 33–50, has argued that the Salome whom Aristobulus married was the daughter of Antipas and his Arab wife, the daughter of the Nabataean king Aretas.

[19] On Jotape and her family see Grace H. Macurdy, "Iotape," *Journal of Roman Studies* 26 (1936), 40–2.

[20] Berenice, the daughter of Mariamme, King Agrippa's daughter, is mentioned as the only daughter of her father, Julius Archelaus, but her mother had children afterwards from a different marriage (*AJ* 20.140; 147); we cannot know whether her father had other children from other marriages. Mariamme, the daughter of Joseph the son of Joseph (Herod's brother) and Salome (Herod's daughter), who was married eventually to Herod of Chalcis, the brother of King Agrippa, is also mentioned as an only child, but in this case it is likely that the sources bothered to mention only her because she married into Agrippa's immediate family, without which even she would not even have been noticed. Thus she may have had siblings. Two of Herod's wives also had only daughters: Roxane, daughter of Phaedra, and Salome, daughter of Elpis (*AJ* 17.21), but they were only two of Herod's many children.

[21] Y. Yadin, *Bar Kokhba: Rediscovery of the Legendary Hero of the Second Jewish Revolt against Rome* (London 1971) 233.

[22] The New Testament contains the story of Jesus' resurrection of the daughter of the

Mayer[23] noted the prevalence of only children, daughters as well as sons, in Jewish families of the period. The reasons for this phenomenon he explained as a result of infant deaths and the deaths of mothers during their first delivery. This explanation seems to me comprehensive and satisfactory, and I would note further only that the phenomenon indicates that the problem of inheritance by an only daughter (or only daughters) was certainly a real problem and not merely a subject for theoretical discussion, as we will see.

---

leader of the synagogue, Jairus ("Talitha Kumi": *Matt.* 9.8; 23–6; *Mark* 5.22–4; 35–44; *Luke* 8.41–2; 49–56). Only *Luke* 8.41, which is certainly not the original source of the story, indicates that the girl was an only child, and this point could be based on the parallel story of the resurrection of the only son of the widow from Nain (*Luke* 7.12). This is an example of a phenomenon which scholars have noted frequently in *Luke*, namely, that the author relates parallel stories whose central figure is once male and once female: L. J. Swidler, *Biblical Affirmations of Women* (Philadelphia 1979), 164–5; Constance F. Parvey, "The Theology and Leadership of Women in the New Testament," in *Religion and Sexism: Images of Women in the Jewish and Christian Traditions*, ed. Rosemary R. Ruether (New York 1974), 138–40; B. Witherington III, *Women in the Earliest Church* (Cambridge 1988), 129–30. In my opinion, the historical kernel in the story, if there is one at all, is the presence of a daughter, rather than a son; but it is difficult to know how sick the girl actually was, if she in fact had died and what Jesus actually did. Many New Testament scholars have made a special point of stressing that only Jesus is said to have performed miracles which benefited women: Swidler, *ibid.* 180; B. Witherington III, *Women in the Ministry of Jesus* (Cambridge 1982), 67. But this claim may be interpreted in two contradictory ways: a) as proof that the stories have an historical kernel, for otherwise stories with male heroes would have been chosen; or b) as proof that the stories have no historical kernel, for in order to convey Jesus' feminist social message, the New Testament authors deliberately made females an integral part of stories. Yet in any case either claim appears on its face to neglect the similar story of the rescue of the daughter of Nehonia the well-digger by R. Hanina b. Dosa: "It once happened that the daughter of Nehonia the well-digger fell into a large cistern, and people went and reported [the accident] to R. Hanina b. Dosa. During the first hour he said to them: All is well. In the second hour he again said: All is well. In the third he said to them: She is saved" (*bYeb.* 121b; *bBQ* 50a). The story of the rescue of the daughter of a pious well- and cave-digger by Pinhas b. Yair (*ySheq.* 5.2, 48d), which is constructed on the same model, is in fact the same story with different surface details and does not require a separate discussion; and see Rachel Nissim, "The Figure of the Hasid: A Confrontation between R. Hanina b. Dose and R. Pinhas b. Yair in View of the Rabbinic Position on Retribution," *Alei Siah* 12–13–14 (1982), 135–54 [Hebrew]. In this story, as in that of the rescue of the daughter of the leader of the synagogue in the New Testament, the plot of the story does not require that the child be female; Hanina b. Dosa, who was a popular miracle-worker like Jesus, could just as easily have saved the son of Nehonia, thus the daughter is likely part of the historical kernel of the story.

[23] Above, n. 8.

Naming a Daughter

Sons as well as daughters almost always received their personal names from their parents at the time of birth; there was no difference in this practice for boys and girls. Certain patterns emerge from an inspection of the inventory of personal names from the Second Temple period, which reveals the tendency to adhere conservatively to tradition. Hebrew names are generally biblical, not original, while the remainder of names are Greek, Aramaic, and more rarely Latin or Persian. What, then, were the criteria for naming a child? The rabbis were aware of conservatism in naming practices in their time, as they explained by comparison with the biblical period: "The ancients, since they knew their genealogy, named themselves in reference to the events of their times; but we who do not know our genealogy name ourselves after our fathers" (*Gen. R.* 37.7, p. 349 ed. Theodor-Albeck). In other words, boys were named after their fathers or grandfathers while daughters were named after their mothers or grandmothers. This practice may have been influenced by other peoples of the region, for we have no examples from the biblical period of members of the same family being given the same names, in contrast to the Hellenistic practice – especially among royal families, which were the objects of imitation by all strata of society – whereby the same names were used in successive generations. Thus the Jewish practice of naming children after ancestors may be a sign of Hellenistic influence.

So far as it is possible to trace women's names in the same family, we find that the practice of naming daughters after their grandmothers was indeed followed. The two granddaughters of Queen Shelamzion (Alexandra) bore her Greek name; Agrippa I named his daughter Berenice after his own mother and his second daughter, Mariamme, after his grandmother, after whom Agrippa's sister Mariamme was also named; Antipater son of Salome (Herod's sister) named his daughter Cyprus after his grandmother. This same Cyprus named her own daughter Cyprus perhaps after herself. The wife of Agrippa I, also Cyprus, was named after her great-grandmother.

A Roman influence can also be found in the naming of daughters among Jews. As is well-known, Romans were accustomed, principally in the Republican period, to give daughters their fathers' name with a feminine ending.[24] Sometimes Roman sisters would have the same name.[25] The Greeks also gave daughters the

---

[24] E.g. Agrippa-Agrippina, Octavius-Octavia, etc. See Hallet (above, n. 17), 77–81 plus bibliography listed in n. 22.

[25] Hallet, *ibid. John* 19.25 – "standing near the cross of Jesus were his mother and his mother's sister, Mary the wife of Clopas and Mary Magdalene" – can be interpreted to mean that the sister of Mary the mother of Jesus was also named Mary, but the sentence can also be understood as saying that four different women – the mother, the sister, Mary the wife of Clopas and Mary Magdalene – stood at the foot of the cross.

feminine forms of their fathers' names, and this practice can be found already in the Hasmonean dynasty – for example, Alexandra, after Alexander.[26] Another example can be found in the Herodian dynasty: Herodias, derived of course from Herod. The name Yohanna-Joanna (יהוחנה) which is the feminine form of the male name Yohanan, also became very popular in this period, as it is represented by eight examples;[27] a similar case is that of the biblical name Judith (*Gen.* 26.36), the feminine form of Judah, of which three examples survive.[28] In the same vein, it is interesting to note Berenicianus (*AJ* 20.104; *BJ* 2.221), named after his mother, Queen Berenice, daughter of Agrippa I.[29]

The Roman practice of naming girls, which required very little creativity or special attention, led to a striking monotony in women's names during the period under study. The same quality indeed characterizes men's names as well,[30] but is even more prominent among women. Three names only (Salome, Shelamzion[31]

---

[26] In my estimation, Queen Shelamzion Alexandra was not the relative of Shimeon b. Shetah but a descendant of the Hasmoneans, and see S. Safrai, "Tales of the Sages in the Palestinian Tradition and the *Babylonian Talmud*," in *Studies in Aggadah and Folk-Literature* = *Scripta Hierosolymitana* XXII, edd. J. Heinemann and D. Noy (Jerusalem 1971), 229–32; for a different opinion about Alexandra's background, see J. Efron, *Studies on the Hasmonean Period* (Leiden 1987), 152. Alexandra's name probably derives from the Hasmonean Alexander, perhaps even her father; it is reasonable to assume that she was the niece or cousin of Yannai himself.

[27] See my article (above, n. 8), 195.

[28] *Ibid.* and cf. the figure Judith in the book Apocryphal book bearing her name; this Judith might have been so named in order to equate her accomplishments with those of Judah the Maccabee. In the *Palestinian Talmud*, the sister of R. Judah Nasia (not to be mistaken with Judah the Patriarch, his grandfather) is named Yehudinei (יהודיני) (*yNaz.* 4.1, 56a).

[29] On which see my: "Julia Crispina, Daughter of Berenicianus, A Herodian Princess in the Babatha Archive: A Case Study in Historical Identification," *Jewish Quarterly Review* 82 (1992), 374–7.

[30] See my "The Names of the Hasmoneans in the Second Temple Period," *Eretz-Israel* 19 (1987), 238–41 [Hebrew].

[31] We may also note here the utter rarity of original Jewish names from the Second Temple period, even though the names Shelamzion and Salome are themselves innovations of the same period. According to Mayer (above, n. 8), 106–7, 109–10, Salome is a Hebrew name whereas Shelamzion is Aramaic. The Hebrew form of Salome (שלום) is the same as that for a male, Shalom (or "Shallum"), which appears in *2 Kings* 15.10; 22.14; *Jer.* 22.11; 32.7; 35.4; and see also the many instances in *Ezra* and *Nehemiah*, although in the Second Temple period the name is solely female. There may be exceptions, however: a) the brother of Joseph the son of Tobias was named Σολέμιος, Σόλυμος; his Hebrew name is uncertain, either שלום or שלמה (Solomon); but Solomon appears as Σολομών in Josephus and Σολομών or Σαλωμών in the Septuagint. b) An ossuary bearing the inscription שלום (Shalom) contains the remains only of a male; J. Naveh, "The Ossuary Inscriptions from Giv'at ha-Mivtar," *Israel Exploration Journal* 20 (1970), 36 suggested that the word was either a male's name or a blessing for the deceased, but neither need be the case, for the ossuary could have been prepared for a female and then used for a male.

and Mariamme-Maria[32]) account for 122, or 46.5 % (almost half) of all the Palestinian women whose names are known.[33] We can be certain that this is no accident or illusion, for the same frequency of these names is to be found in all the varied sources: they account for 13 out the 40 women's names in Josephus (32.5 %), 6 out of 16 in the New Testament (37.5 %), 9 out of 25 in *tannaitic* literature (36 %), 75 out of 157 in funerary inscriptions (47 %), and 20 out of 27 in documents from the Judaean Desert (74 %). Thus any deviation which these statistics represent can only be marginal.

The choice of the names Mariamme-Maria and Salome-Shelamzion must in any case be explained. I have already demonstrated elsewhere[34] that Hasmonean names – Mattitiyahu (Matthias) and the names of his five sons – became very popular for sons after the successful Hasmonean revolt. Do the popularity of the names Shelamzion and Mariamme also reflect Hasmonean influence? While the two prominent Hasmoneans who had these names – the queen and Herod's wife, respectively – were not connected to any meaningful historical event on the level of the Hasmonean revolt, and both were active after the Hasmonean dynasty had become loathsome to its Jewish subjects, it is likely that both these figures were named after Hasmonean women from the time of the rebellion who remain unrecorded in the sources. If this theory is correct, then names in the Second Temple period did indeed bear some connection to crucial historical events, although in a different manner from that of the biblical period.

Identifying a Daughter by her Father

Most daughters were identified in the Second Temple period by the father, both in inscriptions and in other documents such as marriage contracts, writs of divorce and deeds of sale. A woman was known as X the daughter of Y.[35] In this light, an ossuary inscription found in a burial-cave in Dominus Flevit on the

---

[32] The popularity of this name was noticed also by J. Luis Diez Merino, "'Maria' en la onomastica Aramea Judia intertestamental (s. II a.C. – s. II d.C.)," *Scripta de Maria* 6 (1983), 29–37, although his sample was much smaller than the one I assembled, and his theological conclusions are irrelevant to our purpose. On the two forms of this name and the Roman influence on its use, see Naomi G. Cohen, "The Personal Name 'Miriam' and its Latin and Greek Transliterations," *Lešonenu* 38 (1974), 170–80 [Hebrew].

[33] A second group of women's names which enjoyed extraordinary popularity includes the Aramaic names Martha (15 examples) and Shapira (11 examples), and the Hebrew name Joanna (8 examples).

[34] Above, n. 30.

[35] Archer (above, n. 5), 267–70 argues that women identified in funerary monuments by the name of their father and not their husband were either divorced or widowed and had returned to their father's house, but the great number of women known by their patronymics makes this explanation statistically improbable.

Mount of Olives, which identifies a father by the name of his daughter, stands out as a rare exception.[36] According to the inscription, the ossuary contained the remains of three people, two women and one man. The women are identified by personal names without mention of any male relative, while the male, Chresimos (Χρήσιμος), is identified as the father of Demarchia (πατὴρ Δημαρχ[ία]ς). This latter name might have been restored in the male form Δήμαρχος had another ossuary bearing the name Δημαρχίας not also been found in the same cave, supporting the assumption that both names belonged to the same woman. This exceptional inscription would indicate that visitors to the burial-cave would have been more familiar with the daughter than with the father.[37]

---

[36] P. B. Bagatti and J. T. Milik, *Gli Scavi del Dominus Flevit = Pubblicazioni dello Studium Biblicum Franciscanum* XIII (Jerusalem 1958), p. 99, no. 41.

[37] On the general phenomenon of men identified by the mothers' names, see my article, "'Man Born of Woman ...' (*Job* 14.1): The Phenomenon of Men Bearing Metronymes at the Time of Jesus," *Novum Testamentum* 34 (1992), 23–45.

Chapter 2:

Marriage

The sources, which we have argued look at the world from a decidedly male point of view, speak of a man's need for a wife and of the problems this dependency causes.

We read in *Ben Sira*: "Where there is no fence, the property will be plundered;/ and where there is no wife, a man will become a fugitive" (36.30)[1] – in other words, marriage brings a certain desired stability to a man's life. *Ben Sira* also says, "I take pleasure in three things, and they are beautiful in the sight of God and of mortals:/ agreement among siblings friendship among neighbors, and a wife and a husband who live in harmony" (25.1–2).[2] In the same style the rabbis taught, "Seven are banned by Heaven; these are they: a man who has no wife ..." (*bPes*. 113b).[3] The same content is expressed in a different style in *Genesis Rabbah*: "He who has no wife dwells without good, without help, without joy, without blessing and without atonement" (17.2, p. 151 ed. Theodor-Albeck). The verse, "willingly lending him enough for his need, whatever it may be" (*Deut*. 15.8), is interpreted as follows: "'him' refers to a wife, as it is stated, 'I will make him a helper as his partner' (*Gen*. 2.18)" (*tPeah* 4.10). Even to the question, what has God been doing since the creation of the world, R. Yose answered, "He sits and makes matches, assigning this man to that woman and this woman to that man" (*Gen. R*. 68.4, p. 772 ed. Theodor-Albeck). Thus both *Ben Sira* and the rabbis thought that, despite the differences between women and men, married life was preferable.

Yet ancient authors distinguish between good and bad wives and daughters who are destined to become wives. *Ben Sira* lays this out rather categorically:

> "A wicked wife to the lot of a fool shall fall / and a righteous woman to a righteous man.
> "A wife who has no shame will do evil / while a daughter who has shame will blush before her husband.

---

[1] See W. C. Trenchard *Ben Sira's View on Women: A Literary Analysis = Brown Judaic Studies* XXXVIII (Chico CA 1982), 24–6.

[2] On this passage see Trenchard, *ibid*. 31–2.

[3] Thus the reading in the MSS; the printed versions read, "A Jew who has no wife ... " R. Rabinovitch attributes the change to the Christian censor; see *Dikdukei Soferim, ad loc*.

"A headstrong wife is regarded as a dog / but a daughter who has a sense of shame will fear the Lord." (26.23–5)[4]

"Happy is the husband of a good wife / the number of his days will be doubled.

"A loyal wife makes her husband put on fat / She will make his years joyful.

"A good wife is a great blessing / she will be granted among the blessings of the man who fears the Lord." (*ibid.* 1–3)[5]

Yet concerning the wicked wife he says:

"Any wound, but not a wound of the heart! / Any wickedness, but not the wickedness of a wife! ..." (25.13)

"There is no venom worse than a snake's venom / and no wrath worse than a woman's wrath.

"I would rather dwell with a lion and a dragon / than dwell with an evil wife.

"The wickedness of a wife changes her appearance / and darkens her face like that of a bear.

"Her husband takes his meals among the neighbors / and in their tastelessness he will sigh.

"Any iniquity is insignificant compared to a wife's iniquity / may a sinner's lot befall her! ..." (25.15–9)

"A dejected mind, a gloomy face / and a wounded heart are caused by an evil wife

"Drooping hands and weak knees / are caused by the wife who does not make her husband happy. ..." (25.23)[6]

"Of three things my heart is afraid / and of a fourth I am frightened: ...

"There is grief of heart and sorrow when a wife is envious of a rival wife ..."

"An evil wife is an ox yoke which chafes / taking hold of her is like grasping a scorpion."[7] (26.5–7)

The rabbis, too, distinguished between the good and the bad wife. To Rabban Yohanan b. Zakkai's question, "Which is the way to which man should cleave?" R. Yose responds, "This refers to the good impulse; but some say it refers to a good wife." And to Rabban Yohanan's question, "Which is the way which man should shun?" R. Yose gives the answer: "This refers to the evil impulse; but some say this refers to the evil wife" (*ARNB* 29, p. 59 ed. Schechter).[8] In the style of wisdom literature, to which genre *Ben Sira*'s maxims belong, the rabbis count the wicked wife among the severest punishments that can be meted out to a man: "R. Judah said: There are fourteen things which are stronger one than the other, and each one is dominated by the next. ... Stronger than them all is a bad wife" (*Eccl. R.* 7.26.2).[9]

---

[4] Compare *bYeb.* 63b. Trenchard (above, n. 1), 12 believes that this passage is not part of *Ben Sira*'s original text, although he acknowledges that the source was nonetheless a Hebrew text composed in the time of *Ben Sira*.

[5] See Trenchard (above, n. 1), 13–4 on the orientation of this text.

[6] According to Trenchard, *ibid.* 243–4, this passage, too, is an interpolation.

[7] Compare *bYeb.* 63b: "a wicked wife is like leprosy (צרעת) to her husband."

[8] But note that this answer does not appear in the original tractate *Abot* in the *Mishnah* and is likely to be of later date.

[9] R. Judah's list in fact includes 15 things; the wife (woman) is an addition to the

1. The Virtuous Wife

The sources provide sparse detail regarding the qualities which make a wife good or bad. *Ben Sira* counts four qualities which make a wife good:

> 1. "Happy is the husband of an intelligent[10] wife / that does not plow with ox and ass." (25.8)[11]
> "A friend or a companion never meets one amiss / but better than both is an intelligent wife."[12] (40.23)

In other words, *Ben Sira* could appreciate a wife's intelligence, although how this quality was manifested is not self-evident. *Ben Sira* provides but little illumination. We do not even know from the text whether women acquired this "intelligence" through formal education which a father provided his daughter. Elsewhere *Ben Sira* says, "A prudent (φρονίμη) daughter obtains[13] her husband" (22.4). One explanation to this verse is that a daughter's intelligence gives her a certain edge in finding a good partner. However, Trenchard understood this to mean "shall accept," that is, a daughter's prudence is manifested in her acceptance of any husband her father chooses for her. If this reading is correct (and the Hebrew word cannot be vocalized in any other way), then a daughter's prudence is nothing more than her obedience to her father.[14]

> 2. "A silent wife is a gift from the Lord / her restraint is more than money can buy.
> "A modest wife has charm upon charm / no scales can weigh the worth of her chastity." (26.16–7)

That is, a wife's wisdom may be, in the opinion of *Ben Sira*, her ability to keep silent.

> 3. "A wife who honors her husband is accounted wise (σοφή) by all." (26.26)[15]

Here as above, it appears that the essence of a woman's wisdom, and perhaps also the kind of intelligence and understanding befitting her, lies in her fulfill-

---

original fourteen, since she is mentioned in a different style, as the sixteenth thing. Yet in any case she is integral to the final redaction, for she is used to clarify the biblical verse, "and I find more bitter than death the woman (wife? אשה)" (*Eccl.* 7.26).

[10] One Genizah manuscript has the letter מ at the beginning of this word. This has been completed by editors to משכלת based on the next text (40.23). The Greek word is συνετή, translated by Liddell and Scott as: "quick at apprehending, intelligent, sagacious."

[11] Trenchard (above, n. 1), 33–4 thinks that the second part of the verse does not concern women.

[12] So in the Hebrew. The Greek has a totally different meaning.

[13] Lit. shall inherit.

[14] Above, n. 1, 138.

[15] According to Trenchard, *ibid.* 11–2, this line was also not part of the original composition.

ment of the natural order of the world, by which a woman is subordinate to a man.

4. Yet the most prominent characteristic of a good woman is:

> "A wife's charm is the delight of her husband / and her knowledge (ἐπιστήμη) puts flesh on his bones. ...
> "As beautiful as the sunrise in the Lord's heaven / is a good wife in a well-ordered home.
> "As bright as the light on the sacred lamp-stand / is a beautiful face up on high.
> "Like a golden pillar on a silver base / is a shapely leg with a firm foot." (26.13–8)
> "A woman's beauty makes a man happy / and overcomes all other desires." (36.27)[16]

That is, a good wife is above all a beautiful woman.

The *tannaim* also thought that beauty was of crucial importance for a wife. The following utterances resemble wisdom literature in style: "Three things increase a man's self-esteem: a beautiful dwelling, a beautiful wife and beautiful utensils" (*bBer.* 57b); "There are three kinds of beauty: the beauty of a wife in her husband's eyes ... (*yYoma* 4.1, 41b).[17] The *Apocrypha* and *Pseudepigrapha* also describe good wives first and foremost as beautiful. Susanna was said to be extremely beautiful (*Susanna* 2; 7; 31). Also described as beautiful are Queen Esther (*Additions to Esther* 4.4), the widow Judith (*Judith* 8.7; 10.7; 19, 23), and Sarah, Tobiah's wife (*Tobit* 6.12). The beauty of the biblical Sarah is especially emphasized in the *Genesis Apocryphon* from Qumran (XX 2–8).[18]

Thus there existed the image of the ideal wife, who was both obedient and beautiful.

2. The Bad Wife

Ben Sira names three prominent characteristics of a bad wife:

> 1. "It is as easy for an old man to climb a sand dune/ as for a quiet husband to live with a nagging wife." (25.20)[19]
> "A strident, garrulous wife is like a terrible trumpet." (26.31)[20]

---

[16] On the importance of beauty in the thought of *Ben Sira*, see Trenchard, *ibid.* 17–8, 21–2.

[17] On the one hand, beauty is so important in the rabbinic value-system that, according to *halakhah*, a woman may demand a *get* in a court solely for aesthetic reasons (*mKet.* 7.10); on the other hand, a woman was forbidden to reveal their beauty to any man other than her husband (see below, chapter 4).

[18] On the importance of female beauty in the Second Temple period, see D. Flusser rev. of Grintz, *Sefer Yehudith* in *Kirjath Sepher* 33 (1958), 273–4 [Hebrew]; C.W. Reines, "Beauty in the Bible and the *Talmud*," *Judaism* 24 (1974), 100–7.

[19] For commentary, see Trenchard (above, n. 1), 76–7.

[20] Cf. above, n. 15.

In direct contrast to the good wife, who keeps silent, the bad wife is a scold ("strident"). Loquacity is defined by the rabbinic sages as one of the leading negative qualities of women: "Ten *kabs* of gossip descended into the world; nine were taken by women" (*bQidd.* 49b). The *Mishnah* defines the scolding woman as follows: "Who is deemed a scolding woman? Whosoever speaks inside her own house so that her neighbors hear her voice" (*mKet.* 7.6). R. Tarfon thought that such a woman should be divorced.

2. "A drunken wife is a great provocation / she cannot keep her excesses secret." (26.9)[21]

Thus drunkenness is counted among the qualities of a bad woman. *Ben Sira* connects wine to prostitution:

"Wine and women rob the wise of their wits / and a frequenter of prostitutes becomes more and more reckless." (19.2)

But elsewhere he says almost the exact opposite:

"Offspring and planting perpetuate a man's name / but better still is a desired woman. "Wine and music gladden the heart / but better still is sexual love (אהבת דודים)." (40.20)

This passage suggests that *Ben Sira* has a double standard regarding wine and women. Similar attitudes towards wine do not appear in *tannaitic* literature, but they can be found in the *Pseudepigrapha*. According to the *Testament of Reuben,* for instance, Bilhah was so drunk when Reuben had intercourse with her that she was not aware of him at all (3.13–14); by this assertion Reuben was trying to assign equal blame to Bilhah. In the *Testament of Judah,* Judah confesses that he decided to marry his Canaanite wife when he was drunk (11.2).[22]

3. The worst characteristic of a bad woman, be it daughter or wife, is considered, naturally, to be the ease with which she can be seduced. Thus *Ben Sira* on daughters:

"Keep close watch over a headstrong daughter / if she finds you off your guard, she will take her chance. "Beware of her impudent looks / and do not be surprised if she disobeys you. "As a parched traveler with his tongue hanging out / drinks from any spring that offers, "She shall sit before every peg / and open her quiver to the arrow." (26.11–4)[23]

---

[21] A discussion of drunkenness in Trenchard (above, n. 1), 65–6. On *Ben Sira*'s apprehensions about drunken and adulterous women, see the humoristic analysis of H. McKeating, "Jesus ben Sira's Attitude to Women," *Expository Times* 85 (1973–4), 85–7.

[22] The problem of women's drunkenness makes an appearance also in Roman sources. See Sarah B. Pomeroy, *Goddesses, Whores, Wives and Slaves: Women in Classical Antiquity* (New York 1975), 153–4 and 243, nn. 9 and 11.

[23] See Trenchard (above, n. 1), 140–6.

And on wives:

> "So too with a wife who is unfaithful to her husband / presenting him with an heir by a different father:
> "First, she disobeys the law of the Most High / secondly, she commits an offense against her husband;"
> "Thirdly, she has prostituted herself by bearing bastard children." (23.36–8)[24]

Rabbinic literature adds another quality of the bad wife: "Three things reduce a man to poverty: ... [one is] being cursed by one's wife to his face" (*bShab.* 62b).

In any case, both *Ben Sira* and the rabbinic sages knew what the judgment on a bad wife had to be. *Ben Sira* says:

> "Do not leave a leaky cistern to drip / or allow a bad wife to say what she likes.
> "If she does not accept your control / divorce her and send her away." (25.29)[25]

The rabbis also thought that a man had to divorce a bad wife: "It is a duty (מצוה) to divorce a bad wife" (*bErub.* 41b).

Marriage and Spinsterhood: Two Different Paths

Although the main Jewish sources presented marriage as the preferred solution to a man's plight, all sources were aware of the difficulties involved in marriage. Thus an ideology that rejected married life completely developed on the *hasidic* fringes of Jewish society. The Essenes, so far as we can make out, came closest to an utter rejection of marriage (*BJ* 2.120; *AJ* 18.21; Philo *Hypoth.* 11.14; Pliny *HN* 5.73), and may even have incorporated this rejection into his legal system.[26] A rejection of married life appears also in the New Testament. In *Matthew* 19.10-11, we find: "His disciples said to him: If such is the case of a man with his wife, it is better not to marry. But he said to them: Not everyone can accept this teaching, but only those to whom it is given." The origin of these verses should be noted: *Matthew* is considered the evangelist most closely related to Judaism, yet these verses do not appear in *Mark* 10.1–12, *Matthew's* source, and therefore are apparently not a genuine teaching of Jesus. The verses in *Matthew* probably reflect a Jewish *hasidic* current close in outlook to the Essenes. The

---

[24] *Ibid.* 99–103.

[25] See Trenchard (above, n. 1), 83–6.

[26] On the connection between Josephus' Essenes and the writings from Qumran, see H. Hübner, "Zölibat in Qumran?" *New Testament Studies* 17 (1970), 153–67. Assuming that the Dead Sea Sect was Essene, he does not believe that the Essenes entirely rejected the institution of marriage; so also A. Isaksson, *Marriage and Ministry in the New Temple: A Study with Special Reference to Mt 19:13–22 and 1Cor 11:3–16 = Acta Seminarii Neotestamentici Upsaliensis* XXIV (Lund 1965), 45–65.

preference of celibacy over marriage eventually became the most striking contrast between Judaism and Christianity, but such a development is late, and the distinction between the two opposing religions with regard to this issue was not so marked during the Second Temple period.[27]

In light of the ambivalent attitude among different Jewish groups towards marriage, it may be instructive to investigate the extent to which marriage was in fact practiced. Rabbinic literature has preserved the case of the bachelor Ben Azzai, whom, when he praised married life and fulfillment of the commandment to "be fruitful and multiply," the rabbis felt compelled to remind that he "is very good at expounding but not at fulfilling" (*tYeb*. 8.4; *Gen. R.* 34.14, pp. 326–7 ed. Theodor-Albeck; *bYeb*. 63b; cf. *ySot*. 1.2, 16c).[28] Another bachelor, whose single status is beyond doubt, is Agrippa II: not only does Josephus never mention that Agrippa II had a wife or children, but he also records the rumor of incestuous relations between Agrippa and his sister (*AJ* 20.145); this gossip found its way into Roman literature as well (Juv. *Sat*. 6.156-60).[29]

The traditional Christian claim is that neither Jesus nor Paul were married,[30] but lately this belief has been challenged. Phipps has claimed that both were

---

[27] On the issue of the tension between Jews who considered marriage "Very good" and those who viewed it as a concession, or a lesser evil, see D. Biale, *Eros and the Jews: From Biblical Israel to Contemporary America* (New York 1992), 34–6. See also the response of Daniel Boyarin, *Carnal Israel: Reading Sex in Talmudic Culture* (Berkeley 1993), 134–66. On the development of monasticism in early Christianity and its appeal to women, see Jo Ann MacNamara, "Sexual Equality and the Cult of Virginity in Early Christian Thought," *Feminist Studies* 3 (1976), 145–58; Ross. S. Kraemer, "The Conversion of Women to Ascetic Forms of Christianity," *Signs: Journal of Women in Culture and Society* 6 (1980), 298–307; B. Witherington III, "Rites and Rights for Women: *Galatians* 3.28," *New Testament Studies* 27 (1980–1), 599–600. On monasticism among Jewish women, see Ross S. Kraemer, "Monastic Jewish Women in Greco-Roman Egypt: Philo Judaeus on the Therapeutrides," *Signs: Journal of Women in Culture and Society* 14 (1989), 342–70.

[28] Ben Azzai's answer to his detractors – "What can I do? My soul lust for the *Torah*; the world can be maintained by others" – explains a phenomenon which we know from early Christianity and thus may have been more widespread in Judaism than our sources suggest. A contradiction regarding Ben Azzai's bachelor status can be found in the *Babylonian Talmud*, which relates that the daughter of R. Aqiba sat and waited for Ben Azzai just as her mother had waited for her father (*bKet*. 63a), but on this see below. And see also Boyarin, *ibid*. 154. In my opinion Boyarin's interpretation is no more than a modern *midrash*.

[29] In her semi-popular book, *Berenice* (London 1974), Ruth Jordan writes that after Berenice was married to King Polemo, Agrippa took two wives (p. 110), but this idea is based on an incorrect reading of a passage in rabbinic literature (*bSukk*. 27a), where it is related that a guardian (אפוטרופוס) of Agrippa had two wives.

[30] See e.g. H. K. McArthur, "Celibacy in Judaism at the Time of Christian Beginnings," *Andrews University Seminary Studies* 25 (1987), 163–81.

married but that the Christian sources neglected to note this fact because it was considered unimportant.[31] And it is certainly true that while the New Testament does not explicitly indicate that any of the apostles were married, Peter certainly was, for he had a mother-in-law, whom Jesus healed (*Mark* 1.30; *Matt.* 8.14; *Luke* 4.38). It would indeed be easier to attribute the utterance rejecting marriage to Jesus himself if he or at least some of his apostles had been bachelors.

The problem of identifying unmarried women is even more complicated. Not a single woman is specifically mentioned in the sources as unmarried, yet in the New Testament the situation of certain women is problematic is a way similar to that of men. Mary Magdalene, Susanna (*Luke* 8.2-3) or the sisters Mary and Martha (*Luke* 10.38-9; *John* 11.1) are never said to have had husbands, and one may surmise that they were not married. Further, the evangelist *John* reports that Mary and Martha lived in the same house with their brother, Lazarus, which means that the house was their father's, even though neither father nor husbands are mentioned.[32] Yet we should also note that Joanna is identified as the wife of Chuza (*Luke* 8.3), despite the fact that Chuza – like the supposed husbands of the other women, if they had them – has no other role at all in the text. Similarly, Mary is said to be the mother of James and Jesus (*Mark* 15.40), although the existence of her husband is never explicitly stated, only strongly implied by the existence of her sons; again, the character of the source was such as not to take pains to indicate the husband's name because he was not considered important. Thus others for whom the existence of husbands is not even hinted may indeed have been married.[33]

A Greek funerary inscription from Tiberias, although of uncertain date, may shed some light on this matter. It is of a 75-year-old woman (her name can no

---

[31] W. E. Phipps, *Was Jesus Married?* (New York 1970); *idem.* "Is Paul's Attitude toward Sexual Relations Contained in *1 Cor.* 7.1?" *New Testament Studies* 28 (1982), 125–31; compare Josephine M. Ford, "Levirate Marriage in St. Paul (*1 Cor.* VII)," *New Testament Studies* 10 (1963–4), 361–5. Phipps repeated much of what Ford said without mentioning her article, which the same journal had published twenty years earlier.

[32] Yet the historicity of their apparently unmarried state, as it emerges from *Luke* and especially from *John*, is doubtful. Elisabeth Schüssler-Fiorenza, "A Feminist Critical Interpretation for Liberation: Martha and Mary: *Luke* 10:38–42," *Religion and Intellectual Life* 3 (1985), 21–36 sets the story in a Christian missionary context. And see also: Adele Reinhartz, "From Narrative to History: The Resurrection of Mary and Martha," *'Women Like This': New Perspectives on Jewish Women in the Greco-Roman World,* ed. Amy-Jill Levine (Atlanta 1991), 161, 179; 183–4. For a very radical view of Mary and Martha and their relation to men, see Mary-Rose D'Angelo, "Women Partners in the New Testament," *Journal of Feminist Studies in Religion* 6 (1990) 65–86.

[33] On this tendency of the New Testament to neglect personal details about its central figures, see Luise Schotroff, "Women as Followers of Jesus in New Testament Times: Exercise in Socio-Historical Exegesis of the Bible," in *The Bible and Liberation, Politics and Social Hermeneutics,* ed. N. K. Gottwald (Maryknoll NY 1983), pp. 418–27.

longer be read on the stone) who was, according to the editors' restoration, ἄγα(μον), i.e. never married.[34] If the restoration is correct, this woman is the only woman whom any source specifically mentions as unmarried for her entire life. Yet this exceptional case is itself qualified by the uncertainty of both its date and restoration.

Thus any claim regarding the prevalence (or even existence) of spinsterhood is perforce an *argumentum ex silentio*, which by nature is malleable enough to conform to almost any point of view. The most that can be said securely at this stage is that during the Second Temple period and afterwards some men are known to have remained bachelors in order to concentrate on study or for less noble reasons, but that nothing is known about the extent or even existence of unmarried status among women.

The Age of Marriage

R. Aqiba interpreted the passage, "Do not profane your daughter by making her a prostitute" (*Lev.* 19.29) as referring to "him who delays in marrying off a daughter who has already passed through puberty" (*bSanh.* 76a). The pubescent was a girl who had passed the age of twelve and a half (*mNidd.* 5.6-8). The problem of preserving a daughter's modesty and chastity was apparently what inspired the rabbinic recommendation to marry a daughter at a very early age.[35] The school of R. Aqiba interpreted the passage "I give my daughter in marriage to this man" (*Deut.* 22.17) as meaning that "a father is permitted to give his daughter in marriage while she is still a minor" (*Sifre Deut.* 235, p. 269 ed. Finkelstein), i.e. before she has reached puberty. And an utterly extreme position is related in the following story: "Our rabbis taught: It is related of Justini the daughter of Aseverus son of Antoninus that she once appeared before Rabbi. Master, she said to him, at what age should a woman marry? At the age of three years and one day, he told her" (*bNidd.* 45a).

The rabbis knew from experience that the coupling of very young girls with much older men is not usually successful.[36] Therefore they recommended that

---

[34] *CII* no. 984.

[35] On the age of marriage, see L. J. Swidler, *Women in Judaism: The Status of Women in Formative Judaism* (Metuchen NJ 1976), 141; Rachel Biale, *Women and the Jewish Law: An Exploration of Women's Issues in Halakhic Sources* (New York 1984), 64–6; D. Mace, *The Hebrew Marriage: A Sociological Study* (New York 1953), 143–4; Isaksson, (above, n. 26), 40; Léone J. Archer, *Her Price is Beyond Rubies: The Jewish Woman in Greaco-Roman Palestine = Journal for the Study of the Old Testament Supplement Series* LX (Sheffield 1990), 151–3.

[36] "If he is a child and she an elderly woman, or vice versa, they should say to him: Go to someone who is of your own age; why should you bring dissension into your house?"

boys, too, marry at a young age. We read in *Ben Sira*: "Do you have sons? Discipline them, and marry them off to women while they are still youths" (7.23). Rabbinic lore relates that in Jerusalem boys were married at age 12 (*Lam. R.* 1.2; cf. *yQidd.* 1.7, 61a). Our rabbis taught: "Concerning ... the man who guides his sons and daughters in the right path and arranges for them to be married near the period of their puberty, it is written, 'And thou shalt know that thy tent is in peace' (*Job* 5.24)" (*bYeb.* 62b). This period of time is specified as "The age of 18 for *huppah* (marriage canopy)" in *Abot* 5.21, which helps explain a teaching of the school of R. Ishmael: "Until the age of twenty, the Holy One, blessed be He, sits and waits. When will he take a wife? As soon as one attains twenty and has not married, He exclaims, Blasted be his bones!" (*bQidd.* 29b).[37] The sources seem unanimous, therefore, in the opinion that marriage should take place at a relatively early age for both sexes.

Yet there existed a somewhat different ideal, according to which a person's suitability and readiness for marriage increase with age and maturity. This is not applied only to men. While the *Book of Jubilees* relates that Jacob was 63 when he married for the first time (25.4),[38] an *aggadah* relates that the daughters of Zelophehad were all above the age of 40 when they married (*Sifre Zuta* 15.32, p. 287 ed. Horovitz; *bBB* 119b). This contrary tradition may reflect the real worry, which is also expressed in the sages' teachings, about marrying a girl at too young an age, lest her body not be mature enough to endure the demands of mar-

---

(*Sifre Deut.* 290, p. 309 ed. Finkelstein); and see also *ARNA* 23 (p. 76 ed. Schechter): "An old man who weds a virgin: she may be suited to him but he is unsuited to her, she may be drawn to him but he withdraws from her."

[37] On the basis of these sources, S. Safrai supposed the age of marriage to be 18: "Home and Family," in *The Jewish People in the First Century* II = *Compendia Rerum Iudaicarum ad Novum Testamentum Section One*, edd. S. Safrai and M. Stern (Assen 1976), 755; but he did not try to determine the age of marriage for girls. D. Kraemer, "Images of Childhood and Adolescence in *Talmudic* Literature," in *The Jewish Family: Metaphor and Memory*, ed. D. Kraemer (Oxford 1989), 65–80, concluded that the accepted age of marriage was 20, while 13 was set as the most extreme bottom limit. Kraemer also does not specifically deal with the age of marriage for girls (see 78 n. 2). For data on Rome, see: K. M. Hopkins, "The Age of Roman Girls at Marriage," *Population Studies* 18 (1964–5), 309–27, who claims that girls in the western Roman Empire married very young. But Hopkins himself contradicts his earlier conclusions when discussing Roman Egypt: *idem.* "Brother-Sister Marriage in Roman Egypt," *Comperative Studies in Society and History* 22 (1980), 333–4. For a recent assessment see B. D. Shaw, "The Age of Roman Girls at Marriage," *Journal of Roman Studies* 77 (1987), 30–46, together with R. P. Saller, "Men's Age at Marriage and its Consequences in the Roman Family," *Classical Philology* 82 (1987), 21–34. In his earlier article Hopkins had noted that with the advent of Christianity, the age of Roman girls at marriage rose (*ibid.* 319–20) and perhaps this could be ascribed to a Jewish influence.

[38] This same tradition is related in the name of an *amora* in *Genesis Rabbah* (68.5, p. 773 ed. Theodor-Albeck). Another *amoraic* tradition claims that Esther only married at 40, or 75 or 80 (*Gen. R.* 39.13, p. 378 ed. Theodor-Albeck).

ried life, above all pregnancy. R. Shimeon bar Yohai said in this regard: "Everyone who lets his daughter be married as a minor diminishes the increase of mankind, loses his wealth and ends up guilty of bloodshed" (*ARNB* 48, p. 131 ed. Schechter), and we can sense here a reference to the widespread death of young mothers in childbirth. The daughter married while still a minor was protected by a specific *halakhah* : "Three kinds of women may use an absorbent [מוֹך- a form a birth control][39]: a minor, a pregnant woman and a nursing woman. A minor, because otherwise she might become pregnant and die as a result. ... And what is the age of such a minor? From the age of eleven years and one day until the age of twelve years and one day. One who is under or over this age must carry on her marital intercourse in the usual manner. This is the opinion of R. Meir. The Sages, however, say: The one as well as the other carries on her marital intercourse in the usual manner, and mercy will be vouchsafed from heaven" (*bYeb.* 12b).[40] Thus the sources depict the ideal of a daughter married quite young to someone only slightly older than she, but a legal provision was made to help avoid risk to life that could result from marriage at such an early age. Now we will examine the extent to which this *halakhic* ideal was in fact realized.

Mayer tabulated all cases of Jewish girls in the Hellenistic-Roman world whose age at the time of marriage is known.[41] His statistical chart is extremely small, containing only five examples, but encompasses an enormously large span of time and geographical area.[42] Only two of Mayer's examples are relevant here. The first is Berenice, daughter of King Agrippa I, who according to Josephus (*AJ* 19.354) was married at age 16 to her father's brother, Herod of Chalcis. Mayer correctly notes that this was Berenice's second marriage, for elsewhere (*AJ* 19.277) Josephus reports that Berenice was first married to Marcus, son of Alexander, the alabarch of Alexandria. Berenice's age at the time of her second marriage adds nothing to our investigation, but it is possible to calculate her age when she was first married. Fuks has maintained that Berenice could not have been married to Marcus before the year 41 CE, when Claudius

---

[39] This form of birth control was known also in Rome; see Pomeroy (above, n. 22), 167; K. M. Hopkins, "Contraception in the Roman Empire," *Comperative Studies in Society and History* 8 (1965) 124–151. On absorbents pp. 134–6. On Jewish practices pp. 142–3.

[40] *Halakhic* birth control is discussed by Biale (above, n. 35), 203–8 and L. Epstein, *Sex Laws and Customs in Judaism* (New York 1948), 145–6; D. M. Feldman, *Marital Relations, Birth Control and Abortion in Jewish Law* (New York 1974), 169–93; 235–44.

[41] G. Mayer, *Die jüdische Frau in der hellenistisch-römischen Antike* (Stuttgart 1987), 52.

[42] Moreover, his conclusions from these finds are unconvincing. In a discussion of Jewish girls' age at marriage in the Diaspora, based on inscriptional evidence, H. R. Horsely (*New Documents Illustrating Early Christianity 1979* [Alexandra, Australia 1987], 222–3), who surveyed much more material, claims that they married in their late teens.

became emperor.[43] There is every indication that Berenice was 13 in that year,[44] which matches the rabbinic ideal. The second example is Mariamme the Hasmonean, who according to Schalit's calculation,[45] was 16 or at most 17 when she married Herod. But this figure is based on the assumption that Mariamme was older than her brother by no more than two years, and this assumption is groundless; on the contrary, if Hyrcanus, Mariamme's grandfather, was eighty years old when he was executed in the year 30 BCE (*AJ* 15.178), and if we assume that his daughter was born when he was already thirty (which would be rather late for that period), then if Mariamme was only 16 in the year 36 BCE, she would have been born in the year 52 BCE, and her mother would have been 28 when Mariamme was born, which was also an unusually advanced age for a first child. It is unclear exactly when Alexandra married Alexander, but even Schalit dates their married life to between the years 55 BCE (in which year Alexandra would have been, according to our calculations, not much younger than 28) and 49 BCE (the date of Alexander's execution).[46] There is no reason to doubt that Mariamme was born in the year 54 BCE. Thus we may conclude that Mariamme could have been 18 or even older when she was married (but not younger than 16).

The Hasmonean dynasty offers an example of a woman being married even at a later age. The age of Queen Shelamzion-Alexandra when she married Yannai can be calculated as follows: her son Hyrcanus was born in 110 BCE if he was 80 at his death in the year 30; but since Shelamzion was 73 when she died in the year 67 (*AJ* 13.430), she was already 30 when her eldest son was born; since her husband Yannai was only 17 when Hyrcanus was born (Yannai died in the year 76 at the age of 51 – *AJ* 13.404), Shelamzion could not have married him before she was at least 27.[47]

Another source informs us that not all girls were married before they were 20. An inscription from Beth She'arim (Cave 20, which falls within our chronological compass) records the burial of two young women, both named Ation, one of whom, the daughter of Rabbi Gamaliel, died a virgin at the age of 22.[48] Two other Jewish funerary inscriptions, which cannot be dated exactly but are from the Roman period, add further information: one, from Asachar near Nab-

---

[43]   A. Fuks, "Marcus Julius Alexander: On the History of the Family of Philo the Alexandrian," *Zion* 13–4 (1948–9), 10–7 [Hebrew].

[44]   See Jordan (above, n. 29), 65; D. R. Schwartz, *Agrippa I: The Last King of Judaea* (Tübingen 1990), 47.

[45]   A. Schalit, *König Herodes: Der Mann und sein Werk* (Berlin 1969), 566, n. 4.

[46]   Schalit, *ibid.* p. 34.

[47]   Shelamzion was probably not the widow of Yannai's brother Aristobulus; see below, chapter 5.

[48]   N. Avigad, *Beth She'arim* III (Jerusalem 1976), 241.

lus,[49] mentions a Jewish mother (Sarah) who was buried with her three daughters; the first, Domna, aged 18, was apparently married, for there is no indication otherwise; the second, Sarah, aged 14, is said to have been a virgin , i.e. unmarried; the third, Malcha, was 13 at the time of death, and although nothing further is mentioned about her, she is likely also to have been unmarried. A second funerary inscription, from Tiberias, reveals a similar picture:[50] Σ[αλ]ώμη was 22 at the time of death, and a νύμφη, which can mean a virgin, engaged but not yet married, or even a young bride. An older mother would not be described by such a term, and certainly not a woman who had been married for a long time; thus we may assume that this Salome had been married only shortly before her death, perhaps at the age of 21.

Rabbinic sources, on the other hand mention five special cases of girls married before the onset of puberty all are fatherless young women whose marriages were arranged by their mothers or brothers and who after puberty refused to remain with their husbands (which Jewish law permitted them to do).[51] Whether these are real or imaginary cases is an open question.

Katzoff has suggested that the wording of the marriage contract of Shelamzion, Babatha's step-daughter – "I have given my daughter in marriage to this man" – is the formula used in the *ketubbah* of a minor, and he finds further support for this interpretation in the fact that the *ketubbah* was found among the papers of her step-mother.[52]

Despite the scarcity of evidence, a negative conclusion is possible: there is no firm indication that 12 was the customary age of marriage for girls. Women older than 20 were still desirable brides, not old maids.

Social Connections and Marriage

In Jewish society, which was class-oriented, highly stratified and extremely conscious of connections to various social groups,[53] the social status of one's wife was considered extremely important.

---

[49] *CII* 1169.

[50] Above, n. 34.

[51] מאון - below, in this chapter.

[52] R. Katzoff, "Legal Commentary," in N. Lewis, R. Katzoff and J. C. Greenfield, "*Papyrus Yadin* 18," *Israel Exploration Journal* 37 (1987), 240–1 and n. 25. I do not find this view convincing; see A. Wasserstein, "A Marriage Contract from the Province of Arabia Nova: Notes on *Papyrus Yadin* 18," *Jewish Quarterly Review* 80 (1989–90), 105–30.

[53] Judith R. Wegner, *Chattel or Person: The Status of Women in the Mishnah* (Oxford 1988), 223, n. 43 called these groups "castes," on the Indian model. See also Mace (above, n. 35), 21.

The different "family stocks" in Jewish society are laid out in detail in the *mishnaic* tractate *Qiddushin*, which uses this as a basis for determining permitted and forbidden marriages (endogamy, exogamy[54]): "Ten family stocks came up from Babylonia: the priestly, the Levitic, and Israelitish stocks, the impaired priestly stocks, the proselyte, freedman, bastard (ממזר) and *nathin* stocks, and the *shetuki* and *asufi* stocks. The priestly, Levitic and Israelitish stocks may intermarry; the Levitic, Israelitish, impaired priestly stocks, proselyte, and freedman stocks may intermarry; the proselyte, freedman, *nathin, shetuki* and *asufi* stocks may intermarry; the proselyte, freedman, bastard, *nathin, shetuki* and *asufi* stocks may all intermarry" (4.1). The indication that these stocks "came up from Babylonia" appears to be historically authentic. As time went on, the social distinctions spelled out in this chapter became too simplistic and did not fit the changing society of the Second Temple period. Two lists in rabbinic literature convey parts of the new system of social strata and relations. The earlier one is found in the *Mishnah* and it lists the social connections of a woman who may marry into the priesthood: "They do not need to trace descent beyond the Altar": that is, if it was found that a girl was the daughter of a priest, there was no need to examine her background further. "... or beyond the Platform": indicating Levitic descent. "... or beyond the Sanhedrin": daughters of sages who sat on the Sanhedrin also did not require further examination. "And all whose fathers are known to have held office as public officers or almoners may marry into the priestly stock and none need trace their descent. R. Yose says: Also any whose name was signed as a witness in the old archives at Sepphoris.[55] R. Hananiah b. Antigonus says: Also any whose name was recorded in the king's army" (*mQidd.* 4.5). This list indicates a narrowing of the group of those whose background was beyond dispute and were therefore eligible to marry priests' daughters: it included now only the wealthy strata and those who had held administrative posts outside the Temple. A certain distance was created between well-connected priestly families and Jews of regular Israelitish descent who did not meet the stricter social criteria. This list seems to preserve an historical memory, for the term "king's army" became archaic after the destruction of the Temple.

A later *tannaitic* list appears in the *Babylonian Talmud* (*bPes.* 49b). In contrast to the two earlier lists from the Second Temple period, this one deals with the subject of social relations not from the point of view of the well-connected priest but from that of a regular Israelite:

---

[54] See Mace, *ibid.* 144–50; L. Epstein, *Marriage Laws in the Bible and Talmud* (Cambridge MA 1942), 145–9.

[55] On this institution, see S. Miller, *Studies in the History and Traditions of Sepphoris* (Leiden 1984), 47–51.

"Our Rabbis taught: Let a man[56] always sell all he has and marry the daughter of a scholar. If he does not find the daughter of a scholar, let him marry one of the great men of the generation. If he does not find the daughter of one of the great men of the generation, let him marry the daughter of the heads of synagogues. If he does not find the daughter of the heads of synagogues, let him marry the daughter of a charity treasurer. If he does not find the daughter of a charity treasurer, let him marry the daughter of an elementary school-teacher, but let him not marry the daughter of an *'am ha-aretz*, because they are detestable and their wives are vermin, and of their daughters it is said, 'Cursed be he that lieth with any manner of beast' (*Deut.* 27.21)."

This list still reflects the great importance which the rabbis attached to good social connections in marriage, but the standards by which such good connections are ranked is obviously different. Not priestly or Levitic status, but membership in the circles of scholars and their relations, is all-important. Obviously this list represents the world-view of a very particular social stratum – that of the rabbis themselves – and thus it must be dated to after the destruction of the Temple.

1. Priests

In the Second Temple period, the group that was the strictest in avoiding any kind of defilement in marriage was the priests. Although permitted by the *Torah* to marry non-priests, extreme rigor was exercised in the choice of marriage partners for the sons of the leading, most socially distinguished priestly families. Josephus twice discusses the women permitted and forbidden to marry priests. In *CA* 1.31, he creates the impression that priests were allowed to marry only the daughters of other priests;[57] in *AJ* 3.276 he gives a somewhat different picture, although even there he lists among women forbidden to priests, aside from divorcées, slaves and war captives (prohibitions known from other sources as well) and women of illegitimate birth (forbidden to all Jews), also peddlers and innkeepers. Obviously priests tried to avoid damaging their honor and position by mingling with the lower classes, whose women had to work for a living.

We read in the sources that a man could attain no greater blessing than to have his daughters marry into the priesthood, for that was the only way his descendants (starting with his grandsons) could serve in the sanctuary.[58] But the *halakhah* heaped up obstacles: the proselyte, for example, could marry his daughter to a priest only if her mother had been born Jewish; if she also was a

---

[56] I.e. a free Jewish man.

[57] Prof. L. H. Schiffman informs me privately that in the composition known as *4QMMT* (מקצת מעשי התורה) the Dead Sea Sect required priests to marry only daughters of priests.

[58] Thus, in the *midrash*, the Rechabites are blessed in that their daughters will marry into the priesthood: *Sifre Num.* 78, p. 73 ed. Horovitz; this is also the blessing R. Joshua gives to Aquila the proselyte: *Eccl. R.* 7.8.1.

proselyte, this honor was withheld from the family (*mQidd.* 4.7, but see R. Yose's opinion there; *yQidd.* 4.6, 66a).

Thus marriage into priestly families was considered to be a great honor. This had a practical side. We find that the court of priests in Jerusalem would levy for priestly daughters marrying into non-priestly families a *ketubbah* of 400 *zuz*, in other words, if they are divorced or widowed priestly daughters receive an amount equivalent to twice that of an Israelite daughter (*mKet.* 1.5); this ensured that only the sons of well-to-do families would marry into the priesthood.

There are several historical examples of socially distinguished non-priestly families trying to arrange marriages with priestly families. Joseph the son of To-bias was the son of the high priest's sister (*AJ* 12.160), which indicates that To-bias himself married into the high priestly family. Ptolemy the son of Abubus, the governor of Jericho, married into the priestly Hasmonean family (*1 Macc.* 16.11), although it is unclear whether he attained his position by virtue of his marriage connection or the other way around. Herod married both Mariamme, the daughter of priests from the Hasmonean house, and Mariamme the daughter of Boethus, from another distinguished priestly house. Rabban Gamaliel the Elder, of the family of Hillel, is said to have married his daughter to Shimeon b. Natanel the priest (*tAZ* 3.10), and even the last high priest, Pinhas b. Habtha, is said by R. Hananiah b. Gamaliel to have been connected to their family by mar-riage (*tKipp.* 1.6).

Priests generally preferred to marry the daughters of other priests. In the Has-monean house, marriage between cousins was the common practice: the daugh-ter of Hyrcanus II married the son of Aristobulus II (*BJ* 1.241; *AJ* 14.300), who in turn was married to the daughter of his uncle Absalom (*AJ* 14.71; *BJ* 1.154). Josephus mentions among his own ancestors priests from two families whose children married each other: a priest on his father's side who married the daugh-ter of Jonathan the Hasmonean (*Vita* 4). Martha, of the priestly family Boethus, was married to the high priest Joshua b. Gamla (*mYeb.* 6.4; *Sif. Emor* 2.6, 95a ed. Weiss). The cases of the high priests from the families Caiaphas and Ze-boim,[59] who were the sons of rival wives, also indicate that marriages were ar-ranged within those families, for otherwise there would have been no *halakhic*

---

[59] The exact reading of the names in this tradition is problematic. Only Caiaphas (קיפא) is a high priestly family known from the Second Temple period; in *tYeb.* 1.10, the family is said to be from the house of Mekoshesh (מקושש). The *Palestinian Talmud* reads: "the family of Nekifi (נקיפי) from the house of Koshesh (קושש)" (*yYeb.* 1.6, 3a), and the *Babylonian Talmud* reads "the family of the house of Kupai (קופאי) of Ben Mekoshesh (בן מקושש)" (*bYeb.* 15b). The name of the second family presents even more difficulties; it is otherwise unknown and appears in various forms: "the house of Alubai (עלובאי) from Zabaim (צבעים)" (*Tosefta*), "the house of Anubai (ענובי) of Zaboim (צבועים)" (*Palestinian Talmud*) and "the house of Zaboim (צבועים) from Ben Akmai (עכמאי)" (*Babylonian Tal-mud*).

problem of the daughter's co-wife. According to *John* 18.13, the high priest Joseph Caiaphas was the father-in-law of the high priest Annas (Hanan). Even the priest Zechariah, the father of John the Baptist, is said to have married one of the "daughters of Aaron" (*Luke* 1.5). R. Tarfon, a known priest (*bQidd.* 71a), relates that his mother's brother was a priest (*yYom.* 1.1, 38d), that is, his father married the daughter of a priest.[60] A funerary inscription from Jerusalem may provide a further example. In the tomb of the family Kalon, of the priestly course Yeshebab, was discovered the ossuary of Shelamzion, who is identified on one side as "the wife of Yehoezer b. Qalon" and on the other as "Shelamzion daughter of Gamala". As we have already seen, Gamala could be the father of the high priest Joshua b. Gamala (Gamaliel), but the name could also be a family name, for high priestly families were especially fond of using family names.[61]

Josephus seems apologetic about the fact the Vespasian forced him to marry a captive (*Vita* 414), for such a marriage would have disqualified any of his sons from the priesthood. The problem of marriage between priests and war captives or other disqualified women hangs like a cloud over Jewish history during the entire Second Temple period and afterwards. John Hyrcanus was slandered for taking up the role of high priest because it was rumored that his mother had been taken captive in Modiin (*AJ* 13.292).[62] The offspring of the marriage between a priest and a war captive or any other disqualified woman were themselves disqualified from the priesthood. Rabbi met one such person in Akko, who in response to his question said, "My father was ambitious and he married a woman who was inappropriate for him and caused that man (i.e. the speaker) to lose his priestly status" (*yShebi.* 6.1, 36c).[63]

---

[60] In the *aggdot* of the Destruction, it is related that 80 priests married 80 daughters of priests in Gophna and all died when the place was destroyed (*yTaan.* 4.8, 69a; *Lam. R.* 2.3; *bBer.* 44a). Priestly families were concentrated in Gophna, and a burial cave, identified as belonging to the priestly course Bilgah, was discovered there: E.L. Sukenik, "An Ancient Jewish Cave Near the Highway Jerusalem-Nablus," *Bulletin of the Israel Exploration Society* 1 (1933–4), 7–9 [Hebrew]; but the *aggadic* character of the rabbinic source cannot be doubted.

[61] *CII* 1351. On priestly family names, see M. Stern, "Aspects of Jewish Society: The Priesthood and Other Classes," in *The Jewish People in the First Century* II = *Compendia Rerum Iudaicarum ad Novum Testamentum Section One*, edd. S. Safrai and M. Stern (Assen 1976), 603–9.

[62] In *bQidd.* 66a, the same slanderous rumor is spread about Yannai, although in light of the political situation into which Yannai was born, the woman mentioned in the source could scarcely have been his mother; Josephus thus seems to be a more reliable source, but see G. Alon, *Jews, Judaism and the Classical World* (Jerusalem 1977), 26–8, n. 22; I. L. Levine, "The Political Struggle between Pharisees and Sadducees in the Hasmonean Period," in *Jerusalem in the Second Temple Period: Abraham Schalit Memorial Volume*, edd. A.Oppenheimer, U. Rappaport and M. Stern (Jerusalem 1980), 70–7 [Hebrew].

[63] A slanderous *amoraic* tradition relates that in the city Mesha in Babylonia priests had the custom of marrying divorced women; see *yQidd.* 4.1, 65c; *yYeb.* 1.6, 3b. Notice that this tradition is only related in a Palestinian source.

For this reason, the sources during the entire *tannaitic* period, up to the time of Rabbi, deal with the permission for daughters to marry into the priesthood. R. Yohanan b. Nuri permits an infant who had been raped to be married later to a priest (*mKet.* 1.10), but disqualifies the wife of a priest who "climbed to the top of an olive tree, and fell and wounded one of his testicles and then died while having sexual relations with her" (*tYeb.* 10.3) from marrying a priest again. In another instance, we hear of a women who came before R. Aqiba and tells him that she had had sexual intercourse before she was three years and one day old, and he permits her to marry a priest (*bNidd.* 45a); but in the sequel he reverses his decision, on the basis of her own testimony ("I will give you a comparison; to what may the incident be compared? to a baby whose finger was submerged in honey; the first time and second time he cries about it, but the third time he sucks it"). Of special interest are the cases in which R. Judah the Patriarch himself confronted the question of permitting women to marry priests. In one instance, he allows such a marriage for a woman who had been penetrated by a dog while she was sweeping the floor (*bYeb.* 59b). In another, he allows a captive to be married to a priest on the basis of the testimony of her son, "When I went out to draw water, my mind was on my mother; when I went out to gather wood, my mind was on my mother" (*bKet.* 27b; *bBQ* 114b). Finally, he allowed such a marriage for a woman proselyte from Rhodes (*yYeb.* 8.2, 9b) or Darom (*yQidd.* 4.6, 66b) who had been a slave but liberated before the age of three years and one day.

All of these *halakhic* cases happened after the destruction of the Temple, and they may indicate a certain easing of restrictions which the priests allowed themselves after their service in the Temple existed no more. On the other hand the solutions to the problem preserved in rabbinic literature may be no more than the rabbis' own proposals, not necessarily accepted by the priests themselves. In fact, one tradition has been preserved which seems to show the priests refusing to accept the sages' dictates. The controversy concerns marriage to a widow of someone from "Isah (עיסה) stock," that is, an Israelite woman of perfectly legitimate ancestry who had been married to a man from a family disqualified from marrying into a priestly family and was then widowed; the rabbis ruled that she may marry a priest, but they acknowledge that the priests themselves refused to marry such women (*mEduy.* 8.3; *bKet.* 14a).[64]

---

[64] See, on this matter, A. Büchler, "Family Purity and Family Impurity in Jerusalem before the Year 70 C.E.," *Studies in Jewish History = Jews College Publications* n.s. I (London 1956), 90–8.

2. Marriage within the Family

Especially in light of the complicated factors outlined above, it was easiest for parents to find a partner for their child from within the family (endogamous marriage). The biggest obstacle to such matches was of course the prohibitions against incest spelled out in the Bible (*Lev.* 18.6-18).[65] The rabbis considered these prohibitions to be particularly painful. They interpret: "'Moses heard the people weeping throughout their families' (*Num.* 11.10). R. Nehorai used to say: It teaches you that the Israelites grieved when Moses told them to abandon incest, and it teaches you that a man would marry his sister and the sister of his father and the sister of his mother, and when Moses told them to abandon incest, they grieved" (*Sifre Num.* 90, p. 91 ed. Horovitz; *Sifre Zuta.*, *ibid.* p. 270). Especially interesting is the following parable: "It is like the king who had an only daughter of whom he was exceedingly fond, so that at first he called her 'daughter', until not satisfied with that he called her 'sister', and still not satisfied with that he called her 'mother'" (*Song of Songs R.* 3.11.2). This parable points to a kind of hierarchy in the loves which one man has for the women in his own family. Most of his love is for his mother, then comes his sister, and his daughter holds only third place.[66] The rabbis, for example, believed that Cain and Seth had no choice but to marry their sisters in order to beget sons (*Sif. Qedoshim* 10.11, 92d ed. Weiss; cf. *Book of Jubilees* 4.9-11).[67] It may be that the address to a wife as "sister" in *Tobit* (5.21; 7.15; 8.4; 10.13) reveals an unconscious desire for the law of incest to be nullified.[68] Yet on the other hand, incest is censured in

---

[65] See Mace (above, n. 35), 150–63; Epstein (above, n. 54), 220–63.

[66] Brother-sister relations are discussed only incidentally in rabbinic literature and sources from the Second Temple period, but all signs point to great affection as common. In the *Apocrypha* we find a man calling his wife "my sister" in order to express a greater level of intimacy (*Additions to Esther* 4.9; *Tobit* 5.21; 7.15; 8.4), and a mother-in-law even calls her son-in-law "my brother" (*Tobit* 10.13). Strong bonds of love between a brother and sister are demonstrated in the story about R. Ishmael's son and daughter, who were captured and met in captivity (*bGitt.* 58a). An inscription on an ossuary from Jerusalem also gives witness to affection between brother and sister "למרים אחותי בלבדא": N. Avigad, "A Hebrew Ossuary Inscription," *Bulletin of the Israel Exploration Society* 25 (1961), 143 [Hebrew]. In the Hellenistic world, especially Egypt, marriages between brother and sister were common. This "longing" could reflect the influence of the lands neighboring Palestine. On the question of a daughter preferring the family of her brother to that of her husband in the East, see Heleen Sancisi-Weerdenburg, "Exit Atossa: Images of Women in Greek Historiography on Persia," in *Images of Women in Antiquity*, edd. Averil Cameron and Amélie Kuhrt (Detroit 1985), 20–33.

[67] The *Book of Jubilees* (33.14–6) explains that Cain's marriage to his sister preceded the laws against incest, which were the result of Reuben's relations with Bilhah. The *Bibl. Ant* 2.1 gives the name of Cain's sister but ignores the problem.

[68] In Roman law, a *manus* marriage has the legal effect of making a woman her husband's daughter; see J. M. Guttmann, "Acquisition of Women According to the Bible and

the strongest terms by the Pharisaic author of *Psalms of Solomon* (8.10), who condemns his opponents (perhaps Sadducees) for practicing it.

In sharp contrast to the widespread practice of marriage between brothers and sisters within royal families in neighboring cultures[69] – especially Egypt, but also Adiabene and Commagene – the Hasmonean and Herodian dynasties, despite their openly Hellenizing tendencies, strictly obeyed the laws of incest spelled out in the Bible; they had, after all, to avoid disqualifying themselves as rulers in the eyes of the people. Agrippa II and his sister Berenice came closer to such a forbidden marriage, but made no official declaration.[70]

The closest family relationship which stood outside the prohibitions against incest was that between cousins[71] or uncle (principally the mother's brother, but also possibly the father's brother) and niece. The *Book of Jubilees* stresses that from the fourth generation of mankind (from Mahalalel), men could marry their cousins instead of their sisters (4.15; 16; 20; 27; 28); *Bibl. Ant.* emphasizes that this was possible from the second generation (2.5). Of the two, the rabbis prefer marriage between niece and uncle, as we find expressed in the following passage: "About him who marries the daughter of his sister, it is written, 'Then, if you call, the Lord will answer; if you cry to Him, He will say, Here I am' (*Is.* 58.9)" (*bYeb.* 62b–63a; *bSanh.* 76b). And further: "A man should not marry a woman until his sister's daughter has reached maturity" (*tQidd.* 1.4). In this matter the Dead Sea sectarians differed from other currents in Judaism of the Second Temple period, opposing marriage between uncle and niece as incestuous.[72]

Talmud," *Yediot ha-Makhon le-Madaei ha-Yahaduth* 1 (1925), 28–9 [Hebrew]. Jewish law generally was strict in such matters, even in doubtful cases: "A step-daughter reared with her step-brothers is forbidden to marry one of them because she appears to be their sister" (*bSot.* 43b). In other words, a man is forbidden to marry even a step-sister, because of her emotional closeness to him. Similarly regarding the mother: "It once happened that a woman came to Jerusalem carrying an infant on her back; she brought him up and he had intercourse with her, whereupon they were brought before the *Bet Din* and stoned, not because he was definitely her son, but because he clung to her" (*bQidd.* 80a). A similar moral problem is probably reflected in the case of the son who has taken his father's (second) wife, in the Pauline epistle *1 Cor.* 5.1.

[69] On which see, e.g. Grace H. Macurdy, *Vassal-Queens and Some Contemporary Women in the Roman Empire* (Baltimore 1937), 8–9. Apparently incestuous marriage was practiced even in the Nabataean royal house; see G. W. Bowersock, *Roman Arabia* (Cambridge MA 1983), 74.

[70] See Jordan (above, n. 29), 102–3, 111; Macurdy, *ibid.* 87–8.

[71] See Mace (above, n. 35), 163–4.

[72] Cf. *Damascus Covenant* V 7–11 and the *Temple Scroll* LXVI 16–7, and see Y. Yadin, *The Temple Scroll* I (Jerusalem 1983), 371–3. Even before the discovery of the scrolls, S. Krauss noticed that the Samaritans and Karaites oppose marriage between uncle and niece. He explained this as influenced by Roman law, which contains the same prohibition: "Die Ehe zwischen Onkel und Nichte," *Studies in Jewish Literature Issued in Honor of Prof. Kaufman Kohler* (Berlin 1913), 165–75. In this light it is interesting to note

Royal families adopted the same classic solution to the problem of keeping property within the family, namely, the marriage of girls to uncles and cousins. The Hasmoneans married cousins, and in the Herodian dynasty uncles married nieces. Salome, the sister of Herod, married her uncle Joseph (*AJ* 15.65). Herod himself married the daughter of one of his brothers (*BJ* 1.563; *AJ* 17.19), and he wanted to give his daughter in marriage to his brother (*AJ* 16.194; *BJ* 1.483). His granddaughter, Mariamme the daughter of Aristobulus, married her uncle Antipater (*BJ* 1.565; *AJ* 17.18), and her sister Herodias was married twice to uncles, Herod son of Herod (*BJ* 1.558; *AJ* 18.136) and Herod Antipas (*AJ* 18.136). Herodias' daughter, Salome, was married to Philip, her uncle on her father's side (*AJ* 18.137). Berenice the daughter of Agrippa was also married to her uncle, Herod of Chalcis (*AJ* 19.277). Even more common in the Herodian family was marriage between cousins. Herod himself married a cousin (*BJ* 1.563), and all of his daughters were married to cousins: Cyprus to Antipater the son of Salome (*AJ* 17.22), Shelamzion to Phasael son of Phasael (*ibid.*), Olympias to Joseph son of Joseph (*BJ* 1.562; *AJ* 17.20), and Roxane and Salome to the two sons of Pheroras (*AJ* 16.228; 17.322). Herod's son Aristobulus was married to Berenice, the daughter of his aunt Salome (*BJ* 1.446; *AJ* 16.11). Agrippa I married Cyprus, a cousin on his father's side (*AJ* 18.131). Salome the daughter of Herodias married (in her second marriage) Aristobulus, the son of her uncle Herod of Chalcis (*AJ* 18.137).

Marriage between more distant relations was also accepted. A marriage was arranged between the daughter of Pheroras, who apparently was younger than the generation of Herod's sons, and a son of the next generation, Tigranes the son of Alexander and grandson of Herod (*AJ* 17.14), but in the end she seems to have married the son of Antipater son of Herod (*BJ* 1.565).

Marriage with cousins and uncles was the best way for most families to ensure a socially compatible partner and also to preserve property within the family. There are even further examples of marriage to uncles: Joseph the son of Tobias and the daughter of his brother (his second wife: *AJ* 12.188-9); R. Eliezer raised and married his sister's daughter (*yYeb.* 3.1, 13c; *ARNA* 16, p. 63 ed. Schechter); R. Yose the Galilean married his sister's daughter (*Gen. R.* 17.3, p. 152 ed. Theodor-Albeck); and Rabban Gamaliel's daughter married his brother (*bYeb.* 15a). One source records the case of a man who took a vow of abstinence from his sister's daughter and then married her after R. Ishmael released him from his vow (*bNed.* 66a-b). Matrona, who often disputed with R. Yose,[73] tells

---

that, according to the *Book of Jubilees* (4.33), which was considered practically canonical by the Dead Sea Sect, Noah married the daughter of his sister (according to some versions). On the place of the *Book of Jubilees* in the literature of the Dead Sea Sect, see L. H. Schiffman, *The Halakhah at Qumran* (Leiden 1975), 40–1.

[73] See chapter 7 below.

him that she was supposed to be married to her father's brother (*Gen. R.* 17.7, p. 158 ed. Theodor-Albeck).[74] These examples will suffice to illustrate how the ideal described in conceptual works was realized in fact.[75]

The *Babylonian Talmud* emphasizes a different aspect of marriage between family relations. As many examples illustrate, the families of the sages made an effort to intermarry, and this effort extended even to those who were closely related by world-view or ideology. R. Eliezer, e.g. is said to have established a marriage connection with the family of Rabban Gamaliel by marrying his sister, Imma Shalom (*bShab.* 116a; *bBM* 59b). However, as we have seen, the Palestinian Talmud relates that R. Eliezer b. Hyrcanus married the daughter of his sister. R. Meir is said to have married the scholar Beruriah, the daughter of the sage R. Hananiah b. Tardion (*bPes.* 62b; *bAZ* 18a). Yet the *Palestinian Talmud* identifies R. Meir's father-in-law as a certain Ben Ziroz (*yDem.* 2.1, 22c; and cf. *bShab.* 147a);[76] R. Aqiba is reported to have married his daughter to one of two sages, either Ben Azzai (*bKet.* 63a) or R. Joshua b. Kefusai (*bShab.* 147a). But Ben Azzai is presented in the Palestinian rabbinic sources as an example of an outstanding bachelor. The *Babylonian Talmud* also contains accounts of wealthy aristocrats trying to draw closer to the sages through marriage. The wealthy Ben Elasa married the daughter of R. Judah the Patriarch (*bNed.* 51a), despite the opposition of Bar Qappara. The daughter of the wealthy Kalba Sabua was married to R. Aqiba (*bKet.* 62b; *bNed.* 50a). Yet the *Mishnah* mentions "R. Yohanan b. Joshua, the son of the father-in-law of R. Aqiba" (*mYad.* 3.5).[77] This can be understood in one of two ways: either R. Yohanan is the son of R. Aqiba's father-in-law, in which case the name of the father-in-law is Joshua (the same name as that of R. Aqiba's son), or Joshua is the son of R. Aqiba's father-in-law, in other words, his brother-in-law – in which case R. Aqiba's son was named after his uncle. Had this been correct, the sources would have mentioned Kalba Sabua, who was a well known personality, by name, but this connection is unknown to the Palestinian traditions in which the *Mishnah* developed. The *Babylonian Talmud* is also the only source which mentions marriage connections between the Hasmoneans and the house of the Pharisaean *nasi* of that time,

---

[74] See also *ARNB* 8 (pp. 23–4 ed. Schechter), where however Matrona tells the story to R. Joshua, which in my opinion is undoubtedly the result of an ancient copyist's mistaken interpretation of the abbreviation resh-yod (ר״י).

[75] *Contra* S. Belkin, "Levirate and Agnate Marriage in Rabbinic and Cognate Literature," *Jewish Quarterly Review* 60 (1969–70), 275–329, who argues that while levirate marriage was still practiced during the period under discussion, marriage between close relatives "belonged to the records of the past" (p. 298). As we will soon see, both parts of this argument are in error.

[76] On Beruriah's family connections see D. Goodblatt, "The Beruriah Traditions," *Journal of Jewish Studies* 26 (1975), 68–85.

[77] See L. Finkelstein, *Akiba: Scholar, Saint and Martyr* (New York 1936), 22–3.

Shimeon b. Shetah, whose sister Yannai is said to have married (*bBer.* 48a).[78] Yet these reports of marriage matches are sometimes contradicted by information in Palestinian sources. This tendency to create fictional connections between the families of sages and other figures who receive favorable treatment in the *Babylonian Talmud* goes hand-in-hand with the elevation of the ideal of marriage connections with the families of scholars above all others just mentioned above – a concept which developed towards the end of our period. In Babylonia itself, at any rate, intermarriage between sages' families is a recorded phenomenon. For example, the daughter of Rav Hisda married Rabba, the *amora* (*bKet.* 85a). The Babylonian *amoraim* probably extrapolated from their own experience the conditions in Palestine during the time of the *tannaim*.

3. Choosing a Husband

Throughout the Hellenistic-Roman period, and according to all relevant sources, marriage was a matter to be settled by the parents of the bride and groom, on the basis of social connection and status. When children married they had absolutely no right to choose their partner, especially if such a choice would fall outside the criteria dictated by society. On the contrary, the rabbis saw in the marriage of a well-matched couple a kind of guarantee of a peaceful married life full of love. R. Meir says: "Anyone who marries a woman unsuitable for him violates five negative commandments: 'Do not take vengeance' (*Lev.* 19.18), 'Do not bear a grudge' (*ibid.*), 'Do not hate your brother' (*ibid.* 17), 'and you shall love your neighbor as yourself' (*ibid.* 18), 'that your brother may live with you' (*ibid.* 25.36), and the consequences are nothing less than removing fertility and increase from the world" (*tSot.* 5.11). This illustrates the belief that love is the natural product of marriage between a well-matched couple. Two people who marry but do not have well-matched lineages are doomed to live lives without love and perhaps even without children.

Although the marriage of a daughter was theoretically controlled entirely by her father it can be assumed that the reality was somewhat different and that such rigorous control over the marriage of children was exercised more in wealthy families, which had to take into account rather complicated economic and political factors. A good illustration is the Herodian dynasty. Josephus tells us that Herod arranged the engagement of his children with family members whom he highly esteemed and canceled the engagements when the intended partners fell out of favor (*AJ* 17.14–8). The attempt by Herod's sister Salome to

---

[78]   For this entire subject, I have relied on the article by S. Safrai, "Tales of the Sages in the Palestinian Tradition and the *Babyloniann Talmud*," *Studies in Aggadah and Folk-Literature* = *Scripta Hierosolymitana* XXII, edd. J. Heinemann and D. Noy (Jerusalem 1971), 229–32. The *Babylonian Talmud* relates that the practice continued into the *amoraic* period; e.g. R. Yohanan married the sister of Resh Laqish (*bBM* 84a).

arrange her own marriage to the Arab diplomat Syllaeus (*BJ* 1.487; *AJ* 16.221–6) was unsuccessful simply because the decision was not hers to make, even though she was twice a widow and her father was long dead; her brother Herod was the one with the authority to decide, and he ruled against the match.[79] Yet discipline within the family regarding this matter appears, at least from Josephus' descriptions, to have become more lax after Herod's death. Herodias acted as a fully empowered party in the cancellation of her marriage with Herod the son of Herod and her subsequent marriage to his high-ranking brother, Antipas (*AJ* 18.110). This incident, according to Josephus' sources, had serious political consequences for Antipas (*ibid.* 112–5): the Nabataean king, unable to bear the humiliation to his daughter, provoked war with the tetrarch and defeated him (*AJ* 18.109–15). If the family discipline had been maintained, it might have been possible to prevent this disaster, although Josephus relates elsewhere that the tetrarch and the king were involved in a border dispute and that the divorce served merely as a pretext for war (*AJ* 18.113). Berenice, daughter of Agrippa I, is the last woman in the Herodian house known to have arranged a match for herself; she was already twice a widow when she arranged her marriage to Polemo king of Cilicia (*AJ* 20.145). But we can assume that her brother, Agrippa II, who was at that time head of the family, had control over her actions and simply chose not to oppose the match, even if it did turn out unsuccessful (*ibid.* 146). Josephus also tells the stories of Berenice's two sisters, Drusilla and Mariamme, who both left their husbands (Azizus and Julius Archelaus, respectively) to marry other men (the governor Felix and Demetrius the alabarch of Alexandria: *ibid.* 141, 147); but the hostile nature of Josephus' source throws into doubt, at least in the case of Mariamme, whether the match was really made by the woman herself or by her family.[80]

Rabbinic literature from the *tannaitic* period mentions three different women who chose husbands without the mediation of a relative. One of these cases clearly involves a widow or divorcée, for she is seeking a husband in order to cope with the difficulties caused by her son (*tBQ* 8.16; *bBQ* 80a); her attempt to find a good match for herself did not turn out well, however, for she failed to get married. The case may nevertheless indicate that a widowed or divorced woman had an easier time arranging her own match than did a young first-time bride,

---

[79] The reliability of the story of Salome's relations with the Nabataean dipolomat is a highly complicated question. Nicolaus of Damascus, Josephus' source for it, had personal reasons to hate the king's sister and missed no opportunity to speak ill of her; I intend to deal with this issue more fully elsewhere. In any case, if the story is true, Herod's prohibition of the marriage was perhaps the worst political mistake of his entire career, for Syllaeus became his bitterest and most dangerous enemy (cf. *BJ* 1.574–7; *AJ* 16.286–8).

[80] On the nature of Josephus' source, see D. R. Schwartz, "KATA TOYTON TON KAIPON: Josephus' Source on Agrippa II," *Jewish Quarterly Review* 72 (1981–2), 241–68.

even though in this particular instance certain obstacles were thrown in the woman's path. The second instance involves "a great woman who was great in beauty," who chose her husband herself; her personal status is unclear (*bKet.* 22a). The third case is the most famous of the three – that of Rachel,[81] the daughter of Kalba Sabua, who married R. Aqiba on her own initiative and against her father's wishes (*bNed.* 50a; *bKet.* 62b).

R. Aqiba lived during the period under study, but the story of his love and marriage – appearing first in the *Babylonian Talmud* in Aramaic (*bKet.* 62b– 63a; *bNed.* 50a), and then in abbreviated and updated form in *Abot de Rabbi Nathan* (A 6; *ARNB* 12, pp. 29–30 ed. Schechter) lies outside the present chronological framework. We can, however, try to extract from the late story some information about the concepts and notions prevalent in our period. A daughter of Kalba Sabua was, by definition, the daughter of a wealthy family, and in violation of all social norms as well as the wishes of her father (who punished her for it) she married a commoner and ignoramus. That is, her actions amounted to a kind of heresy, a complete rejection of all the ideology motivating family connections as presented here. Yet astonishingly the teller of the rabbinic story identifies with the woman, and while her father punishes her the storyteller heaps blessings upon her. There is absolutely no parallel to this among rabbinic stories.[82] I do not intend here to determine when the story took shape, but it

---

[81] If this indeed was the name of R. Aqiba's wife. The name appears only in *ARNA* 6, p. 29 ed. Schechter; there is no mention of it in Palestinian or *tannaitic* sources. The name Rachel appears in a late funerary inscription from Beth She'arim, see M. Schwabe and B. Lifshitz, *Beth She'arim* II (Jerusalem 1974), 93 (= a Rachel from Eilat). It could be that the name is merely a *midrash* on the part of the author of *Abot de Rabbi Nathan*, based on the end of the story of R. Aqiba and the daughter of Kalba Sabua (*bKet.* 63a): "The daughter of R. Aqiba acted in a similar way toward Ben Azzai. This is indeed an illustration of the proverb: Ewe (רחילא) follows ewe, a daughter's acts are like those of her mother." On this issue see Boyarin (above, n. 27), 150–4.

[82] On the *aggadic* motifs in the story, see I. Bin-Gorion, *The Paths of Legends: An Introduction to Folktales* (Jerusalem 1970), 61–2 [Hebrew]; Zipporah Kagan, "The Loyal Wife in the Folkloristic Story," *Mahanaim* 98 (1965), 134–6 [Hebrew]. D. Zimmerman included this story in his *Eight Love Stories from the Talmud* (Tel Aviv 1981), 66–72 [Hebrew], but in contrast to the other seven, the love in this story is not at the outset love between husband and wife whose marriage was presumably arranged by their families. I have been able to find only one other story of this kind in *tannaitic* literature but its central figures are not known personalities but an anonymous pupil of R. Hiyya (or R. Meir: Z.W. Harvey, "The Pupil, the Harlot and the Fringe Benefits," *Prooftexts* 6 [1983], 259–64, and see also A. Goshen-Gottstein, "The Tzitzit Commandment, the Harlot and the Homily," in *Rabbinic Thought: Proceedings of the First Conference*, edd. M. Hirshman and T. Gronner [Haifa 1989], 45–58 [Hebrew]) and a prostitute; see *Sifre Num.* 115, pp. 128–9 ed. Horovitz; *bMen.* 44a. From a literary point of view, the story of the prostitute and the pupil of R. Hiyya resembles the Hellenistic Egyptian Jewish "novel" *Joseph and Asenath* (on the connections between the story and the *midrash*, and on the possibility of a late date for the composition, see V. Aptowitzer, "Asenath the Wife of Joseph: A *Haggadic* Literary-

should be emphasized that it involves the daughter of a wealthy family who chooses as her husband a man who would, eventually, become one of the greatest scholars, i.e. a man who would fit into the top category in the last list of desirable family connections discussed above. Thus the story developed at a time in the world of the sages when accepted values were being turned on their head and, as we see in the list from *bPes.* 49b (see above), money and aristocracy were giving way to accomplishment in *Torah* scholarship as the criteria for good family connections, at least in the circles which produced rabbinic literature. The choice made by the daughter of Kalba Sabua turned out to be extremely intelligent, the kind of choice her parents should have made for her.[83]

This is, as it were, the ideological background for the story. Does it also have an historical one? There is a source which seems to suggest not only that a woman's own choice of her own husband was accepted in certain situations, but also that an institution was established to aid women (and men) towards that end. This, at least in my opinion, is the only way to understand the following passage from the *Mishnah*:

> "Rabban Shimeon b. Gamaliel said: There were no happier days for Israel than the 15th of Ab and the Day of Atonement, for on them the daughters of Jerusalem used to go forth in white raiments; and these were borrowed ... and the daughters of Jerusalem

---

Historical Study," *Hebrew Union College Annual* 1 [1924], 239–306; on the connections between the story and the *Pseudepigrapha* and a possibly earlier date, see E. W. Smith Jr., "Joseph Material in Joseph and Asenath and Josephus Relating to the Testament of Joseph," in *Studies on the Testament of Joseph = Society of Biblical Literature Septuagint and Cognate Studies* V, ed. G. W. Nickelsberg Jr. [Missoula, MO 1975], 133–7; on the connections between the story and the Hellenistic novel, see R. I. Pervo, "Joseph and Asenath and the Greek Novel," *Society for Biblical Literature Seminar Papers* 10 [1976], 171–81; and see also H. C. Kee, "The Socio-Religious Setting and Aims of Joseph and Asenath," *ibid.* 183–92; Ross S. Kraemer, *Her Share of the Blessings: Women's Religion among the Pagans, Jews and Christians in the Greco-Roman World* [Oxford 1992], 110–3). This story, just like the story about the prostitute, involves a woman of exceptional, much-praised beauty and a modest Jew who is not seduced by her and leads her to abandon her life, join Judaism and, in the end, marry him.

[83] Prof. Dov Noy has suggested to me in a private conversation that the story of R. Aqiba and the daughter of Kalba Sabua is the version of R. Aqiba's history which women told, consequently a woman is the central figure. If this is correct, a comparison of the two formulations in the *Babylonian Talmud* should point to the kernel of the tradition, i.e. the elements common to both formulations (such as the woman's biblical quotation in both: "A righteous man knows the soul of his beast"). Moreover, the later story in *Abot de Rabbi Nathan*, in which the woman's role is much less significant, would be the male version of the same story, composed in reaction against the earlier version told by women. Noy's entire approach is based on folkloristic studies and on a general distinction between stories transmitted orally by women and those told by men. For the suggestion that the version in *bKetubbot*, where the woman is clearly the central figure in the story, is earlier than the version in *bNedarim*, where R. Aqiba himself is the hero of the *aggadah*, see A. Aderet, "The Story in *Sefer Ha-Aggadah* B," *Alei-Siah* 4–5 (1978), 122–9 [Hebrew].

went forth to dance in the vineyards. And what did they say? Young man, lift up your eyes and see what you would choose for yourself; set not your eyes on beauty, but set your eyes on family; for 'Favor is deceitful and beauty is vain, but a woman who fears the Lord she shall be praised' (*Prov.* 31.30)." (*mTaan.* 4.8)

The *Mishnah* does not provide enough information to interpret this event with any certainty, but the purpose of the event becomes clear in a *baraita* which fills in what is missing: "It is taught: Whoever did not have a wife repaired to there" (*bTaan.* 31a). In other words, the event was designed to enable unattached men and women to meet each other. The *Talmud* expands the *Mishnah's* report of what the daughters of Jerusalem would say to their intended grooms: "Our rabbis have taught: The beautiful among them called out: Set your eyes on beauty, for the quality most to be prized in a woman is beauty" (*ibid.*). The women from good families would say what the *Mishnah* records, while the ugly ones would cry out, "Carry off your purchase in the name of Heaven, only on one condition that you adorn us with gold" (*ibid.*). The abbreviated version of the women's remarks in the *Mishnah* is an indication of the emphasis the *tannaim* placed on good family background.[84]

This incident may afford a glimpse into the world of the lower classes in Jewish society of the period. Although generally our sources were written either by aristocrats (Josephus and his sources), or by members of the middle class (the sages), it is quite probable that the freedom to choose one's marriage partner was more common in the poorer classes. The present instance is reminiscent of an agricultural festival (note the dancing in vineyards), and we can sense a certain antiquity in the custom (cf. *Judges* 21.19-21) as well as perhaps a slight nuance of a pagan wine festival. Here we may gain another insight into the story of R. Aqiba and his wife, for we must remember that R. Aqiba, who was selected by his wife, came from the same poorer classes. It is true that in the *aggadah* in the *Babylonian Talmud* his wife becomes the daughter of the rich Jerusalemite Kalba Sabua, but as we have noted the Palestinian tradition seems unaware of her distinguished background.[85] Other sources which relate the story of R. Aqiba and his wife without bringing in the part about his going away to study *Torah* confirm that both were wretchedly poor and that his wife helped R. Aqiba a great deal (*ANRA* 6, pp. 29–30 ed. Schechter; *ARNB* 12, p. 30 ed. Schechter), even to the extent of selling her own hair in order to support themselves (*yShab.* 6.1, 7d; *ySot.* 9.16, 24c). It may well be that R. Aqiba's wife was able to choose him as her husband precisely because of the low social standing of both of them.

---

[84] Archer (above, n. 35), 120, n. 5 thought that this description was of a custom from the First Temple period which was not revived in the Second Temple period, but if this is right, why is Rabban Shimeon b. Gamaliel the one who transmits the tradition? And indeed, why would the tradition be recorded at all?

[85] See Safrai (above n. 78), 227–9.

4. Refusal

How successful were marriages arranged by parents?[86] There is in fact one way to gain a glimpse into this problem. According to Jewish law, a marriage which a father arranges for his daughter was binding, but if the father died and the daughter, while still a minor, was married off by her mother or brother, she could repudiate the match on reaching maturity. The sources have preserved five instances of a woman refusing to remain in a marriage arranged by her mother or brother. Already in the Second Temple period the wife of Pishon the camel-driver did just such a thing, and the Schools of Shammai and Hillel disputed the case (*yYeb.* 13.1, 13c; *bYeb.* 107b). The *Tosefta* relates the case, brought before R. Judah b. Baba, of an orphan who repudiated a marriage arranged for her (*tYeb.* 13.5). According to the *Palestinian Talmud*, R. Ishmael's daughter-in-law repudiated her marriage before the sages "while her son was sitting on her shoulders" (*yYeb.* 1.2, 2d; *ibid.* 3.1, 13c); thus it appears that a woman's right to repudiate her marriage was still good even if she had had children from her husband.[87] Finally, there are two cases of daughters repudiating their marriages before R. Judah the Patriarch. One concerns the daughter-in-law of Abdan, a close associate of R. Judah the Patriarch himself (*bYeb.* 108a); in the second case, the woman's husband went to "a country beyond the sea" and she repudiated her marriage before both R. Judah the Patriarch in Beth She'arim and R. Ishmael b. R. Yose in Sepphoris (*bYeb.* 107b). Although these cases are cited in rabbinic literature only to illustrate certain *halakhic* points, they nonetheless reflect historical reality and demonstrate that marriages arranged by parents did not always succeed, even though many women in the end will have agreed to them.

---

[86] Falk has proposed that the law requiring a women to celebrate the first festival after her marriage in her father's home, and preventing the husband from forbidding her to do so (*mKet.* 7.4), provided a means for the bride to express her opinion before her family on whether and to what degree the marriage was succeeding; see Z. Falk, *A Wife's Divorce Action in Jewish Law* (Jerusalem 1973), 15 [Hebrew].

[87] According to the version in the *Babylonian Talmud,* the woman was not R. Ishmael's daughter-in-law but his daughter: "It once happened that the daughter of R. Ishmael came to the *bet midrash* to repudiate her marriage, and her son was riding on her shoulders" (*bNidd.* 52a). R. Ishmael's daughter is mentioned above (n. 66) as having been taken captive together with her brother. Those who wish to keep both versions could conceivably argue that the stories involve different daughters, or that the daughter was taken captive at a later time in her life. But the version in the *Palestinian Talmud,* which identifies the woman as R. Ishmael's daughter-in-law, is to be preferred, for the *Babylonian Talmud* changed the identification in order to raise an ethical question: "The Rabbis wept bitterly, saying: Over a ruling which that righteous man had laid down should his offspring stumble!" (*ibid.*); and see above, chapter 1, n. 22, the story of Nehonia the well-digger and his daughter who fell into a cistern.

Thus both the theory and practice of marriages arranged by parents, who took pains to find a partner for their children from within the family or at least from the same social class, applied principally to aristocratic and middle-class families, because the status of the future husband or wife had decisive economic and political importance. In the lower social classes, so far as we can glimpse into their more poorly documented practices, the choice of a marriage partner was much more flexible.

Polygamy

In the Second Temple period, Jewish society was, at least theoretically, polygamous, like other oriental societies of the time but in contrast to the neighboring Greek and Roman societies. Polygamy appears to be the custom in the Hebrew Bible. *Ben Sira*'s advice, "Never consult a woman about her rival" (37.11), also implies the custom of keeping more than one wife. A similar situation is reflected in rabbinic parables, e.g. "R. Hiyya taught: A priest who had two wives, one the daughter of a priest and the other the daughter of an Israelite ..." (*Lev. R.* 4.5, p. 90 ed. Margulies); or "this is like a man who marries a woman in the presence of his existing wife ..." (*bAZ* 55a).

Generally speaking, the *halakhic* literature deals with many problems arising from the practice of polygamy, even if such discussions have a somewhat theoretical cast and may have had no practical application, their purpose being only for training and sharpening one's skills. Thus many *halakhot* in the tractate *Yebamot* deal with the status of the co-wife. The very practice of *yibbum* (levirate marriage) rests on the permissibility of marrying two wives, even though, as we shall see, the practice of *yibbum* gave way to *halitzah* (the ceremony by which such marriage is averted) toward the end of the Second Temple period. The practice of polygamy is implied in all of the following *halakhot* "a woman whose husband and co-wife went beyond the sea ..." (*mYeb.* 16.1); "one who was married to two women ... and died" (*mKet.* 10.1; cf. 2.4–6); "if a man consummated marriage with his deceased brother's wife, and her co-wife went and married another ..." (*mGitt.* 8.7); "if a man betrothed two women with what was worth a *perutah* ..." (*mQidd.* 3.6).

But even if polygamy was permitted by *tannaitic halakhah*, other *halakhic* systems counseled otherwise. During the Second Temple period, monogamy was preferred even on the conceptual plane by, above all, the Dead Sea Sect whose *halakhah* explicitly prohibited polygamy. In the reworked version of the statutes of the king in the *Temple Scroll,* it is stated: "he shall not take another wife in addition to her, for she alone shall be with him all the days of her life" (LVII 17–8). In the *Damascus Covenant*, criticism is leveled against the "builders of the wall" (Pharisees?) in the following terms: "they shall be caught in fornication twice; once by taking a second wife while the first is still alive ..." The

prooftext for this *halakhic* argument is none other than the biblical story of creation: "the principle of creation is, 'Male and female created He them' (*Gen.*
1.28)," and to this another supporting text is added: "those who entered the Ark
went in two by two" (*CD* IV 20–V 2).[88]

Even the ancient rabbis probably preferred monogamy on ethical grounds.
Abot de Rabbi Nathan, although a late work, contains a *midrash* whose early
date may well be confirmed by its connection to the passage from the *Damascus
Covenant* cited above. Job is made to say: "If the first man was supposed to be
given ten wives, they would have been given him. But it was proper only that he
be given one wife. So I am contented with my wife and my portion" (*ARNB* 2, p.
9 ed. Schechter). Just as the *Damascus Covenant*, *Abot de Rabbi Nathan's* Job
refers to the story of creation which describes the ideal situation of one man and
one wife, creation as made by the perfect God.[89]

Polygamy in rabbinic literature is discussed at length by Lowy,[90] who argued
that although it was known in Jewish society as represented in rabbinic literature, polygamy was not widespread in practice, especially not among the sages
themselves. Lowy dealt only with rabbinic literature, and so all of his examples
of polygamy or bigamy are cited from there. He mentions the sons of co-wives
in high priestly families of the Second Temple period (*bYeb.* 15b); Abba, the
brother of Rabban Gamaliel, who had two wives and whose death caused Rabban Gamaliel to take his wife in levirate marriage thus bringing into his house a
second wife; and Agrippa's guardian, who had two wives (*bSukk.* 27a). Lowy
also cites cases which exemplify how the *halakhah* can be carried *ad absurdum*
and doubtfully describe historical reality: R. Tarfon betrothed 300 women during a famine in order to support them with *terumah* (sacrificial offerings: *tKet.*
5.1; *yYeb.* 4.12, 6b); a man betrothed seven women with a basket of figs
(*mQidd.* 2.7); R. Judah the Patriarch required a man to marry by levirate marriage the widows of his twelve brothers, all of whom had died (*yYeb.* 4.12, 6b).[91]

---

[88] This passage is the keystone in Vermes' argument that the Dead Sea Sect opposed
polygamy but not divorce: G. Vermes, "Sectarian Matrimonial *Halakhah* in the *Damascus
Role*," *Journal of Jewish Studies* 25 (1974), 197–202.

[89] It is interesting to note that Jesus used the story of creation to justify his prohibition
of divorce; see *Mark* 10.6–7; *Matt.* 19.4–5.

[90] S. Lowy, "The Extent of Jewish Polygamy in *Talmudic* Times," *Journal of Jewish
Studies* 9 (1958), 115–38.

[91] *Ibid.* 118–9. Additional cases of polygamy in the world of the sages could be discovered if evidence from the *Babylonian Talmud* could be accepted as historical. We have
already seen, for example, that R. Eliezer had married into the family of the *nasi*, for his
wife was the famous Imma Shalom, the sister of Rabban Gamaliel; but elsewhere we read
that he married his sister's daughter after she spent years growing up in his own house
(*yYeb.* 13.1, 13c; *ARNA* 16, p. 63 ed. Schechter). If the *Babylonian Talmud's* information
is reliable, then the contradiction between it and the *Palestinian Talmud* could be resolved
by assuming that R. Eliezer married his sister's daughter only after the death of Imma

Following Epstein and Mayer[92] we can add to this list the prominent examples from Josephus: Herod apparently had nine wives at the same time;[93] Joseph son of Tobias married his brother's daughter while still married to another woman (*AJ* 12.186-9); King Alexander Yannai is said to have been feasting with his concubines (παλλάκιδες) while his political rivals were being crucified (*AJ* 13.380).[94] Another instance in the Herodian house may be unearthed by close scrutiny of the sources. Herod's son Antipater was apparently married to two women at the same time, for in different places Josephus tells us that Antipater married the daughter of his brother Aristobulus (*AJ* 17.18) and that, on his return from Rome Antipater, was greeted at the dock by his mother and his wife, the daughter of Antigonus the Hasmonean (*AJ* 17.92). We can assume that he was married to both these women at the same time for it is unlikely that he divorced the daughter of Aristobulus before marrying the daughter of Antigonus; by the end of his life the Herodians found no political benefit in marriage to members of the Hasmonean house, and nevertheless the Hasmonean woman was Antipater's wife when he died. Neither Josephus nor his sources say specifically that Antipater son of Herod had a bigamous marriage, but the fact is that no source lays out the family tree of Antipater.

Mayer also mentions the case of Babatha,[95] whose second husband was Judah Khthusion, who himself was already married to another woman, Mariamme, and had even had a daughter from her, Shelamzion.

Shalom; this is the approach of A. Hyman *Biographies of Tannaim and Amoraim* I (London 1910), 173 [Hebrew]. But bigamy is equally likely, since neither interpretation is favored by the evidence. Yet there is a third possibility. While it is true that R. Eliezer's marriage to Imma-Shalom appears already in a *tannaitic midrash-halakhah* (*Sif. Shemini Makhilta de-Miluim* 33, 45c ed. Weiss), her connection to Rabban Gamaliel appears only in the *Babylonian Talmud* (*bShab.* 116a; *bBM* 59b); thus chances are that Imma Shalom herself is the daughter of R. Eliezer's sister, but not really the sister of Rabban Gamaliel. Similar arguments can be made in the cases of R. Aqiba and R. Meir, see above p. 78. It may be relevant in this regard that, as Gafni has established, polygamous marriages were accepted more in Babylonia than in Palestine, and the creators of *aggadot* there were less troubled by such family connections for their stories' central figures; see I. M. Gafni, "The Institution of Marriage in Rabbinic Times," in *The Jewish Family: Metaphor and Memory*, ed. D. Kraemer (Oxford 1989), 21–5.

[92] Mayer (above, n. 41), 58; Epstein (above n. 54), 17.

[93] Epstein has argued that Herod's sons Archelaus and Antipas were each married to two women simultaneously, but this is based on a mistaken reading of the sources. Antipas is said to have promised Herodias that he would divorce his first wife in order to marry her (*AJ* 18.110), and we have to assume he would have done so had she not abandoned him first; and the evidence is very clear that Archelaus did divorce his wife Mariamme in order to marry Glaphyra (*BJ* 2.116; *AJ* 17.350).

[94] Although the story has an obvious Hellenistic character, and the dramatic touch may be the result of creative license taken by Nicolaus.

[95] N. Lewis, *The Documents from the Bar Kokhba Period in the Cave of the Letters II: Greek Papyri* (Jerusalem 1989), 22–6.

Thus it is apparent that while the sources document polygamous marriages primarily for the royal Herodian house, the phenomenon was widespread among other social strata, as the case of Babatha demonstrates. My findings here indicate that the question of multiple marriage was not an ethical issue. Those groups who did object to polygamy on moral grounds (such as the Dead Sea Sect) forbade it by law. The main issue in polygamy was rather economic, and thus we find bigamous and even polygamous marriages mainly among the well-to-do. Babatha's second husband, who already had a wife, is entirely unknown to us, except for the fact that he was a man of means. We can suppose, for example, that it was the well-off man who had not yet produced descendants, or who no longer felt attracted to his wife, that took a second wife. A man of poorer means in the same situation would have divorced his wife before taking another one.[96]

Economic and Legal Arrangements

1. Betrothal (qiddushin)

The transfer of the woman from the authority of her father to the authority of her husband was viewed conceptually by the rabbis as the transfer of property by purchase. This did not differ from the convention in the ancient world whereby a daughter was the property of her father and then of her husband.[97] That this was the rabbis' mindset is evident from the fact that the acquisition of a wife is discussed together with the acquisition of a Hebrew slave, a Canaanite slave, large cattle, secured property and unsecured property (*mQidd.* 1.1–5). The law is formulated identically in each of these cases (X is acquired by means of A, B, C, etc.)[98] but the formulation also reveals that the rabbis considered the acquisition of a wife different from that of the other kinds of property, whose market-value varied according to their quality whereas a bride's value is non-negotiable. A bride's price is nominal, and the Schools of Shammai and Hillel debated only

---

[96]   Safrai (above, n. 37), 748–50, tries to downplay the significance of this.

[97]   Mace (above, n. 35), 191–3 argues against the idea that the husband acquired ownership of his wife just as he acquired ownership of a slave, for otherwise it would not have been important to distinguish between wife and slave. Mace thinks that the husband acquired from the father exclusive rights to his wife's sexuality. Wegner (above, n. 53), 19 follows Mace on this. See further D. H. Weiss, "The Use of קנה in Connection with Marriage," *Harvard Theological Review* 57 (1964), 244–8; P. V. M. Flesher, "Are Women Property in the System of the *Mishnah*?" in *From Ancient Israel to Modern Judaism: Intellect in Quest of Understanding, Essays in Honor of Marvin Fox = Brown Judaic Studies* CLIX, edd. J. Neusner, E. S. Frerichs, N. S. Sarna (Atlanta 1989), 219–31.

[98]   In Roman law, a wife would also be "acquired" in one of three ways: *confarreatio, coemptio* or *usus* (intercourse); see Pomeroy (above, n. 22), 152.

the minimum price without imposing any need to pay more: the School of Shammai set this minimum at one *denarius*, a fairly low sum of which the collection and payment nonetheless required some effort and could be taken as a measure of the seriousness of the payer's intentions; the School of Hillel set the sum even lower, at a *perutah*, which anyone could produce without any effort whatsoever (*mQidd.* 1.1). Thus the acquisition became merely symbolic, devoid of any real monetary value, and became also more egalitarian, so that theoretically every bride became acquirable by every groom.[99] This development, we can assume, goes hand-in-hand with the development described above, whereby social status deriving from wealth was gradually replaced, in the world of the rabbis, by status based on spiritual riches and accomplishment in *Torah*-study. The law which abolished the bride-price customarily paid by grooms was liable to cause economic harm only to the father.

Just as the actual act of acquisition lost any real substance as a result of the rabbinic reform, so the word "acquisition" (קִנְיָן) lost significance when applied to a bride. After the reform, the action was called "consecration" (*qiddushin*). Although scholars have tried to make a lot of the fact that, in contrast to sacramental marriage among Christians, marriage in Judaism remained a contractual transaction between the bride and groom,[100] the use of the word "consecration" (*qiddushin*) to describe both the *talmudic* tractate which deals with the taking of a bride and the action itself indicates that betrothal took on, in addition to its technical legal meaning, a spiritual connotation as well.[101]

2. The Marriage Contract (ketubbah)

The marriage contract (*ketubbah*) is not mentioned in the Bible; yet a *ketubbah* is mentioned already in *Tobit* (7.14), dated as early as the beginning of the Second Temple period.[102] The *ketubbah* was essentially a monetary arrangement between the bride and groom with the purpose of ensuring the bride's maintenance in the event of divorce or the husband's death. The various stages in the *ketubbah*'s development, as understood by the rabbis, are described in *tannaitic*

---

[99] This is the opinion of Guttmann (above, n. 68), 25–39.

[100] S. Baron, *A Social and Religious History of the Jews* II (New York 1952), 217–8; L. Epstein, *The Jewish Marriage Contract: A Study in the Status of Women in Jewish Law* (New York 1927), 1; M. D. Herr, "The Socio-Economic Status of Marriage According to the *Halakhah*," *The Families of the House of Israel* = *Proceedings of the Conference on Jewish Thought* XVIII (Jerusalem 1984), 37–46 [Hebrew]; I. M. Gafni (above, n. 91), 13–4.

[101] And see, e.g. S. Y. Horovitz, "R. Aqiba and the Laws of Matrimony in Israel," *Hashahar* 12 (1884), 180–2 [Hebrew]; J. Neusner, *A History of the Mishnaic Law of Women* V (Leiden 1980), 13; 268; Guttmann (above, n. 68), 38–9.

[102] For an analysis see Z. Falk, *Introduction to the Jewish Laws of the Second Commonwealth* I (Leiden 1978), 280–1.

sources in both *talmudim* and in the *Tosefta*,[103] from which it is clear that even the rabbis were conscious of changes introduced into the *ketubbah* during the Second Temple period, although they cannot agree on the precise nature of those changes. One possibility is that originally the value of the *ketubbah* was given by the groom to the father of the bride as a bride-price, and in the event of divorce the woman returned to her father's house (*tKet.* 12.1; *yKet.* 8.11, 32b). This may be hinted at in *Ben Sira*, who speaks of the father whose anxieties about his daughter continue after she is married, lest she be divorced and return to his house. Various rabbinical parables illustrate the custom of the divorced woman returning to her father's house: "They illustrated by a parable. To what is the thing similar? To a woman who disgraced her husband. Where does he send her? He sends her to her father's house" (*tBQ* 7.3); "It is like a king of flesh and blood who got angry at his wife and threw her out, sending her to her father's house" (*Sifre Deut.* 43, p. 102 ed. Finkelstein). The need to raise the funds specified in the *ketubbah* before the wedding led to the observation that "they would get old without marrying women" (*bKet.* 82b), in other words, that many men could not raise the required sum of money needed to perform the religious duty of marriage.

All sources attribute the change in the character of the *ketubbah* to a reform promulgated by Shimeon b. Shetah. According to the Palestinian Talmud, Shimeon b. Shetah determined that "a man should negotiate his wife's *ketubbah*," but this change did not solve the two problems we raised above, namely, that the *ketubbah* remained in the house of the bride's father and that the money had to be paid *before* the wedding. The *Babylonian Talmud* defines the second stage in the development of the *ketubbah* in its being deposited in the house of the bride's father-in-law; this is at least a solution to one of the two problems. The second problem was not solved even by the decision (related by all sources) that the *ketubbah* money should be used to purchase household utensils for the bride. Thus we should prefer the version of Shimeon b. Shetah's reform found in the *Tosefta* and the *Babylonian Talmud*: "The husband would write for her: all my property is a guarantee for the value of your *ketubbah*" (*Tosefta, ibid.*).[104]

This reform was clearly the first step, followed in turn by the reforms made by the Schools of Shammai and Hillel regarding betrothal, by which the act of marriage became something other than a simple act of acquisition by purchase. Every man, regardless of his means, can get married: he does not have to pay the value of the *ketubbah* before the wedding, nor is he obligated to pay a bride-price to the bride's father. The problem of payment was postponed until the time

---

[103]   An analysis of sources can be found in Falk, *ibid.* 295–8.

[104]   For a comparison of this formulation with contemporary Egyptian material, see M. J. Geller, "New Sources for the Origins of the Rabbinic *Ketubbah*," *Hebrew Union College Annual* 49 (1978), 227–45.

of divorce. If, as all sources indicate, the minimum amount of the *ketubbah* was 200 *zuz* for a virgin and 100 for a widow or divorcée (*mKet.* 1.2), only a man of considerable means could afford to get divorced.

The bride's father was the one hurt most by the reforms. He no longer received either a bride-price or the value of the *ketubbah* so long as his daughter was under her husband's authority much less after her divorce. Consequently many fathers understandably did not want to furnish their daughters with dowries, which had the effect of turning their daughters, who had lost all market-value, into a bothersome worry. Yet the *halakhah*, as part of the series of changes in the marriage contract, came to obligate the father to include a dowry in his daughter's *ketubbah* – at least 50 *zuz*, a sum of more than symbolic significance (*mKet.* 6.5). Yet the law also took account of certain fathers' financial position, allowing a father to reach a determination with the husband that he would pay nothing into his daughter's *ketubbah* (*ibid.*).

The *ketubbah* is cited by many scholars as evidence of an improvement in women's status during the Second Temple period, as compared to the period of the Bible. A more cautious conclusion is to be preferred: the various stages through which the *ketubbah* passed testify to a change in women's legal status. Women's rights were henceforth much more firmly anchored in law. The practical force of the *ketubbah*, and the extent to which the judiciary system was able to enforce its provisions on both marriage partners, are different questions entirely. The *ketubbah*, is a contractual agreement between two marriage partners.[105] In the following lines I shall study the expectations of married couples from the *ketubbah* by comparing the actual marriage contracts discovered in the Judaean Desert (and dating to just a few years before the Bar-Kokhba revolt) with the literary samples in *tannaitic* sources, whose genuineness can thereby be measured.

The various wordings and formulations of the *ketubbah*, as preserved in the fourth chapter of the *mishnaic* tractate *Ketubbot*, represent some of the only Aramaic sentences in the entire *Mishnah*: "All my goods are surety for your *ketubbah*" (4.7); "If you are taken captive, I will redeem you and take you again as my wife" (8); "Male children which you shall have by me shall inherit your *ketubbah* besides the portion which they receive with their brothers" (10); "Female children which you shall have by me shall dwell in my house and receive maintenance from my property until they marry husbands" (11); "You shall dwell in my house and receive maintenance from my property so long as you remain a widow in my house" (12). One may conclude from this that the word-

---

[105] On the various components of the *ketubbah*, see Epstein (above, n. 100). New material found after the publication of Epstein's work has been discussed by other legal scholars. See M. A. Friedman, *Jewish Marriage in Palestine* (Tel Aviv 1979). For more bibliography, see below.

ing of the *ketubbah* solidified into tradition only in Aramaic, and that the tradition did not necessarily take shape in the same circles in which the *Mishnah* developed, where for ideological reasons only Hebrew was used in *halakhic* texts. The marriage contracts which were discovered in the Judaean Desert and have so far been published only lend strength to this argument. These documents were written in Greek or Aramaic, none is in Hebrew. The Greek examples are: 1) the contract of Salome, daughter of Yohanan b. Galgoula, and sister of one of Bar Kokhba's commanders (the document in fact records her second marriage to the same man who had previously divorced her);[106] 2) another marriage contract from Wadi Muraba'at;[107] 3) the contract of Shelamzion, Babatha's stepdaughter, discovered in the Cave of Letters in Nahal Hever;[108] 4) the marriage contract of Salome Komais, also discovered in the Cave of Letters.[109] Next to these, two Aramaic marriage contracts from the Judaean Desert have so far been published.[110] In addition, according to Yadin, Babatha's *ketubbah* is also in Aramaic,[111] despite the implication in the *Mishnah* that the custom in Judaea (in contrast to Jerusalem and the Galilee) was to write the *ketubbah* in Hebrew (cf. the Hebrew formula in *mKet.* 4.12); a section of Babatha's *ketubbah* in Aramaic, representing the Judaean version, was published by Yadin.[112] Both the Greek and Aramaic marriage contracts from the Judaean Desert contain some but not all of the Aramaic formulae which appear in the *Mishnah*.[113] We can see in this material the stages in which the formulation of the *ketubbah* took shape.

---

[106] P. Benoit, J. T. Milik and R. de-Vaux, *Les Grottes de Muraba'ât = Discoveries in the Judaean Desert* II (Oxford 1961), 243–54.

[107] *Ibid.* 254–6.

[108] Lewis (above, n. 95), 76–82.

[109] *Ibid.* 130–3.

[110] Benoit *et al.* (above, n. 106), 109–17.

[111] Y. Yadin, *Bar Kokhba: Rediscovery of the Legendary Hero of the Second Jewish Revolt against Rome* (London 1971), 237–9.

[112] *Ibid.*

[113] For example, in no *ketubbah* does the formula "If you are taken captive, I will redeem you and take you again as my wife" (*mKet.* 4.8) appear. For an attempt to reconstruct the historical development of this section of the *ketubbah*, see Y. Gilat, "'If you are taken captive, I will ransom you and take you back as my wife'," *Bar-Ilan* 13 (1976), 58–72 [Hebrew], who argues that this section was introduced in the wake of the Bar-Kokhba revolt. Papyrological evidence thus provides strong support for this theory. On the other hand, Archer (above, n. 35), 67–8 claims that this section was an unconditional clause enforced by rabbinical courts and that the husband was liable even if the words were not written into his wife's *ketubbah*. By the same reasoning Archer tries to confirm the historicity of the provision in the *ketubbah* obligating a father to maintain his daughters: such a provision would not have been set by a rabbinical court and anyone wanting to guarantee it would have had to write it into the *ketubbah*. To my mind this is a sophistic argument which relies too heavily on the belief that the *halakhah* existed then in all its details just as it appears today in rabbinic sources.

The crystallization of formulae in the *ketubbah* can be traced back a few generations before the Bar-Kokhba rebellion. The sources record, with great admiration, Hillel's interpretation of "common speech" in the wording of the *ketubbah*, that is, he used biblical exegetical methods to expound a text written for secular purposes in order to legitimize children who were potentially bastards. The case is as follows: apparently some women in Alexandria who were betrothed by certain men were kidnapped and married by others. Hillel used the wording of the *ketubbah*, "when you enter my house you will be my wife according to the religion of Moses and Israel" (*tKet.* 4.9; *yYeb.* 15.3, 14d; *yKet.* 4.8, 28d; *bBM* 104a), to rule that the bride officially became her groom's wife only when she entered his house, thereby legitimizing any children from the union with a bride kidnapped before nuptials took place.

The marriage contracts discovered in the Judaean Desert also provide information on their changing monetary values. The value of the contract of Salome daughter of Yohanan Galgoula was the standard 200 *denarii*,[114] and that of Salome Komais was a lower sum (96 *denarii*),[115] but the value of the contract of Shelamzion, Babatha's step-daughter, was fully 500 *denarii*,[116] and in another contract from the Judaean Desert the value is set at 2000 (!) *denarii*.[117] A woman whose *ketubbah* was worth such a large sum could certainly not be easily divorced. *Tannaitic* sources emphasize that rabbinical courts were especially strict in enforcing payment of the *ketubbah* :

> "It once happened that a man vowed to have no benefit from his wife, whose *ketubbah* was 400 *denars*. She came before R. Aqiba and he declared him liable to pay her her *ketubbah*. He said: Rabbi, my father left but 800 *denarii*, and my brother took 400 *denarii* and I took 400; is it not enough that she should take 200 *denarii* and I 200? R. Aqiba said to him: Even if you are forced to sell the hair of your head you shall pay her her *ketubbah*. The husband answered: Had I known that this was so, I would not have made my vow, and R. Aqiba permitted her (to him, i.e. released him from his vow)." (*mNed.* 9.5)

The same strictness in enforcement by the rabbis is illustrated in another, less pleasant story from the *Babylonian Talmud:*

> "There was a man who wanted to divorce his wife but hesitated because her *ketubbah* was worth a great deal. He accordingly invited his friends and gave them a good feast and made them drunk and put them all in one bed. He then brought the white of an egg and scattered it among them and brought in witnesses ..." (*bGitt.* 57a)

The man in this story wants to get around paying his wife's *ketubbah* by framing his wife for adultery and thereby deceiving the rabbinical court, for this was the only way he could avoid paying in full. But of course this story has a happy end:

---

[114] Benoit *et al.* (above, n. 106), 248.
[115] Lewis (above, n. 95), 131.
[116] Lewis *et al.* (above, n. 52), 231.
[117] Benoit *et al.* (above, n. 106), 255.

"There was a certain elder there of the disciples of Shammai the Elder, named Baba b. Buta, who said: This is what I have been taught by Shammai the Elder, that the white of an egg contracts when brought near the fire, but semen becomes faint from the fire. They tested it and found that it was so, and they brought the man to the rabbinical court and flogged him and made him pay her *ketubbah*.."

The mention of Shammai the Elder dates the story to the Second Temple period. It can be assumed that in that period the rabbinical courts had the power to enforce their rulings, but the degree to which this power was impaired after the destruction of the Temple, when the same courts served more as arbitrating bodies than as governmental authorities, cannot be known. This may in fact help us understand the Greek marriage contracts. A contract in Greek could be presented in a Roman court, which could force the husband to meet its provisions. Lewis has pointed out the clearly visible transition in marriage contracts from Aramaic to Greek between the first generation after the Destruction (Babatha's generation) and the second (the generation of her step-daughter, Shelamzion), but he attributes this phenomenon merely to fashion.[118] It seems to me that the Jewish character of Shelamzion's marriage contract and that of Salome Komais, although both are in Greek, can be understood as a sign of changing times and a diminution in the power of Jewish courts.[119] The external form of such a *ketubbah* – language and legal formulae – was indeed appropriate for a Roman court,[120] but its content is essentially Jewish. A recurring clause in both, whereby the husband obligates himself to maintain his wife according to Hellenic custom (Ἑλληνικὸς νόμος), may indicate an attempt to avoid the obligation of paying the value of the *ketubbah* when it was brought to a gentile court – a condition which is emphasized and rigidly enforced in Jewish law.

The Marriage Ceremony

Rabbinic sources provide some impression of the customs attending the marriage ceremony and wedding festivities. The marriage ceremony was the last stage in the process by which the bride was transferred to the authority of her husband. The procession in which the bride was led from her father's to her husband's house was apparently rather easy to recognize, for R. Judah, on seeing just such a procession pass before him, is said to have bade his students to cease their studying in order to fulfill the obligation of praising the bride (*yHag.* 1.7,

---

[118] Lewis (above, n. 95), 130.

[119] On the Jewish character of Shelamzion's marriage contract, see Lewis *et al.* (above, n. 52), 236, 240–7. But see also the answer by Wasserstein (above, n. 52), 160.

[120] For example, the *stipulatio* in ll. 25–7, 66–7 (*ibid.*). On the connection between *stipulatio* and Jewish law, see A. Gulak, "Deed of Betrothal and Oral Stipulations in *Talmudic* Law," *Tarbiz* 3 (1932), 361–76 [Hebrew].

66c; *bKet.* 17a; *ARNA* 4, pp. 18-9 ed. Schechter; *ARNB* 8, p. 22 ed. Schechter).[121] We read even that King Agrippa "made way for a bride, and the sages praised him for it" (*bKet.* 17a). What were these outstanding characteristics of the wedding procession? First of all, the bride was carried in a litter to her husband's house; this custom, according to the *Mishnah*, ceased after the Bar Kokhba revolt (*mSot.* 9.14; *tSot.* 15.9). Some brides would wear a crown on their heads, a custom which ended after the destruction of the Temple (*Mishnah, ibid.*; *Tosefta, ibid.* 8). The bride's hair would also be arranged in a certain way. In one *halakhah* the rabbis determine that one indication of a woman's virginity on her wedding day is her procession from her father's to her husband's house accompanied by marriage-hymns,[122] and her appearance, with her hair unbound. R. Yohanan b. Broqa adds that it was also a custom to share out roast corn to passers-by when a virgin was being married (*mKet.* 2.1; cf. 10). The *Babylonian Talmud* mentions a ritual with some similar points – קצצה – when the bride was considered to be beneath the groom's social rank, in that instance the groom's family distributes fruit to passers-by on the wedding-day so that the memory of the event would be linked with the defect (*bKet.* 28b). We can imagine that another element of the bridal procession was the groomsmen who accompanied her to her husband's house – the groomsmen (שושבינים) who are mentioned as assisting the groom (and the bride) during the marriage ceremony itself (cf. *tKet.* 1.4; *tBB* 10.9).[123]

One tradition in the *Babylonian Talmud* makes a connection between events which led to the rebellions against Rome and popular wedding customs. In Tur Malka a hen and a rooster were carried before the bride and groom. In Betar cedars which had been planted at the births of the bride and groom were cut down to be used for the wedding canopy or bridal chamber – *huppah* (*bGitt.* 57a). The stories in which the details of these customs appear are certainly fictitious, but the customs themselves are not necessarily fictitious, and may in fact represent historical *realia*.

Very little is known about the actual wedding celebration after the bride arrived at the groom's house. The *huppah* was by all indications quite a different thing from what it is today. Büchler thought that it was a room which the groom

---

[121] On this see in detail Shulamit Valler, *Women and Womanhood in the Stories of the Babylonian Talmud* (Tel Aviv 1993), 23–38 [Hebrew].

[122] הינומה perhaps from Greek ὑμέναιος see Safrai (above, n. 37), 758.

[123] On the concept of שושבינים see N. H. Tur-Sinai, "Shoshvin," in *Sefer Asaf: Research Articles Presented to Prof. Simha Asaf on his 60th Birthday*, edd. M. D. Kasouto, J. Klausner and J. Guttman (Jerusalem 1953), 316–22 [Hebrew]. Safrai (above, n. 37), 757 identifies it as a charitable institution designed to provide financial aid to impoverished grooms. See also Ofra Meir, "The Wedding in Kings' Parables (in the *Aggadah*)," *Studies in Marriage Customs = Folklore Research Center Studies IV*, edd. I. Ben-Ami and D. Noy (Jerusalem 1974), 16–7 [Hebrew].

would add on to his father's house for himself and his future wife.[124] It can be assumed that there was a marriage ceremony in which the blessing for bridegrooms was said, for this blessing is mentioned in the *Babylonian Talmud* (*bKet.* 7b), but the different versions of the blessing which the *Talmud* mentions are all attributed to *amoraim*, most of them Babylonian.[125] The evangelist *John* relates the story of a wedding in the Galilean village Cana, to which Jesus' mother was invited, indicating that women were permitted to participate in weddings (*John* 2.2–5). Yet whether this was true for Palestine in our period is less clear, for as noted, that gospel was written far from Palestine and in other ways is less reliable as an historical source than the three synoptic gospels.

---

[124] A. Büchler, "The Induction of the Bride and the Bridegroom into the חופה in the First and Second Centuries in Palestine," *Livre d'hommage à la mémoire du Dr. Samuel Poznanski (1864–1921)* (Warsaw 1927), 83–97.

[125] A fragmentary text discovered in Cave 4 at Qumran has been identified by its editors as a blessing said during a nuptial ceremony: M. Baillet, *Qumrân grotte 4 III = Discoveries in the Judaean Desert* VII (Oxford 1982), 81–105. The text is in very bad condition, and even if its identity as a marriage blessing were certain, the extent to which it reflects common practice would still be unknown, seeing that the Dead Sea Sect which produced it was marginal in the extreme. But see also an entirely different interpretation of the text by J. M. Baumgarten, "$4Q_{502}$ Marriage or Golden Age Ritual?" *Journal of Jewish Studies* 34 (1983), 125–35.

Chapter 3:

A Woman's Biology

The biological differences between men and women, their causes and significance, are the subject of extensive discussion in our sources.

Virginity

One of the main and most obvious biological differences between men and women is that the woman is the one who bears children. As a result, a woman can always be sure that the children she is raising are her own, whereas the identity of the father is theoretically never certain.[1] But there is one part of a woman's anatomy which can serve as a fairly sure indicator of paternity – her hymen. If a woman is a virgin when married, her husband can be sure at least that his wife was not pregnant before the wedding.

1. Loss of Economic Significance

Some have thought that *Ben Sira*'s advice on how a father should treat his daughter does not leave much room for love. This is because *Ben Sira* is not exactly subtle about a father's main worry regarding his daughter, namely, his responsibility to protect her virginity until she is married. In antiquity, virginity was a commodity with a price. In the Bible the father is the main beneficiary of his daughter's virginity, for he received her bride-price.[2] But as we have seen, by the Second Temple period virginity held monetary value not for the father but only for the daughter herself.

---

[1] As noted by A. Isaksson, *Marriage and Ministry in the New Testament: A Study with Special References to Mt. 19:13–22 and 1Cor. 11:3–16 = Acta Seminarii Neotestamentici Upsalensis XXIV* (Lund 1965) 23. The matter is well illustrated in a rabbinic debate on betrothal and marriage; the opinion is expressed that a man should not even betroth a woman before three months have passed from the time of his decision to marry her, in order to ensure that she has not initially been impregnated by someone else (e.g. *bErub.* 47a).

[2] On the origin of the bride-price, see D. Mace, *Hebrew Marriage: A Sociological Study* (New York 1953), 168–74.

On becoming married, a woman had immediately to undergo defloration. A late *midrash* viewed this as punishment for the sin of Eve: "Just as three things were decreed against Adam, so three things were decreed against Eve, as it is said, 'To the woman He said, I will greatly increase your pangs in childbearing' (*Gen.* 3.16): when a woman has intercourse for the first time, it is painful for her ..." (*ARNA* 1, p. 7 ed. Schechter). Perhaps this is the reason why, over the course of time, virginity became so much more than merely an element in a woman's physical anatomy, turning rather into a symbol of purity and innocence. For example, the virginity of girls who died unwed is usually noted on their tombstones.[3]

It is against this background that we may properly understand the story of Jesus' virgin birth (*Matt.* 1.18–20; *Luke* 1.26–38). Only a virgin, that is a woman who could prove that she had never had sexual relations with a man, was fit to be the mother of the savior. But this raises the problem of a pregnant unmarried woman falling immediately under suspicion of having been seduced by a man. This is what happened to the tradition of Mary's virgin conception outside of Christianity, and may in fact reflect the historical reality of Jesus' birth.[4] Mary's virginity is the unique creation of the evangelists, although another account of immaculate conception which similarly raises suspicion of adultery is found already in the strange story of the birth of Melchizedek in the Slavonic *Apocalypse of Enoch* (71.1–20).[5] This may suggest Jewish inspiration for the story of Mary's virginity.

Thus it appears that virginity in the Second Temple period, while losing all economic value in Jewish law, took on a symbolic significance .

2. Legal Significance

Several rabbinic sources shed light on the legal aspects of the problem of virginity. In various cases brides are accused of having already lost their virginity but the sages invalidate the accusation. All these cases appear in two collections of *baraitot*, one in the *Palestinian Talmud* and the other in the *Babylonian Talmud*,

---

[3] E.g. N. Avigad, *Beth She'arim* III (Jerusalem 1976), 242; *CII* 1169.

[4] See recently: Jane Schaberg, *The Illegitimacy of Jesus: A Feminist Theological Interpretation* (New York 1990).

[5] Of the character and purpose of that composition, see F. I. Anderson, "2 (Slavonic Apocalypse of) *Enoch*," in *The Old Testament Pseudepigrapha*, ed. J. H. Charlesworth (Garden City NY 1985), 94–7. The *Protoevangelium Jacobi* also mentions a similar miracle birth, that of Mary herself (1–5), but this story was undoubtedly composed under the direct influence of the virgin birth of Jesus and stands outside the scope of the present work. The *Protoevangelium* is also the first to mention that Jesus' miracle birth left Mary's hymen intact (19–20) – but it is a Christian work with no trace of Jewish influence, see M. Mach, "Are There Jewish Elements in the *Protoevangelium Jacobi*?", *Proceedings of the Ninth World Congress of Jewish Studies*, Div. A (Jerusalem 1986), 215–22.

and the sages who appear in them, with the exception of R. Ishmael b. R. Yose, are all from the house of the *nasi*. In the first story, in which the protagonist dates from the Second Temple period, a man went before Rabban Gamaliel the Elder and claimed that he failed to find the signs of virginity in his wife, but Rabban Gamaliel believed the wife, who claimed that she came from the *Dorkti* family, which was a family in which women were known not to bleed when they lose their virginity (*bKet.* 10b). The same claim was twice brought before Rabbi, who accepted the wife's explanation and rejected the husband's complaint in both cases: in the first, the wife attributed her failure to bleed to years of famine (*Ibid.*), and in the second the wife maintained that her hymen fell from the rigor of climbing the steps of her father's house (*yKet.* 1.1, 25a). R. Ishmael b. R. Yose, when he heard the case of the woman "whose signs of virginity were no larger than a mustard-seed," ruled in her favor and even said a blessing over her, "May there be many in Israel like you" (*yKet.* 1.1, 25a). A most extreme position was taken by Rabban Gamaliel of Yavneh[6] who, when a man came before him and claimed, "I found the entrance open already," did not even ask the wife for her explanation but immediately said to the man: "Perhaps you moved aside. I will give you an illustration: To what is this like? To a man who was walking in the deep darkness of the night [and came to his house and found the door locked]; if he moves aside [the bolt to the door] he finds it open, if he does not move [it] aside he finds it locked" (*bKet.* 10a). There are absolutely no counter-examples of the husband winning his suit. The meaning of all these cases is uncertain: the rabbis may have made an effort to solve the problem of virginity through leniency, even though the *halakhah* laid great stress on virginity, but it may also be true that the stories represent a literary collection composed to justify the woman's position in every instance, even though the rabbinic courts generally ruled in favor of the husband. The unmistakable literary character of the material rules out a single clear answer to this question.[7]

Most of the *tannaim* after the Bar-Kokhba revolt who came from the Galilee, and lived and were active there, were of the opinion that in Judaea a man could not make a claim against the virginity of his wife because of the custom there to allow the groom and bride to spend time alone together before their wedding. This critique of the Judaean practice, appearing in many sources (*mKet.* 1.5; cf. *tKet.* 1.4; *yKet.* 1.1, 25a; *bKet.* 9b, 12a), perhaps affords a glimpse into the different practices in different parts of Palestine regarding the right granted members of the opposite sex to meet before marriage. The approach in Judaea was to

---

[6] Although there is a good chance it was really Rabban Gamaliel b. Rabbi, for the story is related in Aramaic. In that case the story would not be relevant for the present study.

[7] On the literary character and purpose of the Babylonian chain of stories, see: Shulamit Valler, *Women and Womanhood in the Stories of the Babylonian Talmud* (Tel Aviv 1992), 39–55 [Hebrew].

afford potential marriage partners the opportunity to veto a proposed match; but the critique of this practice represents a more puritanical approach, based on the fear that such a meeting between male and female would cause excessive temptation and cast doubt on the intended bride's virginity. The marriage contract of Jesus b. Menahem and Salome Komais, both of Maoza (discovered by Yadin in the Cave of Letters and published recently), records that the married couple were continuing to live together as husband and wife just as they had done previously (συμβιῶσαι τ[ον] Ἰησοῦν μετ᾽ αὐτῆς ω[ς κα]ὶ πρὸ τούτου τοῦ χρόνου).[8] We see from this not only that bride and groom in Judaea were allowed to get acquainted with one another by being left alone together, but also that the custom extended to a kind of cohabitation without a *ketubbah* and perhaps even without an official marriage. This may be the proper background for understanding an opaque *talmudic* passage relating a reform at the time of religious persecution in Judaea. The word used by the rabbis to describe the circumstances which led to this unfortunate event is *shemad* (שמד), a term usually employed in the description of the Bar Kohkba aftermath. At that time a measure was adopted by the Romans which resembles what was known in medieval Europe as the *jus primae noctis*, that is, the right of Roman officers to deflower Jewish virgins prior to their entry into wedlock. The rabbis thus decreed that in the presence of this emergency, "her (the Jewish bride's) husband would have intercourse with her while she was still in her father's house (and would thus avert the suspicion of the authorities that a wedding was taking place)" (*yKet.* 1.5, 25c); and in the same place we find that the daughter-in-law of R. Hoshaya entered the *huppah* pregnant. The note at the end of this passage is highly interesting: "although the persecutions ended, the custom continued".[9]

The Menstruant (*niddah*)

Menstruation was correctly understood in antiquity as a sign of a girl's arrival at sexual maturity (in the rabbis' language, "she saw blood"), but its biological purpose was not at all clear then, and as a result a woman's monthly discharge

---

[8] N. Lewis, *The Documents from the Bar-Kokhba Period in the Cave of the Letters II: Greek Papyri* (Jerusalem 1989), 130.

[9] Patai has argued that the tradition concerning *jus primae noctis* in these sources represents historical reality, although he acknowledges that examination of similar sources from medieval Europe has revealed that those traditions have no factual basis; see R. Patai, "Jus Primae Noctis," *Studies in Marriage Customs = Folklore Research Center Studies* IV, edd. I. Ben-Ami and D. Noy (Jerusalem 1974), 177–80; and see now my "Premarital Cohabitation in Ancient Judea: The Evidence of the Babatha Archive and the *Mishnah*," *Harvard Theological Review* 86 (1993), 247–64.

was treated as a subject of fear and abomination. It was believed, for example, that menstrual blood had magic powers. Josephus relates that in the Judaean Desert there grew a special plant which could be uprooted only by applying to it menstrual blood or a woman's urine; this plant was prized for its power to drive away evil spirits (*BJ* 7.180–5).

Biblical law, probably following an ancient taboo, strictly prohibits sexual relations with a menstruant.[10] Those who violated this prohibition were denounced in both the Pharisaic *Psalms of Solomon* ("and with menstrual blood they defiled the sacrifices as if they were common meat" 8.12) and the *Damascus Covenant* of the Dead Sea Sect ("they profane the Temple because they do not observe the distinction [between clean and unclean] in accordance with the Law, but lie with a woman who sees her bloody discharge" V 7). The rabbinical ethical code expands the biblical law through interpretation. The schools of both R. Ishmael and R. Aqiba agreed that the correct interpretation of the verse, "You shall separate the children of Israel from their uncleanness" (*Lev.* 15.31), implied separation from women before their period: "R. Yoshayah said: From this we deduce a warning to the children of Israel that they should separate from their wives when they are near their periods. ... R. Shimeon bar Yohai: He who does not separate from his wife near her period, even if he has sons like the sons of Aaron, they will die, even as it is written: 'Thus shall you separate the children of Israel from their uncleanness' (*ibid.*) ... 'of her that is sick with her impurity' (*ibid.* 33); and next to it, 'after the death [of Aaron's two sons]' (*ibid.* 16.1)" (*bShebu.* 18b). In other words, even if this is not specified by *halakhah*, a man is warned to "build a fence around himself" to keep a safe distance from impurity. This recommendation to extend the days of separation from a woman by including some days before her period, is complemented by another recommendation, *viz.*, to extend the period of separation on the other side as well: "There are three things which R. Ishmael b. R. Yose commanded Rabbi: ... Do not have marital relations with your wife the first night after she immersed" (*bPes.* 112b). The seriousness of transgression in this matter is illustrated by a *tannaitic aggadah*:

> It once happened that a certain scholar had studied much Scripture and *mishnah*, and had served scholars much, yet died in the prime of life. His wife took his *tefillin* and carried

---

[10] On this taboo see, e.g. Rachel Adler, "Tumah and Taharah: Ends and Beginnings," *The Jewish Woman: New Perspectives*, ed. Elizabeth Koltun (New York 1976), 63–71; Rachel Biale, *Women and the Jewish Law: An Exploration of Women's Issues in Halakhic Sources* (New York 1974), 147; Léone J. Archer, "'In Thy Blood Live': Gender and Ritual in the Judaeo-Christian Tradition," in *Through the Devil's Gateway: Women, Religion and Taboo*, ed. Alison Joseph (London 1990), 22–49; but see now Tirzah Z. Meachem, *Mishnah Tractate Niddah with Introduction: A Critical Edition with Notes on Variants, Commentary, Redaction and Chapters in Legal History and Realia* (Ph.D. diss. The Hebrew University of Jerusalem 1989), 154–70 [Hebrew], who denies the connection to any taboo.

them about in synagogues and schoolhouses ... . On one occasion I [Elijah] was a guest at her house and she related the whole story to me. I said to her: My daughter! How was he to you in your days of menstruation? She said to me: God forbid! He did not touch me even with his little finger. And how was he to you during your days of white garments [between the end of her period and her ritual immersion]? He ate with me, drank with me and slept with me in bodily contact, and it did not occur to him to engage in sex. I said to her: Blessed be the Omnipresent for slaying him ... (*bShab.* 13a-b)

Menstrual blood, like most of the biological phenomena unique to women, was interpreted by the rabbis as part of the punishment meted out to Eve because of the sin in Eden (*yShab.* 2.4, 5b; *Gen. R.* 17.8, p. 160 ed. Theodor-Albeck).

In order to avoid a menstruant woman's temptation of her husband, "The Early Sages (זקנים ראשנים) would say: She shall use neither kohl nor rouge [= cosmetics] until she has immersed in water" (*Sif. Metzora, Zabim* 9.12, p. 79c ed. Weiss). R. Aqiba, however, disapproved of this approach stating: "The matter causes feelings of enmity and he may wish to divorce her" (*ibid.*).

The sources give witness to the rigor and intensity with which the separation between ritually clean men and menstruant women was carried out. The laws of impurity were quite complicated, and in order to maintain strict purity women had to be careful about some matters of which they were not always fully aware. Thus women sometimes sought advice from the sages, generally in instances when they discovered a discharge of blood outside their regular cycle and could not decide whether the blood was menstrual, which causes uncleanness, or blood from some other source, which would not cause uncleanness. R. Eliezer b. R. Zadok relates that his father had trouble deciding about the irregular bleeding of two women, as the bleeding appeared in unusual forms ("red hairs," "red peelings"). Other sages in Yavneh could not solve the puzzle without the help of physicians, who finally determined that the cause of the bleeding in both cases was an internal injury, not menstruation (*tNidd.* 4.3–4; *yNidd.* 3.2, 50c, where the case is handled by *amoraim*; *bNidd.* 22b). In the same vein we find that when a woman who was experiencing bleeding came before R. Aqiba, he decided, after investigating the possibility of an internal injury, that the blood was clean, to the surprise of his students (*mNidd.* 8.3). Likewise, when a woman with irregular bleeding came before Rabbi, he had his associate, Abdan frighten her suddenly, which was an unusual solution to the problem, but a solution all the same (*bNidd.* 66a). These cases illustrate that sages sometimes ruled leniently in cases of women's irregular bleeding. On the other hand, Rabbi was not always so accommodating, for elsewhere it is related that in the instance of a woman with irregular bleeding "it happened that Rabbi granted her four nights in twelve-months" (*bNidd.* 65b), i.e. her continuing impurity was such that she was declared ritually clean for her husband and could have sexual relations with him only four nights a year.

Irregular bleeding was not the only problem that required the sages' intervention. Also bloodstains on objects with which women regularly came into contact made those objects suspect of having been polluted with menstrual blood. It is related that R. Judah the Patriarch and R. Meir allowed two such stained objects to be used, by attributing the stains to other causes (*tNidd.* 6.17). By contrast, we hear elsewhere of bloodstains found on objects with which women had come into contact and which the sages declared impure (*tNidd.* 7.3).

The sources indicate that there were also women who specialized in inspecting blood-stains. Rabbi mentions an extreme example: "A deaf woman lived in our vicinity. Not one who only checks herself,[11] but her friends would see (blood) and would show her" (*bNidd.* 13b). It is true that Rabbi cites the case in order to demonstrate that a deaf woman is not unfit to understand matters concerning *niddah*, but incidentally we learn that if a deaf woman could make the examination and decide on the bleeding of other women, *a fortiori* a woman who was not deaf and who was an expert in such matters.

Since menstruant woman transferred their impurity to household utensils and their contents, female slaves were also obligated to adhere to the laws of *niddah*. Tabitha, the maidservant of Rabban Gamaliel, is said to have examined herself regularly, using her full knowledge of the laws of *niddah* (*yNidd.* 2.1, 49d; *bNidd.* 6b; *Lev. R.* 19.4, pp. 426–7 ed. Margulies). Rabbi's maidservant is also reported to have known and adhered to the laws of impurity regarding woman (*yBer.* 3.4, 6c).

The fear of impurity from menstrual blood accompanied a woman to the grave. The corpse of a woman who died during her period had to undergo a special ceremony of purificatory immersion, as the following story illustrates: "The practice at first was to immerse on account of those women who died during their period; then the practice changed to immersing on account of all out of concern for the women's honor" (*tNidd.* 9.16; *bNidd.* 71a; *bMQ* 27b).[12]

The rabbis regarded the whole subject of menstruation as of the highest importance, and the wives of the Pharisees, like the wives of rabbinic sages afterwards, obviously acted in this matter according to their husbands' dictates and consulted rabbinic experts in every case which they could not decide themselves. It is natural to wonder whether this phenomenon extended beyond Pharisaic circles, and whether, or to what extent, it characterized all Jewish society in the Second Temple period. Other sources, some rabbinic and some not, afford a glimpse into the lives of the other segments of Jewish society.

Rabbinic sources on *niddah* deal with two other groups from that period: Samaritan (Cuthean) and Sadducee women. Samaritan women were judged to bear the ritual uncleanness of the menstruant from their day of birth (*mNidd.* 4.1; *tNidd.* 5.1). This of course does not mean that the Samaritans neglected the bib-

---

[11] The word is דיה (only). Other manuscripts have דוה = menstruant.

[12] The meaning is, all utensils which a menstruant touched before her death would be immersed; Rashi explains that women were ashamed that some of them were being subjected to a different practice from that of other dead women.

lical laws of purity regarding menstruation, merely that the Pharisaic sages of Palestine dismissed the Samaritans' fulfillment of those laws.[13] The Samaritans are not part of the present study and are mentioned here only as a point of comparison with the Sadducees.[14] The rabbis' attitude toward the Sadducees is less clear-cut and more complicated. Sadduccean women were judged *a priori* to be unclean just like Samaritan women (*mNidd.* 4.2; *tNidd.* 5.2; *bNidd.* 33b), but rabbinic sources record that most Sadducee women followed the rulings of the Pharisaic sages and thus were considered to be clean. The *Tosefta* relates the story of a high priest who spoke with a Sadducee in the market and became unclean from his spittle; in response to this, the Sadducee's wife said to the high priest: "My good priest, although we are Sadducean women, we all are examined by a sage" (*tNidd.* 5.3).[15] R. Yose also reports that sages were well-versed in the Sadducean women's fluxes because "they were all examined by a sage, except for one, who died" (*ibid.*).

This case may cause some surprise. The high priest, more than any other Jew, was expected to be Sadducean, since it is well-known that most of the priests at the end of the Second Temple period belonged to the Sadducean sect[16] and also that the priests serving in the Temple were especially strict in matters of ritual purity. Yet it is the high priest who is anxious about contracting impurity from the Sadducees. It was highly unlikely that a priest would arrive at the Temple in a state of ritual impurity as a result of contact with his wife who had not followed *niddah* regulations to the letter. Thus it is difficult to accept the sources' claim that the problem was solved by having the wives of the important figures of that generation defer to advice of the Pharisaic opposition.[17] More probably, in light of the need to legitimate the service in the Temple, the sages declared Sadducean women clean *ex post facto*, even if the laws of purity which the same women followed were without doubt not those of the Pharisees. It is not a coincidence that R. Yose, the pupil of R. Aqiba, who certainly had never seen a Sad-

---

[13] Just as the Dead Sea Sect rejected the Pharisaic rulings on *niddah* : see *Damascus Covenant* V 7.

[14] The Sadducees have been discussed by Meachem (above, n. 10), 191. According to her interpretation, the Sadduccean *halakhah* permitted intercourse with a menstruant, following the general principle that such was permitted in the Bible.

[15] Compare *bNidd.* 33b, where, however, the high priest (rather than the Sadducee)'s wife is the one who tells him that the fluxes of Sadducean women are examined by the sages. Obviously the version in the *Tosefta* is to be preferred.

[16] See M. Stern, "Aspects of Jewish Society: The Priesthood and other Classes," in *The Jewish People in the First Century II = Compendia Rerum Iudaicarum ad Novum Testamentum Section One*, edd. S. Safrai and M. Stern (Assen 1976), 609–12.

[17] Just as it is difficult to accept the sages' claim that the Pharisees were the ones who controlled the Temple service; for the state of the question and a fair assessment of the sources see: E. P. Sanders, *Judaism: Practice and Belief – 63 BCE-66 CE* (Philadelphia 1992), 399–404.

ducee in his life, is the one who reports on the purity of Sadducean women, saying: "They may ever be deemed like the women of the Israelites unless they separate themselves and follow after the ways of their fathers" (*mNidd*. 4.2).

Finally, the New Testament contains two stories which could be interpreted as anti-Pharisaic polemics in this matter. In the first, Jesus heals a woman who for twenty years had suffered a constant discharge of blood which had rendered her unclean by Pharisaic standards (*Mark* 5.25–34; *Matt*. 9.20–2; *Luke* 8.43–8). The woman's contact with Jesus is what healed her, instead of making him unclean.[18] Jesus may by this act be rejecting the idea that one must avoid contact with a menstruant or a woman suffering a discharge. A similar interpretation is given the story about Jesus meeting a Samaritan woman next to the well (*John* 4.7–42).[19] As we have noted, Samaritan women were considered always unclean as menstruants. Jesus drinks from the jar she had been holding, and thus allows himself to contract impurity.[20] This action, too, challenges the rabbinic laws of purity in the matter of *niddah*. The question is whether these stories reflect Christian polemics against Judaism or rather the personal opinion of Jesus and thus are anti-Pharisaic polemic internal to Judaism; unfortunately an answer is unavailable.[21]

In conclusion, the large number of stories which describe women who seek the advice of sages regarding their *niddah* emphasizes the high importance which the Pharisees and, after them, the *tannaim* attached to this matter. But outside the world of the sages there were other groups who behaved according to different standards – like the Sadducees, certainly the Samaritans, and perhaps even Jesus' movement and the social strata from which it sprang.

"Be Fruitful and Multiply"

The concept of procreation – to "be fruitful and multiply" – is central in Judaism, appearing already in the first chapter of Genesis. Josephus says quite explicitly that for Jews the sole purpose of marriage is to produce offspring (*CA* 2.199). Even the rabbis proclaimed: "The world was created for no other pur-

---

[18] On this interpretation, see L. J. Swidler , *Women in Judaism: The Status of Women in Formative Judaism* (Metuchen NJ 1976), 180–1, and B. Witherington III, *Women in the Ministry of Jesus* (Cambridge 1984), 72–3.

[19] On the historicity of the story, see Witherington, *ibid.* 58–9.

[20] For this interpretation, see D. Daube, "Jesus and the Samaritan Woman: The Meaning of συνχράομαι," *Journal of Biblical Literature* 69 (1950), 137–47.

[21] Recently it has even been suggested that the early church was more stringent than Judaism in its treatment of menstruating women, see: S. J. D. Cohen, "Menstruants and the Sacred in Judaism and Christianity," in *Women's History and Ancient History*, ed. Sarah B. Pomeroy (London NC 1991) 271–99.

pose than to be fruitful and multiply, for it is stated, 'he created it no empty void, but made it for a place to dwell in' (*Is.* 45.18)" (*mGitt.* 4.5). And similarly: "Ben Azzai says: whoever does not make an effort to 'be fruitful and multiply', the biblical text charges him as if he were diminishing the divine image, as it is stated: 'For in the image of God made He man ... and as for you, be fruitful and multiply' (*Gen.* 1.27–8)" (*tYeb.* 8.4). Ben Azzai cites the story of creation to prove the universal duty of procreation.[22] According to Josephus, even the Essenes, who idealized bachelorhood as a way of avoiding sexual temptation, were divided over the issue of procreation: one group extolled the need to marry women, but only to produce offspring (*BJ* 2.160–1).

But the rabbis did not rest content merely to encourage procreation; they made it a commandment whose fulfillment was obligatory.[23] Thus we read in the *Mishnah*: "No man may abstain from keeping the law 'Be fruitful and multiply' unless he already has children: according to the School of Shammai, two sons; according to the School of Hillel, a son and a daughter, for it is written, 'Male and female created He them' (*Gen.* 1.27)." And it continues: "If he married a woman and lived with her for ten years and she bore no child, he is not permitted to abstain" (*mYeb.* 6.6). The *Tosefta* adds: "If one of [his sons] died, he is not permitted to abstain" (*tYeb.* 8.4).

The rabbis were well aware that the process of procreation involved both man and woman: "'With the help of the Lord I have brought a man into being' (*Gen.* 4.1) ... Before that, Adam had been created from clay and Eve from Adam. From then on, 'in our own image and likeness' (*ibid.* 1.26), not man without woman or woman without man" (*Gen. R.* 22.2, p. 206 ed. Theodor-Albeck). And further: "Our rabbis taught: There are three partners in man, the Holy One blessed be He, his father and his mother. His father supplies the semen of the white substance out of which are formed the child's bones, sinews, nails, the brain in his head and the white in his eye; his mother supplies the semen of the red substance out of which is formed his skin, flesh, hair, blood and the black of his eye ..." (*bNidd.* 31a; cf. *Eccl. R.* 5.10.1). Yet the rabbis viewed

[22] The source continues as follows: "R. Eleazar said to him: Some are good at expounding, others at fulfilling. Ben Azzai is good at expounding but not at fulfilling. He said to him: What can I do? My soul lusts for *Torah*; the world can be maintained by others." On this issue see now: D. Boyarin, *Carnal Israel: Reading Sex in Talmudic Culture* (Berkeley 1993), 134–6; 165–6.

[23] On the transition from recommendation to commandment, see D. Daube, *The Duty of Procreation* (Edinburgh 1977), who tries to demonstrate that laws on procreation are promulgated when fertility rates fall below normal. In the Hellenistic and Roman world, for example, a sharp drop in natural demographic growth was what spurred Augustus to promulgate his laws encouraging procreation. The rabbis, according to Daube, may have been influenced by Roman legislation when they turned procreation into a commandment. And see further: J. Cohen, *'Be Fertile and Increase, Fill the Earth and Master It': The Ancient and Medieval Career of a Biblical Text* (Ithaca NY 1989), 67–165.

the *commandment* to procreate as incumbent only on the male. In the *Mishnah* we read: "The man is commanded to fulfill the law 'Be fruitful and multiply', but not the woman" (*mYeb.* 6.6), and the *Tosefta* adds: "A man is not permitted to marry a barren woman ... or a woman who is unfit to bear children, but a woman is permitted to marry even a eunuch. A man is not permitted to drink a cup of contraceptive potion in order that he may not impregnate a woman, but a woman is allowed to drink a cup of contraceptive potion in order not to conceive" (*tYeb.* 8.4). Yet this legal ruling did not escape criticism. R. Yohanan b. Broqa angrily attacked its inherent absurdity: "Regarding both man and woman it says: 'And the Lord blessed them and said to them ... Be fruitful and multiply' (*Gen.* 1.28)" (*mYeb.* 6.6)[24] Yet the supporters of this *halakhah* also knew how to use prooftexts: "It has been taught: 'Be fruitful and multiply and fill the earth and subdue it' (*Gen.* 1.28). It is written 'and subdue it.' And in whose nature is it to subdue? The man's and not the woman's" (*yYeb.* 6.6, 7c).

Sexual Relations

The sources are divided about the amount of pleasure permitted in sexual relations between married partners. *Ben Sira* says: "Wine and music gladden the heart, but better still sexual love" (40.20). In a similar style, typical of wisdom literature, the rabbis say: "Our rabbis taught: ... Three things benefit the body without entering it: washing, anointing and sexual intercourse (תשמיש);[25] three are like the world to come: Sabbath, Sun and sexual intercourse" (*bBer.* 57b). In rabbinic literature the opinion is also prevalent that procreation is not the only purpose of sexual intercourse. For example, the rabbis permitted sexual intercourse with a pregnant woman:

> "Our rabbis taught: During the first three months intercourse is hard on the woman and it is also hard on the fetus. During the middle ones it is hard on the woman but beneficial to the fetus. During the last months it is beneficial for both the woman and the fetus, since on account of it the child becomes well-formed and of strong vitality." (*bNidd.* 31a)

This is a kind of folk-wisdom, a popular prescription as to when to have sexual relations during the course of a pregnancy, but in any case it does not prohibit it. Sexual relations are permitted even with a nursing woman, even though in such

---

[24] D. Daube, in his "Johanan ben Broqua and Women's Rights," in *Jewish Tradition in the Diaspora: Studies in Memory of Prof. Walter J. Fischel*, ed. M. M. Caspi (Berkeley 1981), 57–8, suggests that the purpose of the law in the *Mishnah* was to allow women who have not yet borne children to be married to men who are not obligated to do so; R. Yohanan b. Broqa opposed this, adopting what Daube calls a "liberal" position.

[25] Obviously, since intercourse is not viewed as entering the body, the transmitter of the tradition has only a man's body in mind.

a case it was understood that every step should be taken to prevent the woman from becoming pregnant again in order not to jeopardize her infant's nourishment: "Three women may use an absorbent [as a contraceptive]: a minor, a pregnant woman and a nursing woman ... . R. Meir says: during the 24 months [when she is nursing], he threshes inside and sews outside" (*tNidd.* 2.6), that is, the husband is permitted to perform *coitus interuptus*, the very thing for which Onan the son of Judah was killed in the book of Genesis.[26] Thus it is apparent that the *halakhah* not only does not limit sexual relations to fulfilling the commandment "be fruitful and multiply," but even recommends procedure in situations in which sex is permitted but pregnancy is to be avoided.

Yet there is another opinion to be found in the sources, according to which sexual relations were created solely for the purposes of procreation and not for bodily pleasure. In the *Testament of Issachar* (2) it is stated that Rachel earned the privilege of bearing Jacob two sons because she renounced sexual relations with him and because she married him in order to have children and not for sexual enjoyment. Josephus, as we have already seen, says that those Essenes who married women had sexual relations only for the purpose of producing descendants and would separate from their wives as soon as they became pregnant (*BJ* 2.161). Joseph Baumgarten, who is editing fragments from the *Damascus Covenant* from Cave 4 at Qumran, has related that in this text too sexual relations with a woman are prohibited after she becomes pregnant.[27] Sectarian literature also includes prohibitions against sexual relations on the Sabbath (*Book of Jubilees* 40.8) and in the city of the Temple (עיר המקדש) (*Temple Scroll* XLV 11). Of the *Hasidim Rishonim* we read: "It has been taught: *Hasidim Rishonim* would have sexual relations on Wednesday in order to prevent their wives from desecrating the Sabbath" (*bNidd.* 38a-b); this means that sexual relations limited to Wednesdays would ensure against a birth on the Sabbath.[28]

The rabbis generally agreed that sexual relations, even between husband and wife, should be restricted in certain ways. As we have already noted (above, p. 101), they advised against sex a few days before the woman was expected to begin menstruating and one day after she had purified herself. The rabbis even expressed an opinion on the best time of night for sexual relations: "It has been taught: R. Eliezer says: The night is divided into three watches ... and during the third a woman 'converses' (i.e. has sex) with her husband" (*bBer.* 3a). The rabbis also held views on the nature of "proper" sexual relations: "R. Yohanan b.

---

[26] On the meaning of Onan's death, see Daube (above, n. 23), 4–7. On *coitus interuptus* in antiquity see: K. M. Hopkins, "Contraception in the Roman Empire," *Comparative Studies in Society and History* 8 (1965), 142–3.

[27] J. M. Baumgarten in a lecture at the World Congress for Biblical Archaeology, Jerusalem 1990.

[28] And see J. Preuss, *Biblical and Talmudic Medicine*, translation F. Rosner (New York 1978), 383–4.

Dahabai said: The ministering angels told me four things: People are born lame because they [*scil.* their parents] overturned their table [*scil.*, either the woman is on top of the man, or anal sex[29]]; dumb because they kiss 'that place'; deaf, because they converse during sexual intercourse; blind, because they look at 'that place'" (*bNed.* 20a).[30] To sum up the information from this and previous sections, although no *halakhah* existed in this matter, the rabbis did take an ethical stand and viewed deviant sexual behavior as a punishable sin, the punishment being an injury to the children. The rabbis' ethical guidelines thus admonished anyone who was not considerate of his wife during sex or did not separate himself from his wife as her menstrual period neared, as well as anyone who engaged in "licentious" sexual practices. All are punished with regard to their yet unborn children: failure to separate from the menstruant results in stillborn babies licentiousness produces children with defects and failure to satisfy one's wife sexually leads to the birth of daughters. We can assume that the seriousness of the punishments – death, defects and daughters – reflects, in descending order, the seriousness of the offense according to the rabbis' ethical code.

What was the woman's role supposed to be in sexual relations? The rabbis assumed that the woman enjoyed sex as the man did. The biblical verse, "... desire fails" (*Eccl.* 12.5), provoked the comment: "This is sexual desire, which brings peace between husband and wife" (*Lev. R.* 18.1, p. 396 ed. Margulies). And as we have seen, the rabbis urged the man to encourage the woman to participate actively in sexual relations, which was, they taught, the only way sons could be born (*bNidd.* 31a). In Jewish law, sexual relations are often one of a woman's rights (*mKet.* 5.6; *tKet.* 5.6; *yKet.* 5.8, 30a; *bKet.* 71a).[31]

Thus it appears that there were two schools of thought in the Second Temple period. According to one, the purpose of sexual relations is only to fulfill the commandment to "be fruitful and multiply," whereas the other held that sex had value *per se*. The tension between these two approaches is evident in all the sources.[32]

The literature of the Second Temple period contains very few actual descriptions of sexual relations. This is not because the authors of the period were embarrassed by the subject; they simply found few occasions to describe such a banal matter. The rabbis assumed that problems and crises that tend to arise between men and women do not bear on a couple's sexual relations. A unique

---

[29] For this explanation, see Biale (above, n. 10), 137–8.

[30] On this text see Boyarin, (above, n. 22), 109–22.

[31] Biale (above, n. 10), 125–32. The question of the level of a woman's sexual desire, compared to that of the man, was a subject to which the Greeks devoted considerable attention; see Sarah B. Pomeroy *Goddesses, Whores, Wives and Slaves: Women in Classical Antiquity* (New York 1975), 146–7.

[32] On these two schools see: D. Biale, *Eros and the Jews: From Biblical Israel to Contemporary America* (New York 1992), 36–4; Boyarin (above, n. 22), 165–6.

description of the sexual relations between husband and wife is put in the mouth of a woman, Imma Shalom, the wife of R. Eliezer. Her remarks represent the violation of a kind of taboo, for it was presumably not accepted custom for women to discuss such matters in public, and moreover what she says borders on pornography in the modern sense:[33] "Imma Shalom was asked: Why are your children so beautiful? She replied: Because he [my husband] 'converses' with me neither at the beginning nor at the end of night, but only at midnight,[34] and when he 'converses' he uncovers a handbreadth and covers a handbreadth, and is as though he were possessed by a demon. And when I asked him, what is the reason for this, he replied: So that I may not think of another woman[35] lest his (her husband's) children be bastards" (*bNed.* 20a-b).

Sexual relations between husband and wife are described in two other places, in each case because of certain odd features. 1) "... It once happened that a man flung his wife under a fig tree (and lay with her); they brought him before the *bet din* and they punished him by flogging" (*bSanh.* 46a; *bYeb.* 90b). In this case sexual relations in public were dealt with severely, even though the sages themselves admitted that no particular law was violated, simply that "that specific time (i.e. generation) required such measures," which is to say that the ethical standards of Jewish society of that time were offended. 2) A woman came before R. Judah the Patriarch to complain about her husband's behavior: "She said to him: I set his table and he turned it over," that is, her husband had sex with her in a manner other than the missionary position. Rabbi's response was: "My daughter, the *Torah* permits you to him, what can I do for you?" (*bNed.* 20b).[36]

---

[33] "Pornography" as defined by the *Encyclopedia Americana* 22 (Danbury CT 1985), 417: "graphic written or other forms of communication intended to arouse sexual desires. Under the assumption that pornography tends to deprave or corrupt and lead to sexual crimes..."– is a product of the post-Victorian values of the twentieth century. Erotic depictions were not at all unusual in Greek art; see, e.g. Eva Keuls, *The Reign of the Phallus: Sexual Politics in Ancient Athens* (New York 1985), 2–3, and the many pictures reproduced in that book. By contrast, Suetonius is critical of the emperor Tiberius for covering the walls of the rooms of his palace at Capri with erotic pictures in order to arouse his companions to erotic pleasures, and for commissioning erotic art for considerable sums of money (*Tib.* 43–4). Even in Jewish art, although statues and pictures are forbidden, the act of copulation is probably one of the few motifs recognizable in the plastic art in the Temple; a late Babylonian tradition describes what festival pilgrims saw in the Temple: "Rav Qatina said: At the time of Israel's pilgrimages [to Jerusalem], they would pull aside the Temple curtain and reveal the *cherubim* whose bodies were intertwined with one another, and they would say to them: See, your love before the Almighty is like the love of man and woman" (*bYoma* 54a). On the sculpted image of copulating *cherubim*, see R. Patai, *The Hebrew Goddess* (New York 1967), 111–32.

[34] See above for the view of R. Eliezer, Imma Shalom's husband, on the ideal time for sexual relations between a man and a woman at night.

[35] See also *bTaan.* 23b, where Abba Helqia makes a similar statement.

[36] But see above, Yohanan b. Dahabai's statement that he who acts in such a manner will receive punishment from heaven.

In these two instances we witness sexual relations between husband and wife which are considered abnormal. The rabbis, despite the strangeness of such relations and their criticism of them, do not outlaw them by *halakhah*, indicating that sexual relations between husband and wife, or how a husband treats his wife sexually, lie beyond their authority. These are clearly solitary examples and offer no more than a fleeting glimpse into this world. Their paucity suggests that the rabbis dealt relatively seldom with sexual problems of this nature.[37]

Pregnancy and Childbirth

1. Infertility

Sexual relations should lead to pregnancy, yet conception is extremely difficult to control. *Ben Sira* formulated this quite well, as we have seen: the daughter is a constant annoyance to her father, who worries that she may become pregnant before marriage ("in her father's house, lest she become impregnated"), or conversely, that after marriage she may turn out to be barren ("in her husband's house, lest she be barren" 42.10).

As in the instances we have already presented, authors of Second Temple period sources wondered why some women could not become pregnant. Is it the woman's fault? the man's? We find two answers to this question in the sources. In the Ethiopian *Apocalypse of Enoch* (98.5) we read about the connection between a woman's barrenness and her sins. A barren woman is a sinner, and there is no need to discover the actual sin; the fact that she is unable to bear children is a strong enough witness to this. Yet we find a different opinion in rabbinic literature. In the tractate *Derekh Eretz Zuta* (9) we read the warning of R. Eliezer ha-Qappar: "... be respectful of your wife's honor, lest she become infertile". Barrenness is thus presented as the result of a man's disrespectful treatment of his wife.

---

[37] It is appropriate to mention here the "practice of Herod" (*Sifre Deut.* 241, p. 271 ed. Finkelstein), although in the Hebrew manuscripts, הורדוס ("Herod") is only one of many variants; see Finkelstein, nn. *ibid.* Herod is without doubt the correct reading, as we will see. The case is brought up in connection with a law regarding adultery which determines that he who engages in the "practice of Herod" cannot be expected to receive the same punishment as an outright adulterer. The *tannaitic* sources do not explain what the "practice of Herod" is, but the *Babylonian Talmud* does: "He kept his wife for seven years in honey; some say, he had intercourse with her ... " (*bBB* 3b). Josephus does not mention this, but his report that Herod felt terrible longing for his dead wife might have inspired the *aggadah*; see *AJ* 15.240–2. On the way to preserve bodies in honey, see *BJ* 1.184; *AJ* 14.124. A similar story about a king who had intercourse with the body of his dead wife is given by *Herodotus* (5.92). The story is important here because it demonstrates that even sexual relations of this nature, although they involved offense to a corpse, were not totally forbidden by the rabbis.

Infertility is intolerable in a world in which one of the framing notions is that the sole purpose of marriage is to produce offspring. To be sure, the Hebrew Bible contains many examples of righteous but barren women whose patience and the patience and faith of their husbands were rewarded in the end by children, and this literary genre appears again in the story of the birth of John the Baptist (*Luke* 1) and in the *Apocalypse of Ezra* (*IV Ezra*), which presents a woman who gave birth after thirty infertile years (9.43–5);[38] but Jewish law demonstrates absolutely no forgiveness for the failure to carry out the commandment to "be fruitful and multiply." We have already seen that a man who lives with a woman for ten years and produces no offspring is required to divorce her. The *halakhah*, the purpose of which is not to teach moral lessons but to set behavioral norms, recognizes the possibility that not the woman but her husband may be to blame if she fails to become pregnant. Accordingly, a woman is allowed to remarry twice and to live another ten years with each of her two subsequent husbands until her own infertility is beyond doubt (*tYeb*. 8.4). If she then marries a man who has not yet fulfilled the commandment of procreation, she is punished by the loss of her *ketubbah*. It should be noted that this provision deals with only very rare cases, for a woman is no longer young after thirty years of marriage and is not exactly a prime choice for a young man who has not yet produced offspring. This law, or one similar to it, is reflected in a story in *Bibl. Ant.* where we read that Manoah, the father of Samson, wanted to divorce his wife when she failed to become pregnant after many years (42.1).

By contrast, the *tannaitic aggadah* treats this law a bit more critically, exhibiting sympathetic understanding for the woman who is thrown out of the house lacking everything and suffering from the great disappointment of failing to fulfill her duty to become a mother. One story concerns a husband and wife who truly love each other but nonetheless plan to obey the law and divorce after ten years without children.[39] The authors of the *aggadah* find this human predicament unbearable, but since they cannot change the *halakhah* they must resort to a miracle: R. Shimeon bar Yohai prays and the woman becomes pregnant (*Song of Songs R*. 1.4).[40] Similarly, it is related that the wife of R. Shimeon, son of R.

---

[38] A similar story appears in the *Proto-evangelium Jacobi* (1–5) in connection with the birth of Mary to aged parents who had suffered many years from the inability to produce a child. On the non-Jewish character of this text, see Mach (above, n. 5).

[39] This story, together with eight others dealing with the relations between a husband and his wife, is analyzed by D. Zimmerman, *Eight Love Stories from Talmud and Midrash* (Tel Aviv 1981), 44–7 [Hebrew]. The *aggadic* character of the story emerges also from an incidental comparison which Zirndorf makes with a similar literary motif from the Middle Ages: H. Zirndorf, *Some Jewish Women* (Philadelphia 1892), 214.

[40] In this connection we should note the Roman funerary inscription which mentions the woman who suggested to her husband that he divorce her after 43 years of childless marriage: Pomeroy (above, n. 31), 158.

Judah the Patriarch, failed to become pregnant for a rather prosaic reason: after R. Shimeon married her, "he departed and spent twelve years at the academy; by the time he returned his wife become barren," in other words, she had passed out of her childbearing years. This put the Patriarch and his family in a rather delicate position, which Rabbi himself describes: "What shall we do? Should we order him to divorce her, it would be said, This poor soul waited in vain!" that is, even if R. Shimeon has not violated *halakhah*, his actions will provoke public criticism which the house of the *nasi* can ill afford. "Were he to marry another woman, it would be said: The latter is his wife and the other his harlot;" R. Shimeon would still provoke public criticism if, in order to fulfill the commandment to "be fruitful and multiply," he were to marry a second wife without divorcing his first one, for it would give the impression that he was keeping the first wife solely for corporal pleasures. Rabbi had only one way out of this dilemma: "He prayed for mercy to be vouchsafed to her, and she recovered" (*bKet.* 62b); that is, the sages could solve such complications only by means of a miracle.[41] There is one more barren woman mentioned in the sources: Elizabeth, the mother of John the Baptist (*Luke* 1.7), although even she is eventually able to conceive (*ibid.* 24). The *aggadic* nature of these sources should arouse our suspicion regarding their historical authenticity.

Yet barrenness can be studied from a different angle. Some information can be culled by examining the relatively complete family tree we have for the Herodian house. We find there certain women who died childless: two of Herod's wives (*AJ* 17.19; *BJ* 1.563) and Alexandra, daughter of Phasael b. Phasael (*AJ* 18.131). Were these women barren, or did they perhaps die in childbirth? Similarly Herod's son Philip (*AJ* 18.137) and Tigranes king of Armenian son of Alexander (*AJ* 18.139) are both specifically reported to have died childless (as opposed to other males in the Herodian house for whom simply no descendants are mentioned). Philip is known to have been married, and his wife, Salome the daughter of Herodias, produced descendants for her second husband, Aristobulus the son of Herod, king of Chalcis. Tigranes, as king of Armenia, can be assumed to have been married, even if there is no specific information to that effect. Were either Philip or Tigranes partially or completely sterile, or perhaps children born to them died while young, or even in childbirth?

Rabbinic sources also mention Judith, the wife of R. Hiyya, who sterilized herself after giving birth to two pairs of twins (Judah and Hezekiah; Tavi and Pazi) and suffered terribly in childbirth (*bYeb.* 65b-66a). She performed the

---

[41] In contrast to the previous *aggadah*, which is in Hebrew and is marked by a distinct *tannaitic* character, this one is in Aramaic, involves late *tannaim*, and is thus apparently *amoraic*, relevant here only because of its similarity to the first one. On the issue of Barren women in rabbinic Judaism, see Judith R. Baskin, "Rabbinic Reflections on the Barren Wife," *Harvard Theological Review* 89 (1989), 101–14.

sterilization by means of a special potion after her husband granted her permission, based on the *halakhah*, that women are exempt from performing the commandment to "be fruitful and multiply."[42]

2. Miscarriage

The greatest risk in pregnancy is miscarriage. The sages found a moral reason for miscarriages: "It has been taught: R. Nehemiah says: As a punishment for causeless hatred, strife multiplies in a man's house, his wife miscarries ..." (*bShab.* 32b). This assertion falls into the category of punishments meted out to a man's children because of his own immoral behavior – in this case the punishment is death before birth.

Yet the rabbis also supplied a practical explanation to miscarriage. In a kind of medical diagnosis they proposed that a strong or unpleasant odor could cause women to miscarry. It was considered miraculous, for example, that women never miscarried in the Temple as a result of the odor from the burning sacrificial meat (*mAbot.* 5.5). Moreover, various regulations, such as the law exempting pregnant and nursing women from all fasts but those of Day of Atonement and the ninth of Ab, aimed to diminish the chances of miscarriage (*tTaan.* 3.2; *yTaan.* 1.5, 64c; cf. also *tMiqv.* 7.6). Even the law, promulgated (by all indications) after the Bar-Kokhba revolt, prohibiting the Jews from wearing nailed sandals on Sabbath was explained as a preventive measure, since pregnant women would hear hobnails of sandals and may miscarry out of fear since such was the style of footwear of the Roman soldiers (*yShab.* 6.2, 8a).

Yet the rabbinical sources still maintained that no practical precautions could be effective without heavenly aid. One *aggadah* relates that during the 13 years in which Rabbi suffered from a toothache no woman miscarried in Palestine (*Gen. R.* 33.3, p. 305 ed. Theodor-Albeck).[43] In the end of days, according to IV *Ezra,* the danger of miscarriage will be avoided by the ability of fetuses born in the third or fourth month of pregnancy to continue to live outside the womb (4.21).

Today it is known that a fetus is aborted naturally when it is not developing properly. The appearance of the aborted fetus, which often has a different form from that of a healthy infant, was of great interest to the sages. Thus the daughter-in-law of R. Hananiah, the nephew of R. Joshua, is said to have aborted "a

---

[42] The sterilization potion is known to us also from Roman literature, see Pomeroy (above, n. 31), 167. And see also on this D. M. Feldman, *Marital Relations, Birth Control and Abortion in Jewish Law* (New York 1974), 235–44.

[43] The idea is that the role of the Messiah (as Rabbi sees himself in this story) is to suffer for the sins of others and to prevent them from undergoing their punishment – the same explanation offered for the crucifixion and death of Jesus, compare *Mark* 14.23–4; *Matt.* 26.27–8; *Luke* 22.17–20.

kind of serpent" (*bNidd.* 24b); another woman in Simonia is said to have aborted a fetus that looked like a lilith (*ibid.*); and it is related that a woman in Saidan (צײַדן)[44] thrice aborted a fetus that looked like a crow (*tNidd.* 4.6).

The sources describe two more instances of miscarriage. The first attracted Josephus' interest because of its strange nature. In a general description of the horrors wrought by the Roman artillery stones during the siege of Jotapata, Josephus relates that when one stone struck a pregnant woman, causing her immediately to miscarry, her fetus went flying and landed half a stadion away (*BJ* 3.245). The second story concerns a Roman tax-collector's maidservant who miscarried in Rimon and threw the fetus into a cistern (*bNidd.* 15b). The rabbis use this story as a point of departure for discussing the purity of a priest who was present at the scene, but there is a historical kernel to be found here: a maidservant became pregnant and then deliberately disposed of her infant when it was born prematurely. The same matter comes up in the *Tosefta*: "The mounds of earth close to cities, whether between two cities or a city and a road ... are unclean, because women bury their aborted fetuses there" (*tOhol.* 16.1). Together, these two cases indicate that it was the woman's responsibility to dispose of her aborted fetus.

3. Premature Birth

A premature birth in the final months of pregnancy is not considered a miscarriage. The belief was prevalent among the Jews, as in the entire ancient world, that while a fetus born in the seventh month had a good chance to survive, an eight-month fetus did not.[45] This is explained in *Bibl. Ant.* Isaac was born in the seventh month, and consequently every person born thereafter in the seventh month was granted life (23.8). Despite the authoritative medical opinion that

---

[44] This name apparently refers to Bet Saida north of the Sea of Galilee (see *Matt.* 11:20; *Luke* 10:13; cf. S. Klein, "Hebräische Ortsnamen bei Josephus," *Monatsschrift für Geschichte und Wissenschaft des Judentums* 59 [1915], 167–8), but sometimes to Sidon in Lebanon. The name Saidan appears quite often in formulae introducing exemplary legal cases. We will presently examine the case of a man from Saidan who made a vow to divorce his wife (*mGitt.* 4.7). And in another case involving bills of divorce, "It once happened in Saidan that a man said to his wife, Here is your bill of divorce on condition that you give me my cloak, and the cloak was lost; but the sages said: Let her give him its value." (*mGitt.* 7.5). Thus, things which are said to have happened in Saidan may be only legal fictions disguised as precedents.

[45] P. W. van der Horst, "Seven Months Children in Jewish and Christian Literature from Antiquity," *Essays on the Jewish World of Early Christianity* = *NOTA* XIV (Göttingen 1990), 233–47; Preuss (above, n. 28), 393–4; see also Pomeroy (above, n. 31), 168. Needless to say, this belief has no scientific basis. A rabbinic *midrash* on this matter, although a bit later, is related by R. Abbahu (*Gen. R.* 14.2, p. 127 ed. Theodor-Albeck); see S. Lieberman, *Greek in Jewish Palestine* (New York 1942), 22–3.

eight-month-old babies were doomed, the general hope was that every premature infant would survive; this may help us understand the following law: it is
forbidden to carry an infant born in the eighth month of pregnancy on the Sabbath because it is treated as an inanimate object; "but his mother bends over him
and nurses him" (*tShab.* 15.5). Lieberman explains this law as permitting a
woman to nurse in order to relieve her own suffering, for she is full of milk and
is forbidden to milk herself on the Sabbath (*tShab.* 9.22),[46] but it may well have
been intended to allow the child to prove its vitality and the mother to save her
child, contrary to the judgment which the medical establishment had already
pronounced.

4. Childbirth

The moment of birth is the most dangerous moment of the entire nine months of
a normal pregnancy. The rabbis offered the following answer to the repeated
question, why women died during childbirth: "For three transgressions do women die in childbirth: for heedlessness of the laws of *niddah*, the dough-offer-
ings and the lighting of the [Sabbath] candle" (*mShab.* 2.6).[47] These three commandments, which women and only women are obligated to carry out, are
viewed not as a reward, but as punishment for the sin in the Garden of Eden.[48]
Their non-fulfillment is viewed as a matter of life and death and carries a very
heavy penalty. In the *Tosefta* R. Nathan adds another element: "Because of their
vows women die in childbirth" (*tShab.* 2.10; cf. *bShab.* 32b).

By the same token, a painless childbirth is interpreted as the reward of a
righteous woman. Josephus relates that Yochebed gave birth to Moses without
any birth pangs (*AJ* 2.218), and Moses' parents interpreted this as a sign of
God's favor.[49] A woman's birth pangs appeared to the male authors of our

---

[46] S. Lieberman, *Tosefta kifeshuta* III (New York 1962), 247 [Hebrew].

[47] The version in the *Babylonian Talmud* is slightly different: "For three sins women
die in childbirth (יולדות). R. Eleazar said: women die young (ילדות) here the connection is
clear between the pre-adolescent girl and death in childbirth; a girl, after all, is not obligated to fulfill the three commandments enumerated) ... R. Yose said: Three death scruti-
neers (בדקין) were created in woman; others state: Three causes (דבקין) of death: *niddah*,
hallah, and the kindling of the [Sabbath] candles" (*bShab.* 32a).

[48] "And why was the precept of *niddah* given to her? Because she shed the blood of
Adam, therefore was the precept of *niddah* given to her. And why was the precept of *hallah* given to her? Because she corrupted Adam, who was the *hallah* of the world, therefore
was the precept of *hallah* given her. And why was precept of the Sabbath candles given to
her? Because she extinguished the soul of Adam, therefore was the precept of the Sabbath
candles given her" (*Gen. R.* 17.8, p. 160 ed. Theodor-Albeck; *yShab.* 2.4, 5b; *ARNB* 42,
p. 117 ed. Schechter).

[49] Also Mary, according to the *Proto-evangelium Jacobi* (19), gave birth to Jesus without any birth pangs; on this text, see above, n. 5.

sources as quite horrible. The matter is taken up by R. Shimeon bar Yohai and his students: "R. Shimeon bar Yohai's disciples asked him: Why does the *Torah* say, a woman who has given birth must bring a sacrifice? He told them: When a woman kneels down to give birth she swears impetuously that she will not have sex with her husband again; for that reason the *Torah* says, she will bring a sacrifice" (*bNidd.* 31b). The sage here is obviously trying to put himself in the place of a woman in labor, and imagines that if he were to suffer to the same extent, he would in the future want to avoid any activity that would eventually bring the suffering back.

Jewish law equates helping a woman in childbirth with saving a life: both override the Sabbath (*mShab.* 18.3). Jewish women may even employ gentile midwives, even though gentile women in the rabbis' eyes are under suspicion of bloodshed (*mAZ* 2.1; note once more the sages' stereotyping a foreign group). Jewish law also specifies that "if a woman is having a difficult childbirth, they cut up the fetus in her womb, even on the Sabbath, and take it out limb by limb, because her life takes precedence over the life of the fetus" (*tYeb.* 9.4). Thus, although in one respect the woman serves merely as a vessel for a man to fulfill the commandment to "be fruitful and multiply," with the fetus as the desired product, in the critical hour the sages preferred the mother's life over the fetus'.[50]

Except for Judith the wife of R. Hiyya, mentioned above, the written sources do not mention specific cases of women who suffered during childbirth, and even Judith would not have been mentioned had she not sterilized herself to prevent the pains from recurring. The reason for silence in this matter is that pain in childbirth was such a common phenomenon, too banal to mention. The absence of specific cases of death during childbirth can be attributed to the same cause. Yet information is not totally unavailable.

In contrast to literary sources, funerary inscriptions preserve information about several cases of women dying in childbirth. The most famous is Salome daughter of Saul, whose ossuaary was discovered on Givat Hamivtar.[51] Not only does her inscription identify the cause of her death (דשברת), but the ossuary was found to contain her bones together with those of her infant still in her birth canal.[52] Next to the woman's name appear the words, "Salome her daughter," which presumably refer to the infant who died before being fully born. Although Naveh[53] claims that another daughter of hers is meant, no other bones were

---

[50] Roman law contains a similar ruling, see Pomeroy (above, n. 31), 168–9.

[51] J. Naveh "The Ossuary Inscriptions from Givat ha-Mivtar," *Israel Exploration Journal* 20 (1970), 36–7.

[52] See N. Hass, "Anthropological Observations on the Skeletal Remains from Givat ha-Mivtar," *Israel Exploration Journal* 20 (1970), 48.

[53] Above (n. 51), 37.

found in the ossuary (thus the inscription may be read, "Salome [and] her daughter"). A funerary inscription, from Byblos in Phoenicia, describes a woman's death in childbirth quite clearly: Σαλόμη ἥ ἔτ(ε)κεν ᾿Αρτήρ.[54] The exact date of this inscription is unknown, but the name Salome was no longer commonly given to women in the *amoraic* period.[55] Other ossuary inscriptions mention women buried with their children: "Sarah and her daughter" (סרה ובֿרתה);[56] "The wife of Mattiah and her son"(אתת מתיה ובֿרה);[57] Salome and her daughter" (שׁלֹוס ובֿנה).[58.] Another ossuary is identified as that of Marylla, buried with her children (Μαρύλλας/τῶν παιδιῶν); one child probably died young and the other, with his mother, during birth; or else the inscription refers to twins.[59] And further, Cave 20 in Beth She'arim, dated by its excavators to the end of the second century CE, contained the funerary inscription of "Mariamme, daughter of Rabbi Jonathan, with her two daughters;" this case may reflect death in a plague or during the birth of twins.[60] Thus we find that, since in the epigraphical evidence a mother's death coinciding with that of her child was not unduly rare, and presumably this double death sometimes occurred during childbirth, it is likely that some of the women in the Herodian house who are said to have had only one child in fact died in childbirth.

Mayer has pointed out that 54% of the women whose age of death is known died in childbearing years,[61] and he implies that most of these women died in childbirth. This number seems extremely high, and I may be justified in suggesting a different method for calculating the number of women who died in childbirth. The number of ossuaries of women buried with their children, compared to the total number of ossuaries on which women are named, represents fairly closely in my opinion the real percentage of women who died in childbirth,

---

[54] *CII* 874.

[55] The name appears on only two inscriptions from that period: J. Naveh, *On Mosaic and Stone: Aramaic and Hebrew Inscriptions from Ancient Synagogues* (Jerusalem 1978), 33; A. Negev, "Inscriptions Hébraiques, Grecques et Latines de Césarée Maritime," *Revue Biblique* 78 (1971), 248. Both occurrences are interpreted as a man's name, which is possible in the Hebrew but probably wrong in these instances.

[56] *CII* 1222.

[57] *CII* 1362.

[58] P. B. Bagatti and J. T. Milik, *Gli scavi del Dominus Flevit = Pubblicazioni dello Studium Biblicum Franciscanum* XIII (Jerusalem 1958), 79 no. 8.

[59] M. Kochavi, "The Burial Caves of Ramat Rahel 1962 Season," in *Excavations at Ramat Rahel Seasons 1961 and 1962*, ed. Y. Aharoni (Rome 1963), 72. Another ossuary identifies the twins Joseph and Eliezer (᾿Ιωσήφ καὶ ᾿Ελιέζερ διδύμοι) without naming the mother: E. L. Sukenik, "Jewish Burial-Caves in the Vicinity of the Kidron Valley," *Kedem* 2 (1945), 29 [Hebrew].

[60] See Avigad (above, n. 3), 93.

[61] G. Meyer, *Die jüdische Frau in der hellenistisch-römischen Antike* (Stuttgart 1987), 93.

assuming of course that there were also women who died in childbirth while the baby survived; this yields the figure of about five percent (six ossuaries out of 130), a figure which is high by any standard. There is thus no reason to accept Mayer's highly inflated figure of about 50 %, a figure which more accurately reflects the low life-expectancy in that period,[62] when the causes of death were many and varied, including disease, plague, war, famine, and so forth.[63]

5. Nursing

A child is never more dependent on its mother than right after birth, for at that stage she is its only source of nourishment.[64] It should be remembered that before the invention of the artificial nipple and bottle, nursing was the only way to feed an infant.[65] This is the proper context for understanding the blessing a woman gave Jesus over the breasts that nursed him and sustained him (*Luke* 11.27; cf. *Job* 3.12).[66] For this reason, the sources abound in discussions and determinations regarding the nursing of children[67].

---

[62] Hass found a variety of causes of death for the human remains he examined from Givat ha-Mivtar (above, n. 52), 43.

[63] Another interesting topic is child mortality. Mayer (above, n. 61), 93, figured that 24 % of all Jewish women (not just those from Palestine) whose names are mentioned on their tombs died before the age of twelve. A similar mortality rate would be found for boys. Josephus mentions that Mariamme the Hasmonean had a boy who died as a child in Rome (*BJ* 1.435). Agrippa I also had a son who died before reaching maturity (*AJ* 18.132). Josephus himself had two sons who died as children (*Vita* 426). This may have been the fate of other sons in the Herodian house whom Josephus mentions without indicating that they had wives or children, like the three children of Phasael the son of Phasael or Herod the son of Herod, son of the Jerusalemite Cleopatra; although other explanations are of course possible. Anthropological evidence is a far more impressive indicator of child mortality. In two Jewish burial-caves of the period it was found that fully a third of the skeletons belonged to children – 12 out of 35 in the cave on Givat Hamivtar (Hass, above n. 52, 39), and 10 of 30 in a cave in Jericho (Patricia Smith and Rachel Hachlili, "The Genealogy of the Goliath family," *Bulletin of the American Schools for Oriental Research* 235 [1979], 67–70). It is thus not surprising to find many stories of child deaths in rabbinic literature, where we find that Rabbi Judah the Patriarch lost a daughter (*bMQ* 21a Munich MS, see *Dikdukei Soferim ad. loc.*; that R. Judah lost a son, as did R. Yose (*ibid.*); that R. Aqiba lost a son (*Semahot* 8.13); and that R. Meir lost two sons (*Midrash on Proverbs* 31.1). This is naturally not a full list.

[64] By one view, the woman in Judaism is not thought of as the one who brings the child into the world (a role which is assigned the father), but only as the one who nurses it: Rachel Adler, "A Mother in Israel: Aspects of the Mother-Role in Jewish Myth," in *Beyond Androcentrism = Aids for the Study of Religion* VI, ed. Rita M. Gross (Missoula, MO 1977), 237–55.

[65] Preuss (above, n. 28), 409–10 shows that the bottle was not used until modern times.

[66] Jesus' answer to the woman is wrongly understood as feminist, see L. J. Swidler, *Biblical Affirmations of Woman* (Philadelphia 1979), 193, 273.

[67] On nursing see Gail P. Corrington, "The Milk of Salvation: Redemption by the

The rabbis viewed mother's milk as a kind of miracle: "R. Meir said: The entire nine months in which the woman does not see blood, in truth she should do so; but what does the Holy One, blessed be He, do? He directs it upward to her breasts and turns it into milk, so that the fetus may come forth and have food ..." (*Lev. R.* 14.3, p. 305 ed. Margulies).

This opinion is further reflected in some sources. Josephus records the story of Moses refusing to nurse from an Egyptian woman, requiring his mother to be brought in (*AJ* 2.226). Obviously this sort of statement encourages mothers to nurse their infants. Jewish law provides what appear to be material incentives for women to nurse their children: 1. "If she was nursing a child they should lessen her handiwork and increase her maintenance" (*mKet.* 5.9). 2. The nursing mother, together with the pregnant woman, is exempt from certain fasts. 3. The nursing mother has a right to have sexual relations even if not strictly for the purpose of procreation. The *aggadah* quoted above, associating menstrual blood with mother's milk, may well indicate an awareness on the part of the rabbis that nursing serves as a contraceptive. Nevertheless, one opinion in rabbinic literature allows a nursing woman to use birth control in order to ensure the safety of her nursing infant. Yet it is clear that all the special allowances and privileges granted a nursing woman were intended principally to protect the infant; for a nursing woman is not permitted, for example, to relieve her engorged breasts by milking herself on the Sabbath (*tShab.* 9.22).

However, nursing is not unambiguously required by Jewish law. Clearly, an infant needs to nurse from some woman, but a wet-nurse could easily fulfill this function. Thus the Schools of Shammai and Hillel were split on the question of whether a woman who vowed not to nurse her child was required to do so in spite of her vow or whether she was allowed to abide by it; and the School of Shammai granted the woman the right to decide what to do (*tKet.* 5.5; *yKet.* 5.6, 30a). Similarly, a woman whose husband has divorced her is exempt from nursing her infant, and her husband is required to find a wet-nurse to take her place (*yKet.* 5.6, 30a). Yet Jewish law is less moderate when a nursing infant knows his mother: in the case of a divorced woman, "if her child knows her, she is required to nurse and she is given compensation as a wet-nurse because a life is in danger" (*tKet.* 5.5; *yKet.* 5.6, 30a). That the sages did not view nursing as a matter of life and death (*pikuah nefesh*) may be indicated by the statement that "a man cannot force his wife to nurse the son of his friend;" in this way the law protects the woman against damage to her figure. "And a woman cannot force her husband to let her nurse her friend's child" (*ibid.*), or in other words, both marriage partners have joint ownership over the woman's ability to nurse. In addition, a Jewish woman is not allowed under any circumstances to nurse the

---

Mother in Late Antiquity and Early Christianity," *Harvard Theological Review* 82 (1989), 393–420.

child of a Gentile woman (m*AZ* 2.1). It seems to me, then, that nursing was viewed as a need not to be despised, but not as a great privilege.

The rabbis debated how long a woman should continue to nurse an infant. R. Eliezer taught that after 24 months nursing was comparable to consuming an abominable thing (שקץ), while R. Joshua saw nothing wrong with a child nursing even until the age of five (*bKet.* 60a). This controversy concerns the maximum nursing period; a different controversy arose over the question of minimum permissible time for nursing, and there the opinions ranged from 24 to 18 months (*ibid.*; cf. *tNidd.* 2.1; 4).[68]

It would be interesting to know the extent to which Jewish women, specifically in Palestine, nursed their own children, employed wet-nurses for this purpose or engaged in wet-nursing as a profession. Unfortunately, there is no information on this subject.[69] But it seems to me that the way *halakhic* and *aggadic* literature treat this practice has to do with social circles from which this literature emerged. A wet-nurse was a luxury which not everybody could afford; moreover, a mother could better preserve the form of her breasts from harm by hiring someone else to nurse her children. These concerns typify the upper-middle and aristocratic classes, the very circles responsible for the literature of the period under study. It is no surprise, therefore, that the nursing mother was not idealized by the rabbis. Yet we can safely assume that most mothers in the period nursed their own infants for lack of other means to maintain them.

---

[68] Note that a nursing period of 18 months was specified in a contract from Egypt. See next note.

[69] Two documents from Egypt illustrate the custom of employing wet-nurses and the employment of Jewish women in that profession. In a contract from the year 13 BCE, Phamenoth (Φαμενώθ) hires Theodotis the daughter of Dositheos, called "Persian," to nurse a foundling child for 18 months. The woman is obligated not to nurse any other child and to abstain from sexual relations during that period: *CPJ* no. 146. The editors of *CPJ* determined that a woman with such a name, despite her being called "Persian" (or maybe because of it), must be Jewish. The second document, from the year 14 BCE, is a cancellion of a contract for nursing beween a woman named Marion and a woman with a classic Jewish name, Martha (*ibid.* pp. 19–20, no. 147).

Chapter 4:

Preserving a Woman's Chastity

In the opinion of our sources, the world has been fashioned along certain hierarchical lines, according to which men rule women. Josephus explains that in Judaism a woman is supposed always to obey her husband (*CA* 2.201). A late *midrash* finds the basis for women's subordination to men in the story of the Garden of Eden: "Ten decrees were ordained ... for Eve. ...The fourth is that her husband would rule over her" (*ARNB* 42, pp. 116–7 ed. Schechter); yet it is not clear here whether Eve's subordination was the result of her sin or the cause of it, for the same *midrashic* work also relates, in reference to the story of the Garden of Eden, that "From the beginning Eve called her husband only 'rabbi' ['my master']" (*ARNB* 1, p. 6 ed. Schechter). In any case, the author of the *midrash* finds women's subordination to men in the cosmic order established by Creation itself, and the question, whether this situation preceded or succeeded the original sin, is reduced to a mere quibble.

The remarks by Zerubbabel to Darius in *III Ezra* should be interpreted in this light. The passage belongs to the literary *topos* in which a courtier is required to prove his wisdom before the king by using clever arguments to demonstrate as true what is patently ridiculous and absurd.[1] Zerubbabel is given the test of proving that the king is ruled by women, and he demonstrates his wisdom by establishing a fact, as it were, which contradicts the real situation familiar to his audience. His successful arguments run as follows: A woman gave birth to the king; every man desires a woman and is willing to go to great lengths, sometimes to do anything, to win her. These arguments excite surprise and admiration in Zerubbabel's audience (*III Ezra* 4.13–41; cf. *AJ* 11.49–58). Similar utterances are to be found in the *Testament of Judah* (15.5–6): "And the Angel of God showed me that women have mastery over both king and poor man. From the king they will take away his glory; from the virile man, his power; and from the poor man, even the slight support that he has in his poverty." The difference in

---

[1] C. C. Torrey, *The Apocryphal Literature* (New Haven 1945), 48–50. Further on this work and its relation to Palestinian literature of the Second Temple period, see A. Schalit, "The Date and Place of the Story about the Three Bodyguards of the King in the Apocryphal Book of *Ezra*," *Bulletin of the Israel Exploration Society* 13 (1947), 119–28 [Hebrew].

this text is that the remarks are made in earnest; that is, the author really believed that women, by their cunning, rule the world in direct contradiction to divine ordinance.[2]

Thus it is the way of the world that when the natural order of things is inverted a man's life (that is, the life of a free Jewish male) is liable to turn to destruction. *Ben Sira* warns his readers: "To son or wife, to brother or friend, do not give power over yourself, as long as you live" (33.19).[3] Similar statements can even be found in Josephus' historical writings. For example, Josephus (originally Nicolaus, in my opinion) asserts about the rule of the Queen Shelamzion Alexandra that "matters turned out so unfortunately for her house ... because of her desire for things unbecoming a woman" (*AJ* 13.431). Nicolaus blames the ultimate fall of the Hasmonean dynasty on those members of the royal house who disturbed the stable natural order by allowing a woman to hold power.[4] Josephus records the same explanation for the exile with which the emperor Caligula punished Herod Antipas: "God visited this punishment upon ... Herod for listening to a woman's frivolous chatter" (*AJ* 18.255). Similar estimations can be found in rabbinic literature. Ben Azzai ruled: "There are three whose life is no life at all: ... everyone whose wife lords over him" (*ARNA* 25, p. 82 ed. Schechter). Yet it should be noted that both the rabbinic teaching that a man should dominate his wife and also the warning against the danger hidden therein are found in Abot de Rabbi Nathan, a late work, and may reflect the opinion of the author more than that of the earlier sages themselves.

In all these sources the operative assumption, quite often explicitly expressed, is that there are basic differences between men and women. *Ben Sira* makes a general qualitative judgment: "Better is the wickedness of a man than a woman who does good" (42.14).[5] Other sources make an effort to define more precisely the points in which a woman differs from a man. The *Testament of Re-*

---

[2] On women as the embodiment of sin in the *Apocrypha* and *Pseudepigrapha*, see B. P. Prusak, "Women: Seductive Siren and Source of Sin? *Pseudepigraphical* Myth and Christian Origins," in *Religion and Sexism: Images of Women in the Jewish and Christian Traditions*, ed. Rosemary R. Ruether (New York 1974), 89–97; Léonie J. Archer, "The 'Evil Woman' in *Apocryphal* and *Pseudepigraphical* Writings," *Ninth World Congress of Jewish Studies*, Div. A (Jerusalem 1986), 239–46.

[3] For the importance of a man's control over his property in Mediterranean societies and in *Ben Sira*'s ideology see, Claudia V. Camp, "Understanding a Patriarchy: Women in Second Century Jerusalem through the Eyes of *Ben Sira*," *'Women Like This': New Perspectives on Jewish Women in the Greco Roman Period*, ed. Amy-Jill Levine (Atlanta 1991), 1–40.

[4] Josephus himself places the blame on Shelamzion's sons, Hyrcanus and Aristobulus (*AJ* 14.77–8).

[5] On this passage as typical of *Ben Sira*'s world-view, see W. C. Trenchard, *Ben Sira's View on Women: A literary Analysis = Brown Judaic Studies* XXXVIII (Chico CA 1982), 158–60.

uben declares that women are more susceptible than men to promiscuity (5.3). Similarly, we find in *Mekhilta de-Rabbi Shimeon bar Yohai*, "A woman can be seduced, a man cannot" (p. 208 ed. Melamed). The opposite opinion, however, is expressed in *Genesis Rabbah* "Why is a man inclined to yield to seduction while a woman is not?" (17.18, p. 159 ed. Theodor-Albeck).

We read further in the *Testament of Reuben* that women are deceitful and cunning but weak-hearted and fragile (5.1–2) – clearly implying the opposite, i.e. that men are courageous and strong and therefore do not need to resort to deceitful tricks.[6] Similarly, Josephus' Samson, paraphrasing *Judges* 14.18 ("If you had not plowed with my heifer you would not have found out my riddle"), says "there is nothing more deceitful than a woman" (*AJ* 5.294).

There are many places in *halakhic* literature which describe women's characteristics in order to justify different laws for men and women. Thus the determination that "women are light-headed" (*bQidd*. 80b) is meant to explain why it is prohibited for a man to be alone with two women; it is understood from this that men are not light-headed and thus one woman is permitted to be alone with two men.[7] In a discussion on the execution of women it is stated that a woman may not be stoned or hung naked because "all of her nakedness is illicit" (*Sifre Deut.* 221, pp. 254-5 ed. Finkelstein); by contrast men's nakedness is not "all illicit" and thus it is not only permitted but obligatory to hang them naked. "A woman's shame is greater than a man's" (*tKet.* 6.8; 12.3) and therefore a girl orphan is married off before a boy orphan. The determination that "a woman is niggardly" (*Sifre Num*. 110, p. 115 Horovitz) and therefore must separate a greater portion of hallah-dough than the baker is required to do, stands in opposition to the assertion that "men are generous." From R. Eliezer b. Pila's declaration that "women are gluttonous" (*mToh*. 7.9; *tToh*.8.16) and are thus under suspicion of having tasted food while it was being cooked, the opposite is implied, i.e. that men are not gluttonous. To be sure, we find it explicitly stated in *Abot de Rabbi Nathan* (*B* 45, p. 126 ed. Schechter) that gluttony (together with jealousy and the habit of eavesdropping) is a quality distinguishing women from men, but R. Yose immediately objects that precisely the same qualities are found in men as well (*ibid*.).[8]

---

[6] Similarly we read in the *Letter of Aristeas* (250) that a Palestinian sage remarked to King Ptolemy that "the female sex is rash, energetic in pursuing their desires, talkative, easily liable to change its mind because of poor reasoning powers, and of naturally weak constitution." The resemblance to the *Testament of Reuben* is clear, but the *Letter of Aristeas* has not been included in the present study since it appears to have been written in Alexandria and bears the marks of that Diaspora community.

[7] The notion that women are light-headed was in fact universal, appearing in some form in other cultures as well, see A. A. Halevi, *The World of the Aggadah* (Tel Aviv 1972), 249–52 [Hebrew].

[8] "There are four things characteristic of women but not of men: women are gluttonous, jealous, lazy and eavesdroppers. Gluttonous, as it stated: 'And the woman saw that

The *aggadic* tradition adds more qualities peculiar to women: they give off a strong odor of perspiration ("she must use perfume"), they have a higher voice ("her voice is penetrating"), they behave differently in sexual relations ("a woman ⟨comes forth⟩ with her face turned upwards" whereas "a man ⟨comes forth⟩ with his face turned downward;" "the man makes demands on the woman whereas the woman does not make demands on the man;" "a man deposits sperm within a woman whereas a woman does not deposit sperm within a man"), and they dress differently ("a man goes out bareheaded while a woman goes out with her head covered" – all examples from *Gen. R.* 17.8, p. 159 ed. Theodor-Albeck). The rabbis explained all these differences on the basis of the story of creation, as R. Joshua explained to his disciples (*ibid.*): women have a bad odor because they were created from flesh and not, like men, from earth; they have higher voices because they were created from bone, which by itself makes a clanking sound in a pot; they lie on their backs and face the man during intercourse in order to look towards the place of their creation (the man's rib) while men face the place of their own creation (the earth). R. Joshua explains all the other differences in a similar manner, on the basis of the creation story and the expulsion from the Garden of Eden. The creation story is thus seen as the source not only for men's domination over women according to the natural order of things, but also for the biological and psychological differences between men and women.

Thus a woman was the subject of constant worry for her husband: another man might meet her, talk with her, look her up and down, and in the end seduce her. Looking and talking, as opposed to sexual relations, were naturally not considered culpable offenses, but since they could very well lead to the sin of adultery, which at least theoretically carried the death penalty, or even worse to pregnancy and the birth of bastard children, a need was felt to "construct a fence around the *Torah*", that is, to institute safeguards against coming too close to the opportunity to transgress. These safeguards fall into two categories: a) the admonition against a man's speaking with a woman not related to him; and b) the more serious admonition against a man's even looking at another woman.

---

the tree was good for eating' (*Gen.* 3.6). Jealous; as it is stated: 'And Rachel was jealous of her sister' (*ibid.* 30.1). Eavesdroppers, as it is stated: 'And Sarah was listening at the tent-door behind him' (*ibid.* 18.10). Lazy, as it is stated, 'make ready quickly three measures of fine meal' (*ibid.* 18.6). R. Yose says: Just as four things are characteristic of women, so they are characteristic of men. Men are gluttonous, jealous, eavesdroppers and lazy, etc. "

Talking with a Woman

"Talk not much with womankind" is the famous saying of Yose b. Yohanan of Jerusalem, of one of the Pairs (*mAbot* 1.5).[9] If Yose b. Yohanan meant originally to make a general statement, his *tannaitic* colleagues took pains to clarify what he meant by adding: "They said this of a man's own wife; how much more of his fellow's wife!"[10] The later *tannaim* added: "He that talks much with womankind brings evil upon himself and neglects the study of the Law and at the last will inherit *Gehenna*". But clearly a man will not "inherit *Gehenna*" because of a mere conversation with a woman or even neglect of *Torah*-study; the sin is neither of these, but rather the seduction of the woman with whom a man talks excessively. The *Talmud* states this explicitly: "It was taught: Do not speak excessively with a woman lest this ultimately lead you to adultery" (*bNed.* 20a).[11]

A disciple of the sages would exercise special care not to enter into conversation with a woman. An example is the following, expressed in the style of wisdom literature: "Our rabbis taught: Six things are a cause of reproach to a disciple of the sages: ... he shall not converse with a woman in the market ..." (*bBer.* 43b), which is not *halakhah* but only a recommendation regarding ideal behavior. Naturally not every man can behave in ideal fashion, but a higher standard was expected from a disciple of the sages. The same recommendation appears in the later compilation *Abot de Rabbi Nathan*, but there it is extended to all males, and an additional reason is provided: "A man should not speak with a woman in the market, even if she is his wife, much less another woman, because the public may misinterpret it" (*ARNA* 2, p. 9 ed. Schechter). Here we find concern for the less than pleasant consequences that may ensue for both the man and the woman. Accordingly, conversation with a woman became the subject for *aggadah*. God, it turns out, does not converse with women: "In the name of R.

---

[9] For the possible social background to this saying see: J. Goldin, "The First Pair (Yose ben Yoezer and Yose ben Yohanan) or the House of the Pharisee," *Association of Jewish Studies Review* 5 (1980), 41–62.

[10] On this addition, see C. Albeck, *The Mishnah* IV (Jerusalem 1953), 493 [Hebrew]. The wording in the Kaufmann MS is: "Anyone who speaks excessively with a woman while she is menstruating."

[11] A parable illustrates that ideally even the father should not speak too much with his sexually mature daughter: "R. Judah bar Ilai said: It is like a king who had a little girl. Before she grew up and showed the signs of sexual maturity, he would see her in the market and speak with her in public, in alleyways and in courtyards. But after she grew up and showed the signs of sexual maturity, the king said: It is not good for my daughter's reputation that she be seen speaking with me in public; rather, make her a tent, and when I need to speak with her, I will speak with her in the tent" (*Song of Songs R.* 3.7.1).

Eliezer b. R. Shimeon: We have not found that the Almighty spoke to a woman, except Sarah" (*ySot.* 7.1, 21b).[12]

The only critical voice raised against this dictum to be found in rabbinic literature comes from an ironic *amoraic* source and belongs to a woman of the *tannaitic* period, Beruriah: "R. Yose the Galilean was once on a journey when he met Beruriah. By what road, he asked her, do we go to Lod? Galilean fool, she replied, did not the sages say this: 'Talk not much with womenkind?' You should have asked: By which to Lod?" (*bErub.* 53b). It is of course because R. Yose knows the sages' admonition that he puts his question in briefest form, avoiding all polite formalities. Beruriah, who is also aware of the admonition, presses R. Yose to adhere to it, but at the same time, her very instruction violates the same precept by creating an extended conversation.[13]

Looking at a Woman

Another restriction, more severe in nature and revealing an extreme pietistic tendency, forbids men to look at women. We have seen that *Ben Sira* completely forbids looking at any woman other than one's wife (9.5; 8; 41.21). The danger of observing women, particularly beautiful women, is mentioned three times in the Testaments of the Twelve Patriarchs. Reuben avows that had he not looked at Bilha he would not have sinned (*Test. Reub.* 3.10–2; 4.1). Judah, too, lamenting that he fell into the net of the Canaanite woman because of her beauty, warns his sons against looking at women (*Test. Jud.* 17.1). Finally, Benjamin tells his sons that pure thoughts (καθαρὸς νοῦς) require not looking at any woman not one's own (*Test. Ben.* 8.2).

Similar warnings can be found in rabbinic literature: "Our rabbis taught: He who pays a woman by counting out coins from his hand to hers in order to gaze at her, even if the level of his *Torah*-knowledge and good deeds has reached that of Moses our teacher, he will not escape the punishment of *Gehenna*" (*bBer.* 61a); it is further stated that, for the same reason, a man is forbidden to walk behind a woman, even if she is his wife. Elsewhere the rabbis declare: "He who looks at a woman's heals, it is as if he looked at the place of her pudenda, and if he looks there, it is as if he had intercourse with her" (*yHal.* 2.4, 58c). It thus seems that voyeurism is equated with adultery.

More pietistic circles took this idea to even further extremes. In Jesus' Sermon on the Mount, which is a declaration of the central tenets of Matthew, the

---

[12] See further L. J. Swidler, *Women in Judaism: The Status of Women in Formative Judaism* (Metuchen NJ 1976), 123–5.

[13] For this interpretation see: Rachel Adler, "The Virgin in the Brothel and other Anomalies: Character and Context in the Legend of Beruriah," *Tikkun* 3/6 (1988), 30.

evangelist closest to Judaism, we find the admonition against looking at women expressed as law: "You have heard that it was said, 'Do not commit adultery'. But I say to you that everyone who looks at a woman with lust has already committed adultery with her in his heart" (*Matt.* 5.27–8). Here, as we have seen in previous examples, a moral exhortation by the rabbis becomes law in the fringe pietistic groups.

The Woman at Home

Both conversation with and looking at a woman could be prevented by secluding the woman in her house. According to Josephus, the Levite concubine was raped at Gibeah (*Judges* 19) after the residents of the place saw her in the market-place (*AJ* 5.143). In their interpretation of the biblical laws on rape, the rabbis rule assert: "'And a man finds her in the city' (*Deut.* 22.23), If she had not gone out into the city he would not have happened upon her" (*Sifre Deut.* 242, p. 272 ed. Finkelstein). We have already quoted the opinion of R. Yohanan b. Broqa, that both men and women are obligated to fulfill the commandment to "be fruitful and multiply." The word "subdue [the earth]," which his opponents cite to prove that the commandment falls only on the man, is interpreted by R. Yohanan b. Broqa in a manner pertinent to the present discussion: "[Was it written] 'And [you, pl.] subdue it'? No, it was written 'subdue [you, sing.] it' (*Gen.* 1.28). The man subdues the woman so that she will not go out into the market-place, for the inevitable end of every woman who goes out into the market-place is to fall into sin" (*Gen. R.* 8.12, p. 66 ed. Theodor-Albeck).

Thus the ideal was that a woman would remain concealed in the house and not show her beauty in public (= the market-place). This ideal is illustrated in the *Book of Judith* by the beautiful widow, Judith, who for many years after she was widowed did not leave her house (*Judith* 8.4); and when she finally did go out, having even adorned herself, everyone was amazed at her beauty, for they were used to her deliberately hiding it (10.7). An unmarried woman who adorns herself and goes out into public immediately becomes a subject of public talk, as we see in the following illustration: "It is like a woman without a husband: whether she adorns herself or not, everyone looks at her" (*tQidd.* 1.12; cf. *ARNB* 21, p. 44 ed. Schechter).

In this light we can understand *Ben Sira*'s remark that one must shut up a daughter behind sealed windows, lest she appear in public (42.11), even though this advice seems extreme. Such a man, according to R. Meir, acts as "Pappus b. Judah, who locked the door on his wife." By more normal standards, R. Meir continues, a husband "allows his wife to speak with her siblings and neighbors," although the "wicked man," he maintains, is one "who sees his wife go outside with her head uncovered ... and she spins in public and bathes with men" (*tSot.* 5.9; *ySot.* 1.7, 17a; *bGitt.* 90a). The *halakhah* is quite definite on this matter:

"These are they that are put away without their *ketubbah*: a wife that transgresses the law of Moses and Jewish custom. ... And what is Jewish custom? If she goes out with her hair unbound, or spins in public, or speaks with any man. Abba Saul says: Also if she curses his children at his face. R. Tarfon says: Also if she is a scolding woman" (*mKet.* 7.6). The *Tosefta* adds: "and she who goes out with both her sides (shoulders) bare ... and bathes in a public bath with any man" (*tKet.* 7.6). Further, the *Babylonian Talmud:* "she who eats in public, drinks in public, nurses in public" (*bGitt.* 89a). These laws highlight the qualms caused by a woman who performs in public activities which should be restricted to the home. Thus R. Meir's description of the wicked man is based on these laws and pertains to a man who allows his wife to do things for which he is obligated to send her away without her *ketubbah*.[14]

The *halakhah* specifies that a woman's chastity should be guarded even after her death: "They may not set down the bier in the open street on festivals, and the bier of a woman they may never set down, for reasons of honor" (*mMQ* 3.8).

One wonders about the extent to which the rabbinic ideal, that a woman never be found in the market-place (in public), reflects historical reality. This question can be investigated through incidental references in the sources. For example, one law determines that spots of blood found on a woman's garments are not necessarily menstrual blood, for she could have been splattered in the butchers' market (*tNidd.* 6.17). In addition, the *Babylonian Talmud* relates the following story: "R. Judah's wife went out to buy wool, from which she made an embroidered garment; subsequently she would don this garment when she went out to the market, and her husband would cover himself in it when he went out to pray" (*bNed.* 49b). This story of a husband and wife sharing a garment in poverty, incidentally mentions that the wife requires the garment in the market-place. From these traditions we learn that women actually went out into the market-place to do shopping. Also those women whose husbands set them up as shopkeepers (on which see below) in their shops obviously had to be seen in public.

Head-Covering

Several other sources, in addition to the ones we have already cited, specify that when a woman does go out in public, her head should be covered.[15] For example: "The house of R. Ishmael: a warning to the daughters of Israel, that they not

---

[14] See Swidler (above, n. 12), 118–21; L. M. Epstein, *Sex Laws and Customs in Judaism* (New York 1948), 70–4.

[15] S. Krauss argued, in a learned but tendentious article, that Jewish law does not require a woman to cover her head: "The Jewish Rite of Covering the Head," *Hebrew Union*

go out with their heads uncovered (lit. unbound) …" (*bKet.* 72a); and in *Sifre* we find the following interpretation of the passage "and he shall let loose the hair on the woman's head" (*Num.* 5.18): "of the daughters of Israel, that they cover their heads" (*Sifre Num.* 11, p. 17 ed. Horovitz). And in fact, we find in the *aggadah* examples of truly modest women who cover their heads even indoors. Thus Qimhit, when asked by the sages how it happened that seven of her sons served in the high priesthood, gave the following answer: "The beams of my house never saw the hair on my head" (*yHor.* 3.5, 47d; *bYoma* 47a; *ARNA* 35, p. 105 ed. Schechter).

Unbound hair on a woman is depicted as compromising her modesty. The worst of Susanna's humiliations occurred when the elders, who were accusing her of adultery, demanded that her head be uncovered (*Susanna* 32). R. Judah even says, regarding the suspected adulteress (*sotah*) whom the *Torah* specifically says must be examined by, among other things, loosening her hair: "If her hair was attractive he did not loosen it" (*mSot.* 1.5; *Sifre Num.* 11, p. 17 ed. Horovitz). According to *halakhah*, "if a man loosened a woman's hair … he is liable to pay her 400 zuz" (*mBQ* 8.6; cf. *Sif. Emor* 20.1, 104d ed. Weiss).[16]

In this light we may understand the contempt of women expressed in certain *aggadot* of the period. We read in the *Testament of Job,* for instance, that when Job had sunk to the depths of his poverty and suffering his wife was forced not only to wander the market-place to earn bread for both of them (22.3), but also to sell her own hair in order to support her husband (23.7–10) as is also told of R. Aqiba's wife (*yShab.* 6.1, 7d; *ySot.* 9.16, 24c). In *Luke*, the woman sinner who washes Jesus' feet in oil and tears and dries them with her hair is also apparently without a head-covering (*Luke* 7.38; cf. *John* 12.3). The public's reaction to the woman's deed indicates the contempt they felt for the woman. The same picture emerges from the rabbinic story about the meeting between the daughter of Naqdimon b. Gurion and Rabban Yohanan b. Zakkai.[17] The crudest version ap-

---

College Annual 19 (1945–6), 154–62. The custom in ancient Greece was also for women to cover their heads: Eur. *Hec.* 924–6; *Phoen.* 1485–6.

[16] The early Christians also discussed whether and when a woman should cover her hair. Paul, who usually stresses the need for liberation from Jewish law, counsels women to cover their heads as part of the cosmic order, by which a woman is subordinate to her husband because woman was created from man, and also because women were the ones who seduced the angels (*Gen.* 6.2) by leaving their heads uncovered (*1 Cor.* 11.3–10). A sharp debate has recently developed around this passage, see above, Introduction, n. 31, and also M. D. Hooker, "Authority on her Head: Examination of *1 Cor.* XI 10," *New Testament Studies* 10 (1963–4), 410–16; W. O. Walker, "*1 Corinthians* 11:2–16 and Paul's View Regarding Women," *Journal of Biblical Literature* 94 (1975), 94–110; Bernadette J. Brooten, "Paul and the Law: How Complete was the Departure?" *The Princeton Seminary Bulletin Supplementary Issue* 1 (1990), 71–89; Anoinette C. Wire, *The Corinthian Women Prophets: A Reconstruction through Paul's Rhetoric* (Minneapolis 1990), 116–34.

[17] The transmission of these *aggadot* is extremely complicated and has been the subject of extensive scholarship: Ofra Meir, "The Story as a Hermeneutic Device," *Associa-*

pears in the *Mekhilta de R. Ishmael* (*Bahodesh* 1, pp. 203–4 ed. Horovitz-Rabin): Rabban Yohanan goes up to Maon in Judaea and sees "a young woman picking barley grains out of horse dung," but she is not identified. The version in *Sifre Deuteronomy* (305, p. 325 ed. Finkelstein) is somewhat more sophisticated, and more relevant to the matter at hand: Rabban Yohanan arrives at an unspecified place riding on a donkey, and when he turns to the young woman "she wrapped herself in her hair and stood before him." Obviously she covers herself to hide her nakedness and/or her identity, but her hair is itself unbound. The same story appears in the *Babylonian Talmud*, where it is specified that Rabban Yohanan "went out from Jerusalem" (*bKet.* 66b), and in *Abot de Rabbi Nathan*, where "once Rabban Yohanan b. Zakkai was walking in the market-place" (*A* 17, p. 65 ed. Schechter). In this example, the intention was to emphasize the depth of humiliation to which the woman had sunk: not only is she in the market-place, where no respectable woman would dare be found, but her head is uncovered, as learnt from the detail that she hid beneath it.[18]

A different source makes the specific connection between women seen in the market-place and those without head-coverings. One woman whose hair had been unbound against her will in the market-place appeared before R. Aqiba and demanded satisfaction. R. Aqiba commanded the offender to pay high compensation; in order to avoid paying, the offender poured expensive oil at the door of the woman's house, and she came out, unloosed her hair and anointed her head (*mBQ* 8.6).[19] This source censures a woman appearing in public without her head covered, but assumes without judgment that a woman would appear in the market-place.

But the question remains: was it the accepted custom for women to cover their hair? Unfortunately, no Jewish images have survived in plastic art from the

tion of Jewish Studies Review 7–8 (1982–3), 243–56; B. L. Visotzky, "Most Tender and Fairest of Women: A Study in the Transmission of *Aggada*," *Harvard Theological Review* 76 (1983), 416–8; and see also Naomi G. Cohen, "The Theological Stratum of the Martha b. Boethus Tradition: An Explication of the Text in *Gittin* 56a," *Harvard Theological Review* 69 (1976), 187–95. The stories seem nevertheless to contain an historical kernel; the glory of the daughters of the wealthy Jerusalem families faded after the Destruction as they fell into captivity and suffered much, and this was etched into the memories of that generation. One can see this, for example, in the use of the place-name Akko in several *aggadot* which deal with the capture of these women, although their fates are variously reported, e.g. *Lam. R.* 1.49, Mariamme (!) the daughter of Boethus falls captive, as opposed to *yKet.* 5.13, 30b-c, where Martha daughter of Boethus is described as picking barley grains from between the hooves of horses and Mariamme daughter of Shimeon (!) b. Gurion as being tied to a horse's tail in Akko. Other sources, however, set the story in different locations; e.g. *Lam. R.* 1.47 relates that Mariamme (!) daughter of Boethus was tied by her hair to a horse's tail and dragged from Jerusalem to Lod.

[18] See further, Swidler (above, n. 12), 121–3.

[19] For a literary analysis of this story, see H. Licht, *Ten Legends of the Sages in Rabbinic Literature* (Hoboken, NJ 1991), 27–47.

Second Temple period, and so this form of determining women's habits of dress is lost to us.[20] We can gain a different glimpse into reality from another, rather peculiar angle. The *Palestinian Talmud* relates that the wife of R. Aqiba sold her tresses in order to support her impoverished family and enable her husband to study *Torah* (*yShab.* 6.1, 7d; *ySot.* 9.16, 24c). A similar story, as we have seen, is told in the *Testament of Job* about Job's first wife. Women's hair was clearly used for wigs,[21] and that this was a widespread practice is evident from the following *halakhah*: "If a woman was put to death her hair may be used" (*mArakh.* 1.4). If we take this one step further and ask why the demand for wigs was so great, we discover an attempt, true to human nature, to cheat while adhering to an ethical code: wearing a wig allows a woman to cover her head and to be seen with flowing hair.[22] Yet we discover another thing as well: wigs were a luxury which only women of means could afford; thus they represent yet another example of a provision in the moral code which seems to belong to the middle and upper social classes.

By the terms of this moral code, then, a woman was expected to remain concealed inside her house. She was forbidden to walk in the market-place and speak with strange men, and required to wear only clothes becoming her modesty, including a head-covering. It would be instructive to inquire at this point the extent to which these requirements represent the actual practices common in the period, or a set of demands which most women could not meet.

Archaeological Evidence

Strict separation of men and women was practicable only if houses of the period were built in the fashion which *Ben Sira* describes: "See that there is no lattice in her room, no spot that overlooks the approaches to the house" (42.11). This naturally raises the question, whether houses in Palestine during the period under study had separate quarters for women. Jeremias thought so,[23] relying on the descriptions in *2 Macc.* 3.19 ("the young women who were kept indoors") and *3 Macc.* 1.18 ("young women who had been secluded in their chambers"); but Jeremias ignored the fact that both of these texts were composed in Egypt and

---

[20] Women in the Herodian royal house had their portraits painted (*AJ* 15. 26–7) and sculpted (*BJ* 1. 439); none have survived. We do have one coin of Salome, the daughter of Herodias, who was married to Aristobulus, son of Herod king of Chalcis, and became the queen of Armenia; see T. Reinach, "Le mari de Salomé et les monnaies de Nicopolis d'Arménie," *Revue Études Ancien* 16 (1914), 143. On this coin Salome wears a crown in the form of a hat, but her hair hangs down loose underneath.

[21] This subject is discussed at length by *amoraim* at *bArakh.* 7b.

[22] On the use of wigs, see Epstein (above, n. 14), 53.

[23] J. Jeremias, *Jerusalem in the Time of Jesus* (Philadelphia 1969), 360–1.

cannot be used as sources for the situation in Palestine.[24] Yet we should note that Josephus, in his description of the siege of Jerusalem, reports that because of the famine men died in the streets but women on the roofs of their houses (*BJ* 5.512).

Susan Walker has studied the plans of houses from the classical period excavated in and around Athens in an attempt to locate what could have been women's quarters: an area which is separate from the public rooms where banquets and receptions were held, does not look out on a main street and could be reached only through the inner courtyard.[25] Walker was able to identify sections which could have been used for the women's quarters, but she had to admit that such an investigation must remain incomplete because most of the structures presumably had second stories which would have been the most logical location for the women's quarters.[26]

In his archaeological and ethnographic studies of dwellings in Palestine during our period, Yizhar Hirschfeld has assembled the plans of many houses from all parts of the country;[27] from these plans, although Hirschfeld himself did not discuss the question, it is possible, using Walker's criteria, to discern certain areas of the dwellings which could be identified as women's quarters. Among the plans from major Jewish settlements, I have been able to identify certain isolated quarters in houses from Hurvat Kanaf,[28] Meron[29] and Capernaum.[30] I would suggest that these secluded areas of the houses could have served as women's quarters, but I do so with due caution, since I have not seen the structures myself, houses in Palestine probably also had second stories[31] which were the most likely location for women's quarters, and excavations generally turn up the ample houses of the wealthy, so that my identification of women's quarters would apply, if at all, only to the houses of the upper social classes.

The ethnographic part of Hirschfeld's study involved a comparison of the housing conditions of traditional Arab families in the Hebron mountains today

---

[24] Cf. Philo, *De spec. leg.* 3.169; *Flacc.* 89, evidence for seclusion of Jewish women in Alexandria.

[25] Susan Walker, "Women and Housing in Classical Greece: The Archaeological Evidence," in *Images of Women in Antiquity*, edd. Averil Cameron and Amélie Kuhrt (Detroit 1985), 81–91.

[26] In an interesting case from fourth-century Athens, a husband describes how, after the birth of his son, he moved the women's quarters in his house from the top to the ground floor. See Sarah B. Pomeroy, *Goddesses, Whores, Wives and Slaves: Women in Classical Antiquity* (New York 1975), 81–2; Eva C. Keuls, *The Reign of the Phallus: Sexual Politics in Ancient Athens* (New York 1985), 212.

[27] Y. Hirschfeld, *Dwelling Houses in Roman and Byzantine Palestine* (Jerusalem 1987) [Hebrew].

[28] *Ibid.* 12.

[29] *Ibid.* 15.

[30] *Ibid.* 34. The same can be found in house-plans from non-Jewish settlements.

[31] *Ibid.* 166.

with the archaeological finds from the earlier period, on the assumption that the traditional way of life in this region did not change substantially in the last 2,000 years. As noted, Hirschfeld did not look for women's quarters in the dwellings he excavated or surveyed, and in fact the comparison with life of contemporary peasants shifted his focus away from such a search, for those families are accustomed to live and even sleep all in one room, in order (among other reasons) to exploit their own body heat to keep warm;[32] naturally there are no separate men's and women's quarters to be found in them. Hirschfeld's unstated assumption is that the standard form of the house in the Second Temple period is the same as the ones he studied in the Hebron region. This assumption may not be very far from the truth, for while the Arab houses in the Hebron region may preserve the ancient material culture of the lower classes, the abodes of the wealthy are what tend to be uncovered in archaeological excavations.

S. Safrai has suggested[33] that the reason for separate men's and women's quarters in Jewish houses of the period is not moral but *halakhic*, i.e. the menstruant woman had to be secluded so as not to contaminate the utensils in the house or the other people who lived there.[34] Safrai found evidence of the existence of separate quarters in a late *amoraic* source (*bQidd.* 81a) which is open to different interpretations. Safrai in fact rejects the assumption that the second floor was used for the women's quarters, for that was the place of the "upper chamber" (עליה) where sages, i.e. males, would often meet.[35] Rather, Safrai concludes that in the houses where extended families lived, one room was allotted to each nuclear family, which explains the large number of rooms discovered in houses excavated in Palestine. Poorer families, in Safrai's opinion, would have all lived in one room.[36]

Research of this subject is still in its infancy; thorough archaeological study is required. From the investigations of both Hirschfeld and Safrai it is evident that in Palestinian houses women's quarters would have been a luxury which only rich families could afford. In this light we may very cautiously offer the suggestion that the moral requirement that men and women be separated was formulated by and for the well-established classes, who could in fact obey such a requirement. This illustrates once again that rabbinic and other sources represent the middle and upper classes, and neither relate to nor show much consideration for the lower classes.

---

[32] *Ibid.* 164.

[33] S. Safrai , "Home and Family," in *The Jewish People in the First Century* II = *Compendia Rerum Iudaicarum ad Novum Testamentum Section One,* edd. S. Safrai and M. Stern (Assen 1976), 730–5.

[34] *Ibid.* 732.

[35] *Ibid.* 731.

[36] *Ibid.* 732.

Chapter 5:

Crises in Married Life and the Breakdown of Marriage

Adultery

Commission of adultery by the woman could lead to the most severe crisis in a couple's marriage. *Ben Sira* conveys in full detail the seriousness of such a disaster, warning against even looking at another man's wife to avoid the slightest possibility of adultery (9.8; 26.24; 41.20–1);[1] to the same end he counsels against spending time with a woman and her husband at events at which wine is consumed and music is played.[2] The greatest danger in adultery, *Ben Sira* says, is that the illicit relationship could produce offspring, who live in the husband's house as if they were his legitimate heirs when in fact they have no right to be there (*ibid.*).

Jewish law contains no definition of or provision against adultery by the husband against his wife, since he may marry more than one woman; the wife, on the other hand, must remain strictly faithful to her husband. The only way a man can commit adultery is with another man's wife.[3] Jesus seems to have departed from this standard. Since he forbade divorce, he taught that the man who has divorced his wife and marries another also commits adultery (*Mark* 10.11; *Luke* 16.18).[4]

The Bible prescribes death for both the adulterous woman caught in the act and the man who shared her offense (*Lev.* 20.10; *Deut.* 22.20–1). The extent to which this was actually put into practice in the Second Temple period has been

---

[1] See W. C. Trenchard, *Ben Sira's View on Women: A Literary Analysis* = *Brown Judaic Studies* XXXVIII (Chico' CA 1982), 95–108.

[2] The *Bibl. Ant.* (2.7–8) also makes a connection between music and adultery, after the section on Yuval, father of all players on violin and organ: *cum inciassent habitantes terram operari iniqua unusquisque in uxorem proximi sui contaminantes eas.*

[3] See L. M. Epstein, *Sex Laws and Customs in Judaism* (New York 1948), 194–5; Rachel Biale, *Women and the Jewish Law: An Exploration of Women's Issues in Halakhic Sources* (NewYork 1984), 183–4; L. J. Swidler, *Women in Judaism: The Status of Women in Formative Judaism* (Metuchen NJ 1976), 148.

[4] But in *Matthew* 5.32 and perhaps also 19.9, only the man who marries a divorced woman commits adultery because she is still considered her former husband's wife; note that once again the version in *Matthew* is closer to Jewish law.

the subject of considerable debate.[5] The passage in *Ben Sira* which says that the adulterous woman "shall be taken out in front of the public" (23.39) does not help, for it can be interpreted either way.[6] Conflicting attitudes, if not information on actual practice, can be found in two apocryphal books: the story of *Susanna* demonstrates full approval of the death penalty for an adulterous woman (44–5), whereas the Slavonic *Enoch* relates that Noah's brother, Nir, discovering that his wife is pregnant and knowing with certainty that he is not the father, divorces her but does not condemn her to death (71.6–7). Thus it appears that the proper penalty for the adulterous woman was the subject of controversy in the Second Temple period.[7]

The main problem with adultery is that it is difficult to prove. A test for this can be found already in the Bible.

The Suspected Adulteress (*sotah*)

One of the more interesting developments in the Second Temple period is the revocation of the trial by bitter water. The *sotah* is a woman whose husband suspects her of having had sexual relations with another man but cannot prove it. The Bible prescribes that this woman must stand in the Temple and undergo a test in which the husband's claim is either vindicated or disproved by divine judgment. The *sotah* must first bring a meal-offering; then the priest speaks to her words of reproof, and loosens her hair and her clothes; finally the woman drinks water which has been mixed with dust from the floor of the Temple. The woman who has sinned is supposed miraculously to die from this trial. The whole method is extremely odd, in that it departs from the standard Jewish legal processes based on evidence and on the assumption of innocence until guilt is proven. Neusner[8] has noted that the *mishnaic* tractate *Sotah* contains no *halakhic* additions to the Bible, which he explains by the fact that the *Mishnah* was

---

[5] Epstein (above, n. 3), 209–12 argues that a great effort was made to avoid capital punishment; on the other hand, Swidler (above, n. 3), 148–51 thinks that the death penalty was imposed on the adulterous woman during the entire Second Temple period. Note that the one with the lenient views is Jewish while the one with the stringent view is Christian.

[6] According to A. Büchler, "Die Straffe der Ehebrecher in der nachexilischen Zeit," *Monatsschrift für Geschichte und Wissenschaft des Judentums* 55 (1911), 196–206, this passage is a proof of capital punishment, but Trenchard (above, n. 1), 103–7 rejects the passage as reliable evidence for either view. Here, interestingly, the Christian and Jew have exchanged positions.

[7] The Jews' right to decide capital cases in the Second Temple period was already a topic for discussion, centered around this passage in *Susanna*, among the church fathers; see Origen, *Epistola ad Africanum de Historia Susanna* 14, *Patrologiae Graecae* XI: *Origines* I, col. 81–4.

[8] J. Neusner, *A History of the Mishnaic Law of Women* V (Leiden 1980), 140.

edited more than 150 years after the destruction of the Temple, during which time, of course, no *sotah* trial was held; thus all discussions of the *sotah* were presumably restricted to the realm of theory and represent neither historical reality nor *halakhah* in practice. He argues that the tractate *Sotah* should not interest the serious student of *halakhah*. This view is mistaken, however, for it neglects other aspects of the same tractate. Although most of the surviving material on the trial of the *sotah* is *tannaitic* and post-Destruction, it nonetheless contains clear signs that the whole matter was the subject of controversy towards the end of the days of the Second Temple.

First of all, we read: "Rabban Yohanan b. Zakkai says: ...when adulterers became many, the [rite of bitter] water ceased, for they do not make the women drink except in cases of doubt" (*tSot.* 14.2), but further on we find: "When women who were supercilious [lit. had stretched-out necks] and painted their eyes became many, bitter water increased" (*ibid.* 9).[9] These two contradictory traditions are evidence of a controversy between Rabban Yohanan b. Zakkai and another sage or sages, regarding the actual test of the *sotah*. Both sides cited the same reason for, respectively, the cessation and the increase in the use of the test.

The matter is stated more explicitly in the *Mishnah*: "When adulterers became many [the rite of] the bitter water ceased; and Rabban Yohanan b. Zakkai brought it to an end, for it is written, 'I will not punish your daughters when they commit prostitution nor your daughters-in-law when they commit adultery, for they themselves [go apart with whores ...]' (*Hos.* 4.14)" (*mSot.* 9.9). From this we learn that the controversy over when the trial by bitter water ceased was not strictly theoretical, and it was not the destruction of the Temple which diminished the importance of the rite; rather, an attempt was made to stop it altogether before the Destruction.

Rabban Yohanan b. Zakkai's opposition is anonymous not only in the sources cited above but also in an interesting historical episode: the proselyte Queen Helene from Adiabene, who was Rabban Yohanan's contemporary, donated to the Temple a golden table on which were inscribed the biblical verses pertaining to the *sotah* (*mYoma* 3.10). Helene's donation cannot be simply dismissed as the action of a zealous convert who acted on her own advice and consequently embarrassed the Temple officials. It is more likely that one of Rabban Yohanan's opponents, serving as Helene's guide and counselor in spiritual matters, stood behind her action.

Why was Rabban Yohanan opposed to the trial of the bitter water? The reason cited in the *Tosefta*, that adulterers had multiplied and the test was used only in cases of doubt, is not terribly convincing since his opponents based their support

---

[9] The sentence ends with the words "but they ceased," which is obviously an editorial attempt to harmonize the two texts.

of the test on the same grounds. On the other hand, in both the *mishnaic* tractate *Sotah* and the exegetical-*halakhic* commentaries (*midrashei halakhah*) on *Numbers* we find echoes of different debates regarding the *sotah*, going back to the Second Temple period. In the *Mishnah* we read: "As the water tests her so does it test him...; so R. Aqiba. R. Joshua said: So Zechariah b. Haqatzab used to expound" (*mSot.* 5.1). This tradition illustrates the discomfort some sages felt from the inequality in the prescribed trial of the *sotah*: two committed adultery and only one must suffer the ordeal. The *Mishnah* attributes this teaching to R. Aqiba but R. Joshua claims that it belonged to Zechariah b. Haqatzab, a sage from the time of the Second Temple; thus the tradition is quite ancient.[10] What is not clear from the *Mishnah* is which man is tested, her suspected partner or her jealous husband. An answer may be suggested by a *baraita* which appears many times in the *Babylonian Talmud*: "'And the man shall be free from iniquity' (*Num.* 5.31), so long as the husband is free from iniquity the water tests his wife, but if the husband is not free from iniquity the water does not test his wife" (*bYeb.* 58a; *bSot.* 28a; *bShebu.* 5a). Although this *baraita* is not attributed to any particular sage, it nonetheless clarifies, albeit in a roundabout way, which "man" undergoes the trial: if the husband commits adultery with another woman and thereby injures not only the woman's husband but also (although Jewish law does not state this specifically) his own wife, the ordeal of the water will not test his wife. The overriding concern here is for symmetry, i.e. that the rite fall on the man and the woman equally.[11]

Another interesting controversy regarding the *sotah* concerns "merit which holds punishment in suspense." The *Mishnah* states: "If she had any merit, this holds her punishment in suspense. Certain merits may postpone punishment for one year, others for two years, others for three years" (*mSot.* 3.4). Here we find that any meritorious deeds previously performed by the guilty adulteress postpone her penalty, i.e. death at the hands of heaven when her credit is used up.

Can this tradition, which is another sign that belief in the trial of the *sotah* was beginning to falter, also be dated to the Second Temple period? A comparison of various texts yields an answer. In the *Mishnah* we find: "R. Shimeon says: Merit does not hold in suspense the punishment of the bitter water; for if you say, Merit holds in suspense the punishment of the curse-giving water, you will make the water of little effect for all the women that drink, and you will bring an evil name against all undefiled women that have drunk, for it will be

---

[10] *Sifre Zuta* 5.22 (p. 236 ed. Horovitz) attributes the teaching to Rabban Gamaliel.

[11] Judith Hauptman, "Women's Liberation in the *Talmudic* Period: An Assessment," *Conservative Judaism* 26/4 (1972), 22–4, studies this Second Temple period controversy and concludes that the rabbis were trying to improve women's position from what it had been in the biblical period. See also: Adriana Destro, *The Law of Jealousy: Anthropology of Sotah* = Brown Judaic Studies CLXXXI (Atlanta 1989).

said: They are in truth defiled but merit has held their punishment in suspense" (*mSot.* 3.5; cf. *Sifre Num.* 8, p. 15 ed. Horovitz). The same appears in *Sifre Zuta* with slightly different wording: "R. Shimeon says: The matter involved desecration of the Holy Name, for if the water did not actually test her on the spot, when she went down from the Temple she would have said to her friends: Do not steer clear of sinning (= adultery); for I drank and the water did not harm me. Apparently there is no need for it at all" (5.31, p. 239 ed. Horovitz). The difference between these two version lies in the reason given for the cessation of the rite: in the *Mishnah*, it is to protect undefiled women against acquiring a bad name; in *Sifre Zuta* it is to avoid encouraging women to sin who would then drink the water without effect. R. Judah the Patriarch, the editor of the *Mishnah*, debated the issue with R. Shimeon bar Yohai, who was a disciple of R. Aqiba: "Rabbi says: Merit holds in suspense the punishment of the curse-giving water; but nevertheless she will not bear children nor continue in comeliness, but she will waste away by degrees and in the end will die the selfsame death" (*mSot.* 3.5). And in the parallel version in *Sifre Num.*: "Rabbi says: I will decide; if she was undefiled, she will end up dying a normal death, but if she was defiled, then she will end up dying 'and her belly swells and her thigh falls' (*Num.* 5.27)" (8, p. 15 ed. Horovitz).[12] R. Shimeon and Rabbi are both late *tannaim*, but they are not the ones who initiated the controversy, for it was already going on in previous generations, as the tradition in the *Mishnah* indicates in a debate on a different problem: "Hence Ben Azzai says: A man ought to give his daughter a knowledge of the *Torah* so that if she must drink she may know that the merit will hold her punishment in suspense" (*mSot.* 3.4). Ben Azzai has no doubt that merit holds punishment in suspense; this knowledge must be applied by teaching one's daughters. His elder, R. Eliezer, who saw the Temple when it was still standing, answers: "If any man gives his daughter knowledge of the *Torah*, it is as though he taught her lechery" (*ibid.*).[13] R. Eliezer objects only to Ben Azzai's recom-

---

[12] But R. Shimeon has an answer even for this: "And who informs all those standing around [to witness the trial by bitter water] that this woman's end is to die 'and her belly swells and her thigh falls' (*Num.* 5.27)? Rather, when she drinks, her face grows pale and her eyes bulge ..." (*ibid.*).

[13] "Lechery" is only one of many English translations that have been suggested for תפלות. M. Meiselman, *Jewish Women in Jewish Law* (New York 1978), 34 gives the Hebrew term a double definition, one neutral – "trivial and irrelevant things" – and the other sexual and pejorative – "immorality". The translations of other scholars follow one or both of these senses. S. Zucrow, *Women, Slaves and the Ignorant in Rabbinic Literature* (Boston 1932), 75 translated, alternately, "nonsense" and "something indecorous." Recently, B. Witherington III, *Women in the Ministry of Jesus* (Cambridge 1984), 6 has rendered the term as "extravagance" and "lechery". Biale (above, n. 3), 33 translates "nonsense;" others have opted for the more sexual connotation, such as Swidler's "lechery" (above, n. 3, 93) and Judith R. Wegner's "lasciviousness" (*Chattel or Person: The Status of Women in the Mishnah* [Oxford 1988], 161). Those who have given the term a sexual connotation

mendation to teach one's daughter *Torah*, not to the idea that merit holds punishment in suspense. In other words, the idea dates from the Second Temple period because R. Eliezer accepts it as a fact. It is thus contemporary with the debate on the bitter water, in which Rabban Yohanan b. Zakkai was involved.[14]

In sum, the controversy over the trial of the *sotah* at the end of the Second Temple period seems to have been internal to the Pharisees, and those who objected to the rite, led by Rabban Yohanan b. Zakkai, seem to have held the upper hand and may even have succeeded in abolishing it. This is at least the impression one gets from later sources which try to present the Pharisees as managing the affairs of the Temple. The validity of the rite was questioned on the basis of two doubts: a) whether the water could accurately test a woman whose husband was having sexual relations with other women, and b) whether the water afforded a fair test for women who behaved modestly all their lives and lapsed only at the end. We can assume that behind the entire controversy stood actual cases in which the test was negative but adultery was proven afterwards by other means.[15] The controversy at its height thus dealt with an actual problem, but by the time the *Mishnah* was redacted the entire subject was ancient and no longer real, a theoretical problem from the Bible demanding interpretation but having no practical consequences. The fact is that the "truth" which was so clear and indisputable to the early *tannaim* – i.e. that merit postpones punishment – became the subject of debate once more at the end of the *tannaitic* period because the practical problems which lay behind the exegetical issues were no longer in the front of anybody's mind.

We should mention one more controversy regarding the *sotah*: "'And a jealous spirit come over him' (*Num.* 5.14): This means that it is voluntary [to subject the wife to the trial of the bitter water], in the opinion of R. Ishmael; but in the opinion of R. Eliezer, he is obligated." (*Sifre Num.* 7, p. 12 ed. Horovitz). According to the version in the *Babylonian Talmud* (*bSot.* 3a), the discussants are R. Ishmael and R. Aqiba, but this seems more like a set formula than a reliable tradition. At first sight, this debate seems to follow the same line as the others, beginning with an attempt by R. Ishmael to reduce as much as possible the use of the trial of the *sotah* by making it the husband's option. But in this instance the debate seems in fact strictly theoretical, for R. Ishmael was still a

---

have relied on R. Joshua's remarks in the continuation of the *mishnah*: "A woman has more pleasure in one *kab* with תפלות than in nine *kabs* with abstinence" (*mSot.* 3.4), which beginning with Rashi has been interpreted to mean that women prefer regular sexual gratification combined with humble living conditions to abstinence combined with wealth.

[14] The position of Daniel Boyarin (*Carnal Israel: Reading Sex in Talmudic Culture* [Berkeley 1993], 170–4) is that the merit on which the entire argument revolves is the study of *Torah*, but I find this interpretation far-fetched.

[15] Some have imagined that women put through the ordeal died from fear, even if they were not guilty; this of course cannot be proven either way, see Biale (above, n. 3), 187.

child when the Temple was destroyed, and the rite may have ceased even before he was born. His opponent, at least in *Sifre*, is R. Eliezer, an eye-witness to the Destruction and purveyor of a tradition that pre-dated that event; he knew a thing or two about the issue of the *sotah*, as we have seen, and his rejection of R. Ishmael's liberalizing reform indicates that, at least to the best of his knowledge, this had not previously been the practice.[16]

One of the reasons why the ritual trial of the *sotah* was abolished was that it had ceased to be effective, for "adulterers became many." Before it was re-voked, the rites was presumably in regular use, and one should expect to find examples of women whose husbands became jealous of them and forced them to undergo the trial. Yet in all the sources there is mention only of one woman of the Second Temple period – from the days of Shemaiah and Abtalion – who underwent the ordeal. She was a freed slave by the name of Karkemit to whom, surprisingly, not a priest but Shemaiah and Abtalion themselves administered the test (*mEduy.* 5.6; *bBer.* 19a; cf. *ySot.* 2.5, 18b). But the lack of examples in the sources (as opposed, for example, to the multiplicity of cases of women seeking advice from sages regarding their *niddah*) reveals more about the sour-ces than about the practice of the ritual. While the examination of menstruants was, at least after 70, entirely under the institutional authority of rabbis, the trial of the *sotah* lay in the domain of the Sadduccean priests, who by all indications retained exclusive control over it during the Second Temple period until its re-vocation after the destruction of the Temple or perhaps a bit before that. Since the rabbinic sources do not represent the priestly circles from the days of the Temple, and since no legal writings have survived from those circles, the pauci-ty of sources should cause no surprise.[17]

Divorce

Since adultery is difficult to prove, and since the trial of the *sotah* lost its credi-bility and usefulness toward the end of the Second Temple period, the sources tend to recommend punishing the adulterous wife with divorce.

Ben Sira, as we have seen, believed that a wicked wife had to be divorced (25.26). The rabbinic sources contain a whole list of reasons, such as spinning or

---

[16] For an odd view of the controversy between R. Aqiba and R. Ishmael, see S. Y. Hur-witz, "Rabbi Aqiba and the Laws of Matrimony in Israel," *Hashahar* 12 (1885), 383–4 [Hebrew].

[17] Some scholars have asked why Herod did not subject his wife Mariamme to the trial of the *sotah* when he suspected her; see A. M. Rabello, "*Hausgericht* in the House of Herod the Great?" in *Jerusalem in the Second Temple Period: Abraham Schalit Memorial Volume*, edd. A. Oppenheimer, U. Rappaport and M. Stern (Jerusalem 1980), 121–3 [He-brew]. I find the entire question irrelevant as I will show presently.

nursing in public, which require divorcing one's wife and even withholding her *ketubbah* as a fine. To this we should add the opinion of R. Judah the Patriarch: "It was taught: When a pedlar leaves a house and the woman within is fastening her petticoat, since the thing is ugly she must, said Rabbi, go. If spittle is found on the upper part of the curtained bed, since the thing is ugly, she must, said Rabbi, go. If shoes lie under the bed, since the thing is ugly, she must, said Rabbi, go" (*bYeb.* 24b–25a). As opposed to instances we have previously examined, in which divorce perforce followed proven infractions, Rabbi requires a woman not only to be chaste but to appear chaste, and therefore he imposes divorce on the woman who only gives the impression of having betrayed her husband. This ruling by Rabbi does not have the force of *halakhah* but is a recommendation based on strict moral grounds.

If all the cases discussed so far – in which divorce has been either obligatory or at the very least highly recommended – have represented the necessary conditions for divorce, what were the sufficient conditions? This question lay at the heart of a famous controversy between the Schools of Shammai and Hillel: "The School of Shammai say: A man may not divorce his wife unless he has found unchastity in her, for it is written, 'Because he has found in her *indecency* (unchastity) in anything (ערות דבר)' (*Deut.* 24.1)" (*mGitt.* 9.10); by this view, the sufficient condition is, just as we have already seen, sexual licentiousness, which was also, at least according to *Matthew*, the view of Jesus (5.31; 19.9).[18] By contrast, "The School of Hillel say: [He may divorce her] even if she spoiled a dish for him, for it is written, 'Because he has found in her indecency in *anything*' (*Deut.* 24.1)" (*mGitt.* 9.10); by this view, any pretext is sufficient cause for divorce. Yet R. Aqiba outdid them both: "Even if he found another fairer than she, for it is written, 'And it shall be if she find no favor in his eyes …' (*Deut.* 24.1)" (*mGitt.* 9.10; cf. *Sifre Deut.* 269, p. 288 ed. Finkelstein); that is, a man need find no real fault at all in his wife in order to divorce her.[19] A parable illustrates the opinion that a woman may be divorced even for something which can be easily amended: "It is like the king who became angry with his wife. He summoned a scribe to come and write her a bill of divorce. Before the scribe ar-

---

[18] An extremely detailed analysis but rather unconvincing interpretation of this passage in Matthew is offered by A. Isaksson, *Marriage and Ministry in the New Testament: A Study with Special References to Mt. 19:13–22 and 1Cor. 11:3–16 = Seminarii Neotestamentici Upsalensis* XXIV (Lund 1965), 152–66.

[19] Two conflicting attitudes to this saying of Aqiba's can be found in modern literature, both connecting Aqiba's utterance to his own marriage: J. Goldin, "Toward a Profile of the Tanna Aqiba ben Joseph," *Journal of the American Oriental Society* 96 (1976), 38–56, who claims that Aqiba's great love for his wife made loveless cohabitation abominable in his eyes; and *contra*, Roslyn Lacks (*Women and Judaism: Myth, History and Struggle* [New York 1980], 128), who suggests that Aqiba formulated this law because he was insensitive to his wife's love, ungrateful for her loyalty, and probably followed the precept himself in his own career.

rived the king became placated with his wife. The king said: Can the scribe leave here at odds [with us]? Instead he said to him: Come, write that I double her *ketubbah*" (*Sifre Num.* 131, p. 170 ed. Horovitz).

R. Aqiba's approach to divorce is extreme in the eyes of everyone else, and even if it gained *halakhic* standing, the sages voiced their moral disapproval of divorce, seeing it as something better avoided: "R. Eliezer said: Whoever divorces his first wife, the very altar sheds tears for him" (*bSanh.* 22a). Extreme pietist groups during the Second Temple period gave *halakhic* status to this moral precept. In the Gospels we read: "Whoever divorces his wife and marries another commits adultery against her" (*Mark* 10.11; *Luke* 16.18). This may also have been the law for the Dead Sea Sect, but opinions are divided on this question.[20]

Thus far it should be clear that divorce was always the right and responsibility of the husband to initiate. Jewish law was asymmetrical in this respect, as opposed to Roman law, which grants the wife the right to divorce her husband. As Josephus notes in passing, in the middle of Nicolaus' account of the divorce bill sent by Salome to Costobarus: "It is only the man who is permitted by us to [initiate a divorce], and even a divorced woman may not marry again on her own initiative unless her former husband consents" (*AJ* 15.259). This observation, although embedded within an account based on Nicolaus, is Josephus' own, since he says "by us [Jews]," and Jewish law held no particular interest for Nicolaus.[21] A quite clear statement, in any case, is made by the rabbis: "The man who divorces is not similar to the woman who is divorced, for the woman is divorced either willingly or unwillingly whereas the man divorces her only at his will" (*mYeb.* 14.1; cf. *tKet.* 12.3). But even the rabbis were aware of the need in some exceptional cases to force the husband to divorce his wife: "And it should also be said in the matter of women's bills of divorce, they compel the man until he says: It is my will" (*mArakh.* 6.5; cf. *Sif. Dibura Dehoba* 3.15, p. 31 ed. Finkelstein; *bYeb.* 106a).[22] The *Mishnah* contains an interesting list of the exceptional cases in which the husband was in fact forced to grant his wife a bill of divorce: "he that is afflicted with boils, or that has a polypus, or that collects [dog's excrements], or that is a coppersmith or a tanner" (*mKet.* 7.10). These are men who

---

[20] Those who think so include: Y. Yadin, "L'attitude Essénienne envers la polygamie et le divorce," *Revue Biblique* 79 (1972), 98–9; J. A. Fitzmayer, "Divorce among First Century Palestinian Jews," *Eretz-Israel* 14 (1978), *103–*10. Some think that the sectarians opposed only polygamy, not divorce: G. Vermes, "Sectarian Matrimonial *Halakhah* in the Damascus Role," *Journal of Jewish Studies* 25 (1974), 197–202; Isaksson (above, n. 18), 60–1.

[21] Josephus' additional remark could refer to the minority opinion of R. Eliezer in the following: "If a man divorced his wife and said to her: You are permitted to any man, except so-and-so, R. Eliezer permits it but the sages forbid it" (*mGitt.* 9.1).

[22] See Hauptman (above, n. 11), 26–7.

have repulsive bodily defects or bad smell, but we should note that there is nothing in the list about physical or emotional abuse.

Josephus mentions three men who divorced their wives: Herod, his son Archelaus and Josephus himself. Josephus relates that Herod divorced his first wife Doris in order to marry a daughter of the Hasmonean royal house (*BJ* 1.241; *AJ* 14.300), but after he executed Mariamme the Hasmonean Herod brought back Doris (*BJ* 1.451; *AJ* 16.85). In the end, Herod divorced Doris once again when he discovered her part in the plot by her son against himself (*BJ* 1.590; *AJ* 17.68). On the same occasion he divorced another wife, Mariamme daughter of the high priest Shimeon b. Boethus, for complicity in the same plot (*BJ* 1.599; *AJ* 17.78). Herod's son Archelaus is said to have divorced his wife in order to marry his brother's widow (*BJ* 2.115; *AJ* 17.350). Josephus says of himself that he divorced his second wife (*Vita* 426). Pheroras, Herod's brother, is also said by Josephus to have divorced his wife, but he did so against his will and afterwards took her back (*AJ* 16.198–9).

The rabbinic sources also contain but sparse references to actual cases of divorce. In fact, R. Yose the Galilean is the only one we know by name (*yKet.* 11.3, 34b; *Gen. R.* 17.3, pp. 152–5 ed. Theodor-Albeck), and there are in addition two anonymous bills of divorce brought before rabbinical courts, one before Rabban Gamaliel (*mGitt.* 1.5; *tGitt.* 1.4) and the other before R. Ishmael (*tGitt.* 1.3).[23]

Yet the rabbis were quite critical of the biblical law permitting a man who divorced his wife to take her back if she had not married someone else in the meantime (*Deut.* 24.2–4). The following passage, formulated in the style of the lists found in wisdom literature, will illustrate: "Four are they whom the mind

---

[23] And see further, above chapter 3, n. 44. *Tannaitic* literature mentions other bills of divorce and other cases of husbands intending to divorce their wives, but these are not useful as historical evidence. We have already encountered the case, from the days of Baba ben Buta, of the man who wanted to divorce his wife without a *ketubbah*. One of the stories meant to explain the Destruction tells of a man who, on the advice of a friend, divorces his wife because she had apparently betrayed him, whereupon the same friend went and married her (*bGitt.* 58a); the obvious *aggadic* nature of the story renders it unsuitable as hisorical evidence. We have also already examined the story of Rabbi's son, who wanted to divorce his wife after ten childless years, and also a similar case handled by R. Shimeon bar Yohai; in both instances, the divorce was not carried out. All these stories bear the unmistakable signs of *aggadot*. Two more cases of men who divorce their wives – one on his deathbed (*tGitt.* 6.4), and the other with the intention of committing suicide (*mGitt.* 6.6) – are mentioned only to illustrate the *halakhic* principle that the purpose of the bill of divorce (*get*) is to exempt the woman from levirate marriage or to ensure her inheritance; they are not relevant here, for they illustrate exceptional, non-representative uses of the *get*. R. Meir, too, is said to have written a *get* for a woman who came and announced to him and his disciples: "Rabbi, one of you has betrothed me through intercourse" (*bSanh.* 11a), although here the divorce was clearly a formal legal act and not a true divorce by a husband of his wife.

cannot endure.[24] These are they: ... and some say: the man who divorces his wife the first time and the second and brings her back" (*bPes.* 113b). A parable from the period may indicate that since divorce was easy, a man could marry the same woman many times: "It is like the king who got angry at his wife and divorced her. Some time later he became placated towards her. She immediately put on her girdle and her gown and indulged him too much" (*Sif. Shemini, Mekhilta de-Miluim* 5, 43d ed. Weiss).

The return of a divorced wife was not a practice confined to the house of Herod. The *ketubbah* of Salome the daughter of Yohanan Galgoula, whom Elai b. Shimeon took back and remarried after having divorced her, was discovered in the Judaean Desert.[25] Rabbinic literature preserves the case of a man from Saidan who divorced his wife as a result of an oath but the sages permitted him to take her back (*mGitt.* 4.7).[26] We also hear of a girl married as a minor whom her husband later divorced but then remarried (*tYeb.* 13.5).

Josephus' source informed him that Herod Antipas promised Herodias, whom he dearly loved, that he would divorce his wife, the daughter of the Nabataean king Aretas, but before he could do so his wife left him and fled to her father's house (*AJ* 18.110–12). The wife's flight violated Jewish law, but we should not expect the daughter of a foreign king connected to the Herodian house only by marriage to adhere to Jewish law. Yet Josephus found in his sources several other cases of women who abandoned their husbands and went and married other men. For example, it is reported that Berenice, daughter of Agrippa I, left her husband Polemo king of Cilicia (*AJ* 20.146); that her sister, Drusilla, left her husband Azizus king of Emesa to marry the Roman governor of Judaea at the time, Felix (*AJ* 20.143); and that Berenice's second sister, Mariamme, left her husband Julius Archelaus to marry Demetrius, the alabarch of Alexandria (*AJ* 20.147).[27] Josephus relates another case outside the Herodian dynasty, that of himself: his first wife was a Jewish captive whom he married, he says, by order of the emperor Vespasian, but she left him (*Vita* 415).[28] In rabbinic literature we find the case of R. Eliezer b. R. Shimeon, who was abandoned by his wife after he showed a preference for going to the study-house

---

[24] Cf. *Prov.* 30.21: "Under three things the earth trembles, and under four it cannot bear up."

[25] See P. Benoit, J. T. Milik and R. de Vaux, *Les Grottes de Murabaʿât = Discoveries in the Judaean Desert* II (Oxford 1961), 243–54.

[26] On the place-name, see above, chapter 3, n. 44.

[27] The story of Agrippa's three daughters all leaving their husbands bears the stamp of an attempt to malign the king's descendants; the information should not be taken at face value. On the nature of the source, see D. R. Schwartz, "KATA TOYTON TON KAIPON, Josephus' Source on Agrippa II," *Jewish Quarterly Review* 72 (1981–2), 241–68.

[28] Cf. Stein's suggestion (in his Hebrew translation of *Vita*) that Josephus' first wife left him because he was a traitor.

rather than staying with her at home (*bBM* 84b). These examples illustrate that even women, in violation of *halakhah*, left their husbands without first acquiring a bill of divorce. The *halakhic* consequences are not discussed in the sources.

The most extreme case of a wife abandoning her husband is that of Herod's sister Salome, who not only left her second husband Costobarus but also sent him a bill of divorce (*AJ* 15.260). We can assume that Salome, a Roman citizen, based her action on Roman law.[29] Josephus also relates that Herodias married Herod Antipas while still married to Herod son of Herod (*AJ* 18.110), but it is unclear whether she simply abandoned him, sent him a *get* (following Salome's example), or was divorced by him. J. T. Milik claimed[30] to possess a *get*, apparently found by Beduins in Nahal Hever, given by a woman, Salome daughter of Joseph, to her husband, Eliezer b. Huni. This unpublished document has for some time served as a major piece of evidence for the belief that in the Second Temple period women could divorce their husbands by giving them a bill of divorce.[31] J. Greenfield of the Hebrew University, who now controls the document, contends that Milik's reading is mistaken and the *get* was in fact given to the woman by the man;[32] but until the document becomes publicly available no final determination can be made. This whole problem, it should be noted, is a general one that occurs often in the study of women, namely, that scholars force their own readings on documents whose contents seem strange or contradict Jewish law. Obviously a reading cannot be rejected simply because it does not correspond to *halakhah* or the individual scholar's understanding of the status of women.

Divorce was performed by giving the *get*, called "bill of divorcement" (ספר כרתות) in the Bible (*Deut.* 24.1). There are quite detailed provisions in Je-

---

[29] See A. M. Rabello, "Divorce of Jews in the Roman Empire," *The Jewish Law Annual* 4 (1981), 92–3.

[30] J. T. Milik, "Le travail d'édition des manuscrits du Désert de Juda," *Volume du congres Strasbourg 1956 = Supplements to Vetus Testamentum* IV (Leiden 1956), 21.

[31] The debate over whether women in Judaea of the Second Temple period, even if not in Pharisaic circles, were legally permitted to divorce their husbands, is raging in recent years. After Milik's announcement, E. Bammel, "*Markus* 10 11f. und das jüdische Eherecht," *Zeitschrift für Neu Testamentliche Wissenschaft* 61 (1970), 95–101 argued that that *get* was not the only piece of evidence for such a phenomenon. Ten years later, his claims were for the most part repeated by Bernadette J. Brooten, "Konnten Frauen im alten Judentum die Scheidung betreiben? Überlegung zu *Mk* 10, 11–12 und *1Kor* 7,10–11," *Evangelische Theologie* 42 (1982), 65–80. Brooten's article provoked greater interest because it seemed to be motivated not only by scientific interest but also by ideological considerations. See the response by E. Schweizer, "Scheidungsrecht der jüdischen Frau? Weibliche Jünger Jesu?" *Evangelische Theologie* 42 (1982), 294–300; H. Weder, "Perspective der Frauen," *Evangelische Theologie* 43 (1983), 175–8; and Brooten's answer: "Zur Debatte über das Scheidungsrecht der jüdischen Frau," *ibid.* (1983), 466–78.

[32] Greenfield announced this in a public lecture in 1989.

wish law for the giving of the *get* and for dealing with problems that may arise during this process. Much of the discussion in rabbinic literature is theoretical and involves absurd situations far removed from the realities of daily life.[33] We do possess a *get* discovered in a cave in Wadi Muraba'at which a man wrote for his wife in Masada, apparently in the year 72 CE;[34] it is in Aramaic and is the only actual *get* from the Second Temple period.

In sum, the number of actual documented cases of divorce during the period is relatively small, and in many of them the marriage of the two partners was restored. The main reasons for the paucity of actual cases seems to be economic: divorce was very expensive for the man, who had to pay his former wife her *ketubbah*, for which all his property was accountable.[35] Furthermore, the husband always had the option of marrying a second wife, although only those who had the means to support two wives could do this. Divorce, like polygamy, was a privilege which only those with a fairly high income could enjoy. Thus we find in a number of marriage contracts a clause in which husbands commit themselves to supporting their wives "according to Hellenic custom," which may be a means of making divorce easier. By contrast, it is interesting to note the relatively large number of women who are said to have abandoned their husbands, even though most examples of this took place in the Herodian house.

Widowhood

A woman's married life was liable to end, if not by divorce, then by the death of her husband. Already in the biblical period, widows and orphans were treated as the weakest members of society, despite the fact that both divorce and widowhood were a kind of legal liberation for a woman, making her a legal entity unto herself;[36] or as the rabbis put it, "A woman acquires her freedom (lit. acquires herself) in two ways ... by a bill of divorce and by the death of her husband" (*mQidd.* 1.1). The *Testament of Job* relates that Job used to give charity to widows (9.3; 5; 10.3). Jesus admonishes the Pharisees, in the best prophetic tradition, for seeking honor and at the same time "swallowing widows' houses"

---

[33] There is considerable research on this. See in particular, Wegner (above, n. 13), 129–38, and also Daniella Piatteli, "The Marriage Contract and Bill of Divorce in Ancient Hebrew Law," *Jewish Law Annual* 4 (1981), 77–8; Biale (above, n. 3), 70–81; Swidler (above, n. 3), 154–66.

[34] Benoit *et al.* (above, n. 25), 104–9.

[35] "Her *ketubbah* is large," see *bGitt.* 57a; 58a and also the story of the divorce of R. Yose the Galilean quoted above; for a literary analysis of the story, see Y. Fraenkel, "Paranomasia in *Aggadic* Narratives," in *Studies in Hebrew Narrative Art = Scripta Hierosolymitana* XXVII, edd. J. Heinemann and S. Werses (Jerusalem 1978), 28–35.

[36] On this see Wegner (above, n. 13), 14–7.

(*Mark* 12.40; *Matt.* 23.14; *Luke* 20.47), that is, for wronging the weakest and most defenseless element of society. The rabbis maintain that there is a clear difference between the slave who buys his freedom and the woman who acquires hers: "It has been taught: R. Eliezer said: ... A slave gains when he acquires freedom from his master, but for a woman it is a liability, for she becomes disqualified from receiving *terumah* and loses her maintenance" (*bGitt.* 12b); in other words, the divorcée and widow suffer economic loss from their change in status.

For this reason the rabbis viewed remarriage as the best solution for the unfortunate women who were either divorced or widowed. The verse, "And I will slay you with a sword, and your wives shall be widows and your children orphans" (*Ex.* 22.28), was interpreted by the rabbis in the following manner: "What need is there of saying, 'And your wives shall be widows and your children orphans'? It is but to indicate that they will be widowed, and yet not widows, in the same sense as when it is said, 'So they were shut up unto the day of their death, in widowhood, with their husband alive' (*2 Sam.* 20.3)" (*Mekhilta de R. Ishmael, Mishpatim* 18, p. 314 ed. Horovitz-Rabin); in other words, a curse worse than widowhood is that of the *aggunah*, a situation in which the husband has disappeared and no one can be found to testify that he died, so that his wife cannot remarry. Consequently most of the rabbis' attention in the matter of widowhood was focused on *halakhic* means of helping women by proving their widowhood and thus making them eligible for remarriage. Accordingly, only one witness, even a woman (who would normally be ineligible even as one of two witnesses), was required in order to prove the husband's death and free the woman (*mYeb.* 16.5–7; *bYeb.* 115a).

Despite the opinion that the rabbis set the widow's *ketubbah* at a low sum (only 100 *zuz*: *mKet.* 1.2) because she was no longer a virgin,[37] their purpose would also have been, it seems to me, to have made her a more desirable bride, for a smaller initial outlay would be required from her husband. It should be remembered that a widow had already collected her *ketubbah* of 200 *zuz* when her first husband died. A widow's wedding was set for Thursday, "for if he would marry her on any day of the week, he would leave her and go to his work; so they issued a ruling that he should marry her on Thursday: Thursday, Friday and the Sabbath, three days without working: he rejoices with her for three days" (*tKet.* 1.1). Clearly, the idea here is that the man who marries a widow is not thought to be as happy with his acquisition as the man who marries a virgin, and the purpose of the ruling is to ensure that the newlyweds would rejoice with each other.

---

[37] L. M. Epstein, *The Jewish Marriage Contract: A Study in the Status of Women in Jewish Law* (New York 1927), 71–2.

On the other hand, while the rabbis saw the marriage of a widow as aid to a woman in distress, other groups with a more extreme moral outlook idealized the woman who chose to remain a widow and mourn the man of her youth. The best example of this is the rich widow Judith, the heroine in the book of *Judith*, who locks herself away after her husband's death to pray and fast, leaving her house once to save her people from the Assyrian Holofernes but then returning and putting back on her widow's garments, in which she dies.[38] In early Christianity, even in the Palestinian community with its Jewish roots, widowhood gained high respectability, alongside the ideal of not marrying at all. In *Luke* we find in the Temple the widow Anna, daughter of Phanuel, who had remained a widow for 84 years (2.36–8).[39] "Widow" even became the technical term for women who served in the early Christian community (*Acts* 9.39).[40] Only one woman in rabbinic literature is said to have deliberately chosen to remain a widow. When R. Judah the Patriarch proposed marriage to the widow of R. Eliezer b. R. Shimeon, she answered him: "Shall a vessel that was used for a sacred purpose be used for a profane purpose?" (*yShab.* 10.5, 12c; *Eccl. R.* 11.2.1).[41]

By contrast, widowhood in Judaism was in most instances a temporary situation, and the sources describe many cases of widows remarrying; there are only very few cases of women remaining widows long after the deaths of their husbands. The most prominent example is that of the Hasmonean Alexandra, daughter of Hyrcanus II, who was married to Alexander, son of Aristobulus II, and remained a widow in Herod's house after her husband was executed (*BJ* 1.185; *AJ* 14.125), until she herself was sentenced to death (*AJ* 15.247–51). Alexandra's prolonged widowhood could perhaps be explained by the decline of the influence of the Hasmonean dynasty, as a result of which Hasmonean heire-

---

[38] On the choice of a widow as the heroine of the story, see J. Licht, "The *Book of Judith* as a Work of Literature," in *Baruch Kurzweil Memorial Volume,* edd. M. Z. Kaddari, A. Saltman and M. Schwarcz (Ramat Gan 1975), 169–83 [Hebrew]. What the story lacks, in my opinion, is a "happy end" in which the righteous heroine marries a righteous hero; the hero is present – the proselyte Achior the Ammonite – only the marriage is missing, to the sorrow and surprise of the reader. We can assume that the first Christian widows aspired to the same ideal.

[39] On the literary parallel between this legendary character and Judith, see J. K. Elliot, "Anna's Age (*Luke* 2:36–37)," *Novum Testamentum* 30 (1988), 100–2.

[40] See Jo Ann McNamara, "Wives and Widows in Early Christian Thought," *International Journal of Women's Studies* 2 (1979), 575–92. In *1 Cor.* 7.8, Paul counsels the small group of widows in the Christian community in Corinth not to remarry; the city lies outside the geographical limits of the present study. On this topic see: S. Davies, *The Revolt of the Widows: The Social World of the Apocryphal Acts* (Carbondale 1980); Antoinette C. Wire, *The Corinthian Women Prophets: A Reconstruction through Paul's Rhetoric* (Minneapolis 1990), 82–97.

[41] This Palestinian *aggadah* on the righteousness of the wife of R. Eliezer b. R. Shimeon should be compared to the *aggadah* in the *Babylonian Talmud* (quoted above pp. 145–6) on the wickedness of the same woman (*bBM* 84b).

sses were no longer the most desired brides. Herod might even have interpreted marriage to Alexandra as a conspiracy against his own house. Herod's mother, Cyprus, is also not known to have remarried after the death of her husband Antipater (*BJ* 1.226; *AJ* 14.280–1), although this can be explained in opposite fashion, i.e. a husband of sufficient age and honor could not be found for the mother of the king, who could by no means be anyone's second wife. Moreover, as a result of psychological restraints Herod perhaps could not bring himself to seek a match for her as actively and openly as he did for the other women in his family. Thus his sister, Salome, did not long remain a widow after her first husband, Joseph, was executed (*BJ* 1.443; *AJ* 15.87); she was married to Costobarus (*AJ* 15.254), and after his execution (*AJ* 15.252) she remained a widow for some years but in the end had to marry Alexas (*BJ* 1.566; *AJ* 17.9–10). The wives of the sons of Mariamme the Hasmonean both married again after their husbands were killed: Glaphyra, at first Alexander's wife, was remarried twice, first to Juba king of Libya and then to her first husband's half-brother, Archelaus (*BJ* 2.115–6; *AJ* 17.349–50), although this last marriage violated Jewish law, for Glaphyra had had sons with Alexander and her marriage to Archelaus was thus considered to be incest. On the advice of his son Antipater, Herod married off Aristobulus' wife, Berenice the daughter of Salome, to the brother of Antipater's mother Doris (*BJ* 1.553; *AJ* 17.9). Agrippa I's daughter Berenice also did not long remain a widow after the death of her first husband, Marcus son of Alexander the alabarch of Alexandria, but was married to her uncle, Herod of Chalcis (*AJ* 19.276–7), and after his death (*BJ* 2.221; *AJ* 20.104) in turn married Polemo, king of Cilicia (*AJ* 20.145–6). Babatha, whose archive was found in the Judaean Desert, married Judah Khthusion after the death of her first husband, Jesus b. Jesus,[42] although in this case it should be noted that Babatha was her second husband's second wife. The priest Joshua b. Gamla married the widow Martha daughter of Boethus (*mYeb.* 6.4); problems arose when immediately after the engagement he was appointed high priest and he was thence *halakhically* forbidden to marry a widow, but despite the prohibition he brought her into his house as his wife, thus creating a *halakhic* precedent.

Anonymous widows are very rare in the sources. There is a poor widow in the New Testament who contributes a very small sum of money to the Temple (*Mark* 12.42–4; *Luke* 21.2–4), but she appears to be more fictional than real, for the story is built around a saying of Jesus, and it is almost axiomatic in text-criticism of the New Testament that Jesus' sayings pre-date the stories, which in fact were formed around the sayings. Moreover, a similar story is told in the rabbinic *midrash* of *Leviticus Rabbah* (3.5, p. 67–8 ed. Marguleis)

---

[42] Y. Yadin, *Bar Kokhba: Rediscovery of the Legendary Hero of the Second Jewish Revolt against Rome* (London 1971), 237–9.

Rabbinical stories concerning widowhood usually describe the special exertions the rabbis made to confirm that a woman's husband in fact died, in order to permit her to marry another man. R. Tarfon is said to have cross-examined a witness who came to him in order to permit, on the strength of his single testimony, the wife of the deceased to remarry (*tYeb.* 14.10; *yYeb.* 16.5, 15d; cf. *mYeb.* 16.6). Abba Yudan of Saidan[43] relates two instances of women remarrying on the strength of the testimony of gentiles who claimed to have witnessed the deaths of the women's husbands (*tYeb.* 14.7–8; *bYeb.* 126a).[44] On the basis of the testimony of only one witness, Rabban Gamaliel the Elder permitted the widows of the fallen at Tel Azra to remarry (*mYeb.* 16.7); and in two instances the sages allowed widows to remarry on the basis of an "echo (בת קול)," i.e. a mere rumor of their husbands' deaths (*mYeb.* 16.6; cf. *tYeb.* 14.7). Rabbi judged womens' testimony sufficient to allow the widows of men who drowned in a shipwreck to remarry (*bYeb.* 115a); the *Mishnah* preserves the story of a female innkeeper whose testimony of a man's death was considered sufficient to allow his widow to remarry (*mYeb.* 16.7); finally, a brigand sentenced to death by the Roman authorities is said to have confessed, as he was being led to the gallows, to the murder of a certain Jew, in order to permit his widow in Lod to remarry (*tYeb.* 4.5; *yYeb.* 2.11, 4b; *bYeb.* 25b). The sages affirm that the ruling by the School of Hillel which allows the testimony of a woman who comes from the harvest and claims that her husband had died, was based on an actual case (*mYeb.* 15.2; and esp. *bYeb.* 116b). In none of these instances of widows receiving permission to remarry is it known whether they actually did remarry or whether the permission was merely formal and general, for whenever they chose to use it.

Widowhood, then, was a dismal state for a woman to fall into; the rabbis urged widows to remarry and made special efforts to remove obstacles in their way to this goal. To judge from the sources, not many Jewish women remained widows for very long.

---

[43] Note the recurrence of this place-name, and see above, chapter 3, n. 44.

[44] The second instance involves gentiles who witnessed the deaths at Betar, although this source contradicts another which well illustrates the worst situation that could befall a widow: *ARNA* 38 (p. 115 ed. Schechter) reports that not a soul survived at Betar to testify to the deaths of women's husbands and thereby permit them to remarry. This is one of the places in *Abot de Rabbi Nathan* which is difficult to accept.

Levirate Marriage (*yibbum*)

A woman whose husband died childless was required by biblical law to be married by one of the deceased husband's brothers, in order to continue his name.[45] Since the law does not merely appear in the Bible but is highlighted by the story of Judah and Tamar as well as that of Ruth and Boaz, the framers of *halakhah* in the Second Temple period had no choice but to accept it and to try to justify it, and act according to its precepts, despite the fact that the original need answered by the law – to keep the patrimony within the family – had disappeared. The law of levirate marriage is obviously the basis of the account, appearing in all three synoptic gospels, of the Sadducees' question to Jesus regarding the woman who was married to seven brothers in succession, for as each died childless, the next in line was obliged to marry her (*Mark* 12.19–25; *Matt.* 22.24–30; *Luke* 20.28–35).

Members of two high priestly families in Jerusalem were born from levirate marriages (*tYeb.* 1.10; *yYeb.* 1.6, 3a; *bYeb.* 15b). Similarly, Rabban Gamaliel is said to have married the co-wife of his daughter, the widow of Abba (*bYeb.* 15a). The wife of Ben Megusath, although a man-made eunuch in Jerusalem, is said to have been taken by his brother's wife in levirate marriage (*mYeb.* 8.4). We also hear of a priest who died from a wound to his sexual organ after a fall from the roof the Chamber of Hewn Stone, giving rise to the question of whether his widow should be subjected to *yibbum* (*tYeb.* 10.3). The sources contain no evidence of what was actually done in this case, but if the rabbis' precepts were followed, levirate marriage was not performed. From the days of the Temple we know of a very famous and wealthy woman – the daughter or daughter-in-law of Naqdimon b. Gurion – who was waiting for her brother-in-law's decision on whether or not to marry her (*tKet.* 5.9; *bKet.* 65a; *ARNA* 6, p. 31, ed. Schechter),[46] but we do not know what the brother-in-law decided in the end. The last documented case of levirate marriage is that of R. Yose b. Halafta, who married his brother's widow and produced five sons with her (*yYeb.* 1.1, 2b; *Gen. R.* 85.5, p. 1038 ed. Theodor-Albeck; cf. *bShab.* 118b). All these instances but the last happened before the Destruction or immediately afterwards (the case of Rabban Gamaliel). The *Palestinian Talmud* does preserve a story, dating to the time of R. Judah the Patriarch, in which Rabbi convinces a man with twelve de-

---

[45] On the origin and tribal character of this law, see D. Mace, *Hebrew Marriage: A Sociological Study* (New York 1953), 95–117; L. M. Epstein, *Marriage Laws in the Bible and Talmud* (Cambridge MA 1942), 77–89.

[46] On this story, see Ofra Meir, "The Story as a Hermeneutic Device," *Association of Jewish Studies Review* 7–8 (1982–3), 231–62.

ceased brothers to marry all twelve widows (*yYeb*. 4.12, 6b), but this story has a distinctively *aggadic* ring to it.[47]

Josephus explains levirate marriage as an attempt to ease the burden of the widow's crisis (*AJ* 4.254). Yet the *mishnaic* tractate *Yebamot* opens with a list of married women who are exempt from levirate marriage (1.1–2); these women are the "co-wives" of women whom the biblical laws against incest prevent from marrying their brothers-in-law. For example, if a man gave his daughter in marriage to his brother (a match considered very desirable, as we have seen), he obviously cannot take his own daughter in levirate marriage if his brother dies childless; Jewish law also exempts the deceased brother's other wives from levirate marriage in this case.

One indication of the date of this particular law is the controversy it provoked between the Schools of Shammai and Hillel (*mYeb*. 1.4), a controversy which was still alive during the generation of Yavneh and in which quite a few sages took part (*bYeb*. 16a). The position of the School of Hillel, whose victory in the end exempted a daughter's co-wives from levirate marriage, typifies the whole series of laws aimed at reducing so far as possible the force of the biblical law. Another measure of the success of the School of Hillel is the clear preference shown by the *halakhah* for *halitzah*, the biblical alternative to levirate marriage whereby the brother of the deceased discharges his responsibility in a ceremony of public self-humiliation, and at the same time frees his brother's wife to marry any other man. As the *Mishnah* puts it: "Beforetime the duty of levirate marriage came before the duty of *halitzah* when they acted intent on fulfilling a religious duty; but now when they so act, but are not intent on fulfilling a religious duty, they have enjoined that the duty of *halitzah* takes precedence over the duty of levirate marriage" (*mBekh*. 1.7; *bKet*. 64a). That is, the humiliating public ceremony became a merely formal act whose purpose was to relieve society of the restraints of an ancient, obsolete practice.[48]

The *Mishnah*'s language in this passage reveals the rabbis' tendency to embrace the past as a much better time, when everyone acted properly, as opposed to their own time which they viewed as an age of moral decline. Yet on closer inspection, we find that the passage contains a paradox and aims to invalidate levirate marriage under all circumstances. If a man wants to marry his deceased brother's wife by *yibbum*, he cannot be permitted to do so since the expression of his will is taken to be a sign of his desire for the woman herself, and his pur-

---

[47] See, e.g. I. M. Gafni, "The Institution of Marriage in Rabbinic Times," *The Jewish Family: Metaphor and Memory*, ed. D. Kraemer (Oxford 1987), 22.

[48] This development is explained, in part, also by Biale (above, n. 3), 115–6. See also, J. Katz, *Halakah and Kabbalah: Studies in the History of Jewish Religion, its Various Faces and Social Relevance* (Jerusalem 1984), 127–30 [Hebrew].

pose is therefore not limited only to the performance of a religious duty; in such a case, the man must undergo *halitzah*. But if, on the other hand, the man does not want to marry her by *yibbum*, then he certainly does not desire her at all and could then in fact marry her by *yibbum*, except that he himself chooses the alternative of *halitzah*. The same idea appears in less sophisticated form in the *Talmud*: "It was taught: Abba Saul said: If a man marries his deceased brother's wife on account of her beauty, or in order to gratify his sexual desires or with any other ulterior motive, it is as if he has infringed the laws of incest, and I am inclined to think that the child [of such a union] is a bastard" (*bYeb.* 39b). Even the story about R. Yose b. Halafta, who married his brother's widow by *yibbum*, makes a special point of stressing that the sage did so not out of sexual desire but to perform a religious obligation: "R. Yose b. R. Halafta married his brother's [childless] widow, with whom he had intercourse only five times and penetrated through a sheet,[49] and he planted five plants" (*Gen. R.* 85.5, p. 1038 ed. Theodor-Albeck). That is, R. Yose had intercourse with his sister-in-law for the sole purpose of producing offspring, and each instance the sexual act was performed without lust and each resulted in pregnancy. Thus *halitzah* was preferred over *yibbum* for the childless widow.[50]

There are fewer cases of *halitzah* mentioned in the sources, and all are later than the Second Temple period. At the beginning of the *tannaitic* period, we find R. Eliezer b. R. Zadok advising a doctor who is about to depart on a journey to perform *halitzah* for his brother's widow, as she is waiting for his decision on *yibbum* (*tYeb.* 6.8). We also hear incidentally that R. Tarfon and his disciples were witnesses at a *halitzah* ceremony (*tYeb.* 12.15; *Sifre Deut.* 291, p. 311 ed. Finkelstein; *bYeb.* 101b; *bQidd.* 14a). Another case involves a man who performed *halitzah* in prison, apparently after the Bar Kokhba war, and the act was approved by R. Aqiba (*mYeb.* 12.5; *bYeb.* 104a). R. Ishmael is said to have taken a similar action, except that in his case it was done at night, apparently also because of the general state of emergency (*tYeb.* 12.9; *bYeb.* 104a); we might have

---

[49] There are interesting variants to this text - דרך הסדין: 1. "as the *hasidim* do (דרך חסדין)," 2. "as do the righteous (דרך כשרין)," 3. "in the Chaldean manner (דרך כשדין);" see Theodor-Albeck *ad loc.*; one can see how each variant grew out of the text and out of each other. The question is, which is the original. Without deciding on this matter, we should note that "as the *hasidim* do" suggests an approach to sex common to pietistic groups in the Second Temple period.

[50] S. Belkin, "Levirate and Agnate Marriage in Rabbinic and Cognate Literature," *Jewish Quarterly Review* 60 (1969), 298 viewed the size of tractate *Yebamot* and the extensive discussion on the subject by the rabbis as evidence that the institution of *yibbum* was widespread in the Hellenistic-Roman period. By contrast, he argued, the marriage of relatives is discussed far less in rabbinic literature and thus was far less practiced. This second claim, as I have shown, is in error. Now I will demonstrate that the first half of the argument is also false.

here a duplicated tradition of the same event. R. Hiyya is said to have deemed a *halitzah* valid in which the woman actually paid her brother-in-law to perform the ceremony and liberate her (*bYeb.* 106a). A tale is told about a woman from Saidan who had been married to a tanner and refused to marry his brother, who was also a tanner, and the sages obligated him to perform *halitzah* for her (*mKet.* 7.10).

To conclude: it appears that in the Second Temple period, *yibbum* or levirate marriage was more frequently practiced than *halitzah*, the rite by which a man renounces any intention of marrying his deceased brother's widow. Most known cases of *yibbum* date from then, and there is not even one instance of *halitzah* datable to the period. Yet in the *tannaitic* period, the situation reversed and *halitzah* was practiced instead of *yibbum*; we know of only two instances of levirate marriage from this period, that of Rabban Gamaliel who followed the *halakhah* according to the School of Shammai and married his daughter's co-wife, and that of R. Yose, whose levirate marriage is presented as exceptional and marvelous in its piety. Both are sages, who acted according to the strictest interpretation of the law; everyone else who consulted the sages received the advice to perform *halitzah*. Thus the preference for *halitzah* developed only after the destruction of the Temple. It is impossible to know whether the change in behavior preceded its appearance in law; they probably were mutually influential. In most instances, the rite of *halitzah* was the easiest course for both the widow and the brother-in-law; it would also have been a way to avoid polygamy that would result from *yibbum*. But these were not the reasons the sages used to justify their preference for *halitzah*; they argued rather that the man who wanted to contract levirate marriage was suspected of having improper thoughts and intentions, although we can assume that this argument was thought of after *halitzah* had already become preferred in practice.

Excursus - Probably the most famous case of *yibbum* from the Second Temple period is that of King Alexander Yannai. From the beginning of modern research it has been believed that the wife of Judah Aristobulus I, after she aided in the murder of her husband's brother Antigonus (*BJ* 1.76; *AJ* 13.308) and after the death of Judah Aristobulus himself, freed his other brother, Yannai, from prison (*BJ* 1.85; *AJ* 13.320) and married him.[51] Josephus never says any

---

[51] So, among others over the past 150 years: I. M. Jost, *Geschichte der Israeliten* I (Berlin 1820), Anhang: 29–31; F. Hitzig, *Geschichte des Volkes Israel* II (Leipzig 1869), 476; H. Ewald, *History of Israel* V (London 1880), 386, n. 5; E. Renan, *Histoire du peuple d'Israël* V (Paris 1893), 11, n. 2; E. Schürer, *Geschichte des jüdischen Volkes im Zeitalter Jesu Christi* I³ (Leipzig 1901), 277, n. 2; J. Wellhausen, *Israelitische und jüdische Geschichte*⁷ (Berlin 1914), 263; R. Marcus, *Josephus with an English Translation* = *Loeb Classical Library* VII (Cambridge MA 1958), 388–9; S. Zeitlin, "Queen Salome and King

such thing, but the belief is common even today. It is based on the fact that Aristobulus' wife, according to Josephus, was named Salina (Σαλίνα, *AJ* 13.320) Alexandra, and Yannai's wife's name, again on Josephus' evidence, was Alexandra (*BJ* 1.107; *AJ* 13.405), or Shelamzion according to rabbinic literature.[52] Scholars simply assumed that the names Salina and Shelamzion were identical and belonged to the same woman. There are two problems with this, the first onomastic and the second chronological: a) The name Salina is not in fact at all similar to Shelamzion, and the coincidence of the name Alexandra proves nothing since it was the most common name for women in the Hasmonean dynasty. It is true that the *Babylonian Talmud* reports that Shelamzion was the sister of Shimeon b. Shetah (and thus she could perhaps not have been from the Hasmonean house), but as we have demonstrated, all family relations reported only in the *Babylonian Talmud* are suspect, and we should assume that Yannai married his cousin. b) If Josephus is right that Hyrcanus II was at least 80 years old when executed by Herod in the year 30 BCE (*AJ* 15.178), then he was born to Yannai in the year 110 BCE at the latest; but Yannai, according to the best of our knowledge, rose to the throne only in 103 BCE, when the son would already have been seven. Thus it is difficult to imagine that if Yannai and Shelamzion were the parents of Hyrcanus, Shelamzion had been previously married to Aristobulus. Needless to say, Hyrcanus would not likely have been the son of Shelamzion and Judah Aristobulus, for then there would have been no need for a levirate marriage. This particular case, therefore, cannot be considered an example of *yibbum*,[53] and there is no point in all the detailed argumentation concerning the propriety of Yannai's marriage to his brother's widow, for "as for a high priest ...others can contract

---

Jannaeus Alexander," *Jewish Quarterly Review* 51 (1960–1), 5; Alyn Brodsky, *The Kings Depart* (New York 1974), 196; J. Klausner, "Judah Aristobulus and Jannaeus Alexander," in *The World History of the Jewish People VI = The Hellenistic Age*, ed. A. Schalit (New Brunswick NJ 1972), 225.

[52] The name appears in several variants in rabbinic literature: שלמצו in *Sif. Behuqotai* 1.1, 110d ed. Weiss; *Sifre Deut.* 42, p. 89 ed. Finkelstein; *Lev. R.* 35.10, p. 829 ed. Margulies (which mentions also the variants שלמצי and שלמצה). The form של ציון appears in *bShab.* 16b; שלמתו in *Eccl. R.* 7.11; שלמינון in a *scholion* to *Meg. Taan.* 28 Tebet (and also *ad loc.* שלמרון and של-ציון); 2 Shebat (and also *ad loc.* שלמנצון and שלמרון). C. Clermont-Ganneau, *Archaeological Researches in Palestine* I (London 1899), 386–92 was the first to suggest that the name is Shelamzion (שלמציון), after the discovery of the first ossuary with this name inscribed on it; since then many other inscriptions and documents have been discovered which confirm this reading.

[53] For a fuller treatment, see my article, "Queen Salamzion Alexandra and Judas Aristobulus I's Wife: Did Jannaeus Alexander Contract Levirate Marriage?" *Journal for the Study of Judaism* 24 (1993), 181–90.

levirate marriage with his widow, but he cannot contract levirate marriage," and "a king ... cannot contract levirate marriage, nor can his widow be contracted in levirate marriage" (*mSanh.* 1.1–2).[54]

---

[54] Cf. *mYeb.* 6.4: "If a woman awaited levirate marriage with a common priest and he was appointed high priest, although he had bespoken her he may not consummate the union." On this *halakhic* "problem," see Ewald (above, n. 51), 386, n. 5; H. Graetz, *Geschichte der Juden* III[5] (Leipzig 1905), 121, n. 2; I. Deutsch, *Die Regierungszeit der judäischen Königin Salome Alexandra und die Wirksamkeit des Rabbi Simon ben Schetach* (Magdeburg 1901), 13–6; M. Z. Segal, "Notes on the History of the YHD sect (Based on *CD*)," *Tarbiz* 22 (1951), 141 [Hebrew]; Klausner (above, n. 51), 225.

Chapter 6:

Women and the Legal System

Most sources on the legal aspect of women's lives are *tannaitic* and reflect only the attitudes of the world from which they came – that of the Pharisees of the Second Temple period and their heirs.

Punishments and Judgments

The absolutely equal treatment of women and men in regard to legal punishments stands out in stark contrast to their unequal treatment in Pharisaic and, subsequently, *tannaitic* law in other matters. The school of R. Ishmael gave this equality a legal definition: "'And if men contend' (*Ex.* 21.18). I thus know only about men. How about women? R. Ishmael used to say: All laws about damages found in the *Torah* are not explicit on this point. But since in the case of one of them Scripture explicitly states (*Num.* 5.6) that women are to be regarded like men, it has thus made it explicit in regard to all the laws about damages found in the *Torah* that women are to be regarded like men" (*Mekhilta de R. Ishmael, Mishpatim* 6, p. 269 ed. Horovitz-Rabin; cf. *ibid.* p. 275). And in the *Talmud* it is more simply stated: "It was taught at the school of R. Ishmael: ... Scripture equated the woman to the man in respect of all punishments in the *Torah*" (*bYeb.* 84b; *bTem.* 2b; *bQidd.* 35a).[1]

This teaching is strengthened by the fact that indeed in only a very few cases does *halakhah* specifically distinguish between judgments against a man and against a woman. The exceptions generally involve what the rabbis perceived as injury to the woman's modesty, e.g. "When he was four cubits from the place of stoning they stripped off his clothes. A man is kept covered in front and a woman both in front and behind. So R. Judah. But the sages say: A man is stoned naked but a woman is not stoned naked" (*mSanh.* 6.3); or again: "A man is hanged with his face to the people and a woman with her face towards the gallows. So R. Eliezer. But the sages say: A man is hanged but a woman is not

---

[1] And also from the school of R. Eliezer, *ibid.*: "Scripture equated the woman to the man in respect of all damages in the *Torah*;" and the school of R. Hezekiah: "Scripture equated the woman to the man in respect of all capital punishments in the *Torah*."

hanged" (*ibid*. 6.4; cf. *Sifre Deut*. 221, p. 253 ed. Finkelstein). The *Sifre* adds by way of explanation: "Because all of her nakedness is illicit" (*Ibid*. pp. 254–5 ed. Finkelstein). In another context the rabbis debated whether a woman condemned to flogging should receive more leniencies than a man. We read in the *Tosefta*: "If after he was flogged he had loose bowels, they do not flog him anymore. And in what does his dirtying himself consist? Both man and woman with excrement. This is the opinion of R. Meir" (*tMakk*. 5.14). In other words, flogging is stopped only if the man or woman being flogged soils him/herself. But there was another opinion in this matter: "R. Judah says: The man [who soils himself] with excrement, the woman with urine" (*ibid*.); that is, a more lenient standard for a woman. Yet: "The sages say: the man and the woman are the same: if they dirty themselves either with excrement or with urine, the flogging is stopped" (*ibid*.); in this ruling, man and woman are treated with complete equality.[2] The *tannaim* were obligated to discuss in some detail one particular case of women sentenced to death, for it involved biological characteristics peculiar to women: "If a woman was condemned to be put to death they may not wait until she has given birth, but if she had already sat on the birth-stool they wait until she has given birth" (*mArakh*. 1.4; *tArakh*. 1.4).[3]

Despite all this material supporting R. Ishmael's definition, there is one exceptional law indicating that a woman's status was different from a man's in the matter of fines: "A slave or a wife are dangerous: he that injures them is culpable, but if they injure others they are not culpable" (*mBQ* 8.4).[4] This exemption, of course, derives from the fact that a wife's entire property is controlled by her husband (as is a slave's by his master), as is illustrated by the continuation of the passage: "Yet they may need to make restitution afterward – if the wife was divorced or the slave freed they are liable to make restitution" (*ibid*.). That is to say, a woman gains full legal entitlement only upon divorce,[5] a status which ironically is considered here to be a liability and not an advantage.

No actual cases of women suffering a lesser punishment than death survive in the sources,[6] but there are indeed from the Second Temple period certain instances of women being condemned to death after a trial of some form or other.

---

[2] Interestingly, the *Mishnah* in this case presents the sages' view as *halakhah* and R. Judah's as the minority view, with no mention of R. Meir's view (*mMakk*. 3.14; cf. *Sifre Deut*. 286, p. 304 ed. Finkelstein).

[3] The Romans had a similar law, see Sarah B. Pomeroy, *Goddesses, Whores, Wives and Slaves: Women in Classical Antiquity* (New York 1975), 168.

[4] This was a point of controversy between the Pharisee and Sadducees, see *mYad*. 4.7, which however deals only with male and female slaves without mentioning wives *per se*.

[5] Or widowhood, see above, chapter 5.

[6] A *tannaitic* parable recounts that two women, one who committed adultery and the other who ate unripe figs of the sabbatical year, were condemned (in one version) to be flogged (*Sifre Num*. 137, pp. 183–4 ed. Horovitz) or (in another version) to be paraded

The most notorious case is that of Herod's wife, Mariamme the Hasmonean. Josephus reports that "Herod, calling together those who were closest to him, brought an elaborately framed accusation against her" (*AJ* 15.229). The exact content of Herod's indictment is not clear. In one place Josephus states that Herod's sister Salome framed Mariamme through her servants for an attempted poisoning of the king (*AJ* 15.223–6). If this is correct, then Mariamme was tried for attempted murder. But then Josephus says that Herod accused her of adultery with her bodyguard Soemus (*ibid.* 228–9).[7] Elsewhere Josephus says again that Herod executed Mariamme on charges of adultery (*AJ* 16.185). If this information is correct, it means only that adultery is the charge brought against her at her trial; it can be assumed that the execution of Mariamme by Herod, like that of the other Hasmoneans, was ultimately motivated by political considerations.[8] As soon as Mariamme had fulfilled the purpose for which Herod married her – providing legitimacy for his own reign – Herod got rid of her just as he did with the rest of the Hasmoneans. This becomes especially clear when we consider that her fate was decreed after the fall of Cleopatra, the close friend of Mariamme's mother Alexandra. With Cleopatra gone, Herod did with the two Hasmonean women as he wished. In court – i.e. in public – Mariamme was tried for adultery, perhaps even as a priest's daughter (for she belonged to the priestly Hasmonean family) who prostituted herself and was liable to execution by fire. How she was in fact executed is unknown. Yet since her trial and sentencing followed neither Pharisaic procedure as reflected in rabbinic literature nor apparently even Sadducean procedure, but Hellenistic custom,[9] her execution presumably was also not carried out according to *halakhah*, at least not the Pharisaic version. A less notorious case is that of Mariamme's mother, Alexandra, who

---

around in public disgrace (if that is the correct interpretation of this punishment: *Lev. R.* 31.4, pp. 719–20 ed. Margulies), but this story cannot be accepted as an historical case; at most it may indicate that women were indeed subjected to other kinds of punishments.

[7] Cf. *BJ* 1.443, where Mariamme is accused of adultery with Joseph, Salome's husband. On this source-problem see A. Schalit, *König Herodes: Der Mann und sein Werk* (Berlin 1969), 67–8. Schalit gives a good overview of the sources and concludes that *BJ* and *AJ* report different incidents, but I find this difficult to accept. It seems to me that, given the fact that in *BJ* the story is told once whereas in *AJ* the second appearance of the story is presented as a flashback (15.202–17), we are dealing with one story taken from two different sources preserving different traditions. The solution of this historiographical problem cannot be presented here.

[8] See E. Mary Smallwood, *The Jews Under Roman Rule: From Pompey to Diocletian: A Study in Political Relations*[2] (Leiden 1981), 71. The exiles of Augustus' daughter Julia and his granddaughter for adultery can be seen in the same light, i.e. the results of the intrigues of Augustus' wife Livia, who wanted to guarantee the throne to her son, see Suet. *Aug.* 65 and Tac. *Ann.* 1.2. I thank Hannah Cotton for drawing my attention to this parallel.

[9] See A. M. Rabello, "*Hausgericht* in the House of Herod the Great?" in *Jerusalem in the Second Temple Period: Abraham Schalit Memorial Volume*, edd. A. Oppenheimer, U. Rappaport and M. Stern (Jerusalem 1980), 119–36 [Hebrew].

was apparently brought up on charges of rebellion before the same tribunal as her daughter (*AJ* 15.251).

During the Second Temple period executions were carried out according to the Sadducean, not the Pharisaic interpretation of the law. This we learn from R. Eliezer b. R. Zadok, who recalls witnessing as a child the execution of a priest's daughter by burning, in the Sadducean manner (*mSanh.* 7.2; cf. *tSanh.* 9.11; *bSanh.* 52b).[10] The New Testament recounts that Jesus was present at the execution of an adulteress condemned to death by stoning, and he was able to save her (*John* 8.3–11). Whether this story is historical, wholly or partially, or even just realistic, is difficult to decide.[11] The *Babylonian Talmud* preserves a story, transmitted only by figures from Palestine (R. Shimeon b. Pazi in R. Joshua b. Levi's name on Bar Qappara's authority), of an execution in Jerusalem: "It once happened that a woman came to Jerusalem carrying an infant on her back; she brought him up and he had intercourse with her, whereupon they were brought before a *Bet Din* and stoned. Not because he was definitely her son, but because he clung to her" (*bQidd.* 80a). The historicity of this story is also hard to gauge, especially since the first generations of Palestinian *amoraim* liked to use anecdotes of things that supposedly happened in Jerusalem in order to strengthen their own *halakhic* arguments.

Also quite well-known is Shimeon b. Shetah's execution of eighty women in Ashkelon by hanging (*mSanh.* 6.4). Despite Shimeon b. Shetah's status as a Pharisaic leader, his action contradicted the Pharisaic law which determined that "two shall not be condemned on the same day" (*ibid.*). An *amoraic aggadah* which appears twice in the *Palestinian Talmud* asserts that the eighty women were witches (*yHag.* 2.2, 77d-78a; *ySanh.* 6.9, 23c), but there is no sign of this in the *Mishnah*. According to the same *aggadah*, the women were executed by crucifixion, not hanging as in the *tannaitic* version. *Sifre* asserts that the executions violated *halakhah* but were carried out because "the times required it, to serve as a lesson for others" (*Sifre Deut.* 221, p. 253 ed. Finkelstein; and cf. *ySanh. loc. cit.*).[12] This strange story contains many surprising details, particu-

---

[10] For a discussion of when this actually happened, see D. R. Schwartz, *Agrippa I: The Last King of Judaea* (Tübingen 1990), 118–9.

[11] Although the story appears only in *John*, linguistic peculiarities and the textual tradition have led most scholars to reject a *Johanine* origin. L. J. Swidler, *Biblical Affirmations of Women* (Philadelphia 1979), 275 has, on linguistic grounds, identified the story as belonging to the *Lukanic* stratum in the New Testament. In this instance, at least, the origin of the story is chronologically closer to the events it purports to describe, but this does not add any more certainty about its historicity, for its fictional qualities are manifestly clear. B. Witherington III, *Women in the Ministry of Jesus* (Cambridge 1982), 21 contends that story is historically reliable.

[12] This odd expression is also used in two stories, one about a man who had sexual relations with his wife in public and was sentenced to flogging (see above, chapter 3), the

larly the setting, for Ashkelon was never under Jewish sovereignty.[13] The whole episode is an unsolved puzzle, and it is difficult to know how heavily to lean on it as historical evidence.[14]

Most of these examples from the Second Temple period involve the execution of a woman for adultery. Even the Hasmonean Mariamme, who as stated was executed for political reasons, was nonetheless formally accused of adultery. Far more executions of men are known to us from the same period, but in nearly every case the motive was political: King Alexander Yannai put to death 800 of his political opponents (*BJ* 1.97; *AJ* 13.380); under Queen Shelamzion the Pharisees executed Diogenes, a Sadducee who had been Yannai's counselor and the Pharisees' opponent (*BJ* 1.113; *AJ* 13.411); Herod killed Hyrcanus II; (*AJ* 15.165–76) as well as three of his own sons for political reasons. Political considerations also were the prime reason for Herod Antipas' execution of John the Baptist (*AJ* 18.116–9); the Roman governors' execution of Jesus, of the false prophet Theudas (*AJ* 20.97–9) and the two sons of Judas of Galilee (*AJ* 20.102); and the execution of Jesus' brother James by a Sadducean Sanhedrin (*AJ* 20.200).[15] This is only a partial survey. The only example I have been able to find of a man executed for any other reason is that of a false witness whom Shimeon b. Shetah (or Judah b. Tabbai) put to death (*Mekhilta de R. Ishmael, Mishpatim* 20, p. 327 ed. Horovitz-Rabin; *tSanh.* 6.6). The imbalance appearing in the sources, which record executions of women in this period mostly for adultery and of men almost always for political reasons, simply cannot be accepted as historical fact. More reasonably, the imbalance reflects the interest of the sources themselves: the politically motivated executions of men and the execu-

---

other about a man who rode his horse on the Sabbath and was stoned (*bSanh.* 46a; *bYeb.* 90b); also the rabbis' decision in the case of the menstruation of a young woman from Hitlu is defined as "an instruction befitting the hour" (*tNidd.* 1.9; *yNidd.* 1.5, 49b).

[13] See M. Stern, "The Political Background of the Wars of Alexander Jannai," *Tarbiz* 33 (1964), 330, n. 27 [Hebrew].

[14] For one interpretation, see J. Efron, "The Deed of Simeon ben Shatah in Ascalon," in A. Kasher, *Jews and Hellenistic Cities in Eretz Israel* (Tübingen 1990), 318–41. Recently, M. Hengel, *Rabbinische Legende und frühpharisäische Geschichte: Schimeon b. Schetach und die achtzig Hexen von Askalon = Abhandlung der Heidelberger Akkademie der Wissenschaft philisophisch-historischen Klasse* (Heidelberg 1984), has interpreted the story as an allegory masking a polemic against the purges of Shimeon b. Shetah in the days of Pharisaic ascendancy under Queen Shelamzion; the women are supposed to represent men. Hengel could find one other example of an allegorical use of a woman, namely, Mariamme daughter of Bilgah, who in rabbinic literature appears as an apostate during the days of the Kings of Greece (*tSukk.* 4.28) but really represents a man from the division of Bilgah, Menelaus, who participated in the Hellenizing movement and helped enforce the religious decrees of Antiochus against the Jews.

[15] Even the two men crucified with Jesus are called λησταί, (*Mark* 15.27), which could mean a common brigand but in the context of first-century Palestine probably refers to political agitators.

tions of women for adultery were incidents considered worth relating. Political rebellion was a criminal activity punishable by death for men similar to adultery for women.

Women as Witnesses

Women were involved in the legal system not only as defendants, yet their role in other capacities, such as giving testimony, is complicated and requires careful investigation.⟩ ⊢ ∨ ∙ ⎸∙

Josephus asserts that by Jewish law women are disqualified as witnesses (*AJ* 4.219), and the rabbis made the same determination, as we find stated quite explicitly in *Sifre Deuteronomy*: "Is a woman also qualified to give testimony? It is stated: 'two [witnesses]' (*Deut.* 19.15), and further on, 'the two [men]' (*ibid.* 17). As the meaning of 'two' in the one instance is men and not women, so the meaning of 'two' in the other instance is men and not women" (*Sifre Deut.* 190, p. 230 ed. Finkelstein; and cf. *Sif. Vayiqra*, 7.1, p. 150 ed. Finkelstein). The view of the Dead Sea Sect is not so decisive. In the *Rule of the Congregation* (*1QSa* I 10–1), we find the following: "He is not to have carnal knowledge of a woman until he is twenty years old and has reached the age of discretion. Furthermore, it is only then that she is eligible to give testimony regarding him in matters involving the laws of the *Torah* or to attend judicial hearings." Some scholars have interpreted these words to mean that women were eligible witnesses in the sect.[16] Others have emended the text, reasoning that the sectarians, who were generally strict, would not permit what "even" the "more lenient" *tannaitic halakhah* does not allow.[17] In my opinion, the jury is still out, so to speak.

According to Josephus, the reason why women were disqualified as witnesses was their lightheadedness and brazenness, in other words their questionable morality cast doubt on their testimony. The rabbis held a similar view. A *baraita* which spells out a number of minor offenses which can disqualify a witness (dice-playing, raising doves [apparently some street magician], selling produce of a sabbatical year), adds the following: "Every testimony which a woman is not qualified to give, these [petty offenders] are also not qualified to

---

[16] See H. N. Richardson, "Some Notes on *1QSa*," *Journal of Bibilical Literature* 76 (1957), 108–22; A. Isaksson, *Marriage and Ministry in the New Testament: A Study with Special References to Mt. 19:13–22 and 1 Cor. 11:3–16 = Acta Seminarii Neotestamentici Upsalensis* XXIV (Lund 1965), 56–7.

[17] J. M. Baumgarten, *Studies in Qumran Law* (Leiden 1977), 183–6. Even scholars who generally shy away from textual emendations have accepted Baumgarten's change of "she" to "he" and "regarding him" to "according to," emendations which the text itself in no way justifies. See L. H. Schiffman, *Sectarian Law in the Dead Sea Scrolls: Courts, Testimony and the Penal Code = Brown Judaic Studies* XXXIII (Chico CA 1983), 62–3.

give" (*yRH* 1.9, 57c; *bSanh.* 27b). This would imply that there are specific instances in which a woman's testimony would be accepted, or as we find in a
more positive statement of the same ruling, "testimony which a woman is qualified to give, so they [the petty offenders] also are qualified to give" (*tSanh.* 5.2),
and there the kinds of testimony which a woman is ineligible to give are spelled
out: the observation of the new moon and intercalation of the year and judgments involving money and capital cases. Thus it seems that a woman's testimony was acceptable in other sorts of cases.

Gershon Holzer, in his article "Women's Testimony in Jewish Law,"[18] assembled a list of many matters for which, by the rabbis' own evidence, a woman's
testimony could be accepted. A woman could testify to: a) the origin of a swarm
of bees (*mBQ* 10.2; *tKet.* 3.3);[19] b) the death of someone's husband, in order to
permit the widow to marry another man (*mYeb.* 16.5; *bBekh.* 46b);[20] c) the chastity (*mKet.* 2.9)[21] or defilement (*mSot.* 6.2; cf. *Sifre Zuta* 5.21, p. 234 ed. Horovitz)[22] of a woman war captive; and d) a midwife who helps in the delivery to
twins can testify as to which is the elder (*tBB* 7.2).[23] We can add that a woman
could also confirm by her testimony that a man was a priest (*mKet.* 2.3).

The rule which can be derived from the above examples was formulated by
R. Nehemiah: "In every instance in which the rabbis permitted it, a woman's testimony was on equal footing with that of a man" (*tYeb.* 14.1). This would mean
that when a woman's testimony could be accepted, it was subject to normal rules
of evidence; but "if not, the majority opinion is followed" (*ibid.*, and also *bYeb.*
117b; *yYeb.* 15.6, 15b). This "majority" was given a specific interpretation: the
evidence of "two women against that of one woman is given the same validity as
that of two men against one man" (*bYeb.* 117b),[24] i.e. in cases in which a woman's testimony would not normally be accepted, the evidence provided by two
women witnesses is accepted if it is not contradicted by that of two women.

Further deductions can be made in two cases by pointing out internal incon-
sistencies in dry legal texts. a) Rabban Shimeon b. Gamaliel was of the opinion
that the daughter of a priest is qualified to testify about the first-born animals of
priests (namely, whether they were accidentally maimed and may thus be con-

---

[18] *Sinai* 67 (1970), 94–112 [Hebrew].

[19] *Ibid.* 100, 102–4.

[20] *Ibid.* 99.

[21] *Ibid.*

[22] *Ibid.* 100, 108–9.

[23] *Ibid.* 100, 105–6.

[24] The *Palestinian Talmud* preserves the *amoraic* ruling in this matter: "That rule
which you have stated applies to a case in which there was one woman against two women, but if there were a hundred women and a single male witness, all the women are
deemed equivalent to a single male witness" (*ySot.* 6.4, 21a), where "a hundred" means
simply "many."

sumed, or whether they were intentionally maimed, in which case they may not); if so, then *a fortiori* so can a woman who is unrelated to him (*bBekh.* 35b). b) In *Mishnah Sotah* 9.8, we read: "If a woman said: I saw him [the murderer], and another said: You did not see him, they must break the heifer's neck."[25] This text deals with the procedure to be followed when a corpse is discovered in a field and no witnesses to the murder can be found. Scripture prescribes an elaborate ceremony to be performed by the community (*Deut.* 21). The *halakhah* here deals with the decision which the elders of the community must take, i.e. whether to proceed with the ceremony, or whether to postpone it on the chance that witnesses may turn up after all; thus the *halakhah* deals with evidence given in a criminal case. If indeed one's woman's testimony regarding a murderer was enough to offset another woman's testimony, then clearly a woman's testimony in the same matter is accepted when it is not contradicted.

The sages even accepted the testimony of a woman about herself in personal matters when she clearly has no interest in lying, e.g. "If a woman said: I have been married and now I am divorced, she may be believed, since the mouth that forbade is the mouth that permitted. ... If she said: I was taken captive yet I remain chaste, she may be believed, since the mouth that forbade is the mouth that permitted" (*mKet.* 2.5; *tKet.* 2.2; cf. *mEduy.* 3.6; *bBekh.* 36a). In other related instances the rabbis debated whether a woman's testimony about herself could be accepted:

"If a man married a woman and 'found not in her the tokens of virginity' (*Deut.* 22.14), and she said: After you betrothed me I was raped ... Rabban Gamaliel and R. Eliezer say: She may be believed. But R. Joshua says: We may not rely on her word. ...If she said: It was through an accident ... Rabban Gamaliel and R. Eliezer say: She may be believed. But: R. Joshua says: We may not rely on her word. ... If she is seen speaking with some man in the street, and they said to her: What manner of man is this? [and she answered]: His name is so-and-so and he is a priest. Rabban Gamaliel and R. Eliezer say: She may be believed. But R. Joshua says: We may not rely on her word. ... If she was found with child and they said to her: What manner of child is this?, [and she answered]: It is by one named so-and-so and he is a priest, Rabban Gamaliel and R. Eliezer say: She may be believed. But R. Joshua says: We may not rely on her word ..." (*mKet.* 1.6–9)

We may conclude that the specific law disqualifying women as witnesses was formulated as a general *halakhic* principle, just as in other matters such as punishments, but that many exceptions arose from actual custom and practice. During a normal trial in court, women's testimony was not sought out and was in fact avoided whenever possible because "no man wants his wife to degrade herself in court" (*bKet.* 74b), but testimony which could not otherwise be obtained was by all means accepted.[26]

---

[25] See Holzer (above, n. 18), 100.

[26] For this reason, the Christian theological debate regarding testimony by women, particularly that of Mary Magdalene, of Jesus' resurrection – testimony which of course

In the Second Temple period, we find the specific case of a woman serving once as a witness and once perhaps even as a judge, in the trial of the conspirators against Herod. At least, Josephus says that Herod's sister Salome sat as the judge in the trial of Herod and Mariamme's two sons (*BJ* 1.538), and that in the trial of Antipater she was brought in to testify against him (*AJ* 17.93). Needless to say, both these trials were not transacted according to the Pharisaic interpretation of the law.[27]

In another case from the Herodian house, the maidservants of Pheroras's wife (*BJ* 1.584–90; *AJ* 17.64) and Antipater 's mother (*AJ* 17.65) were tortured in order to force them to incriminate their mistresses in the plot against Herod. This story contains two interesting elements: first, that evidence was collected by means of torture, a procedure which was generally employed only on slaves,[28] and second, that evidence procured in such a manner, from both a woman and a slave, was accepted in court. We do not know how Jewish law treated such a procedure or such evidence, but we may note that Josephus, who was trained in Jewish law, adds no comment to the story as he found it in Nicolaus.

Thus the Jewish judicial system was not monolithic in the Second Temple period, and in some quarters of Jewish society women's testimony was considered perfectly acceptable in court.

---

was not given in a courtroom – is not relevant here. Some scholars have stressed that the evangelists were compelled to find male witnesses for the resurrection since the women's testimony was not sufficient according to Jewish law. See, e.g. M. Hengel, "Maria Magdalena und die Frauen als Zeugen," *Abraham Unser Vater: Festschrift für Otto Michel = Arbeiten zur Geschichte des Spätjudentums und Urchristentums* (Leiden 1963), 246–8, 255–6; E. L. Bode, *The First Easter Morning: The Gospel Account of the Women's Visit to the Tomb of Jesus = Analecta Biblica* XLV (Rome 1970), 40–1; Evelyn and F. Stagg, *Women in the World of Jesus* (Philadelphia 1978), 157–8; Swidler (above, n. 11), 200–1. For a fresh insight into the issue see now Antoinette C. Wire, *The Corinthian Women Prophets: A Reconstruction through Paul's Rhetoric* (Minneapolis 1990), 159–63.

[27] Rabello (above, n. 9), 127–35.

[28] Although Josephus says (*AJ* 17.64) that torture was also used on free women, among them the mother of Antiphilus, the friend of Antipater (*ibid.* 77). This method of torturing slaves to procure evidence was widely used in Greece and Rome, see e.g. Tac. *Ann.* 3.23; and see on this e.g. J.A. Crook, *Law and Life of Rome 90 BC-AD 219* (New York 1967), 274–5; T. Wiedemann, *Greek and Roman Slavery* (Baltimore 1981), 9 and various documents there.

Inheritance

1. Bequeathing Property

As we have seen, the rabbis viewed both widows and divorcées as women who had suffered a decrease in the standard of living to which they had been accustomed. This view was based on the fact that the woman, according already to biblical law, cannot be her husband's heir, nor can a daughter be her father's heir except when she has no brothers. In such circumstances a woman would only rarely own property – that is, beyond what her husband and father had provided her in her *ketubbah*, and even that she received only after divorce or the death of her husband. The assumption was that the property which the woman received from her father in her *ketubbah* was managed by her husband, who had the right to enjoy the profits from the property (*mKet.* 6.1) and even to lose against it (*ibid.* 8.5); and if the woman died, the property went to her husband and his family (*bBQ* 42b; *bBB* 111b-112a), but if her husband died she was entitled as a widow only to the sum of her *ketubbah* and no more (*mBB* 8.1). Yet the close contact between the Jews of the Second Temple period and the neighboring cultures, particularly Roman, in which a daughter was considered an heir on equal footing with a son, gave rise to a sharp controversy between the Pharisees and Sadducees (or the Boethusians, according to the *Tosefta*) regarding a daughter's inheritance, despite the clearly stated biblical law. "The Boethusians say: we complain against you, Pharisees: If my son's daughter, who inherits on the strength of my son, who inherits on my account, thus inherits me, isn't it right that my daughter, who comes on my account, should inherit me? The Pharisees say: No. If you have said so in regard to the daughter of the son, who shares with the brothers, will you say so of the daughter who does not share with the brothers?" (*tYad.* 2.20). The *Palestinian Talmud* also preserves this controversy, and adds: "The sages of the Gentiles say: A son and a daughter have equal footing as heirs" (*yBB* 8.1, 16a), which precisely identifies the source of the Sadducean idea.[29] The Pharisees, and the *tannaim* after them, could find no good reason to void the biblical law: "If a man said: Such a man shall inherit from me, and he has a daughter; or: My daughter shall inherit from me, and he has a son, he has said nothing, for he has laid down a condition contrary to what is written in the *Torah*" (*mBB* 8.5).[30] The same controversy seems to have raged also

---

[29] On the Sadduceans and the Roman law, see J. Le Moyne, *Les Saddecéens* (Paris 1972), 305.

[30] *tBB* 7.18 records this in the name of R. Yohanan b. Broqa, whom D. Daube ("Johanan b. Broqua and Women's Rights," in *Jewish Tradition in the Diaspora: Studies in Memory of Prof. Walter J. Fischel*, ed. M. M. Caspi [Berkeley 1981], 55) has surprisingly called a liberal and a crusader for women's rights. On biblical law and a daughter's inheritance, see Z. Falk, "The Inheritance of the Daughter and Widow in the Bible and *Talmud*,"

between Jews and early Christians. The *Babylonian Talmud* records the story of
Rabban Gamaliel and his sister (!) Imma Shalom who, with the purpose of proving the greed of a Christian judge, each approached him privately, offered bribes
in return for a ruling on whether Imma Shalom could share in the inheritance
their father left (*bShab.* 116a-b); yet the historical value of this story is not very
high. A similar story appears in the Palestinian *midrashic* compilation, *Pesiqta
de-Rav Kahana* (*Eicha* 9, p. 260 ed. Mandelbaum), except that its central figures
are not Rabban Gamaliel and Imma Shalom but an anonymous man and woman
who appear before a corrupt judge; this version contains no mention of women's
right to inherit, nor is the judge identified as Christian. These two stories obviously represent a *topos*. The *Babylonian Talmud* combines this with another
topos which we have already discussed, that of the woman who bewails the un-
fairness she suffers under Jewish law. As we noted, this literary form is a kind of
rabbinical self-criticism; it does not help us decide the historicity of the alleged
controversy between Jews and Christians. Another self-critique within Judaism
can be found in the book of *Judith*, according to which Judith came into her
wealth through a bequest from her husband (8.7).

The rabbis tried to find strictly legal ways to bestow property on a woman after the death of her husband, even if she is not his direct heir. The most accepted
method of transferring property to a daughter was simply to write it into her
ketubbah, although as we have noted, this method had two flaws: when a woman
was married she enjoyed only nominal ownership of these assets, which her husband managed, benefited from and could even lose without being held accountable (*mKet.* 8.5); and if the woman died before her husband, the property went
over to him and his family, and was thus lost completely to her family. Some
sages were aware of these problems in the law. According to a *baraita*, R. Yohanan b. Broqa attempted to provide correction: "They taught: R. Yohanan b.
Broqa says: a man who inherits from his wife shall return [the property in her
ketubbah] to her family after deducting fees and expenses" (*bKet.* 84a).

A daughter could also receive property as a gift. A father would write his
daughter a deed of gift, although this property would be subject to the same fate
as that provided in her *ketubbah*. The eighth chapter of the *mishnaic* tractate
Ketubbot, dealing with a husband's right to manage his wife's goods, records a
controversy between the Schools of Shammai and Hillel, concerning a woman's
right to manage property she had acquired during the period of betrothal; both
schools apparently agreed that property which a woman acquires after marriage
is transferred to the custody of the husband, as is even property in her possession

Tarbiz 23 (1952), 9–15 [Hebrew]; P. Neeman, "Inheritance of the Daughter in *Torah* and
Halakhah," *Bet Miqra* 47 (1971), 476–89 [Hebrew]; Judith Hauptman, "Women's Liberation in the *Talmudic* Period: An Assessment," *Conservative Judaism* 26/4 (1971–2),
24–6.

before the betrothal, once the marriage takes place. Yet despite the law's specific provisions, we do hear the discordant voices of some sages who resented
the limitations their predecessors set on women's rights: "(Rabban Gamaliel)
said to them: We are at a loss [to find reason for giving him right] over her new
[possessions], and would you even burden us with the old also!" (*mKet.* 8.1);
that is, the law's direction to the husband to manage his wife's property is somewhat humiliating. As a consequence, the *Mishnah* contains a formula whereby a
husband can exempt himself from managing his wife's property: "If a man declared to his [betrothed] wife in writing, I will have neither right nor claim to
your property ... if she sold it or gave it away her act is considered valid" (*mKet.*
9.1, which provides also the formulae by which a man exempts himself from inheriting his wife). But in cases where the husband claimed his right to his wife's
property and did not cooperate, a devise was formulated and is recorded in the
Tosefta, for a wife to put her property beyond his reach: "They write a fictional
deed of transfer[31] to another person, in the opinion of Rabban Shimeon b.
Gamaliel. And the sages say: ... they write a deed of gift, from today to whenever I determine" (*tKet.* 9.2).

Aside from her *ketubbah* and a gift, a daughter was eligible to receive other
kinds of inheritances: a) from her mother, if the latter died after the father ("R.
Zechariah b. Haqatzab ... says: the son and the daughter are on equal footing
when it comes to the possessions of the mother," *bBB* 115a); Rabbinic literature
does not contain many actual cases of women inheriting property, aside from
that of the mother of the Rokhel sons, who is said to have bequeathed a very
valuable possession to her daughter (*mBB* 9.7), which provoked the ire of R.
Eliezer, who angrily exclaimed, "May their mother bury the sons of Rokhel!" b)
The daughter could also inherit from her father, if she has no brothers. But in
both cases, as we have pointed out, this property remains in her husband's custody until she is either divorced or widowed.

Despite *halakhic* limitations, a wife also had certain rights to inherit property.
a) Although a wife does not inherit more than her *ketubbah* when her husband
dies, a critically ill husband, shortly before his death, can bequeath to his wife
part of his property in addition to her *ketubbah* (*bBB* 138a-b).[32] b) In the opinion
of R. Judah b. Shimeon, "By biblical law, a father is heir to his son and a woman
is heir to her son, as it is said, 'tribes' (*Num.* 36.9). The mother's tribe is comparable to the father's tribe. Just as in the father's tribe the father is heir to his son,
so in the mother's tribe the woman is heir to her son" (*bBB* 114b). All of these
measures were intended to circumvent biblical law and insure that the divorcée

---

[31] The Hebrew expression (פסים שטר) here comes from the Greek πίστις see S. Lieberman *Tosefta kifshuta* IV (New York 1967), 325 [Hebrew].

[32] R. Yaron, *Gifts in Contemplation of Death in Jewish and Roman Law* (Oxford
1960), 18–9.

and especially the widow could acquire property as soon as they were left without a man.

Finally, various remedies were instituted for the benefit of a woman and her daughters when the husband dies impoverished. The widow, for example, could opt to remain in the house of her husband's heirs (either her children or her husband's children by another woman) and be maintained by them for as long as she liked (according to the practice in the Galilee and Jerusalem) or until her *ketubbah* was paid in full (according to the practice in Judaea) (*mKet.* 4.12; cf. 12.3; *mBB* 9.1; *tKet.* 4.8; 6.1). A similar remedy protected the daughters: "If a man died and left sons and daughters, and the property was great, the sons inherit and the daughters receive maintenance; but if the property was small the daughters receive maintenance and the sons go begging" (*mKet.* 13.3). This law, dating by all indications from the end of the Second Temple period, caused some bitterness, as Admon, complained: "I suffer a loss just because I am male?" (*ibid.*).

In conclusion, the laws and remedies we have cited enabled a father or a husband to transfer to his daughters or wife as much of his property as he wanted, and also to rest assured that in the event of his death they will be able to maintain a respectable standard of living – and all this despite the quite specific biblical laws against inheritance and property ownership by women.

We must search outside the rabbinic corpus for examples of large bequests bestowed on women. Herod wrote a will in Roman (not Jewish) fashion and bequeathed to his sister Salome the tax-revenues of three important cities in Palestine: Yavneh (Jamnia), Ashdod (Azotus) and Phasaelis (*BJ* 1.646; 2.98; *AJ* 17.147; 189; 321). Babatha's father Shimeon gave all his property by a deed of gift to his wife Mariamme, in accordance with rabbinic law; by this measure Shimeon ensured that his assets would go to his wife after his death.[33] Babatha's second husband, Judah Khthousion, also wrote a deed of gift for his daughter, Shelamzion, by which he bequeathed to her all of his property in Ein Gedi except for a small courtyard.[34] These two instances illustrate that *tannaitic* legislation was not completely detached from actual practice, although chronologically, which preceded which is not clear.

Babatha was not the only woman of the period who was left with considerable assets after the death of her husband. Queen Berenice, for example, owned fields near Beth She'arim (*Vita* 119). Herodias, also: when Caligula exiled Herod Antipas and confiscated his property, he proposed to Herodias that she

---

[33] Y. Yadin, *Bar Kokhba: Rediscovery of the Legendary Hero of the Second Jewish Revolt against Rome* (London 1971), 236–7.

[34] N. Lewis, *The Documents from the Bar Kokhba Period in the Cave of Letters II: Greek Papyri* (Jerusalem 1989), 84. And see R. Katzoff, "*P. Yadin* 19: A Gift after Death from the Judaean Desert," *Proceedings of the Tenth World Congress of Jewish Studies* Div. C/1 (Jerusalem 1990), 1–8 [Hebrew].

keep her own assets (*AJ* 18.253), which seems to indicate that she owned something worth keeping. Further, in *Acts* we read that the mother of the apostle John Mark (not he or his father) owned a house in Jerusalem (12.12). On various deeds of sale from the period, the wife's signature confirming the sale appears next to that of her husband, indicating without doubt joint ownership of the house.[35] Next to the date orchard, of which Babatha declared her ownership before the authorities in Rabbat-Moab, there was another orchard owned by a woman, Tamar daughter of Thamous.[36] Storage jars with women's names on them were discovered in Masada, which could be evidence for property owned by women or even for women merchants.[37]

The ownership of property by women independently of their husbands also emerges from an examination of charitable contributions to public institutions during the Second Temple period. Unfortunately the many synagogue dedicatory inscriptions which document women's contributions of entire buildings, parts of buildings, or even furnishings or equipment,[38] are not relevant here since they generally lie outside the geographical and chronological limits of this study. But the literary sources contain various indications that women contributed money for similar purposes during the days of the Second Temple. The *Mishnah* records that a certain Domitia[39] contributed her daughter's weight in gold to the Temple after she vowed to do so and her daughter recovered from an illness (*mArakh.* 5.1; *tArakh.* 3.1). This incident recalls the donations recorded in the later dedicatory Synagogue inscriptions, in which the women donators specify their purpose as being to ensure the health and well-being of family members. Two *baraitot* in the *Babylonian Talmud* allude to charitable practices

---

[35] P. Benoit, J. T. Milik and R. de Vaux, *Les Grottes des Muraba'ât* = *Discoveries in the Judaean Desert* II (Oxford 1961), 142, 145; J. T. Milik, "Un contract juif de l'an 134 après J.-C.," *Revue Biblique* 61 (1954), 183. Léonie J. Archer, *Her Price is Beyond Rubies: The Jewish Woman in Graeco-Roman Palestine* = *Journal for the Study of the Old Testament Supplement Series* LX (Sheffield 1990), 184–5 has suggested that women's signatures on these deeds signified their release of the purchaser from any obligation to pay the woman's *ketubbah* if she is widowed or divorced, for a *ketubbah* normally provides that all of the husband's property is accountable for payment of it. This interpretation adheres entirely to rabbinic *halakhah*, which Archer assumes everyone followed.

[36] Lewis (above, n. 34), 67. This is the first occurrence of the name Tamar in the Second Temple period. It appears again in the *Palestinian Talmud* (*yMeg.* 3.2, 74a). But the name in the document could also signify not a personal name but a kind of date which grew in the orchard adjacent to Babatha's. This matter requires further study.

[37] Y. Yadin and J. Naveh, *Masada I: The Aramaic and Hebrew Ostraca and Jar Inscriptions from Masada* (Jerusalem 1989), 21–2.

[38] For discussion, see Bernadette J. Brooten, *Women Leaders in the Ancient Synagogue: Inscriptional Evidence and Background Issues* = *Brown Judaic Studies* XXXVI (Chico CA 1982), 157–65.

[39] The printed editions give "ירמטיה" but the Cambridge manuscript has the more reliable Roman name "דמטיה"; see H. Danby, *The Mishnah* (Oxford 1933), 547, n. 6.

supported exclusively by women who are called "worthy women of Jerusalem". One was the wine administered to condemned prisoners before they were executed (*bSanh.* 43a). The other was the maintenance of women whose sons were raised to assist the high priest in the burning of the red heifer, and therefore could not incur any ritual impurity (*bKet.* 106a).[40] It is clear that in these cases the moneys belonged to the women themselves and were donated on their own initiative without their husbands' involvement.

2. Guardianship

Even if a man could not bequeath his estate to his wife, Jewish law did permit him to appoint her guardian over his property. This is not in fact stated explicitly but is implied in the law which determines that "if a man ... appointed his wife a guardian, he may exact of her an oath whensoever he will. ... If she went from her husband's grave ... and was made a guardian, the heirs may extract an oath of her ..." (*mKet.* 9.4; 6; cf. *tKet.* 9.3; *bKet.* 86b).

An interesting question related to this topic is a woman's right to be guardian over her own children, as is specifically described in the following law: "A *bet din* does not take the initiative in making women and slaves guardians, but if their (i.e. the woman's children's) father appointed her guardian while he was still alive, the *bet din* makes her a guardian" (*tTer.* 1.11; *mBB* 8.17). The same appears in a slightly different form in a *baraita* in the *Babylonian Talmud*: "They do not make women, slaves or minors guardians, but if the father of 'orphans' appointed them, they are (or in another version: he is) entitled" (*bGitt.* 52a). The wording of this law reveals a certain discomfort on the part of its framers. Guardianship is not a Hebrew institution but was adopted by Judaism during the Second Temple period from classical models[41] in an effort to make the Jewish legal system fit better with the international environment of that time. It is true that in the Greek and Roman systems, women did not serve as guardians,[42] but the rabbis felt more comfortable leaving responsibility for fatherless children in the hands of the mother rather than transferring the legal right over them to a strange male. Since there was no biblical law which forbade this, they provided the father the opportunity before his death to make the mother guardian over the children.[43] Jewish law also provided a widow, even without prior

---

[40] On wealthy women in the Hellenistic period, and on this type of public assistance, see R. van Bremen, "Women and Wealth," in *Images of Women in Antiquity*, edd. Averil Cameron and Amélie Kuhrt (Detroit 1985), 223–42.

[41] Pomeroy (above, n. 3), 62–3, 127, 150–5.

[42] *Ibid.*

[43] And see S. Assaf, "Appointment of Women as Guardians," *Hamishpat Haivri* 2 (1927), 75–81 [Hebrew], although most of this article deals with a practice common in the Middle Ages.

legal appointment, the right to demand that her children live with her and not with her husband's heirs (*tKet*. 11.4; *bKet*. 102b).[44]

The Babatha archive now affords the opportunity to examine some of the more practical aspects of the institution of guardianship. Babatha was widowed by her first husband Jesus at an early age and was left with a child (also named Jesus) whom she calls "the orphan" (ὀρφανός). In the first half of the year 124 CE, a court in Petra appointed two guardians, one Jewish and the other Nabataean, for Babatha's son.[45] There are two possible reasons for this action by the court: Babatha's deceased husband did not appoint her guardian, and/or the court in Petra followed not Jewish but Roman law. Babatha tried to persuade the court to increase her son's income, which she felt had been neglected by his guardians,[46] but her effort apparently did not succeed, for her archive also contains a receipt from the year 132 of maintenance funds from her son's guardians – one of whom had in the meantime died and was replaced by his heir, his son[47] – and the amount of the receipt was the same amount Babatha had been receiving eight years previously when she took the matter to court. In all her court appearances documented in the archive Babatha was accompanied by a guardian, at first her second husband (Judah b. Eleazar Khthousion), then (when she loans him money) Jacob b. Jesus who was perhaps her brother-in-law from her first marriage, then after his death Yohana b. Makhoutha and finally Babelis b. Menahem.[48] Babatha's step-daughter, Shelamzion, also appears in court with a guardian, her husband, Judah Cimber.[49] These two examples illustrate that Roman-Nabataean courts in Palestine upheld the general rule by which a woman neither served as a guardian nor represented herself in court.

Yet the Babatha archive also illustrates that historical *realia* were different from the legislative ideal. The brother of Babatha's second husband, Jesus b. Eleazar, died and left children who brought Babatha to court and demanded that she return them property in her possession. Two guardians represent these or-

---

[44] See Birgit Klein, *Die Stellung der Frau in Judentum: Rabbinische Initiative oder Legitimation? Demonstriert am Beispiel des jüdischen Vormundschaftrechts* (MA thesis, Hochschule für jüdische Studien, Heidelberg 1991).

[45] Lewis (above, n. 35), 47–64.

[46] *Ibid.* 58–64. One wonders whether Babatha tried, for instance, to obtain guardianship over her son. H. J. Wolff thinks not – "Römisches Provinzialrecht in der Provinz Arabia (Rechtspolitik als Instrument der Beherschung)," *Aufstieg und Niedergang der Römische Welt* II.13 (Berlin 1980), 763–806, esp. 798–801 – but he wrote before the full publication of the Babatha archive, and see now: Hannah Cotton, "The Guardianship of Jesus son of Babatha: Roman and Local Law in the Province of Arabia," *Journal of Roman Studies* 83 (1993), 94–108. But see also Klein (above, n. 44), 44–7.

[47] Lewis (above, n. 34), 116–7.

[48] *Ibid.* 55–6, 60–1, 66–7, 71–3, 98–100, 117.

[49] *Ibid.* 88–92.

phans, one male – Besas b. Jesus – and the second a female – Julia Crispina.[50] How or why this woman could appear in court was not clear to Yadin,[51] nor is it now clearly explained by Lewis, who published the documents.[52] Yadin dismissed it as one of the oddities of Roman rule in the East and thought Julia Crispina to be Roman, but we should note that Roman law, even more than Jewish law, prohibited women to serve as guardians.[53] That Julia Crispina was of Roman origin is doubtful, for her father's name, Berenicianus,[54] is Greek and would probably not belong to a Roman. More likely, she was of eastern origin (Jewish, from the context) but Hellenized, and had acquired Roman citizenship, although her role as a guardian of orphans is indeed an odd application of Roman law in the East, revealing mutual influences between the Roman and Jewish systems of law.[55]

3. Succession to the Throne

Could women succeed men to the throne? Rabbinic law contains no provisions for the transfer of power from a king to his heirs, although the verse "By all means you may set a king over yourself" (*Deut.* 17.15) elicits the comment in *Sifre Deuteronomy*, "a king and not a queen" (157, p. 208 ed. Finkelstein). This law probably does not refer specifically to Queen Shelamzion, for the same work mentions her very positively in another context (42, p. 89 ed. Finkelstein). In a short article, C.W. Reines attempted to show that the reference in *Sifre* was not to a queen like Shelamzion, who exercised what was essentially a constitutional monarchy and did not sit in judgment in court, but to an absolute monarch, such as never existed in the form of a queen in Israel.[56] But Reines' arguments sound more like excuses, for there is no way to know that Shelamzion's reign was not absolute or that she did not sit in judgment. But Reines is probably right in his alternative suggestion that the law, "king, not queen," was formulated later than Queen Shelamzion. It was by all indications formulated in the studyhouse of R. Aqiba as an academic problem unrelated to any actual situation.

On the other hand, we know of two Hasmonean rulers who bequeathed their rule to their wives, even though they had mature sons who would have been capable of running the state. The first was John Hyrcanus I, although his plans

---

[50] *Ibid.* 88–91, 108–12.

[51] Above, n. 33, 247–8.

[52] Above, n. 34, 111, n. 2.

[53] Pomeroy (above, n. 3), 150–2.

[54] Lewis (above, n. 34), 108.

[55] See now my article, "Julia Crispina Daughter of Berenicianus, A Herodian Princess in the Babatha Archive: A Case Study in Historical Identification," *Jewish Quarterly Review* 82 (1891–2), 361–81.

[56] "'King and not Queen'," *Sinai* 67 (1970), 327–8 [Hebrew].

failed, as his son, Judah Aristobulus I, usurped his mother's rule and starved her to death (*BJ* 1.71; *AJ* 13.302). The second was Alexander Yannai, whose rule was successfully passed on after his death to his wife Shelamzion Alexandra (*BJ* 1.107; *AJ* 13.399–405). The nine years of the queen's rule were considered, both by the rabbis (*Sifre Deut.* 42, p. 89 ed. Finkelstein; *Sif. Behuqotai* 1.1, 110d ed. Weiss) and by Josephus himself (*AJ* 13.432, contrary to his own source, Nicolaus, *ibid.* 430–1), as the quietest and most peaceful of the entire Second Temple period, despite the attempts by her son, Aristobulus II, to seize power from her (*BJ* 1.117; *AJ* 13.411; 422–8). In bequeathing power to women the Hasmoneans were following Hellenistic models. Several women, even in the presence of eligible sons, became queens in Ptolemaic Egypt by inheriting monarchical power from their husbands; occasionally mothers even fought wars with their sons for possession of the throne.[57] Thus it seems that the practice of women inheriting the throne can be counted among the signs of Hellenization in the Hasmonean dynasty; and the model was one of absolute monarchy in all its aspects. In this light, Herod's motivation for executing Mariamme the Hasmonean becomes clearer: the danger was not that her descendants would as Hasmoneans lay claim to power (which in fact is what did happen), but that Mariamme as a Hasmonean might try to seize power herself, in the absence of any male claimant to the throne (after the deaths of the last of the Hasmoneans, her grandfather Hyrcanus II and her brother Jonathan Aristobulus III). Even the attempted *coup* of Mariamme's mother, Alexandra, after Mariamme's death (*AJ* 15.247–51), should be interpreted as an attempt to seize the Hasmonean throne for herself.

No parallel aspirations to power on the part of women are found in the Herodian house, which can be explained by the fact the dynasty was influenced less by Hellenistic culture than by Roman political culture, in which no woman ever held office.[58]

---

[57] See Grace H. Macurdy, *Hellenistic Queens* (Baltimore 1932), 141–75, 184–223.

[58] And see the remarks of Averil Cameron, "'Neither Male nor Female'," *Greece and Rome* 27 (1980), 63.

Chapter 7:

Women in Public

Commandments

One subject at the center of Jewish feminist studies is women's fulfillment of religious commandments. But most research of this kind, even if it deals with the sources and makes a special effort to put into context all the laws excluding women from divine service, nonetheless is aimed ultimately at understanding the position of Jewish women today. Thus I shall bypass most modern comments on the topic and turn to the sources themselves to try to discover their attitude toward Jewish women's fulfillment of religious commandments in the Hellenistic-Roman period.

A Jewish woman's position in the whole system of religious commandments was exactly the reverse of her position in the Jewish legal system. In the latter, the operating assumption was that women are included in every verdict or punishment described in *halakhah* unless specifically excluded, while in the former, the commandments connected to divine service are assumed to exclude women unless otherwise stated.

There is an important *baraita* on this subject: "R. Judah says: A person must say three blessings every day: Blessed be He who did not make me a gentile, Blessed be he who did not make me a woman, Blessed be he who did not make me an ignoramous ... who did not make me a woman, because women are not obligated to fulfill commandments" (*tBer.* 7.18; cf. *bMen.* 43b, where it is suggested to replace "ignoramus" with "slave").[1] Two notes are in order. First, this

---

[1] In the *halakhah*, women are often grouped together with others who were not independent legal entities, but they were compared principally with slaves, as we have seen. On the equation between the legal status of women and slaves, see J. Jeremias, *Jerusalem in the Time of Jesus* (Philadelphia 1969), 373–5; and now P. V. M. Flesher, *Oxen, Women or Citizens? Slaves in the System of the Mishnah = Brown Judaic Studies* CXLIII (Atlanta 1988). R. Judah's remarks find a parallel in a statement by the pre-Socratic philosopher Thales, or Socrates himself (*Diog. Laert.* 1.33) or Plato (Plut. *Mar.* 46.1), see W. A. Meeks, "The Image of the Androgyne: Some Uses of a Symbol in Earliest Christianity," *History of Religions* 13 (1973–4), 167–8. Some Christians have seen R. Judah's statement as the antithesis of Paul's remarks in his letter to the *Galatians* 3.28, see B. Witherington III, "Rites and Rights for Women in *Galatians* 3:8," *New Testament Studies* 27 (1981), 593–604;

is the main source for the notion that women's exemption from performing commandments is a disadvantage; without this source, one could think that the commandments were not a reward but a form of punishment, such as we found in the *midrash* which presents the three commandments applying only to women – lighting of Sabbath candles, separation of dough and *niddah* – as punishment for the original sin in Eden. Second, the word we have translated as "person" (אדם) means, as we have already seen, a Jewish man, and as a general rule "אדם" is part of the wording of the commandments, the assumption being that they apply only to mature Jewish men. If another group – such as slaves, minors or women – also falls under the obligation to perform a certain commandment, this is specified: "Women, slaves and minors ... are obligated to say the Eighteen Benedictions, to put up a *mezuzah* and to say the blessing over food" (*mBer.* 3.3); "One's son, hired worker, slave and wife may separate *terumah* from what they eat, but they do not separate *terumah* from everything, for a man does not give *terumah* from what is not his" (*tTer.* 1.6); "Everyone may participate in the *minyan* of seven even a woman, even a minor" (*tMeg.* 4.11); "[the commandment to observe a festival with] joy falls on both men and women" (*tHag.* 1.4). Exceptions to this rule are rare. The fact is, however, that many commandments whose basic formulation would exclude women from their performance nonetheless make a special point of stating their exclusion, e.g. "Women, slaves and minors are exempt from saying the *Shema* and from putting on phylacteries (*tefillin*)" (*mBer.* 3.3); "A company [for the Passover sacrifice] may not be made up of women, slaves and minors" (*mPes.* 8.7); "From whom do they exact pledges? From Levites and Israelites ... but not from women, slaves or minors" (*mSheq.* 1.3); "Women, slaves and minors are exempt from residing in the *sukkah*" (*mSukk.* 2.8), and so on.

Thus it appears that since the inclusions and exclusions in *halakhot* are not self-evident, the rabbis took pains to formulate a general rule by which anyone could understand which commandments applied to women and which did not: "The observance of all positive commandments that depend on time is incumbent on men but not on women, and the observance of all positive commandments that do not depend on time is incumbent both on men and on women. The observance of all negative commandments, whether they depend on the time or not, is incumbent both on men and on women ..." (*mQidd.* 1.7). The *Tosefta* provides examples of "positive commandments that depend on time": "Like the

---

Madeleine Boucher, "Some Unexplored Parallels to *1 Cor* 11,11–2 and *Gal* 3,28. The NT on the Role of Women," *Catholic Biblical Quarterly* 31 (1969), 50–8. For a new outlook on Paul and this statement, see Antoinette C. Wire, *The Corinthian Women Prophets: A Reconstruction through Paul's Rhetoric* (Minneapolis 1990), 136–8. On the wording of the blessing, see G. Jochnowitz, "... Who Made Me a Woman," *Commentary* 71/4 (1981), 63–4.

sukkah, the *lulav* and *tefillin*," and of positive commandments that do not depend on time": "Like [the rules of] returning a lost object, letting the mother bird go free (when taking the young), [putting up] a railing and wearing fringes on a garment (*tzitzit*)" (*tQidd.* 1.10). Clearly the first category includes commandments connected to ritual and liturgy, whereas the second category includes those connected to local custom and everyday life, with the exception of the commandment to wear *tzitzit*, which appears in the second group but bears the aspect of religious ritual; in fact we find in the continuation of the passage: "R. Shimeon exempts women from the commandment of *tzitzit*, because it is a positive commandment that depends on time" (*ibid.*); "R. Shimeon said to them: do you not admit that it is a positive commandment that depends on time? But consider, a night-dress does not have to have fringes" (*yQidd.* 1.7, 61c). Apparently the sages eventually did agree with this, for in the version of this *baraita* in the *Babylonian Talmud*, *tzitzit* appears in the list of positive commandments that depend on time and from which women are exempt (*bQidd.* 33b).

The *halakhah* as quoted above from the *Mishnah* can be taken to describe the historical reality of the period, but it did not hold in every case, for we read (*ibid.*): "The observance of all the negative ordinances, whether they depend on time or not, is incumbent both on men and on women, excepting the commandments 'You shall not mar [the corners of your beard]' and 'You shall not round [the corners of your heads]' and 'You shall not become unclean because of the dead'." To these three exceptions the *amoraim* added more: women are obligated to eat *matzah* during Passover, which is a positive commandment dependent on time (*yQidd.* 1.7, 61c); and they are obligated to rejoice at the festivals and to participate in the "meeting day" (הקהל - the convocation of the people at the end of the seven-year agricultural cycle [cf. Deut. 31.10–3], *bQidd.* 34a). And of the positive commandments not dependent on the time of year, women are exempt from the study of *Torah*, procreation and redemption of the first-born (*ibid.*).[2] From all these examples, and from the exceptions in the *Talmudim*, we can see that in practice there was no operative rule which forbade or permitted women's participation in performing the commandments; rather, the *halakhah* reflected custom.

A major exception is *tzitzit*. As we have seen, R. Shimeon in the *Tosefta* holds the minority opinion, as opposed to his colleagues who obligated even women to perform the commandment. The matter is presented with a positive face in a *baraita* in the *Babylonian Talmud*: "Our rabbis taught: Everyone is obligated [to perform the commandment] of *tzitzit*: priests, Levites, Israelites, proselytes and slaves" (*bMen.* 43a). Yet in the tractate *Qiddushin* (33b) of the *Babylonian Talmud*, the commandment to wear *tzitzit* is presented as applying only to men. This

---

[2] See Rabbi S. Goren, "Women in Positive Commandments Dependent upon Time," *Mahanaim* 98 (1965), 10–6 [Hebrew].

apparent contradiction indicates perhaps the gradual process by which the rabbis exempted women from participation in ritual activity.

The historical reality, as opposed to ideal set forth in the *halakhah*, can be partly drawn out by examining those places in which the sources, involved in a discussion of some other matter, incidentally mention women's participation in the commandments. First of all, women were involved in the performance of commandments connected to the Temple service.[3] A *talmudic* tradition relates the custom of women going up to pray in the Temple, more specifically, the daughters of Lod would prepare bread-dough at home, go up to pray in Jerusalem and manage to return home in time to bake bread from the risen dough. The same source relates that the daughters of Sepphoris also had the custom of going up to Jerusalem and hurrying back home, except that they were not able to accomplish what the daughters of Lod could because of the greater distance from the capital (*yMS* 5.2, 56a; *Lam. R.* 3.3). It is true that these women were engaging in voluntary prayer, but other women were obligated to go up to the Temple from time to time in order to bring special sacrifices, such as after childbirth. Of course, such a sacrifice could be brought on any number of occasions, and a ruling by Rabban Gamaliel the Elder allowed a woman one sacrifice, to be brought for several births (*mKer.* 1.7; *Sif. Tazria* 3.7, 59b-c ed. Weiss).[4] This could have been the reason why Jesus' mother Mary went up to the Temple with her husband, who performed the commandment of redeeming his first-born (*Luke* 2.21–39).

Similarly, several sources of *aggadic* origin indicate that women participated in the three annual pilgrimages to Jerusalem, despite the contrary claim in the rabbinic sources. For example, Jesus' mother Mary is said to have been in Jerusalem, along with other residents of her home village Nazareth, for one of the traditional pilgrimage festivals (*Luke* 2.41–50). If *Luke* was working from a historical tradition, Mary's presence in Jerusalem for the festival, together with her husband and sons, indicates that women of the period did make the festival pilgrimages, but unfortunately Luke's evidence is not of the most reliable sort. On the other hand, we might similarly interpret Mary's presence in Jerusalem for Passover when Jesus was executed as evidence of women making the pilgrim-

---

[3] See now Susan Grossman, "Women and the Jerusalem Temple," in *Daughters of the King: Women and the Synagogue*, edd. Susan Grossman and Rivka Haut (Philadelphia 1992), 15–37.

[4] This ruling was motivated by economic considerations, since the cost of sacrifices had risen so high as to be beyond the economic means of most women. According to one *aggadic* tradition, the price of sacrifices dropped as a result of the ruling, but it is more likely that women simply took advantage of the provision and brought one sacrifice for many births. See also S. Safrai, "Home and Family," in *The Jewish People in the First Century II = Compendia Rerum Iudaicarum ad Novum Testamentum Section One*, edd. S. Safrai and M. Stern (Assen 1976), 769.

ages (*John* 19.25; *Acts* 1.14).[5] A story from the *Babylonian Talmud* also indicates that women regularly joined the pilgrimages to Jerusalem: "It once happened (that a man said to his sons: I will sacrifice the Passover-offering with whichever of you goes up first to Jerusalem) and his daughters arrived before his sons, so that the daughters showed themselves zealous, and the sons indolent" (*bNed.* 36a).[6]

Related to the question of pilgrimage is the question of whether women also lay their hands on the offerings sacrificed during the pilgrimage festivals. In this connection we read R. Yose's remarks: "Abba Eleazar told me: We had a calf for a peace offering, and we took it out to the Women's Court and the women lay their hands on it" (*Sif. Dibora Denedaba* 2.2, p. 20 ed. Finkelstein; *bHag.* 16b). The sages do answer him: "Is there indeed laying hands on sacrifices in the Women's Court? Rather, they did it to let the women have the satisfaction of doing so;" but this answer is not necessarily an accurate reflection of the custom in the time of the Second Temple, only the sages' later interpretation of it.

Women took part in the religious obligations and customs of the pilgrimage festival Sukkot. Many sources mention the balcony which was constructed above the Women's Court in the Temple in order to enable men to dance in the court during the celebration of the ceremonial drawing of water (*bet ha-shoeva*) while the women sat above and avoided mixing with the men (*mMidd.* 2.5; *tSukk.* 4.1; *ySukk.* 5.2, 55b; *bSukk.* 51b).[7] The *Tosefta* also states explicitly that before the construction of the balcony, women and men would intermingle dur-

---

[5] It is true that the gospel according to *John* has a theological character and contradicts the accounts of the crucifixion in the other gospels, but *Acts* has a more neutral tone and is thus more reliable. Mary's presence in the "upstairs room" with the apostles after Jesus' death seems to be an incidental detail which may reflect an historical tradition.

[6] Pilgrimage to Jerusalem was stopped after the destruction of the Temple, but it was still viewed as a positive commandment depending on time from which women were exempted. The rabbis, however, had a tradition in which Jonah's wife performed the pilgrimage (*Mekhilta de R. Ishmael, Bo* 17, p. 68 ed. Horovitz-Rabin; *yBer.* 2.3, 4c; *yErub.* 10.1, 26a; *bErub.* 96a). Although Rashi identifies this woman as the wife of the prophet of Jonah b. Amitai, she was probably in fact a woman known from the Second Temple period. In this context the following story is of particular interest: "It once happened that a man made his wife vow not to make a pilgrimage to Jerusalem, and she did go up" (*tNed.* 5.1; *bNed.* 23a) – so far so good, but the continuation of the story is unexpected: "The man came and asked R. Yose about it, and he said: If you knew that she is violating your word, etc." Since there was a problem with a vow, the husband was required to consult a sage and request that he annul the vow; yet the sage being consulted is R. Yose b. Halafta, the disciple of R. Aqiba, who lived after the destruction of the Temple: what pilgrimage could be meant?

[7] Of course, unlike the women's section in the synagogue, the Court of Women did not serve solely women, but marked the boundary beyond which women could not cross into the Temple if they had no sacrifices to offer. See S. Safrai, "Was there a Woman's Gallery in the Synagogue of Antiquity," *Tarbiz* 32 (1963), 329–38 [Hebrew].

ing that ceremony, and this was considered indecent by a Jewish court of law. We may thus suppose that women also participated in the dancing.

A related question is whether women were required to reside in the *sukkah*. In a discussion of the proper size of a *sukkah*, R. Judah related the following story: "It once happened that the *sukkah* of (Queen) Helene was more than twenty cubits high, and elders entered and departed from her (*sukkah*) without saying a word about it to her". The sages answered him: "Because she was a woman, and women are exempt from the obligation of sitting in a *sukkah*" (*tSukk.* 1.1; *ySukk.* 1.1, 51d; *bSukk.* 2b), but this response clearly reflects the period of the tradents and is later than the event itself, which reflects another practice.

Another commandment in which women participated and which had a connection to the Temple was the nazirite vow. Anyone who made such a vow abstained from wine and all other products of the vine, avoided contamination by corpses, let his/her hair grow until the end of the period of the vow, and completed the vow by bringing certain sacrifices to the Temple. Three women are known from the Second Temple period to have made a nazirite vow and to have offered the proper sacrifices at its completion. One is Mariamme of Palmyra (*mNed.* 6.11; *tNaz.* 4.10), the second is Queen Helene (*mNaz.* 3.6; *Sifre Zuta* 6.5, p. 241 ed. Horovitz), and the third is Queen Berenice (*BJ* 2.313). Nothing more is known about Mariamme other than her city of origin, but quite a bit more is known about the other two. Helene's Nazirite vow seems to match her particularly strict observance of the commandments, but Berenice's is a bit odd in light of other things known about her. She did not exactly live a life of religious devotion or abstinence: the gossip was that she had incestuous relations with her brother (*AJ* 20.145; Juv. *Sat.* 6.156–60); she left her third husband, King Polemo of Cilicia, on her own initiative (*AJ* 20.146); and during the siege of Jerusalem and afterward she lived with the Roman general Titus as his conjugal partner, without the benefit of an official marriage (Suet. *Tit.* 7.1–2; *Dio* 66.18.1; *Epit. de Caesaribus* 10.7). But this catalogue of Berenice's sexual sins reveals more about the authors of the sources and their religious outlook than about the religious feelings of the queen herself. The fact is that Berenice did not agree to marry Polemo until he had undergone circumcision, and from the description of his life after she left him ("and when the marriage was annulled he stopped living according to Jewish custom") it appears that while married he had lived a Jewish life for her sake. These three instances seem to indicate that taking a nazirite vow became the fashion primarily among high-class women towards the end of the Second Temple period, a restriction explained partly by the high price of sacrifices at the time. Offering sacrifices would have afforded an opportunity to display wealth and piety. Another woman is said to have made a nazirite vow while drunk (*mNaz.* 2.3), but her vow was not taken seriously by the sages because of her drunken state.[8]

---

[8] It is worth noting that in contrast to these specific cases all male nazirites mentioned

Women fulfilled other commandments, aside from those connected to the Temple, during the period of the Second Temple and afterwards – circumcision, for example. According to some sources, it was the mothers who circumcised their sons. The books of the *Maccabees* tell of women who circumcised their own sons and were put to death for it by cruel tortures (*1 Macc.* 1.60–1; *2 Macc.* 6.10; *4 Macc.* 4.25). *1 Maccabees* does relate the same thing about the other members of the executed women's families, as well as the ones who circumcised them (τοὺς περιτετμηκότας αὐτούς), but the Greek word used for the women's offense is the same word. Rabbinic literature preserves another two stories which seem to indicate that women were the ones who circumcised their sons. It is related that after three sisters from Sepphoris circumcised their sons and the boys all died, Rabban Shimeon b. Gamaliel permitted a fourth sister to postpone circumcising her son (*tShab.* 15.8; *bYeb.* 64b); and R. Nathan allowed a woman from Cappadocia to postpone circumcising her fourth son for quite a while after her first three died as a result of the operation (*tShab.* 15.8; *yYeb.* 6.6, 7d; *Song of Songs R.* 7.2.3). Neither of these stories mentions the father or any other male who performs the circumcision. Although both appear to be different versions of the same incident, their wording seems to suggest a historical kernel.[9] Women's performance of circumcisions fits well with other forms of women's involvement in the medical and para-medical professions, as we will see below.

There is also some evidence for women of the period performing the commandment of phylacteries (*tefillin*). The rabbis preserve the story of Mikhal bat Kushi putting on phylacteries. In the Mekhilta (*Mekhilta de R. Ishmael Bo* 17, p. 68 ed. Horovitz-Rabin), the story is told without further additions, but both the *Palestinian Talmud* (*yBer.* 2.3, 4c; *yErub.* 10.1, 26a) and the *Babylonian Talmud* (*bErub.* 96a) note that the sages warned her against doing so.[10] Thus it seems

---

in the sources are anonymous. Thus the *Mishnah* tells of nazirites (which could have included women) from the Diaspora who went up to Jerusalem and found the Temple in ruins (*mNaz.* 5.4). A better-known story is the one about the 300 poor nazirites who went up to Jerusalem in the days of Shimeon b. Shetah and King Alexander Yannai (*yBer.* 7.2, 11b; *Gen. R.* 91.3, pp. 1115–7 ed. Theodor-Albeck; *Eccl. R.* 7.11); women could also have been among that group. Another nazirite, a youth from the time of Shimeon the Just, is mentioned but not named (*tNaz.* 4.7; *yNed.* 1.1, 36a).

[9] See J. Preuss, *Biblical and Talmudic Medicine*, translation F. Rosner (New York 1978), 35–6.

[10] In the *Palestinian Talmud* (*yErub.* 10.1, 26a), probably on the basis of *Ps.* 7.1, Mikhal is identified as the daughter of Saul. In the *Babylonian Talmud* we find the following *midrash:* "And is Kush really his name? Isn't his name Saul? Rather, just as a Kushite is distinguishable by his skin, so Saul was distinguishable by his deeds" (*bMQ* 16b), and on this see R. R. Hutton, "Cush the Benjaminite and *Psalm Midrash*," *Hebrew Annual Review* 10 (1986), 127–30. The fact that no early rabbinic source and only one late one identifies this woman as Mikhal the daughter of Saul suggests that she was a woman from the Second Temple period who lived only a short time before the rabbis reported her actions.

that there was some historical memory of a woman who put on phylacteries, but this act caused surprise even then, for otherwise there would have been no reason to take note of it.

Women were also involved in making the *erub*. This was not exactly a commandment, but a legal fiction which allowed neighbors to keep the Sabbath jointly and carry objects across common courtyards and alleyways. We find in the sources two instances in which women set the *erub* with their neighbors just before the Sabbath. In the first instance, related by R. Joshua, two women who were hostile to each other made peace when they jointly set an *erub* (*yErub*. 3.2, 20d).[11] The second story appears in both the *Babylonian* and *Palestinian Talmudim*, with slight differences. The version in the *Palestinian Talmud* is quite simple: "It once happened that a woman made an *erub* for her mother-in-law without her knowledge" (*yErub*. 7.11, 24d), whereas in the *Babylonian Talmud* the roles are reversed, the women are from a well-known family and even the reason for the incident is described: "It once happened that the daughter-in-law of R. Oshayah went to the bath-house [before Sabbath], and it became dark [before she left] and her mother-in-law made an *erub* for her" (*bErub*. 80a).[12] In both stories, women set the *erub*; the logical explanation for this is that the *erub* had to be set while the man would normally still be out of the house at work, and so the task fell on the woman.

We may note in this connection that men relied on women's exemption from performing commandments in order that they themselves perform the commandments with greater devotion. For example, we hear of women who incurred ritual impurity so that men could avoid doing so on the eve of Passover: "R. Eliezer says: It once happened in Bet Dagan which is in Judaea, that a man died on the eve of Passover, and the women came and tied a rope to the stone closing the burial-cave (an action that may cause defilement), and the men pulled it away (an action which requires strength but avoids contact with the

---

[11] In *yErub*. 7.10, 24c-d, the story is told by R. Joshua b. Levi. If this is correct, the story falls outside the chronological limits of the present study.

[12] That these are two version of the same incident becomes clear in the continuation of the story. According to the *Palestinian Talmud*, "The matter came before R. Ishamel and he sought to forbid it. R. Hiyya said to him: Thus I heard from your father: Whenever you see an opportunity for relaxing the laws of *erub*, seize it," but in the *Babylonian Talmud* the situation is reversed: "The matter was reported to R. Hiyya and he forbade it. Said R. Ishmael b. R. Yose to him: Babylonian, are you so strict about the laws of *erub*? Thus said my father: Whenever you see an opportunity for relaxing the laws of *erub*, seize it". While it is true that according to the *Palestinian Talmud* the daughter-in-law is the one who sets the *erub* and R. Hiyya is the one who permits and R. Ishmael forbids, whereas in the *Babylonian Talmud* the mother-in-law is the one who sets the *erub* and the roles of the two rabbis are reversed, it is nevertheless clear that both versions are based on the same ruling of R. Yose b. Halafta, and since the main figures are the same in both versions, the errors are errors of transmission; the story is the same.

corpse), and the women entered and buried the deceased (an action which certainly causes defilement) and the men performed their Passover sacrifices in a state of ritual purity" (*Sifre Zuta* 19.16, p. 313 ed. Horovitz; *tOhol.* 3.9). The *Mishnah* offers another example of women performing a commandment for the same purpose: "A woman may take [the *lulab* on *Sukkot*] out of the hand of her son or out of the hand of her husband and put it back in water on the Sabbath (thus observing the Sabbath less stringently)" (*mSukk.* 3.15).

In conclusion, we have found that women sometimes performed certain "positive commandments that depend on time" from which they were later exempt *en bloc*. Most of these commandments were connected to the Temple. The destruction of the Temple brought in its wake a sharp reduction in women's participation in religious ritual. The rabbis variously interpreted the evidence that women performed these commandments while the Temple stood, for the traditions contradicted the ideal picture they were creating of the Temple service. But the historical memory of women's participation in the Temple service does not have to correspond to the interpretation given by later sages.[13]

Occupations and Professions

Many *halakhot* having to do with rearing of children are formulated with feminine verbs – a linguistic feature of Hebrew absent in Indo-European languages – even though the laws are intended for men and women alike. The fact that the mother was mainly responsible for the rearing of children was so obvious that the sources wasted no time stressing the point. Many laws indeed assume it implicitly, although none states it in so many words. For example, "a woman may pull her child along" in the public domain on the Sabbath (*mShab.* 18.2) because the mother is the one who does this the other days of the week; it is not ruled, however, that the father is forbidden to "pull his child along" on the Sabbath. Thus also a woman is permitted to wash one hand on *Yom Kippur* in order to feed her child (*bHull.* 107b), but as the source continues we see that the law specifies "mother" not in order to exclude the father but because she was the one who routinely fed her children: "They said about Shammai the Elder that he did not want to feed [his child] with one hand, and they ruled that he should feed [the child] with both hands". The law specifies the woman, but the illustration involves a man.

---

[13] Hannah Safrai has also drawn attention to women's high level of participation in the Temple. In a public lecture, she explained the apparent contradictions between the *halakhah* and historical descriptions by proposing that women pressured the rabbis to change widespread laws pertaining to the Temple service. Safrai's assumption is that the rabbis' description of the Temple is Second Temple Sadducean and not rabbinic *post eventum*. This approach to the sources, however, is questionable.

On the other hand, the rabbis singled out certain commandments which were the father's obligation to perform for his son: a father had to circumcise his son, teach him *Torah*, teach him a trade, redeem him, marry him to a woman, and so forth (*bQidd.* 29a). The mother is explicitly exempt from all these obligations (*mQidd.* 1.7), but this of course does not mean that the mother had no hand or interest in any of these areas. The difference between these obligations and the ones mentioned in the previous paragraph has to do with the age of the child. The mother took care of the child when he was very young, while the father taught him *Torah* and a trade and married him off when he reached a mature age. It is true that a son was circumcised while still an infant, but as we have seen, the woman often was responsible for doing this herself. The formulation of these *halakhot* as commandments may be explained by the fact that the father, as opposed to the mother, did not view these obligations as self-evident.

Yet the feminine gender is used not only for the language of those laws dealing with the care of children. Many other laws regulating tasks normally assumed by women are similarly formulated, as the following few examples illustrate. "If a woman [who is impure] kneads dough in a kneading-trough, are the woman and kneading- trough unclean for seven days and the dough clean?" (*bHag.* 22b) – which indicates that women were the ones who kneaded dough for bread. Another example: "A woman should not fill a pot with lupine and pounded wheat and put it into an oven as darkness is coming in the evening of the Sabbath" (*tShab.* 3.1). And finally, in a description of how a priest inspects for leprosy-signs (נגעים), the *Mishnah* says that "the man is inspected [while he stands] like one that hoes, and like one that gathers olives, and the woman [while she stands] like one that rolls out bread, and like one that gives suck to her child and like one that weaves at an upright loom ... . R. Judah says: Also like one that spins flax ..." (*mNeg.* 2.4). Thus cooking, baking, spinning and weaving were women's tasks.

The rabbis in their manner defined these tasks as "tasks which a wife must perform for her husband," and these included "grinding flour and baking bread and washing clothes and cooking food and giving suck to her child and making ready his bed and working in wool" (*mKet.* 5.5). And in every instance in which the *halakhah* deals with one of these tasks, the formulation is in the feminine gender. In this context, the difference between a man and a woman is that the woman takes care of household tasks, or, as the *Mekhilta de-R. Shimeon bar Yohai* puts it: "(In Egypt the children of Israel) would perform the tasks of the house and the tasks of the field: men's tasks and women's tasks" (p. 38, ed. Melamed).

This division of labor between work done inside and outside the house is reflected also in the parables of Jesus in *Matthew* and *Luke*, deriving therefore from the anonymous *Q*, which seems to have been a collection of the sayings of Jesus himself. One parable describes two women sitting together and grinding meal (*Matt.* 24.41; *Luke* 17.35). In another, Jesus compares the kingdom of heaven to a woman who mixes yeast into flour (*Matt.* 13.33–4; *Luke* 13.20–1). *Luke* offers a female version of the shepherd and lost sheep in the parable of the woman who scours the house looking for a lost coin (15.8–9).[14]

The rabbis see a woman's performance of these tasks as her compensation to her husband for his maintenance of her, and they even rule that "if he gives her nothing towards her own needs, her handiwork is hers" (*mKet.* 5.9). If she has maidservants, they can perform the work she owes her husband (*ibid.* 5.5), but "R. Eliezer says: Even if she brought him in a hundred maidservants, he should compel her to work in wool, for idleness leads to lechery (זמה)" (*ibid.*). The idea that keeping busy with spinning and weaving protects a woman's chastity and also demonstrates a woman's diligence and high quality originates in classical Greece and can be found throughout Greek literature.[15] R. Eliezer's adoption of this idea may illustrate Hellenistic influence in Palestine. In another context, R. Eliezer is found to say to a woman: "A woman has no wisdom, except in handling her spindle" (*bYoma* 66b).[16]

The rabbis' very clear notion, then, was that the tasks to which women should devote themselves are all confined to the house. That means that the husband had the full responsibility to support the family, which was done outside the house, either through agricultural work in his own field or a trade in his own shop, or as someone else's hired laborer. Even work considered to be a woman's task when performed inside the house, like baking, was a male profession in other contexts (נחתם, e.g. in *mHal.* 1.7; *mPes.* 2.8; *mYad.* 1.5).

But the rabbis' picture is once again idealized and does not necessarily represent historical reality. For one thing, it is known that in agricultural societies, the division of labor between home and field, principally during the harvest and fruit-picking seasons, is not so sharply defined. We even find a *baraita* saying, "Whoever hires a worker, his son and wife will glean after him" (*bBM* 12a); in other words, even the wife of the hired laborer will work in the field with him.

Even certain things which a woman worked at inside her house could turn into an income-producing profession. The *Mishnah* discusses the case of the woman who prepares dough for sale in the market (*mHal.* 2.7; *tHal.* 1.8; *yHal.*

---

[14] On *Luke*'s alleged feminist purpose in this feminine parallel to the male-oriented shepherd parable, see Constance F. Parvey, "The Theology and Leadership of Women in the New Testament," in *Religion and Sexism: Images of Women in the Jewish and Christian Tradition*, ed. Rosemary R. Ruether (New York 1974), 138–46; L. J. Swidler, *Biblical Affirmations of Women* (Philadelphia 1979), 251–84.

[15] Sarah B. Pomeroy, *Goddesses, Whores, Wives and Slaves: Women in Classical Antiquity* (New York 1975), 71–3; Eva C. Keuls, *The Reign of the Phallus: Sexual Politics in Ancient Athens* (New York 1985), 247–58.

[16] Similarly, in the *Iliad*, Hector sends his wife Andromache back to her spindle (6.490–3); in *Odyssey* 1.356–7. Telemachos does the same to Penelope.

2.7, 58d). Elsewhere rulings are made regarding women who sell garments which they themselves made from wool (in Judaea) or linen (in the Galilee) (*mBQ* 10.9). The mention of wool in Judaea and linen in the Galilee seem to lend a shade of reality to the law, beside the fact that a woman's engaging in business contradicts the rabbinical world view, for she would necessarily have come into contact with her customers.

Women's skill in spinning and weaving won official recognition. One group of women, perhaps belonging to the same family, are mentioned as the weavers of the curtain which hung in the Temple. We hear that these women "took their wage from donations in the Temple treasury," just like the family of Abtinos, which prepared all the incense for the sanctuary, and the family of Garmo, which was responsible for the shew-bread (*tSheq.* 2.6).[17] The same women are mentioned in a source closer to the Second Temple period, the Syrian *Apocalypse of Baruch* (10.19), where it is stated. "And you virgins, who weave fine linen and silk with gold of Ophir, take with haste all these things and cast them into the fire".[18]

We also hear that women would sell olives for their husbands: "Rabban Shimeon b. Gamaliel says: It is permitted to buy from housewives olives (in Upper Galilee during the festivals: *Babylonian Talmud*), for sometimes a man is ashamed to sell them at the door of his house and so gives them to his wife to sell" (*tBQ* 11.7; *bBQ* 119a). The act of selling olives for the husband put the woman in an entirely new position, that of shopkeeper who serves customers in the family store. We know that, despite the unsuitability of this occupation for women according to the rabbinic ethical code, women did in fact work as shopkeepers, for certain laws deal specifically with this phenomenon: "If a man set up his wife as a shopkeeper or appointed her a guardian, he may exact from her an oath whensoever he will" (*mKet.* 9.4; cf. *tKet.* 9.3; *bKet.* 86b; and see also *mShebu.* 7.8).

---

[17] This *baraita* also appears in *bKet.* 106a, after its essential contents are related by the *amora*, Rav. Elsewhere (*ySheq.* 4.2, 48a; *Song of Songs R.* 3.6.1), the *amora* Samuel transmits the same things. Then another opinion is expressed: "Rav Huna (חונא; הונה in *SS. R.*) says: (they were paid) from the contributions (תרומות) ("fund" [לשכח]: *SS. R.*) consecrated for Temple repairs." In the *Babylonian Talmud,* this is the opinion of Rav Nahman. *Song of Songs R.* reports that this controversy also had an *amoraic* interpretation: "One authority puts the curtain on the same footing as the building, and the other on the same footing as the offerings." *bKet.* 106a records another *baraita* alongside this one: "The women who brought up their children for the [services of the red] heifer received their wages from the Temple funds." But this provoked a controversy: "Abba Saul said: The notable women of Jerusalem fed them and maintained them;" and see on this above.

[18] The mention of virgins in this context is quite interesting, for virgins had a similar function in the temple of Athena at Athens, see Pomeroy (above, n. 15), 76; Keuls (above, n. 15), 306–8.

Just as we find that a woman's domestic training could be turned into an occupation or profession, and afterwards even make her shopkeeper, so we find
women working in another area that, given their backgrounds, is entirely fitting
– inn-keeping. Since women's place was in the home, they could quite satisfac-
torily provide hotel services in their own homes and contribute thereby to the
support of the household, especially since their husbands normally worked outside the house. Women innkeepers are mentioned in the *halakhic* sources in incidental fashion, such as in the formulation of laws: "If a man gives a woman innkeeper (פונדקית) food to cook for him …" (*tDem.* 4.32); "If a man gave [food to
be cooked] to a woman innkeeper he must tithe what he gives her and also what
he receives back from her" (*mDem.* 3.5). A woman innkeeper was even allowed
to testify that a man died, in order to free his widow to remarry: "It once happened that the sons of Levi went to Zoar, the city of Palms, and one of them fell
sick on the way there so they brought him to an inn. When they returned there
they asked the mistress of the inn, Where is our companion? She told them, He
died and I buried him. And they allowed his wife to remarry" (*mYeb.* 16.7). At
the same time, however, innkeeping was not a respectable occupation for women. The reason the rabbis gave for the need to tithe what one gives and receives
from a woman innkeeper is that "she must be suspected of changing it (with
someone else's untithed food)" (*mDem.* 3.5).   On accepting a woman innkeeper's testimony on the death of a husband, the sages asked R. Aqiba, "Should
a priestess [not be deemed more trustworthy] than the mistress of an inn?"
(*mYeb.* 16.7).[19] We see from this that the priest's wife and the woman innkeeper
stand at opposite ends of the scale of respectability. Josephus, like the *Targum
Jonathan*, relates that the prostitute Rahab (*Josh.* 2.1) was an innkeeper (the
mistress of a καταγώγιον, *AJ* 5.7), and this attribution further darkened the reputation of woman innkeepers, rather than exonerated Rahab.

Finally, we are compelled to note three more professions peculiar to women.
First is hair-dresser. The *Mishnah* states that "the hair-dresser's receptacle for
the flour" is "susceptible to uncleanness as being something that is sat upon,
since girls sit in it to have their hair dressed" (*mKel.* 15.3; cf. *tKel BM* 5.5); thus
dressing women's hair was a profession in which women could work. The demand for women hair-dressers is difficult to gauge, for presumably those women who could pay to have their hair done could also afford to keep slaves who
would do the same thing; at least, the *Mishnah* mentions "a maidservant that is a
hair-dresser" (*mQidd.* 2.3). However that may be, the *Babylonian Talmud* interprets the name Mary Magdalene (*Mark* 15.47; *Matt.* 27.56; *Luke* 8.2; 24.10;
John 19.25) to mean that she was a hair-dresser (גדלת see *bShab.* 104b Munich

---

[19] In the *Palestinian Talmud*, the *amoraim* have qualms about accepting a woman innkeeper's evidence, see the remark of the *amora* Samuel bar Sosatri: "They treated her like
a gentile who was speaking innocently" (*yYeb.* 16.10, 16b).

MS); the interpretation derives from another passage which mentions another woman who could be mistaken for Magdalene: "Mariamme, the women's hairdresser (מרים מגדלא שערא נשיא)" (*bHag.* 4b).

Secondly, the midwife, known as wise woman (חכמה *Sifre Zuta* 19.11, p. 306 ed. Horovitz; *mShab.* 18.3; *mRH* 2.5) or lifegiver (חיה *Mekhilta de R. Ishmael Mishpatim* 8, p. 276 ed. Horovitz-Rabin, although this word also refers to the woman who is giving birth while sitting on the birthing stool *Sifre Deut.* 319, p. 365 ed. Finkelstein; *yKil.* 9.4, 32b; *yKet.* 12.3, 35a). The profession of midwife was of course limited to women, although not necessarily Jewish women (cf. *mAZ* 2.1). Every reference in rabbinic literature to a person involved in midwifery uses feminine forms. The laws dealing with childbirth were better known to midwives than to the sages themselves, as we see in the following story: "The maidservant of Bar Qappara, going to help a Jewish woman in labor on the Sabbath, went and asked Rabbi if it was permitted to cut the umbilical cord. He said to her: Go ask a midwife" (*yShab.* 18.3, 16c); in other words, the sage did not know the correct legal procedure for childbirth on the Sabbath and referred the question to the midwife, who was more of an expert than he. The maidservant responded to Rabbi: "The midwife is out. He told her: Then act according to your local custom" (*ibid.*); that is, in the absence of a midwife expert in the law, the woman had to act as she thought best. That means that if the midwife was a gentile, she followed non-Jewish procedures.

According to Josephus, one of the Zealots during the rebellion against Rome was named Joseph son of a ἰατρίνη (*Vita* 185), "midwife".[20] Midwifery trained women for another profession. If a woman could work as a midwife, she probably could also round out her knowledge of anatomy and work as a physician as well, whether or not she had formal training. A woman's regular experience in cooking would have made her familiar with plants and herbs, and without much extra effort she could learn which had medicinal uses. This sort of informal education is the reason why the knowledge and preparation of poisons were attributed to women (see below). That women had medical knowledge and experience and were customarily consulted regarding the treatment of illnesses, may very well be indicated by a remark in the *Tosefta*: "They do not say: Let these matters be done according to what women say or according to what Samaritans say, but they join the opinion of Israelites with them" (*tShab.* 15.15).

Finally, just as women were the ones who (as midwives) brought children into the world, so also women accompanied people to their graves as professional mourners.[21] The mourner (אליית) always appears in the feminine form in

---

[20] The feminine form of the masculine ἰατρός – physician – is almost invariably translated as midwife, see Preuss (above, n. 9), 12. However I believe a further investigation into this translation is in place.

[21] The language of the sources reveals a subconscious connection between birth and

the sources, for example *mMQ* 3.9: "they sing lamentations," "they clap their hands," "they wail," "one begins by herself and all respond after her" are all expressed in feminine language. By Jewish law a husband must hire at least one female mourner for his deceased wife (*mKet*. 4.4). The musical instrument used by a woman mourner was called a רביעית (*mKel*. 16.7); as also the ארוס (*ibid.* 15.6). R. Joshua finds a connection between women working as professional mourners and the story of the Garden of Eden (*Gen. R.* 17.8, pp. 159–60 ed. Theodor-Albeck). In the gospels, women were the ones who prepared Jesus' body for burial (*Mark* 16.1; *Luke* 23.5; 24.1; in *John* 19.40 it is men who do it).

We may conclude that it was very common for women to work. They helped support their households and worked in professions in which they had special knowledge and training, even if informal.

Study of *Torah*

Closely connected with the question of the occupations appropriate for women is the question of whether women were also permitted to study *Torah*. Lately, this entire matter, like the question of women's participation in the religious commandments, has furnished extensive material for debates on both theological and practical issues within Judaism. My comments with regard to women's participation in the commandments are relevant also here.

Josephus says that among Jews, women and slaves know the *Torah* (*CA* 2.181), although we cannot be exactly sure whether he means that *Torah*-study was open to women if they wanted it, or that women learned just enough *Torah* to know how to keep a proper Jewish household.

---

death. The rabbis occasionally refer to the womb of a pregnant woman by the same word used for "grave" (קבר) (e.g. *mOhol*. 7.4). Tirzah Z. Meachem, *Mishnah Tractate Niddah with Introduction: A Critical Edition with Notes on Variants, Commentary, Redaction and Chapters in Legal History and Realia* (Ph.D. diss. The Hebrew University of Jerusalem 1989), 195 [Hebrew], interprets this as referring only to a womb in which the fetus has died, but later (pp. 213–4) she acknowledges that the word is used to refer even to wombs with healthy fetuses. The identification of birth with death can be found also in Greek culture; see Pomeroy (above, n. 15), 44. Many theories have explained the connection between women and the mysteries of birth and death as resulting from women's presence at both events. See, e.g. E. Neuman, *The Great Mother* (Princeton 1955), 120–208; Sherry B. Ortner, "Is Female to Male as Nature is to Culture?" in *Women, Culture and Society*, edd. Michelle Z. Rosaldo and Louise Lamphere (Stanford CA 1974), 67–87, esp. 85–6; Elise Boulding, *The Underside of History: A View of Women through Time* (Boulder CO 1976), 135–40; Léone J. Archer, "'In Thy Blood Live': Gender and Ritual in the Judeo-Christian Tradition," in *Through the Devil's Gateway: Women, Religion and Taboo*, ed. Alison Joseph (London 1990), 22–49.

Jewish law seems not only to excuse but explicitly to exclude women from the religious obligation to study *Torah*: "'And you shall teach them to your sons' (*Deut.* 11.19), your sons and not your daughters" (*Sifre Deut.* 46, p. 104 ed. Finkelstein; cf. *bQidd.* 30a). This issue was controversial already in *mishnaic* times. In a discussion of whether daughters should be taught the laws and sections of the *Torah* pertaining to *sotah*, so that they would know that "merit holds punishment in suspense," (see above) Ben Azzai says: "A man must give his daughter a knowledge of *Torah* … . R. Eliezer says: Anyone who teaches his daughter *Torah*, it is as though he has taught her lechery" (*mSot.* 3.4). Elsewhere R. Eliezer also says: "They shall burn the teachings of *Torah* rather than convey them to women" (*ySot.* 3.4, 19a; cf. *bYoma* 66b), and we find there also a famous story illustrating R. Eliezer's fierce opposition to teaching *Torah* to women: "A wise woman (Matrona according to the *Palestinian Talmud*) asked R. Eliezer: How is it that, although only one sin was committed in connection with the golden calf, they died by three kinds of executions? He said to her: A woman has no wisdom except in handling her spindle, for it is written, 'And all the women that were wise-hearted did spin with their hands' (*Ex.* 35.25);" in other words, R. Eliezer sends the woman who is occupied with *Torah* back to her traditional household tasks.[22] Similarly R. Eleazar b. Azariah taught: "'Assemble the people together: men, women and little ones' (*Deut.* 31.12). If men come to study and women come to hear, why do the little ones come? To receive the reward for those who bring them" (*tSot.* 7.9). Women attend the assembly (הקהל), which as we have seen is a positive commandment dependent on time but from which women are not exempt (according to specific instructions in the Bible). However, women attend only as listeners whereas men come to study.

Actually, the question of whether some women could read Bible or even reached more advanced stages of study should be preceded by the question, to what extent Jewish women could read and write at all. The answer to this question is not obvious. In many cultures men receive a many-faceted education while women remain illiterate.

---

[22] Already in the last century, S. Y. Hurwitz, "R. Eliezer ben Hyrcanus and the Education of Women," *Hashahar* 11 (1883), 437–41 [Hebrew] determined that rabbinic sources present R. Eliezer as the only aggressive opponent of *Torah*-study for women. Hurwitz thought that R. Eliezer held his hostile attitude because he could not bear the scholarly accomplishment of his own wife, the learned scholar Imma Shalom, who was the sister of Rabban Gamaliel. Even if Hurwitz' first claim is correct, his second claim reveals a certain *naïveté* in the interpretation of the sources. There is no proof that Imma Shalom was in fact Rabban Gamaliel's sister (the only sources for this are Babylonian: *bShab.* 116a; *bBM* 59b), or that she was an accomplished scholar (cf. *ibid.* and *Sif. Shemini, Mekhilta de-Miluim* 33, 45c ed. Weiss; *bErub.* 63a; *bNed.* 20a-b). Those scholars who believe that Imma Shalom was indeed a *Torah* scholar attribute to her two stories (*bSanh.* 39a; 90b-91a) in which the central (unnamed) figure is Rabban Gamaliel's daughter, not his sister; see, e.g. H. Zirndorf, *Some Jewish Women* (Philadelphia 1892), 142–4.

In such places as the royal households women acquired the skill of reading and perhaps also writing. Alexandra wrote letters to Cleopatra (*AJ* 15.24; 45; 62). Antipater's mother, Doris, wrote her son warning-letters that were intercepted (*BJ* 1.620; *AJ* 17.93). A Jewish maidservant of Livia by the name of Acme wrote letters to Antipater and Herod and included therein a forged letter allegedly from Herod's sister Salome (*BJ* 1.641; *AJ* 17.134–41). But examples restricted to royal houses are not representative. We should add that letters written by royal women, which could very well be dictated, are not really evidence for the ability to write.[23]

The documents in Babatha's archive indicate that Babatha, despite her involvement in stormy legal battles in the later years of her life, did not know how to read or write,[24] even though she clearly signed one document.[25] Similarly a deed of sale found in Wadi Murba'at[26] is signed by both a man and his wife (Shapira daughter of Jesus). Next to her signature appear the words "for herself," i.e. she signed the document herself, but the continuation of the line is restored and read by the editors as "she asked for this document (ה]כ[תבין ש]א[לה),"[27] which possibly means that Shapira knew how to sign her name but the document had to be read to her before she signed it. The added words could also be interpreted to mean that Shapira asked for special instruction regarding the way in which she had to sign her name, for she did not know how to do it. Yet there is a third interpretation: it could be that Shapira, although she knew a little Hebrew, did not know enough to understand the document, for her husband, Kleopas son of Eutrapelus, knew no Hebrew (or Aramaic) and signed his name only in Greek; Shapira most likely knew Greek as did her husband.[28]

---

[23] Acme's knowledge of writing is another matter, but does not fit into the geographical limits of this study. And see also Susan Cole, "Could Greek Women Read and Write?" in *Reflections of Women in Antiquity*, ed. Helen P. Foley (New York 1981), 219–45.

[24] N. Lewis, *The Documents from the Bar Kokhba Period in the Cave of the Letters II: Greek Papyri* (Jerusalem 1989), 60.

[25] *Ibid.* 67 and plate 14.

[26] P. Benoit, J. T. Milik, R. de Vaux, *Les grottes de Muraba'ât = Discoveries in the Judaean Desert* II (Oxford 1961), 142.

[27] This reading is quite doubtful (*ibid.*). Milik is confident in the reading because of an unpublished document in his possession, apparently from Nahal Hever which contains a woman's signature with the additional words, "for herself she asked this document (על נפשה שאלה כתב)," *ibid.* 143.

[28] One wonders about the extent to which Jewish women in Palestine knew how to read and write Greek. This question can be partially examined in the *amoraic* period. R. Abbahu is said to have permitted, on the basis of a ruling by R. Yohanan, teaching one's daughter Greek because "this is an adornment to her" (*yPeah* 1.1, 15c; *ySot.* 9.16, 24c). The sages retorted that R. Abbahu based this ruling on his superiors because he wanted to teach his own daughter Greek.

According to Safrai,[29] illiteracy such as Babatha's was not limited to women. He claims that the educational system of the time tried to make reading a universal skill by teaching it to all (male) youths, but writing was studied separately, not as part of elementary education. Yet several laws of the time assume that women could write. For instance: "All are qualified to write a bill of divorce ... a woman may write her own bill of divorce" (*mGitt.* 2.5); "They taught: ... a *Torah* scroll, *tefillin* and a *mezuzah* which ... a woman wrote ... are disqualified" (*bMen.* 42b). These laws take it for granted that women could write bills of divorce and even *Torah* scrolls; the question is only whether they are qualified to do so.

Women studying *Torah* also appear quite incidentally in unrelated discussions in rabbinic sources.[30] In the *Mishnah* we find the following: "If a man is forbidden by vow to have any benefit from his fellow, ... he may teach Scripture to his sons and daughters ..." (*mNed.* 4.2–3);[31] here, without specifically intending to do so, the *Mishnah* reveals that daughters learned Bible with sons. Yet women could learn even more than Bible: "Men and women who have suffered a flux, menstruants and women who have given birth [and all these are ritually unclean] are permitted to read in the *Torah*, the Prophets, and the Writings and to learn *mishnah*, *midrash*, *halakhah* and *aggadah* ..." (*tBer.* 2.12). This *halakhah* assumes that women not only knew and could read the *Torah*, but also had the skills required to study rabbinic literature.[32] A conservative view would hold that the second part of this *halakhah* (the study of rabbinic literature) relates only to men (i.e. who have suffered a flux), but such an interpretation receives no clear support from the text itself. By another ruling, "a woman may not be a teacher of scribes" (*mQidd.* 4.13), i.e. she may not teach writing, for reasons of modesty. Yet just as "a bachelor may not be a teacher of scribes" (*ibid.*) even if he has the skill and knowledge to do so because "the mother [of the pupil] or his sister may come with him" and become a sexual temptation for the teacher (*yQidd.* 4.11, 66c), so also the woman, theoretically, had the skill and know-

---

[29] S. Safrai, "Education and the Study of *Torah*," in *The Jewish People in the First Century* II = *Compendia Rerum Iudaicarum ad Novum Testamentum Section One,* edd. S. Safrai and M. Stern (Assen 1976), 952.

[30] And see also S. Safrai, "Women Learned in *Torah* in the *Mishnaic* and *Talmudic* Period," *Mahanaim* 98 (1965), 58–9 [Hebrew].

[31] The word "daughters" is missing from many manuscripts, but in this case the absence is surely the result of deliberate omission by copyists who could not accept the simple meaning of the text.

[32] This interpretation has also been suggested lately by D. Boyarin, *Carnal Israel: Reading Sex in Talmudic Culture* (Berkeley 1993), 180–1, and see his remarks there about the version of the *baraita* in the *Babylonian Talmud*. Meachem (above, n. 21), 2 argues that the meaning of this *halakhah* is that women were expected to learn well the laws of *niddah* and *zov*, but I cannot accept this interpretation, which seems too far removed from the plain meaning of the text.

ledge to teach writing to children. This conclusion is supported by another *hala-khah*: "A man marries a woman and he makes her promise that she ... will teach him *Torah*" (*tKet.* 4.6). This *halakhah* is illustrated by a story: "It happened with R. Joshua b. R. Aqiba, that he married a woman and made her promise that she would support him and teach him *Torah*" (*tKet.* 4.7; *yKet.* 5.2, 29d). This may mean that the woman will subsidize her husband's *Torah* studies, but the other possibility, that the woman provides actual instruction in the *Torah*, should not be rejected out of hand.[33]

The sources in any case do preserve some actual examples of *Torah*-study by women. One woman is said to have frequented the study-house of R. Meir in order to hear him expound the Bible. Her husband is said to have thought that she thus neglected her household duties (*ySot.* 1.4, 16d). *Luke* (10.38–42) says that Mary of Bethany, the sister of Martha, sat at Jesus' feet to hear his teaching, yet it is evident from the story that Mary's actions were seen to contradict the traditional womanly roles which her sister Martha filled – preparing food and serving it at table.[34] Despite the literary character of the story, Mary and Martha were undoubtedly historical figures and were counted among Jesus' disciples.[35] These two stories demonstrate that opposition to *Torah*-study by women was based on the woman's neglect of her traditional obligations in the house and kitchen that would result as a consequence.

Yet even R. Eliezer thought that some matters of *halakhah* were more suited to women than men, for he taught his wife about the signs of sexual maturity in an adolescent girl so that she could perform examinations and help him in his own work (*tNidd.* 6.8; *bNidd.* 48b). R. Ishmael is said to have done the same thing with his mother (*ibid.*). Thus there were some areas of the law in which women not only were permitted to be involved but even gained more expertise than men. We have already seen that the sages' own knowledge in the laws pertaining to childbirth was extremely limited compared to that of professional

---

[33] Perhaps in R. Aqiba's family it is more reasonable to suppose that his son's wife supported her husband and did not necessarily teach him *Torah*. The *Palestinian Talmud* preserves the tradition whereby R. Aqiba's wife sold her hair in order to enable her husband to go and study (*yShab.* 6.1, 7d; *ySot.* 9.16, 24c). On the same literary motifs applied to both Aqiba and his son, see J. Elbaum, "Models of Storytelling and Speech in Stories about the Sages," *Proceedings of the Seventh World Congress of Jewish Studies 1977* Div. 3 (Jerusalem 1981), 71, n. 2 [Hebrew]. For the theory that Rabbi Aqiba himself probably learnt to read and write from his wife, see Roslyn Lacks, *Women and Judaism: Myth, History and Struggle* (New York 1980), 134.

[34] For discussion see Swidler (above, n. 14), 192; B. Witherington III, *Women in the Ministry of Jesus* (Cambridge 1984), 100–3; Elisabeth Moltmann-Wendel, *The Women Around Jesus* (New York 1982), 18–20. A different interpretation has been suggested by Elisabeth Schüssler-Fiorenza, "A Feminist Critical Interpretation for Liberation: Martha and Mary: *Luke* 10:38–42," *Religion and Intellectual Life* 3 (1985), 21–36.

[35] See Schüssler-Fiorenza's analysis of the appearance of these two women in an entirely different context in *John*, *ibid.*

midwives, and that women were also more versed than men in the laws pertaining to care of the sick. Thus, women also inspected other women in connection with signs of menstruation (*bNidd* 13b).

In the *Tosefta*, two legal rulings are given by women. 1) "A door-bolt (קלוסטרה): R. Tarfon says it is susceptible to uncleanness and the sages say it is not susceptible. And Beruriah says: It may be drawn off one [door][36] and hung on another. On the Sabbath this was told to R. Joshua, he said, Beruriah has said well" (*tKel. BM* 1.6). 2) "Rabban Shimeon b. Gamaliel says in the name of R. Shila: If they plastered an oven while in a state of purity and it became unclean, from what time is its purification? R. Halafta of Kefar Hananiah said: I asked Shimeon b. Hananiah, who asked the son of R. Hananiah b. Tardion, and he said: When one will have moved it from its place. And his daughter says: When it will have disassembled. And when these things were reported to R. Judah b. Baba, he said: His daughter ruled better than his son" (*tKel. BQ* 4.17). In these two instances, both Beruriah and the daughter of Hananiah b. Tardion[37] transmit legal rulings in matters connected to the house (door-bolt) and kitchen (oven), areas of women's expertise, as Goodblatt has shown.[38] Goodblatt cites two more examples illustrating women's superior knowledge of laws pertaining to the kitchen (*yShab.* 4.1, 6d; *yBets.* 4.4, 62c), the first of which is exceptionally appropriate to our purpose: "R. Shimeon b. Rabbi says, I did not learn this from my father, but my sister told me in his name: If an egg is laid during a festival, one may rest a utensil on it so that it does not roll around, but one may not put a utensil over it." In the second instance, R. Hiyya's daughter asks her father about laws pertaining to the kitchen, but we are told that she already knew the answer.[39]

Against this background we can understand a story R. Joshua told about himself: "I have never been defeated, except by a woman, a little boy and a little girl" (*bErub.* 53b; *Lam. R.* 1.19); a woman defeated him in a *halakhic* debate dealing with matters connected to the kitchen. She had cooked him a dish but he refrained from eating it because it was over salted, which provoked her comment: "My master, is it possible that you did not leave a *peah* in the first meals, for the sages said: a *peah* must not be left in the pot, (and you have left a *peah* here because they said): a *peah* must be left in the plate?" The law dealt with

---

[36] Based on the *mishnaic* text (*mKel.* 11.4) which puts the same ruling in the mouth of R. Joshua with a change of one word – פתח instead of פסה, which makes sense if *klaustra*, as Albeck *ad loc.* suggests, does indeed mean door-bolt.

[37] See below on the possibility that they are the same.

[38] D. Goodblatt, "The Beruriah Traditions," *Journal of Jewish Studies* 26 (1975), 83.

[39] Meachem (above, n. 21), 176, discusses a law forbidding a woman to come into contact with her husband for seven clean days after her period, and according to the *Babylonian Talmud* (*bNidd.* 66a) women made this ruling. But this source is apologetic and in any case lies outside the chronological limits of the present study.

here pertains only to kitchen expertise and is not mentioned in the *mishnaic* tractate *Peah* or in any other rabbinic source.

Elsewhere in rabbinic literature, women are found citing the Bible. In the
continuation of his story, R. Joshua mentions a little girl who gave him water to
drink, and when he said to her, "You have done as Rebecca did," she responded,
"I have done as Rebecca did but you did not do as Eliezer did" (*Lam. R.* 1.19; an
entirely different story in *bErub.* 53b). The *Babylonian Talmud* preserves a story about a woman whose husband died and she "took his *tefillin* and carried
them about in synagogues and schoolhouses, and she said to them: It is written
in the *Torah*, 'For this is your life and the length of your days' (*Deut.* 30.20). My
husband, who studied much Bible and *mishnah*, and had served scholars much,
why did he die in the prime of life?" (*bShab.* 13a-b). In the *Babylonian Talmud*'s
version of the story of R. Aqiba's departure from his house to study *Torah*, his
wife who was left alone says to her persecutors who claimed that now her husband has returned as great *Torah* scholar, and will not know her: "The righteous
knows the soul of his beast" (*Prov.* 12.10 – *bKet.* 63a; *bNed.* 50a). Without a
doubt, this passage belongs to an early stratum of the story, for in both versions
of the story in the *Babylonian Talmud* R. Aqiba's wife cites the same biblical
verse in her answer to two different questions from two different detractors.[40]

From *tannaitic* sources we learn that R. Hananiah b. Tardion's wife and
daughter both cited Bible in critical moments in their lives. When R. Hananiah
b. Tardion's son joined a band of robbers and afterwards informed on them and
they took revenge by executing him, "his mother cited the following verse regarding him: 'Foolish children are a grief to their father and bitterness to her
who bore them' (*Prov.* 17.25). And his sister cited the following verse regarding
him: 'Bread gained by deceit is sweet, but afterward the mouth will be full of
gravel' (*Prov.* 20.17)" (*Semahot* 12.13; *Lam. R.* 3.6). And when Hananiah b.
Tardion, his wife and his daughter had heavy decrees laid on them, the mother
and daughter were again able to cite appropriate verses, in order to justify to
themselves the judgment against them: "They said to his wife: It has been decreed that your husband be burnt to death and you to be executed. She cited this
verse: 'A God of faithfulness and without iniquity' (*Deut.* 32.4). They said to his
daughter: It has been decreed that your father be burnt to death, that your mother
executed and that you 'perform labor'. She cited the verse: 'Great in counsel and
mighty in deed, whose eyes are open [to all ways of mortals]' (*Jer.* 32.19)" (*Sifre
Deut.* 307, p. 346 ed. Finkelstein; cf. *bAZ* 17b-18a).

But the events in these stories, as well as in the ones we will presently discuss, did not necessarily actually happen, nor do they demonstrate that the authors of the sources did not hesitate to attribute to women the ability to quote

---

[40] For an analysis of the connection between the two stories, see A. Aderet, "The Story
in *Sefer ha-Aggadah* B," *Alei Siah* 4–5 (1978), 122–9 [Hebrew].

from the Bible, because certain women were able to do just that. In rabbinic literature even animals and inanimate objects quote Scripture. We will now study two specific cases which will help us measure the actual level of women's *Torah*-knowledge.

1. Beruriah

Goodblatt[41] has discussed the identity of the daughter of R. Hananiah b. Tardion and her connection to R. Meir. His conclusions are as follows:

a) As we have seen, the *Tosefta* mentions two women who transmit *halakhah*: Beruriah and the (unnamed) daughter of R. Hananiah b. Tardion.

b) The daughter of R. Hananiah b. Tardion, who can cite Bible, appears in the two *tannaitic aggadot* which we have just quoted. Again, her name is not specified in either place.

c) In the *amoraic* continuation of the second *tannaitic* story in the *Babylonian Talmud*, the daughter of R. Hananiah b. Tardion, who knows how to quote Bible and who was forced to suffer the punishment of labor (here interpreted as sitting in a brothel), is not Beruriah, but her sister, whose salvation is placed by Beruriah in the hands of R. Meir.

d) Beruriah is identified as the daughter of R. Hananiah b. Tardion and the wife of R. Meir only in this *amoraic* Babylonian source (*bAZ* 18a) and in another one which mentions R. Yohanan (*bPes.* 62b). A parallel to this latter source is found in the *Palestinian Talmud* but it does not mention Beruriah at all (*yPes.* 5.3, 32a-b).

e) Beruriah was not necessarily the wife of R. Meir, for one source, albeit late (*Midr. Prov.* 31.1), mentions the wife of R. Meir anonymously.[42] And elsewhere, Ben Ziroz and not Hananiah b. Tardion is said to be the father-in-law of R. Meir (*yDem.* 2.1, 22c; *bHull.* 6b).

Goodblatt sees in the identification of these three women – Beruriah, the daughter of Hananiah b. Tardion and the wife of R. Meir – the kind of harmonization to which the *Babylonian Talmud* seems partial. Only in the *Babylonian Talmud* does a woman named Beruriah quote from the Bible. In a story about criminals living near R. Meir, the latter prayed for their death, but Beruriah cited *Ps.* 104.35, "Let sins be consumed from the earth, and let wickedness be no more," in order to prove to him that one should pray for the disappearance of

---

[41] Above, n. 38, 68–85.

[42] On the *aggadic* character of the story of the death of R. Meir's sons and the activities of his wife, see Alisa Shenhar, "On the Popularity of the Legend of Beruriah Wife of Rabbi Meir," in *Folklore Research Center Studies* III, ed. I. Ben-Ami (Jerusalem 1973), 223–7 [Hebrew], who cites examples of the same literary framework in folk stories among other peoples. Note that Shenhar announces already in title of her piece that R. Meir's wife was named Beruriah, although she has no name in the story she discusses.

sins, not sinners (*bBer.* 10a). It is interesting to note that this story recurs in the *Babylonian Talmud*, but its central figures are Abba Helqiah and his wife (*bTaan.* 23b). This parallel does not exactly instill confidence in the historicity of the same story involving Beruriah and R. Meir.[43] But the story involving the wife of Abba Helqiah includes no biblical citations, for the righteousness of the woman in that version is not measured by her knowledge of Scripture.[44]

Goodblatt has shown that in *tannaitic* sources, Beruriah makes rulings in domestic matters and the daughter of Hananiah b. Tardion is the one who quotes from the Bible. Only the *amoraic* sources have joined the two into one and relate stories about the marvels of Beruriah's deep learning in the *Torah* (*bPes.* 62b); thus the Beruriah of the *Babylonian Talmud* never existed. Goodblatt's arguments are basically convincing, and certainly reduce the *tannaitic* figure to the right proportions; but he fails to explain why, if the Beruriah of the *Babylonian Talmud* did not exist, did the *amoraim* go to so much effort to invent her. Goodblatt's rather unclear suggestion is that this Beruriah somehow reflects an aspect of Babylonian reality, but such a proposal should be supported by examples of women like her from Babylonia, and of course no one can offer such examples.[45]

Beruriah's mastery of the *Torah* turned her into both a symbol for the Jewish feminist movement[46] and, for the movement's opponents, the exception that proves the rule.[47] Adler provided a guarded feminist response to the question

---

[43] Ann Goldfeld, "Women as Sources of *Torah* in the Rabbinic Tradition," in *The Jewish Woman: New Perspectives*, ed. Elizabeth Koltun (New York 1976), 265–9, thinks that the two stories serve as evidence that women's opinions were a source of the teachings of other sages. This suggestion appears to me completely groundless. A repeated literary motif is evidence of a literary *topos*, not a repeated historical event.

[44] Beruriah even cites the verse, "Sing, O barren one who did not bear; ... for the children of the desolate woman will be more than the children of her that is married, says the Lord" (*Is.* 54.1) in a debate with an heretic (*bBer.* 10a). And she quotes *2 Sam.* 23.5, "ordered in all things and secure" to a student who mumbled his lesson instead of declaiming it in full voice (*bErub.* 53b-54a).

[45] And see now Boyarin (above, n. 32), 172–80, who puts forward a claim exactly the opposite of Goodblatt's, i.e. that Beruriah could have been an historical figure from Palestine, not Babylonia. Boyarin himself, however, seems to doubt his own conclusions (see p. 194).

[46] She occupies a central place in the article by Safrai (above, n. 30), 58–9. See also Goldfeld (above, n. 43), 257–71; L. J. Swidler, "Beruriah: Her World Became Law," *Lilith* 3 (1977), 9–12; Lacks (above, n. 33), 129–35; Sondra Henry and Emily Taitz, *Written out of History: Our Jewish Foremothers* (Fresh Meadows, NY 1983), 44–7, 54–8.

[47] L. J. Swidler, *Women in Judaism: The Status of Women in Formative Judaism* (Metuchen NJ 1976), 93–111. It should be noted that Swidler wrote the article mentioned in the previous note as a kind of penance for what he wrote in this book. The article was published in a Jewish feminist journal for a Jewish audience. The book, by contrast, was written for a Christian feminist audience and, to a great extent, against Judaism. For a brief

which Goodblatt left open.[48] She does not reject Goodblatt's conclusions, but in her view the Beruriah of the *Babylonian Talmud* was a kind of nightmare which pursued the *amoriam* because of their oppression of their own women – or as Adler puts it, "What if there were a woman just like us (men)?" Thus she argues that the Beruriah stories represent not a historical reality but a literary creation of which the coping-stone is the story of Beruriah's temptation by one of R. Meir's students. This story appears in neither *Talmud* and in none of the *midrashim* but has been preserved by Rashi in his commentary on the expression "the case of (מעשה) Beruriah ..." in the *Babylonian Talmud*: "Once she mocked the sages' teaching that women are lightheaded (*bQidd.* 80b), and he (R. Meir) said to her: 'By your life! you will end up agreeing with them. And he ordered one of his pupils to tempt her to infidelity. He implored her many days until she consented. And when it became known to her (that it was her husband who had commissioned the pupil) she hanged herself and R. Meir escaped from shame" (*ad bAZ* 18b).[49] Goodblatt rejected the story because of Rashi's late date,[50] but we can assume that Rashi did not invent the tradition. Adler's opinion is that Rashi's source was reliable and the story comes, if not from the *tannaitic* stratum of the Beruriah traditions, then at least from the *amoraic* stratum; the sages agree that if such a learned and wise woman as Beruriah existed, it would have nonetheless been possible to find in her some weak point, even if R. Meir had to "play the pimp" for his own wife in order to discover it. But it seems to me that one does not have to look far to find Rashi's source. Adler herself mentioned it[51] when she drew attention to the parallel story of the temptation of R. Meir himself: "R. Meir used to scoff at transgressors. One day Satan appeared to him in the guise of a woman on the opposite bank of the river. As there was no ferry, he seized the rope and proceeded across." But the end of the R. Meir story is good: "When he had reached halfway along the rope, he let him go, saying, Had they not proclaimed in heaven, Take heed of R. Meir and his learning, I would have valued your life at two cheap coins" (*bQidd.* 81a). Adler explained the discrepancy between the two stories as follows: "Having a place in the rabbinic authority structure, then, entitles one to the help of Heaven, when ones own defenses against temptation have proven inadequate. Hence the rabbi (is) rescued. By

---

but deadly critique of the book, see J. Neusner, *A History of the Mishnaic Law of Women* V (Leiden 1980), 246–7.

[48] Rachel Adler, "The Virgin in the Brothel and other Anomalies: Character and Context in the Legend of Beruriah" *Tikkun* 3/6 (1988), 28–32, 102–5.

[49] This story contains a common folkloristic motif; see H. Schwarzbaum, "International Folklore Motifs in Joseph Ibn Zabara's 'Sepher Sha'shu'im'," in *Studies in Aggadah* = *Folklore Research Center Studies* VIII, edd. I. Ben-Ami and J. Dan (Jerusalem 1983), 66–71, n. 38.

[50] Above, n. 38, 78–9, but see now Boyarin (above, n. 32), 181–93.

[51] Above, n. 48, 103–4.

contrast, no heavenly voice protects Beruriah … she is judged by more stringent standards." But Adler did not perceive that this story, and not "the case of
Beruriah," was related in the *Talmud* in connection with the sages' teaching,
"Women are lightheaded" (*bQidd.* 80b-81a). The two stories are certainly similar: R. Meir, like Beruriah, mocks the sages' teaching, and he also falls into the
trap set for him and gives in to temptation from the same weakness which he had
mocked. But in contrast with Beruriah, Satan, who in the parallel dresses up as a
woman, does not need to importune R. Meir, for he gives in immediately. Thus it
appears that somehow the central figures in these orally transmitted stories became reversed in Rashi or his source. Another possibility is that "the case of
Beruriah" was from the beginning a subtle, sophisticated story like the one
about Beruriah's meeting with R. Yose the Galilean and her admonishment of
him to heed the sages' warning against talking too much with women (*bErub.*
53b – above chapter 4), and in so doing she prolonged their conversation. This
story is an example of the rabbis' self-criticism regarding their own anti-feminist rulings and the original "Case of Beruriah" may have belonged to this same
genre.

We may conclude, then, that the *tannaitic* Beruriah (and/or the daughter of
Hananiah b. Tardion) who is given to quoting Bible or *halakhah*, was no different from those women who, as we have seen, knew even better than the men
did those laws pertaining to domestic matters, and could conceivably quote
Scripture. The great *Torah* scholar who was the *amoraic* Beruriah was the
product of the imagination of the *amoraim*.

2. Matrona

Most women who demonstrate mastery of Bible in rabbinic sources do not quote
prooftexts from Scripture, as did Beruriah. They appear before various sages,
like the "wise woman" who appears before R. Eliezer, in order to clarify an ob-
scure point in the Bible. Most of these women, unlike the woman who queried
R. Eliezer, receive detailed and satisfying answers.

Particularly plentiful in the sources are cases involving a woman named Matrona and the questions she put to R. Yose b. Halafta. The earliest source containing such traditions is *Genesis Rabbah*, which in fact relates seven, all of course
involving the interpretation of a particular passage in the book of *Genesis*.[52]

---

[52] M. D. Herr, "The Historical Significance of the Dialogues between Jewish Sages
and Roman Dignitaries," in *Studies in Aggadah and Folk-Literature = Scripta Hierosolymitana* XXII, edd. D. Noy and J. Heinemann (Jerusalem 1971), 148, n. 134; Rosalie Gershonzon and E. Slomovic, "A Second Century Jewish-Gnostic Debate: Rabbi Jose ben
Halafta and the Matrona," *Journal for the Study of Judaism* 16 (1985), 10, n. 27. Both of
the these articles refer to an earlier source for the story: *Midrash Tannaim* to *Deuteronomy*.
The problem is that the remains of this original *midrash* have not been found, and Hoff-

Neither *Talmud* mentions any such case,[53] but they appear in *midrashim*, from *Leviticus Rabbah* to *Ecclesiastes Rabbah* to much later works such as *Pesiqta Rabbati* and the *Tanhuma*, and ending with medieval commentaries on the Bible, like *Da'at Zekenim*.[54] So far, the scholars who have studied Matrona's questions to R. Yose have concluded that she was not Jewish, but Christian,[55] Gnostic,[56] a "god-fearer" (σεβομένη),[57] or a member of a pagan school such as Stoicism, Epicureanism, etc.[58] These views all rest on 1) the fact that the rabbinic sources, particularly the two *Talmudim*, use the word "matrona" to describe a Roman lady;[59] 2) the strong pagan or gnostic character of Matrona's statement in some of the sources, particularly *Exodus Rabbah* 3.12: "When Moses saw the snake, who is my God, immediately 'Moses fled from before it' (*Ex.* 4.3);" 3) the assumption that Jewish women in Palestine did not know enough Bible to ask such questions, or in Bacher's words: "Für das christlische Bekentniss der "Matrone" spricht auch theilweise ihre Bibelkunde ...".[60]

On each of these points I may offer a comment:

1) In all the best manuscripts of *Genesis Rabbah*, which as I have said is the earliest source for the episodes mentioning of Matrona, she is never called "The Matrona" or "a certain Matrona," but always simply "Matrona".[61] The name

mann's edition (Berlin 1908), which contains the story (p. 262), consists of passages he collected from the *Midrash ha-Gadol* on the assumption that their origin was *tannaitic*. The earliest genuine source for any Matrona-R. Yose stories is *Genesis Rabbah*; at best, the *Midrash Hagadol* is a *terminus post quem* for this tradition.

[53] F. Böhl, "Die Matronenfragen im *Midrasch*," *Frankfurter judaistische Beiträge* 3 (1975), 39–44 has argued that the story of R. Eliezer and the "wise woman," whom the *Palestinian Talmud* calls "Matrona," belongs to the set, but this claim cannot stand: only the question by the woman fits the model I will set out, not the responder, his response or the source. For by the same token, one could identify matrona who pesters R. Judah with embarrassing questions (e.g. *bNed.* 49b) as the same matrona, except that in that setting as well, the central figures and the nature of the questions and answers are very different.

[54] The sources in *Genesis Rabbah* are a. 4.6 (p. 30, ed. Theodor-Albeck); b. 17.7 (p. 158 *ibid.*); c. 25.1 (p. 239, *ibid.*); d. 63.8 (p. 688, *ibid.*); e. 68.4 (p. 771–3, *ibid.*); f. 84.21 (p. 1027, *ibid.*); g. 87.6 (p. 1070, *ibid.*). For the other traditions, see Gershonzon and Slomovic (above, n. 52).

[55] Z. Fraenkel, "Zur Geschichte der jüdischen Religionsgespräche," *Monatsschrift für Geschichte und Wissenschaft des Judentums* 4 (1855), 208–9; W. Bacher, "Ein polemischer Ausspruch Jose b. Chalfthas," *Monatsschrift für Geschichte und Wissenschaft des Judentums* 42 (1895), 505–7.

[56] Gershonzon and Slomovic (above, n. 52), 1–41.

[57] Böhl (above, n. 53), 58–64.

[58] Herr (above, n. 52), 145–8.

[59] For partial lists, see J. Levy, *Wörterbuch über die Talmudim und Midraschim* III (Berlin 1924), 93–4; A. Kohut, *Aruch Completum* V (Berlin 1926), 125; M. Jastrow, *Dictionary of the Targumim, the Talmud Babli and Yerushalmi and the Midrashic Literature* (New York 1950), 769–70.

[60] W. Bacher, *Agada der Tannaiten* II (Strassbourg 1890), 170, n. 2.

[61] Cf. the notes in the relevant *midrashim*, ed. Theodor-Albeck.

Matrona was given to Jewish women in Palestine during the late Roman period, as we find in inscriptions[62] and amulets.[63] The *midrash* which we are dealing with here may very well involve not a Roman matron but a Jewish woman with the name Matrona.

2) All the material on Matrona mentioning Jewish matters of interest to pagans, Christians or proselytes appears in *midrashim* later than *Genesis Rabbah*, the earliest *midrashic* source for the tradition.[64] All the discussions between Matrona and R. Yose in *Genesis Rabbah* deal with what may reasonably be considered matters internal to Judaism, and even the version of the Bible they use is the *masoretic* Hebrew version. What brought the authors of the later *Midrashim* to put in the mouth of the Matrona questions of non-Jewish character was a two-pronged literary development. On the one hand, the many stories about Matrona and R. Yose in *Genesis Rabbah* became a literary model which a later exegete could use as the vehicle for any controversy whatsoever. During the course of transmission the word Matrona in the *midrashim* gradually lost its meaning as a private name for a Jewish woman, and later exegetes, as well as modern historians, understood it as a descriptive term for a Roman matron and thus used the literary model to illustrate debates which were likely to arise between the Jewish sages and non-Jews, or even among the Jewish sages themselves.[65] On the other hand, the conventions of Jewish society permitted women outside that society to do things that were forbidden to Jewish women. We see this especially in the *Babylonian Talmud*. While the wise Jewish woman who comes before R. Eliezer with a question on Scripture, does not receive an answer to her question, gentile women receive a different treatment; in many instances, the sages grant non-Jewish women answers to their questions regarding the Bible. Cleopatra, queen of Egypt, reportedly asked R. Meir about a passage in Scripture ("Queen Cleopatra asked R. Meir: I know that the dead will rise, for it is written, 'And they shall blossom forth out of the city like the grass of the earth' (*Ps.* 72.16). But when they arise, shall they arise nude or in their garments?" [*bSanh.* 90b]) and received an answer to her question; the fictional nature of this story is self-evident, for no queen named Cleopatra existed in the

---

[62] Leah Roth-Gerson, *The Greek Inscriptions from the Synagogues in Eretz Israel* (Jerusalem 1987), 118 [Hebrew]; M. Schwabe, "Notes on the Column Inscription from Ashkelon," *Tarbiz* 13 (1952), 66–7; The name also appears in an Hebrew inscription from the Roman period found in North Africa – "מטרונא בת רבי יהודה" see P. Monceaux, "Épigraphique chrétienne d'Afrique," *Revue Archeologique* 4/3 (1904), 372.

[63] A. Reifenberg, *Ancient Hebrew Arts* (New York 1950), 143.

[64] A discussion of circumcision, a topic of interest to both Aquila the proselyte and Matrona, appears in *Pesiqta Rabbati*; the pagan snake-god is found in *Exodus Rabbah*; etc.

[65] Note, e.g. how a debate between R. Judah and R. Nehemiah in *Genesis Rabbah* (12.4, p. 100 ed. Theodor-Albeck) appears in the *Tanhuma* ed. Buber, *Bereshit* 2 as a debate between Matrona and R. Yose.

time of R. Meir. The emperor's daughter puts a question to R. Joshua based on the Bible ("Your God is a carpenter, for it is written, 'Who layeth the beams of His upper chambers in the waters' (*Ps.* 104.3)" [*bHull.* 60a]) and likewise receives an answer, albeit an unsatisfactory one. Even a female proselyte is preferred over a native-born Jewish woman when it comes to questions about the Bible, according to the *Babylonian Talmud.* The proselyte Beluriah, known from a *halakhic* problem connected to her conversion and discussed in *Mekhilta de R. Ishmael* (*Bo* 15, p. 57 ed. Horovitz-Rabin; *bYeb.* 46a), in the *Babylonian Talmud* turns to Rabban Gamaliel with the question: "It is written in your *Torah*, 'who does not regard persons' (*Deut.* 10.17), yet it is also written, 'the Lord lift up his countenance to you' (*Num.* 6.26)" (*bRH* 17b: in Hebrew the two expressions are almost exactly the same) – and of course she receives the privilege of an answer. Some modern scholars have even thought that Beluriah and Beruriah were the same person, because of the similarity of names and also presumably because a proselyte was more likely than a native Jewish woman to know Bible.[66] I would propose that these two literary developments – the *topos* of the Matrona-R. Yose stories and the *Babylonian Talmud*'s idea that non-Jewish women were more eligible than Jewish women to ask the rabbis questions regarding Scripture – are what led to the change in Matrona, in fact her complete reversal from what she is in *Genesis Rabbah.*

3) The assumption that Jewish women did not know enough *Torah* to ask questions on the level of Matrona's is precisely the point we are examining here. The fact that in all the cases in *Genesis Rabbah* the woman is not an integral part of the story, and the same questions could just as well have been asked by men, and elsewhere are indeed asked by them, means that the presence of the woman is an authentic historical remnant; and moreover, the woman in the stories was almost certainly Jewish.

In *Genesis Rabbah* we find for the first time in rabbinic, particularly *midrashic* literature, seven stories in which Matrona asks R. Yose questions about the Bible. Since all the questions are in Hebrew and R. Yose was the disciple of R. Aqiba, the source is *tannaitic*. Since *Genesis Rabbah* contains no other stories in which women pose questions for sages, the seven existing ones can be considered as a kind of unit, that is, a literary collection from which the editors of the *midrash* could draw relevant material. It is likely that the same collection was at the disposal of the authors of the later *midrashic* compilations like *Leviticus Rabbah* and *Ecclesiastes Rabbah*, although this cannot be proved, especially in light of the fact that the formula "Matrona asked R. Yose" became part of a literary *topos.* The Matrona in the collection used by the editors of *Genesis Rabbah* thus refers to one woman, perhaps an historical figure, most likely not a prototype. The fact that *Genesis Rabbah* nowhere says that Matrona was of

---

[66] J. Leipoldt, *Jesu Verhältnis zu Griechen und Juden* (Leipzig 1941), 20, n. 36.

pagan or Christian origins, or that she was a proselyte, seems to suggest that she was a woman who somehow was occupied with the *Torah* in a Jewish setting.

From the existing evidence, Matrona had no more than a superficial knowledge of the book of *Genesis*. R. Yose's responses to her are drawn from everyday experience and do not involve complex citations from other parts of the Bible, in the normal *midrashic* manner. This may reflect only the condition of the sources, but it may just as well reflect the fact that the book of *Genesis*, the first in the entire Bible, was the only one taught to women.

We may now attempt to summarize a complex discussion in a few statements. There was no official education system for girls. They learnt to read and write at home if there was someone there to teach them. Commandments and laws relevant to keeping a *kosher* Jewish household were meticulously repeated, at least in the households of the Pharisaic and *tannaitic* sages. This intensive training could result in women's specialized knowledge of laws extending beyond the rabbis' own kin. If a woman studied Scripture, she would most probably concentrate on the relatively simple book of *Genesis*. Everything we know about the *Torah* studied by women, including all the information on Beruriah, can be subsumed under these topics.

Chapter 8:

Other Women

So far we have dealt with typical Jewish women: free, and most of them, as was expected, married. This is the kind of woman the sources usually mean when they refer unqualifiedly to "a woman." But naturally in the Second Temple period there were other women who fell outside this normal framework.

Maidservants

Jewish law draws a distinction between a Hebrew slave and a Canaanite slave, and that includes females slaves (e.g. *mQidd.* 1.2–3). We may assume that when the distinction is not specifically made, a source means both kinds of slaves. The Hebrew slave, as long as he was in bondage, was apparently exempt from the same religious obligations as a Canaanite slave, all the more so a Hebrew maidservant, not only because she was a woman but also because by biblical law she did not go free on the seventh year: the *halakhic* sources do not require the liberation of slaves when the Bible does not. In the *Book of Judith* we read how Judith, close to her death, frees her maidservant (16.23); this shows at least that someone thought the action praiseworthy. It is impossible to tell from the story whether Judith's maidservant was Hebrew or Canaanite. However, it is important to note that the authors and editors of other sources at least assumed the theoretical possibility that Jews could hold other Jewish slaves.

Most commandments regarding slaves include female slaves. For example: "slaves and maidservants: ... one does not say for them the blessing for the mourner or the consolation of the mourner" (*bBer.* 16b); "If she inherited old slaves and maidservants, they should be sold and land bought with their price" (*mKet.* 8.5).[1] On the other hand, in discussions about the difference between a

---

[1] Both of these *halakhot* come close to seeing slaves as cattle, but this attitude does not pervade all rabbinic thought. In the second instance, Rabban Shimeon b. Gamaliel answers: "They shall not be sold, for they were the pride of her father's house" (*ibid.*). Again, in a debate between the Sadducees and Pharisees over an owner's obligation to pay for damages caused by his slaves and maidservants, the Sadducees compare slaves to work-animals but the Pharisees answer them: "No. As you argue concerning my ox or ass (which

male slave and a maidservant, a clear conclusion is reached: the slave is a worker, whom his owners acquired with money, whereas the maidservant, aside from
working as a house-servant,[2] is also a sexual object for the males of the house.
Ethical writings of the period view this sexual exploitation of a defenseless
maidservant as a lurking danger. In his essay on women to be avoided, *Ben Sira*
warns: "(Take heed, sons, ... and be warned against) having any relations with
your maidservant" (41.22). Hillel supposedly said, "the more maidservants, the
more lewdness" (*mAbot.* 2.7). And a parable tells of "a royal prince who sinned
with a slave-girl, and the king on learning of it expelled him from court" (*Gen.
R.* 15.7, p. 140 ed. Theodor-Albeck); thus the prince's action was disapproved
of not only by his father but by the authors of the source.[3] A maidservant's sexual availability can also be seen in another rabbinic saying: "Why ... does not
everyone jump to marry a freedwoman? Because ... the liberated maidservant
was by any measure a prostitute. R. Eliezer b. R. Zadok says: Because it is spoken of by society only as a curse" (*tHor.* 2.11–2). Thus it seems that a freed
maidservant's sexual past was a difficult obstacle to finding a match for her.

Jewish law did deal with the problems arising from a maidservant's sexual
availability, but the main concern seems to have been to protect the good name
of the owner (and perhaps even his wife), not of the maidservant. The *halakhah*
tries to root out any emotional involvement between maidservants and their
owners but makes no special effort to use the established system of legal punishments to protect the body of the maidservant. This double-standard is most con-
vincingly illustrated by the fact that a maidservant is not eligible to be married.[4]
Sifra remarks on the verse in *Leviticus*, "You shall not uncover your daughter-
in-law's nakedness" (18.15), as follows: "Even a maidservant ...? But she is referred to as: 'your son's wife' (*ibid.*) ... this excludes the maidservant because
she cannot be married to your son" (*Sif. Qedoshim* 9.13, 92a ed. Weiss). This
seems to permit what in any other circumstances would be considered a serious
violation of the most basic ethical principles (see, e.g. *Amos* 2.7; *bGitt.* 57a): a
father and son may have intercourse with the same woman if she is a maidservant. Jewish law fails to protect even a maidservant's offspring: "If her betrothal
to this man was not valid, and her betrothal with others would also not be valid,

---

have no understanding), would you likewise argue concerning my slave or maidservant
who have understanding?" (*mYad.* 4.7).

  [2] "If she brought him in one maidservant, she need not grind or bake or wash; if two,
she need not cook or give her child suck; if three, she need not make ready his bed or work
in wool; if four, she may sit [all day] in a chair" (*mKet.* 5.5).

  [3] Although we cannot know whether the son was not thrown out of the house because
he usurped the exclusive rights of his father over the sexuality of the women in the house;
see D. Mace, *Hebrew Marriage: A Sociological Study* (New York 1953), 131.

  [4] On the different degrees of marriage, see S. J. D. Cohen, "The Origin of the Matrilineal Principle in Rabbinic Law," *Association of Jewish Studies Review* 10 (1985), 30–4.

the offspring is of her own standing. This is the case when the offspring is by a maidservant ..." (*mQidd.* 3.12). A maidservant's child is not considered to have a father and thus is not included among the real father's heirs; the child is, like his/her mother, a slave. Elsewhere we learn that even the brother of a maidservant's child is not considered legally to be his brother: "If a man has any kind of brother, such a brother imposes on his brother's wife the duty of levirate marriage ... unless he was the son of a maidservant" (*mYeb.* 2.5). We can assume that the main purpose of all these laws is to prevent, so far as possible, any emotional connection from developing between a maidservant and her owner.[5] Criticism of this double standard is put in the mouth of the maidservant of R. Judah the Patriarch, who in rabbinic literature takes the form of the prototypical, perfect maidservant for a rabbinic sage. We have already observed this technique, by which veiled criticism of the sages for their attitudes toward women is put in the mouth of the actual parties concerned. "It once happened that a man came to have sexual relations with Rabbi's maidservant. She said to him: If my mistress does not immerse, I do not immerse," that is, it was inadvisable for him to have sexual relations with her because she was unclean from having her period. "He said to her: Are you not as a beast?" that is, beasts do not need to immerse and become ritually clean. The maidservant answered: "And have you not heard about the man who has intercourse with a beast that he is stoned to death? for it is written, 'Anyone who lies with cattle shall be surely put to death' (*Ex.* 22.18)" (*yBer.* 3.4, 6c). The point is clear: if a maidservant is a person, then she must be granted control over her own sexuality just as every woman is; if she is considered a beast, then she is forbidden sexually to any man.

In conclusion, the way the sources of the Second Temple period relate to the problem of the maidservant among Jews reflects the more universal problem of the enslavement of women: their lack of freedom turned them not only into instruments of labor but also into sexual objects for their owners' use. This situation was bitterly criticized by ethical writers, but the *tannaitic halakhah* dealt with the problem only insofar as was necessary to protect the maidservant's owners, without giving any consideration to anchoring her own rights in law.

The reality is more complicated. Maidservants in Palestine fell into two groups: those who were owned by Jews but were partly (or mostly) not Jewish themselves, and Jewish maidservants sold to non-Jews. The common assumption today is that those slaves and maidservants held by Jews in the Second Temple period were not "Hebrew slaves" but "Canaanite slaves,"[6] but this claim

---

[5] No such emotional connections are known from the Hellenistic-Roman period, but the Genizah contains documents which record the liberation of maidservants with the purpose of marrying them. See M. A. Friedman, *Jewish Polygyny in the Middle Ages* (Tel Aviv 1986), 291–4 [Hebrew].

[6] L. M. Epstein, *Marriage Laws in the Bible and Talmud* (Cambridge MA 1942), 62; S. Safrai "Home and Family," in *The Jewish People in the First Century* II = *Compendia*

seems more apologetic than based on fact. It rests on one single saying which cannot even be certainly identified as *tannaitic* and appears in the *Babylonian Talmud:* "The law of the Hebrew slave applies only as long as the Jubilee applies" (*bArakh.* 29a). I wish to argue here that Hebrew slaves did in fact exist in the period, and that their existence is documented in the sources. For example, the *Babylonian Talmud* contains the story of a slave who was raised to the priesthood during the *tannaitic* period (*bKet.* 28b); naturally this slave had to be a Hebrew slave. The wife of Herod's brother Pheroras is called a slave (δούλη, apparently a freed slave, *BJ* 1.484; *AJ* 16.194) and is said to have been close to the Pharisees (*AJ* 17.42–3); since she is never said to have converted to Judaism, she can be assumed to have been originally a Hebrew slave.

The rabbinic stories about sages and their maidservants present a didactic model of the relations between master and maidservant. *Genesis Rabbah,* for example, relates that R. Yose (Issi in the manuscripts) admonishes his wife in front of his maidservant in order to fulfill the verse, "If I have ever rejected the plea of my slave or my slave-girl, when they brought their complaint to me" (*Job* 31.13) (48.3, pp. 479–80 ed. Theodor-Albeck). Tabitha, Rabban Gamliel's maidservant, was called "Mother (Imma) Tabitha" as a mark of respect and prestige (*bBer.* 16b; cf. *yNidd.* 1.5, 49b).[7] Both *Talmudim* contain stories about the maidservant of R. Judah the Patriarch. She is mentioned with him more often than his wife, and her love for him appears to have been greater than the love others had for him (*bKet.* 104a).[8]

The story of the death R. Eliezer's maidservant also reveals close relations between master and maidservant. R. Eliezer's pupils come to console him over

---

Rerum Iudaicarum ad Novum Testamentum Section One, edd. S. Safrai and M. Stern (Assen 1976), 751; but see E. E. Urbach, "*Halakhot* Regarding Slavery as a Source for the Social History of the Second Temple and the *Talmudic* Period," *Zion* 25 (1960), 141–89 [Hebrew].

[7] On the title "Imma," see Bernadette J. Brooten, *Women Leaders in the Ancient Synagogue: Inscriptional Evidence and Background Issues = Brown Judaic Studies* XXXVI (Chico CA 1982), 64–8. For the view that the title applies only to age, see M. B. Lerner, "Inquiries into the Meaning of Various Titles and Designations: 1. Abba," *Studies in Judaica = Teuda* IV, edd. M. A. Friedman and M. Gil (Tel Aviv 1986), 99–100 [Hebrew], although he acknowledges that age by itself commands respect. For an ossuary with the inscription "ימה מרים" see P. Figueras, *Decorated Jewish Ossuaries* (Leiden 1983), 18.

[8] Some have identified Rabbi's maidservant as one of the most *Torah* learned women during the period. See, e.g. S. Ben-Chorin, *Mutter Mirjam: Maria in jüdischer Sicht* (München 1982), 99, but see also L. J. Swidler's response (*Women in Judaism: The Status of Women in Formative Judaism* [Metuchen NJ 1976], 106–10). The woman's knowledge of archaic Hebrew (*yShebi.* 9.1, 38c; *bErub.* 53b; *bMeg.* 18a) is not necessarily a sign of broad education. From a similar source (*Gen. R.* 79.7, pp. 946–7 ed. Theodor-Albeck) we learn that the word for "broom" (מטאטא), which Rabbi's maidservant explained to the sages, was still a viable word in the Arabic of the period; could this be a sign of her ethnic background (Nabataean) and not her level of education?

her death, but he does not allow them to offer consolation, which is forbidden by law for slaves and maidservants (*bBer.* 16b). This story raises two central questions. First, why did R. Eliezer's pupils want to console him for the death of his maidservant? This question may be answered in two ways, one by making an historical supposition and the other by offering a literary interpretation: either R. Eliezer's disciples knew his real affectionate feelings for his maidservant and decided, despite the strictness of the law, to offer him comfort and consolation after her death, or the whole scene was imagined to stress the strictness with which R. Eliezer held himself to the law, despite his personal pain, which is a motif recurring in other stories involving R. Eliezer. In this second case, of course, R. Eliezer's reported relations with his maidservant would have no historical value. But if the literary approach to the first question is correct, the second question would still remain, *viz.* why did the teller of the story decide that R. Eliezer's maidservant, and not his male slave, should die? This question seems to bring us back to historical reality. The gender of the slave has no structural significance in the story, and thus I accept it as historical fact and accept further that R. Eliezer had close relations with his maidservant.

The Babylonian *amoraim* relate another episode: "Said Rabba to Rav Nahman: Surely Tamar conceived from a first contact! The other answered him: Tamar penetrated with her finger; for R. Isaac said: All women of the house of Rabbi who penetrate are designated Tamar. And why are they designated Tamar? After Tamar who penetrated with her finger" (*bYeb.* 34a-b). The question under discussion is whether a woman can become pregnant the first time she has intercourse and loses her virginity. In order to prove the positive, Rabba cites the case of the biblical Tamar, the wife of Er. Rabbis answer him that Tamar "penetrated with her finger," i.e. she herself tore her hymen before she had intercourse with Judah, and then the *Talmud* relates a peculiar case anonymously: in Rabbi's house there were women called Tamar because they would also "penetrate," or as Rashi explains: "They destroy their virginity with their own fingers." The meaning of this, and the identity of the women in Rabbi's house, cannot be known. Women of the house of the patriarch could be family relatives or maidservants of Rabbi and his immediate family. Since in a society which placed so much value on a woman's virginity when she gets married the daughters or other female relatives of the patriarch would not likely have destroyed their own virginity, the women in the story were probably maidservants kept for purely sexual purposes, especially since that is the only context in which they are mentioned. The exact purpose of their artificially destroying their virginity is not clear, however, and the anonymous nature of the source prohibits any further investigation. These stories, though incomplete, suggest that even the exemplary relations between sages and their maidservants, as presented in rabbinic literature, were not in fact completely spotless.

Outside the narrow world of the sages, we further hear of sexual exploitation of maidservants. For example, the maidservant of a tax-collector got pregnant and miscarried (*tOhol.* 16.13; *bNidd.* 15b). As we have seen, Herod's brother Pheroras married his maidservant (*BJ* 1.484; *AJ* 16.194); we can assume that this marriage took place after Pheroras sexually exploited her, and that the Herodian prince did not think that he would fall captive to his maidservant's charms when he began the sexual adventure with her.

There is hardly any evidence for the liberation of maidservants, and we cannot know the extent to which this was in fact practiced. Pheroras presumably freed his maidservant before he married her. The only *sotah* from the Second Temple period who underwent the trial of bitter waters was, as we have seen, was "Karkemit the freed maidservant" (*mEduy.* 5.6; *Sifre Num.* 7, p. 11 ed. Horovitz; *bBer.* 19a).

The sale of Jewish women into slavery is the other side of the same coin. Josephus reports more than one occasion on which Jewish women captives were sold as slaves during the Jewish revolt. When the Romans captured the Galilean town of Yapha, for instance, they killed all the males and sold the women and children into slavery (*BJ* 3.304); the same policy was carried out in Machaerus (*BJ* 7.208). Josephus also says that the prices of children and women slaves dropped because the fall of Jerusalem flooded the market (*BJ* 6.384).

Jewish women were sold as slaves in contexts other than war. The Zenon papyri mention a Jewish maidservant by the name of Joanna.[9] Zenon was engaged in the slave-trade when he was in Palestine,[10] and Joanna was presumably sold to him on that occasion. A different papyrus from Egypt[11] mentions a freed Jewish maidservant named Martha. The deed of liberation of three Jewish maidservants was found in Delphi[12] and as Urbach has suggested,[13] these women, freed in 156/7 BCE, were likely captured in Palestine during the Hasmonean wars. A well-educated Jewish maidservant by the name of Acme served in the empress Livia's house (*BJ* 1.641, 661; *AJ* 17.137–41; 145; 182).

Three other sources, one a *baraita* in the *Babylonian Talmud* and the other two in *Abot de Rabbi Nathan A*, mention extreme pietists (*hasidim*) engaged in the ransom of Jewish maidservants (*bShab.* 127b; *ARNA* 8, p. 37 ed. Schechter).[14] Even Martha the daughter of Boethus is said to have been captured and ransomed (*Lam. R.* 1.49). Precisely because their purpose is to preach the ran-

---

[9] *CPJ* I, pp. 132–3, no. 7.

[10] V. Tcherikover, "Palestine in Light of the Zenon Papyri," *Tarbiz* 4 (1933), 231–3; 238–41; *ibid.* 5 (1934), 42–3 [Hebrew]. Zenon dealt in Jewish male slaves, as well, for some of his purchases were circumcised.

[11] *CPJ* II, pp. 20–2, no. 148.

[12] *CII* 709.

[13] Above, n. 6, 147.

[14] *ARNB* 19 (pp. 41–2 ed. Schechter) gives the same story with some of the elements different. R. Joshua appears in place of the pietist, and an attractive woman from Ashkalon

som not just of women captives but of all captives, these sources, despite their late date and *aggadic* character, serve as evidence that Jewish society tried to deal with problem of Jewish women falling into captivity and being sold into slavery by the known method of ransoming captives.[15]

Proselytes

In this section I will discuss primarily conversions by women for the purpose of marriage – not that this was the main reason for women converting to Judaism, only that this is the focus of the sources, which are interested in women mainly insofar as they are connected to men. Mixed marriage was an old topic in Judaism, dating from the biblical period, and it comes up in several sources from the Second Temple period. Job, in his final words in the *Testament of Job*, warns his sons against mixed marriage (45.3), even though this topic is completely unrelated to the contents of the rest of the book; nor is it clear which kind of mixed marriage Job has in mind, for Job himself is said to descend from the sons of Esau (1.5) while only his wife Dinah was a daughter of Israel (1.6). The *Book of Jubilees* bases a severe prohibition against mixed marriage on the story of Dinah, prescribing death both for the father who marries his daughter to a gentile and to the daughter herself (30.7; 13). Josephus, even if he seems to find the offense less serious, bases the same prohibition on the mass divorce of gentile wives in the days of Ezra (*AJ* 11.153).[16] A gentile woman's descendants had the same *halakhic* status as descendants of maidservants. Marriage was prohibited between a Jew and a non-Jewish woman, and the laws regarding a maidservant apply also to the non-Jewish woman.[17]

A gentile woman's status changed considerably once she converted. The convert was no longer completely outside the Jewish community, but she was not considered to be a full member, either.[18] A convert's marriage was considered to

---

in place of the captive, which seems to indicate that the basic story structure including the woman captive who had to be ransomed is not after all essential to the story, and therefore perhaps more historically reliable.

[15] For another story of the ransom of women captives, this time by a woman, see *Esther R.* Pref. 3.

[16] See S. J. D. Cohen, "From the Bible to *Talmud:* The Prohibition of Intermarriage," *Hebrew Annual Review* 7 (1983), 23–39. See also the curious piece written by the serious German scholar during the Nazi period, with surprisingly mild conclusions: G. Kittel, "Das Konnubium mit den Nicht-Juden im antiken Judentum," *Forschung zur Judenfrage* 2 (1937), 30–62.

[17] Cohen (above, n. 4), 19–53.

[18] It is not the purpose of this work to define the status of the convert in Judaism, and thus I will deal here only with the differences between the male and female convert.

have an intermediate status between marriage of a full Jew and marriage of any one of the excluded groups: "the Levitic, Israelitish, impaired priestly stocks, proselyte and freedman stocks may intermarry; the proselyte, freedman, bastard, *Nathin, shetuki* and *asufi* stocks may all intermarry" (*mQidd.* 4.1); in other words, a convert, unlike a native Jewish woman, may not marry a priest.[19] Both a fully Jewish woman and a convert may marry Levites and Israelites, but only a convert may marry those who are disqualified from marriage with native Jews, such as the bastard and the *Nathin*.

Despite this intermediate status, there are differences between the convert and the maidservant: "...everyone jumps at the chance to marry a convert ... because she has the status of one who has been preserved (from sexual abuse)" (*tHor.* 2.11). However, this cannot be the only reason why converts were considered desirable partners. Some women apparently converted as a result of romantic entanglements with Jewish men whom they married after the conversion. A good example is the story about the student from R. Hiyya's study-house who captured the heart of a prostitute who serviced the highest ranks in the Roman Empire, and as a result of her romantic involvement abandoned her profession, converted to Judaism and married the student (*Sifre Num.* 115, pp. 128–9 ed. Horovitz; *bMen.* 44a). The Hellenistic poet Meleager of Gadara in Palestine (Transjordan) laments that his beloved Demo (Δημώ) preferred a Jew to him and broke his heart.[20] There is not enough data in the poem to determine whether Demo married the Jew or whether she converted to Judaism; nor can we know whether the situation is real or imagined. Yet this lyric poem does at least represent yet another romantic relationship between a Jewish man and a gentile woman, or if not that, the environment in which such a relationship could develop. Even the law which forbids conversion "for the sake of love, both the conversion of a man for the sake of a woman and a woman for the sake of a man" (*yQidd.* 4.1, 65b)[21] was intended as a safeguard against a phenomenon which the guardians of the tradition viewed as negative.

Thus it seems that there was a double standard with regard to the conversion of women to Judaism. Generally speaking the conversion was welcomed, but the rabbis also wanted to ensure that the conversion was not made for immediate gain in this world.

---

[19] See *mBik.* 1.5; see discussion above of social connections in marriage.

[20] M. Stern, *Greek and Latin Authors on Jews and Judaism* I (Jerusalem 1974), 140.

[21] This law has no recognizable marks of the *tannaim*, but the fact that Rav, the first-generation *amora*, opposes the law – "The law is that they are converts and their marriages are not prohibited" – means that it was formulated before him. On the other hand, the *Babylonian Talmud* says, "It is all the same whether a man converts for the sake of a woman or a woman converts for the sake of a man – they are not true converts; this is the opinion of R. Nehemiah" (*bYeb.* 24b). In this case R. Nehemiah's name places the law in the *tannaitic* period.

The conversion of women to Judaism has been intensely studied by modern scholars. Some have claimed that women were more attracted than men to Judaism because, among other reasons, circumcision was a disincentive to men.[22] Josephus does say, for example, that the women of Damascus were quite enthusiastic about Judaism, in sharp contrast to their husbands (*BJ* 2.560), but this does not necessarily prove the claim, which may not stand up under close scrutiny.

The most famous woman convert of the Second Temple period was Queen Helene, who arrived in Jerusalem from Adiabene around the year 46 and became involved there in good works (*AJ* 20.51–2; *mYoma* 3.10; *tKipp.* 2.3; *yYoma* 3.8, 41a); she earned a name for herself among the sages (*mNaz.* 3.6; *Sifre Zuta*, 6.5, p. 241 ed. Horovitz; *tSukk.* 1.1; *ySukk.* 1.1, 51d), although one would not know from the rabbinic sources that Helene was a convert.[23] We should not forget that Helene's two sons, Izates and Monobazus, converted along with her. Other members of that family may also have converted, but their sex is unknown (*AJ* 20.75). The one woman convert mentioned by name in rabbinic sources is Beluriah (*Mekhilta de Rabbi Ishmael Bo* 15, p. 57 ed. Horovitz-Rabin; *bYeb.* 46a), who according to the *Babylonian Talmud* also knew Bible and posed questions about it (*bRH* 17b). But two male converts of the period are also mentioned by name in rabbinic literature: Aquila the proselyte (e.g. *Gen. R.* 70.5, p. 802 ed. Theodor-Albeck) and Neptaeus the proselyte (*bYeb.* 98a). Rabbinic literature mentions another woman convert, from Rhodes, whose case was dealt with by R. Judah the Patriarch (*yYeb.* 8.2, 9b; *yQidd.* 4.6, 66b), and yet another, who together with her ex-husband converted to Judaism, then asked R. Judah the Patriarch to rule on whether they could marry each other again (*yQidd.* 1.1, 58c). In this second story we find a male convert next to her. Another woman convert appears in a story of rather *aggadic* character which places R. Eliezer's hostility to converts in opposition to R. Joshua's more tolerant attitude (*Eccl. R.* 1.8.4). This in turn is reminiscent of the stories of the potential converts who appear before Hillel and Shammai with the request that they convert them (*bShab.* 31a). Two more converts – Maria and Salome – appear in ossuary inscriptions from

---

[22] D. Daube, *Ancient Jewish Law. Three Inaugural Lectures* (Leiden 1981), 2–3; Ross S. Kraemer, *Her Share of the Blessings: Women's Religions among Pagans, Jews and Christians in the Greco-Roman World* (New York 1992), 106–23. And cf. also the difficult conversion of Izates of Adiabene (*AJ* 20.38–46) compared to the ease with which his mother converted (*ibid.* 35).

[23] In *Gen. R.* 46.10, pp. 467–8 ed. Theodor-Albeck we find the story of the conversion of Helene's two sons, Izates and Monobazus, but no connection is made between the two sons – who are identified as the sons of King Ptolemy – and Helene, even though their mother is mentioned in the story. See L. H. Schiffman, "The Conversion of the Royal House of Adiabene in Josephus and Rabbinic Sources," in *Josephus, Judaism and Christianity*, edd. L. H. Feldman and G. Hata (Detroit 1987), 293–312.

Jerusalem.[24] Four more funerary inscriptions mention male converts.[25] All of this material together suggests that, within the general picture of conversion to Judaism at the end of the Second Temple period, conversion by women in Palestine was widespread, but the number of female converts known to us by name is no greater than the number of named male converts.[26]

Prostitutes

Another woman who falls outside the category of the free Jewish woman who behaves properly, is eligible to be married and contributes to the next generation, is the prostitute. Ancient Jewish sources, which all have an ethical slant, judge all sexual relations outside marriage to be illicit and improper. The married woman, as we have seen, is of primary concern, but the man who has sexual relations with an unmarried woman not his wife also earns a warning or admonition. *Ben Sira* proclaims:

> "Two kinds of men add sin to sin / and a third brings retribution on himself.
> ... To an adulterer every loaf is as sweet as the last." (25.16–7)

And he also issues warnings:

> "Do not go near a foreign woman / for fear of falling into her snares.
> "Do not conceal yourself with a harlot / lest you fall into her snares.
> "Do not keep company with a dancing-girl / or you may be burnt by her tricks.
> "Do not let your mind dwell on a virgin / or you may be trapped into paying damages for her.
> "Never surrender yourself to prostitutes / for fear of losing all you possess,
> "Do not become defiled by your gaze at the deserted corners of her house.
> "Do not let your eye linger on a beautiful woman's figure / or look on beauty not yours to possess.
> "Many have been seduced by women / whose overture kindles passion like fire." (9.3–8).[27]

---

[24] *CII* 1390; P. B. Bagatti and J. T. Milik, *Gli scavi del Dominus Flevit = Pubblicazioni dello Studium Biblicum Franciscanum* XIII (Jerusalem 1958), 95, no. 31.

[25] *CII* 1385; Bagatti *et ql. ibid.* 84, no. 13; *ibid.* 89, no. 21; and see now "Judah the convert" on an ossuary from the Kidron Valley, in my "New Ossuary Inscriptions from Jerusalem," *Scripta Classica Israelica* 11 (1992), 149–59; the cave was excavated by G. Avni and Z. Greenhut.

[26] The Diaspora was another matter. Among the literary sources, see the *Testament of Joseph* (4.5), where Potiphar's wife says that if Joseph grants her request, she will serve his God and also convince her husband to do so. And see also the conversion of Asenath (in the apocryphal *Joseph and Asenath*) for which see also Kraemer (above, n. 22), 110–3. For other women converts in the Diaspora see eadem. "On the Meaning of the Term 'Jew' in Greco-Roman Inscriptions," *Harvard Theological Review* 82 (1989), 35–53.

[27] On this passage see W. C. Trenchard, *Ben Sira's View on Women: A Literary Analy-*

We have here a list of women, married and unmarried, to whom the man is not married and with whom he is warned against having sexual relations. All these illicit sexual relations are viewed as harlotry. Similarly, the Pharisaic *Psalms of Solomon* lambastes apparently Sadducee opponents for their lusting after many women (4.4–5; 8.10). Literature from the circle of Enoch also contains this theme; we find in the *Testament of Levi* a prophetic reproof against his descendants, accusing them of adultery with married women (14.6). In his testament, Benjamin declares that a good man is one who looks at no woman other than his wife (*Test. Ben.* 8.2). Issachar, in his testament, states the same thing the other way around, declaring that he lived a pure and innocent life because he did not have relations with any woman other than his wife (*Test. Issach.* 7.1–2). In the *Book of Jubilees*, Jacob declares that until age 63, when he was married, he had had no experience with women (25.4).[28] The *Biblical Antiquities* maintains that the tribe of Gad was punished because their sons lusted after their neighbors' wives (25.10).

A unique text was preserved in Qumran; it is written in the style of wisdom literature and contains many characterizations of the unmarried seductress.[29] The work recalls, in its own language and style, *Proverbs* ch. 7 on the "foreign woman" and was designated *The Wiles of the Wicked Woman*. The wicked woman of the Qumranic fragment is described as a seductress who lays snares for the simple, unsuspecting man:

"... to track down a righteous man / and a perfect man to make him stumble;
"upright men to divert (their) path / and those chosen for righteousness from keeping the commandment."
"... to make fools of them [...] / and those who walk uprightly to transgress the l[aw]
"to make the humble rebel from God / and to turn their steps from the way of righteousness; ..."
"to lead man astray in the ways of the Pit / and to seduce by flatteries the sons of men."

The woman drags her innocent sacrifices after her to her abode, which is the underworld:

"Her ways are the ways of death. ..."
"Her gates are the gates of death / through the entrance of her house you shall approach *Sheol* ...
"and all who possess her will descend to the Pit."

---

sis = *Brown Judaic Studies* XXXVIII (Chico CA 1982), 118–20, who thinks that *Ben Sira* adopted here without significant modification old traditions which appealed to his hostility towards women.

[28] According to the Jewish Hellenistic novel *Joseph and Asenath,* Joseph was still a virgin at his wedding ceremony (4.9; 21.1).

[29] See J. M. Allegro, "The Wiles of the Wicked Woman: A Sapiental Work from Qumran's Fourth Cave," *Palestine Exploration Quarterly* 96 (1964), 53–5.

The description of her is filled with imagery of darkness:

"... the foundations of darkness, the sins in her skirts are many. ...
"... the depths of night and her clothes...
"Her garments are the shades of twilight..."
[Her lodgings] are the depth of the Pit / and her [do]minions couches of darkness."

This text is very fragmentary. We possess neither its beginning nor its end, thus neither its proper context nor its purpose can be known. Some have explained it as an allegorical work, much like the *pesharim* discovered at Qumran, and have even tried to identify the wicked woman with an historical figure.[30] Others have seen in the composition not a precise allegory but a parable in which the woman represents the personification of evil in the abstract.[31] It is even possible that the woman represents no more than the dangers of a wicked woman in the eyes of the sect or the author of the composition.[32] In any case, my present purpose requires neither knowing the author's original intentions nor determining whether he was a member of the sect. What is important here is the fact that many lines are devoted to the description of a woman (even if she is symbolic) in whom the embodiment of evil represents a sexual temptation to innocent men. The use of the image of the woman in a parable signifies that the author conceived her as such, and the discovery of the composition in Qumran indicates that this conception was close to the hearts of the sectarians. It is not surprising that a text of this nature was produced by the Qumran sect close to (if not actually) Essenes, whose suspicion of women led to a physical distance from them as well as a very limited role for women in the sect. It is difficult to decide whether the absence of women is what led to the development of the extreme idea of the woman as the embodiment of evil expressed in sexual terms, or conversely, whether such an ideology is what led to the distance between men and women in the community.

Even the rabbis took an extreme approach in the matter of extra-marital sex. The biblical passage, "and the land be filled with lewdness" (*Lev.* 19.29), was interpreted by R. Eliezer: "This is the unmarried man who has intercourse with an unmarried woman with no intention of marrying her" (*tQidd.* 1.4).

In view of this gynophobic tendency to view all women as potential seductresses, it should come as no surprise that the sources present the prostitute as a most dangerous woman who is to be shunned. Thus Josephus claims that

---

[30] E.g. A. M. Gazov-Ginzburg, "Double Meaning in a Qumran Work (The Wiles of a Wicked Woman)," *Revue de Qumrân* 6 (1967), 279–85; H. Burgman, "'The Wicked Woman': Der Makkabäer Simon?" *Revue de Qumrân* 8 (1974), 323–59.

[31] R. D. Moore, "Personification of the Seduction of Evil: The Wiles of the Wicked Woman," *Revue de Qumrân* 10 (1981), 505–19.

[32] J. Licht, "The Wiles of the Wicked Woman," in *Bible and Jewish History: Studies in Bible and Jewish History Dedicated to the Memory of Jacob Liver*, ed. B. Uffenheimer (Tel Aviv 1971), 289–96 [Hebrew].

Jewish law forbids marriage to a prostitute (*AJ* 4.245) and he indicts the judge Samson for violating this law (*AJ* 5.306).

The sources identify three kinds of prostitutes: the gentile prostitute with whom a Jewish man was likely to come into contact; the Jewish prostitute whose clients are Jewish; and the Jewish woman captive who is made a prostitute against her will. The rabbis thought that most prostitutes in the world were of the first sort: "It was taught in the name of R. Nathan: ... of the ten parts of prostitution in the world, nine are in Alexandria and the other in the rest of the world" (*Esther R.* 1.17; *ARNB* 48, p. 132 ed. Schechter). Yet version A of *Abot de Rabbi Nathan*, although still expressing the idea that most of the prostitution in the world is not found in Israel, places the emphasis somewhat differently: "R. Nathan says: ... you don't have prostitution like the prostitution of Arabs" (28, p. 85 ed. Schechter) perhaps hinting at the late post-Islamis date of this composition. These rabbinic sources thus did not view the problem of prostitution in Israel as of highest severity.

Yet we find an odd confusion in the sources regarding the Jewish prostitute. On the one hand, in literature from the period of the Temple we find an attitude such as that represented by Jesus: "Truly I tell you, the tax-collectors and prostitutes (πόρναι) will enter the kingdom of heaven ahead of you [priests and elders], for John came to you in the way of righteousness and you did not believe him, but the tax collectors and the prostitutes believed him" (*Matt.* 21.31);[33] or as the author of the *Psalms of Solomon* says, the degeneration and sin of Jerusalem "arose from prostitution in its midst" (ἀντὶ πορνῶν ἐν αὐτῇ, 2.11); or as the *Testament of Levi* says, the priests, the sons of Levi, were responsible for the corruption and crime of that time because they "eat the sacrifices of God ... with prostitutes (μετὰ πορνῶν), and [they] become unclean through the wives of men, and [they] consort with prostitutes (πόρναι) and adulteresses (μοιχαλίδες)" (4.5–6). Even in rabbinic literature, in a discussion concerning the days of the Messiah, we find the following: "They taught: R. Judah says: The generation in which the son of David will come, the House of Congregation (בית הועד) will be filled with prostitutes" (*bSanh.* 97a).[34] All these sources suggest that Jewish women worked as prostitutes, and the last three sources even see Jewish prostitution as a sign of degeneration in which disaster lurks.

---

[33] Interestingly, this remark appears only in *Matthew*, which is the closest to Judaism. We may ask whether *Matthew* describes a typical phenomenon in Jewish society, of which the other evangelists were simply unaware, or whether *Matthew* had a personal stake in the issue. This question cannot be answered decisively. The New Testament also mentions prostitutes, for example, in the parable of the lost son who "devoured his property with prostitutes" (*Luke* 15. 30). On prostitutes in the New Testament, see L. J. Swidler, *Biblical Affirmations of Women* (Philadelphia 1979), 187–8, 250–1.

[34] According to *Dikdukei Soferim*, instead of זונות (prostitutes), the Munich ms. has גנות ("abomination"); according to the *Mishnah*, the word should be זנות (prostitution). But as Rabinovitch has shown, זונות appears in many manuscripts.

On the other hand, the sources mention only one Jewish woman specifically as engaging in prostitution. In the *aggadah* about the destruction of Tur Shimeon, we read: "And why did they destroy it? If you say because of prostitutes, there was only one young woman there, and they removed her from there ..." (*Lam. R.* 2.4). Another *aggadah* does recount that "the disciples of R. Ishmael dissected the body of a prostitute who had been condemned to death by burning" (*bBekh.* 45a), but this story appears in the *Babylonian Talmud* and is transmitted by Rav Judah in the name of Samuel, and thus is far removed from any historical reality that may lie behind it.[35]

Jesus' identification of prostitutes as an oppressed element of the society of his time has led some to identify the sinning woman (ἁμαρτωλός) in *Luke* 7.36–50 as a prostitute; the historicity of this story, however, does not inspire great confidence, especially in light of its synoptic parallels (*Mark* 14.3–9; *Matt.* 26.7–13; *John* 12.3–8)[36] and also the fact that the woman is not specifically identified as a prostitute.

Some have explained the relative absence of prostitutes from rabbinic literature by the embarrassment the topic caused the rabbis.[37] New Testament scholars have even assumed the existence of a large number of prostitutes in Jewish society.[38] It does seem to be the case, however, that Jewish prostitution did not exactly abound, and this can be explained by the fact that Jews in Palestine lived in close proximity to large non-Jewish populations whose prostitutes provided sexual services for Jewish men. We hear, for example, of a house of prostitution in Caesarea (*AJ* 19.356). We have also already seen that R. Hiyya's disciple traveled to cities on the coast to visit a famous prostitute (*Sifre Num.* 115, pp. 128–9 ed. Horovitz; *bMen.* 44a). R. Eliezer b. Dordia is also said to have visited many prostitutes throughout the world (*bAZ* 17a) etc. This seemingly apologetic claim may find support in the fact that moralistic writers such as *Ben Sira* and the author of the *Wiles of the Wicked Woman* identified the archetypal seductress as a foreign woman.

Yet in their legal discussions, the rabbis were unsure as how exactly to define a prostitute. In *Sifra* we read: " 'A woman who is a prostitute' (*Lev.* 21.7), R.

---

[35] This story should be grouped together with another one involving the disciples of R. Ishmael, who again speak of experiments on the bodies of women condemned to death (*bNidd.* 30b). The historical kernel in both stories may be simply that such experiments on condemned criminals were allowed, but this does not necessarily apply to Jewish society, in which no criminals were condemned to death long before the destruction of the Temple.

[36] See Elisabeth Schüssler-Fiorenza, *In Memory of Her: A Feminist Theological Reconstruction of Christian Origins* (New York 1983), xiii-iv, 128–30; R. Holst, "The One Anointing of Jesus: Another Application of the Form-Critical Method," *Journal of Biblical Literature* 95 (1976), 435–46.

[37] Judith R. Wegner, *Chattel or Person: The Status of Women in the Mishnah* (Oxford 1988), 37.

[38] Schüssler-Fiorenza (above, n. 36), 128.

Judah says: A prostitute is a barren woman. And the sages say: A prostitute is none other than the proselyte, the freedwoman and the woman who has intercourse in such circumstances as those of prostitution. R. Eliezer says: Also when an unmarried man has intercourse with an unmarried woman without intending to marry her" (*Sif. Emor* 1.7, 94b ed. Weiss). These definitions of a prostitute have nothing to do with the woman who has sexual relations for profit; rather, the prostitute is the woman who has sexual relations forbidden by Jewish law, and this includes the two categories of women we have discussed above, the maidservant and the proselyte, whose sexual relations are in any case not proven but assumed.[39] The definition seems to embrace every kind of woman who does not fit the criteria of a free-born Jewish woman, as laid out in this chapter. A *baraita* in the *Babylonian Talmud* illustrates the problematic nature of this all-encompassing definition: "It was taught: 'prostitute' (*Lev.* 21.7): a prostitute in the plain sense of the word (כשמה); so R. Eliezer. And R. Aqiba says: A prostitute is a licentious woman (מופקרת)" (*bYeb.* 61b).[40] We learn from this that the rabbis were aware of the definition of "prostitute" as a professional woman who offered sexual services, but some preferred to broaden the definition. In the continuation of the passage, we find an extremely severe definition of prostitute: "R. Matia b. Haharash says: even if her husband was taking her to make her drink [= undergo the trial of the *sotah*] and he had sexual relations with her on the way, he made her a prostitute" (*ibid.*, and then the *baraita* from *Sifra* is quoted in full). These rather broad definitions turn prostitution from a specific profession into an abstract concept which includes all sexual behavior deviating from societal norms. The legal ramifications of this broad definition can be found already in the *Book of Jubilees*. Although generally speaking the legal determinations in that work are based on the stories in *Genesis*, and although *Genesis* contains the story of Tamar, who posed as a prostitute,[41] the *Book of Jubilees*, without any *midrashic* connection to the Bible, decrees death as the penalty for a daughter or wife who turns to prostitution, that is, she who has sexual relations with any man not her husband (20.4). This definition of prostitution, which is not limited to the professional prostitute, is given also by *Ben Sira*: "The haughty stare betrays a prostituting wife; her eyelids give her away" (26.9);[42] that is, even a woman's gaze at a man in a way that could be considered

---

[39] See L. M. Epstein, *Sex Laws and Customs in Judaism* (New York 1948), 167–70; Rachel Biale, *Women and the Jewish Law: An Exploration of Women's Issues in Halakhic Sources* (New York 1984), 190–2.

[40] According to Rashi, R. Eliezer's definition pertains to a woman unfaithful to her husband, while R. Aqiba's definition (מופקרת) refers to the profession. But I think we should take the text to mean the opposite, as translated above.

[41] From this story the *Book of Jubilees* derives the law prohibiting a father from having sexual relations with his daughter-in-law (41.25–6).

[42] On this verse, see Trenchard (above, n. 27), 115–8.

seductive was counted as prostitution. This helps us understand the rabbis' allegation of prostitution in an attempt to blacken the names of biblical women who otherwise appear guiltless: "Our rabbis taught: Rahab was a prostitute in name" (*bMeg.* 15a). Although even according to the Bible Rahab was indeed a professional prostitute, the other women mentioned in the same *midrash* were decidedly not: "Yael (committed prostitution) with her voice, Abigail by her being remembered, Mikhal the daughter of Saul with her appearance" (*ibid.*).[43] This is only another example of the view that a woman does not have to be a professional prostitute to be considered one merely for being unfaithful to her husband. This strict morality is the proper context for understanding Tobiah's prayers the night of his wedding, when he swears that he did not marry his wife for the sake of prostitution (οὐχὶ διὰ πορνείαν, *Tobit* 8.7).

Thus in their disquisition on the destruction of the Temple, inspired certainly by the *Zeitgeist* of the *Psalms of Solomon* and the *Testament of Levi* from the days of the Temple, the rabbis taught that "prostitution and sorcery have made an end of them (Jerusalem and the Temple) altogether" (*mSot.* 9.13). In the same vein we hear that three cities were destroyed, "Kabul because of controversy, Shihin because of sorcery and Migdal Zibia because of prostitution" (*yTaan.* 4.8, 69a). It seems, then, that in the rabbinic view not just prostitutes in the plain sense of the word, but also prostitution in the sense of deviant sexual behavior by individuals in society can bring on moral decline.

The third kind of prostitute, as we saw above, was the women captured in war by gentiles and forced against their will into prostitution. Jewish law treats these prostitutes as war captives, that is, defiled unless they can prove otherwise (*mKet.* 2.9). The sources do not judge or criticize these women, whose fates are related only in *aggadic* literature – for example, "women who were captured for prostitution" and committed suicide in order to escape their lot (*bGitt.* 57b; *Lam. R.* 1.45). Of the same literary type is the story about the daughter of Hananiah b. Tardion who was sentenced to sit in the house of prostitution in Rome but managed by a whole series of pretexts to avoid providing the service for which she had been brought there (*bAZ* 17b-18a).[44] These women's exemplary

---

[43] On the assault on the prestige of respected biblical women, see, e.g. Linda Kuzmack, "*Aggadic* Approaches to Biblical Women," in *The Jewish Woman: New Perspectives*, ed. Elizabeth Koltun (New York 1976), 248–56; Leila Bronner, "Biblical Prophetesses through Rabbinic Lenses," *Judaism* 40 (1990), 171–83. On the opposite phenomenon, i.e. the rehabilitation of negative biblical male figures, see A. Margulies, *The Wicked in the Bible Who are Righteous in Talmud and Midrash* (London 1949) [Hebrew]; the author also mentions in this book Tamar wife of Er and Rahab the prostitute.

[44] The parable which R. Nehemiah tells in *Genesis Rabbah* may also have to do with the same thing: "It is like the virgin who stays in the prostitution market and does not earn a bad name" (*Gen. R.* 30.9, p. 276 ed. Theodor-Albeck, and see notes *ibid.*). See also the article on Beruriah by Rachel Adler, "The Virgin in the Brothel and other Anomalies: Character and Context in the Legend of Beruriah," *Tikkun* 3/4 (1988), 28.

behavior in captivity, by which they avoided engaging in prostitution, is in the rabbis' eyes, the way every daughter of Israel should behave.

However, here is no documented case of a Jewish woman being sold into prostitution. Although the *Babylonian Talmud* reports that the daughter of Hananiah b. Tardion was sentenced "to sit in a house of prostitution" (*bAZ* 17b-18a), the *tannaitic* source describing this event defines her punishment differently as "having to perform labor" (*Sifre Deut.* 307, p. 346 ed. Finkelstein). Nor, clearly, can the *amoraic* continuation in the *Babylonian Talmud*, whereby R. Meir ransoms his sister-in-law, be considered historical. *Abot de Rabbi Nathan* also describes a Jewish woman captive who sits in a house of prostitution (*A* 8, p. 37 ed. Schechter), but this has no more historical value than the passage in the *Talmud*, although there can be no doubt that Jewish female captives were employed in this capacity.

Witches

We have just examined passages in which a close connection is made between prostitution and witchcraft. Both were responsible, according to one source, for the destruction of the Temple (*mSot.* 9.13), and according to another source, while Migdal Zibia was destroyed because of prostitution, Shihin was destroyed because of sorcery (*yTaan.* 4.8, 69a). Moreover, just as the rabbis taught that most of the prostitution in the world is located in Alexandria, so also "of the ten parts of sorcery in the world, nine are in Egypt and the tenth spread out over the rest of the world" (*ARNB* 48, p. 132 ed. Schechter).

During the Second Temple period, magic was often identified with women. On *Ex.* 22.17, "A sorceress shall not live," the rabbis commented, "It is all the same whether it is a sorcerer or a sorceress, except the *Torah* meant to teach you the way of the land, because most women are inclined to sorcery" (*ySanh.* 7.19, 25d; *bSanh.* 67a); or as the *Mekhilta de R. Shimeon bar Yohai* puts it, "Most sorcery is in women" (p. 209 ed. Melamed). Our sources imagine that the origin of the connection between women and sorcery is very ancient. The Ethiopian *Apocalypse of Enoch*, for example, says that the fallen angels are the ones who taught the daughters of men poisons, medicine, spells, invocations, sorcery, the cutting of roots and plants (καὶ ἐδίδαξαν αὐτὰν φαρμακείας καὶ ἐπαοιδὰς καὶ ῥιζοτομίας, καὶ τὰς βοτάνας ἐφδήλωσαν αὐταῖς – 7.1), and this knowledge turned them into the allies of the fallen angels (19.2).[45]

---

[45] On women and magic in the *Apocrypha* and *Pseudepigrapha*, see B. P. Prusak, "Woman: Seductive Siren and Source of Sin: *Pseudepigraphical* Myth and Christian Origins," in *Religion and Sexism: Images of Women in the Jewish and Christian Tradition*, ed. Rosemary R. Reuther (New York 1974), 89–116; Léonie J. Archer, "The 'Evil Woman' in

Several sayings by the rabbis strengthen their claim that "most sorcery is in women". Regarding the verse, "There shall not be a man able to stand against you" (*Deut.* 7.24), *Sifre* asks: "This applies to a single man; what about a nation, a family or even a woman plying her witchcraft?" (*Sifre Deut.* 52, p. 118 ed. Finkelstein); in other words, if anyone stands against the people of Israel with the aid of sorcery, it will be a woman. Elsewhere we read, "The more women, the more sorcery" (*mAbot* 2.7). It seems to be self-evident to the rabbis that women engaged in witchcraft, the problem being only the number of women who did so. An extreme view is found in the *Palestinian Talmud*: "It was taught: R. Shimeon b. Yohai says ... even the most decent woman practices witchcraft" (*yQidd.* 4.11, 66c): no woman is free from suspicion of practicing witchcraft. The rabbis also quote *Ben Sira* on witchcraft, even though the passage exists in neither the Greek nor Hebrew original, at least as they have been preserved. In a passage describing the pains and sorrows a daughter causes her father, the *Talmud* adds: "When she grows old – lest she engage in witch craft" (*bSanh.* 100b); that is, even after his daughter has grown up, married, produced children and grown older, a father cannot rest peacefully because she is liable to turn to sorcery.

Sorcery is considered to be as serious a transgression as adultery, or at least that is the impression from the following parable: "The matter is similar to the king who made a decree saying: All who eat figs of the sabbatical year will be paraded around in public as punishment. A certain woman, from a good family, went and collected and ate figs of the sabbatical year, and they paraded her around in public. She said to him: By your leave, my lord the king, publicize my fault lest people in this country say: It seems that they caught her in adultery or they caught her in sorcery" (*Sifre Deut.* 26, p. 36 ed. Finkelstein).

Our information on the kind of witchcraft Jews practiced is quite limited because of the well-known connection between sorcery and idolatry, although we do have evidence of Jewish witchcraft[46] which did not belong to mainstream Judaism described in rabbinic literature. This material, however, cannot concern us here because it is later than the *tannaitic* period and stems predominantly from the Diaspora. What we do possess is chapters 6 and 7 in the tractate *Shabbat* in the *Tosefta*, which contain a long list of customs called "superstitious practices," or literally "The ways of the Emorite," which in effect are magical practices common in Palestine and forbidden by Jewish faith in its purest form.[47] Of the practices in the list, the language used to describe 25 in chapter

---

Apocryphal and *Pseudepigraphical* Writings," *Proceedings of the Ninth World Congress of Jewish Studies* Div. A (Jerusalem 1988), 239–46.

[46] See, e.g. J. Naveh and S. Shaked, *Amulets and Magic Bowls: Aramaic Incantations in Late Antiquity* (Jerusalem 1987), and note the special role of the mother's name in amulets.

[47] On this passage in *Tosefta*, see S. Lieberman *Tosefta kifeshuta* III (New York 1962), 79–96 [Hebrew].

six and another ten in chapter seven uses the male forms, whereas for only ten in chapter six is the female gender used. These ten activities fall into areas in which women were normally occupied: "she drags her son among the dead" (6.1) is connected to a woman's role as mother; "she who shouts at an oven not to let the bread fall, she who puts charms into the handle of a pot that it should not boil over" (6.14) and "she who imposes silence for lentils and who smacks her lips at rice" (6.15) are connected to a woman's role as baker and cook; "she who sets hens to brood and said: I set them out only in pairs, I set them out only naked, I set them out only with the left hand, I set them out only with both hands" (6.17) and "she who sets out a brood of chicks in a sieve, or puts pieces of iron among a brood of chicks" (6.19) are connected to the woman's responsibility of raising chicks from eggs.[48] Only the practices "she who slaps for a lamp" (6.15) and "she who puts eggs and grass into the wall and plasters them over and counts seven and one" (6.18) do not have a clear parallel in women's normal work. Thus it seems that "the ways of the Emorite" were not considered to be those which women in particular carried out.

We learn from the book of *Enoch* that the study of witchcraft was linked to the knowledge of roots and plants.[49] Women's knowledge of the plant world is what led to the identification of the concoction of drugs and remedies from plants with sorcery. The *Testament of Joseph* describes Potiphar's wife (the Egyptian!) as using magic on Joseph's food in order to make him more seducible (ἀποστέλλει μοι βρῶμα ἐν γοητεία πεφυρμένον – 6.1).

Concocting poisons was closely related to the production of drugs and remedies, and women were naturally considered expert in this field, too.[50] In this light we may recall the story of the poison which Antipater prepared for his father, King Herod. The story, which Josephus relates both in *BJ* 1 and *AJ* 17, was without doubt taken from Nicolaus of Damascus. The wife of Herod's brother Pheroras was accused of killing her husband with poison (φάρμακον) which an Arab woman had prepared and which was brought in by the mother and sister of Pheroras' wife. The woman who concocted the potion was, according to *AJ*

---

[48] Compare *ARNB* 4 (pp. 14–5 ed. Schechter).

[49] Some modern scholars have claimed that the link between women and the plant world originates in the prehistoric period, when human society was organized into groups of hunters and gatherers, the latter function being filled by women. See Elise Boulding, *Underside of History: A View of Women Through Time* (Boulder CO 1976), 76–7, 111–7; and see also the collection: Frances Dahlberg, ed. *Woman the Gatherer* (New Haven 1981).

[50] In the *Testament of Joseph* 5.1, Potiphar's wife suggests that she would poison her husband (ἐγὼ ἀνελῶ τὸν ἄνδρα μου φαρμάκῳ). Women poisoners are mentioned in numerous instances in classical literature. A cursory survey of Tac. *Ann.* uncovered the following instances in which women were accused of poisoning: 2.73–4; 3.7; 17; 4.3; 12.65–6. I am certain that a more thorough survey of Tacitus would produce more evidence just from this one author.

17.62–3, a relative of the lover of Syllaeus the Arab, Herod's enemy, and she was, according to *BJ* 1.583, employed by Syllaeus himself. Thus the story describes a poisoning prepared and carried out, as it were, by five women. Yet it turns out that the entire story was fabricated by men who knew that a plot which combined preparation of poison and women would easily be believed. Slaves of the house, when tortured, not only did not expose such a plot but revealed an entirely different one, the one in which Antipater tried to poison his father. In that plot, the poison had been prepared in Egypt(!) by a male physician and brought into Palestine by Antipater's brother, Antiphilus, then transferred to Antipater's uncle Theudion, who gave it to Pheroras. Pheroras gave the poison to his wife, and it was in the end discovered in her possession (*BJ* 1.592–600; *AJ* 17.69–76). In this instance, the poison was prepared and handled entirely by men. This whole episode is a good example of how women's image as preparers of poison and sorceresses could affect the writing, and even the course, of history.

If the connection between women and magic had any historical basis, we would expect to find many sorceresses in the sources. They are not there to be found. Not one sorceress from the Second Temple period and afterwards is known. It is true that the *Palestinian Talmud* (*yHag.* 2.2, 77d–78a; *ySanh.* 6.9, 23c) identifies the eighty women hanged by Shimeon b. Shetah (*mSanh.* 6.4) as witches, but the historicity of the story is compromised by its clearly late, popular-*aggadic* character.[51]

The *Babylonian Talmud* may be mentioning a witch, by the name of Yohani bat Ratavi (*bSot.* 22a). The present version of the text only mentions her name without any reference to what she did, but Rashi *ad loc.* describes Yohani's activities: she knew magical charms for opening and closing women's wombs afflicted by labor pains.[52] As we have noted, Rashi's sources for such *aggadot* are unknown to us, and it is difficult to know just how important this particular story is for the history of the period we are studying. It may be a *tannaitic baraita* which somehow dropped out of the *Babylonian Talmud*, but this is not very likely. The story Rashi tells about Yohani of the *Talmud* appears in the writings of R. Nissim of Kairouan in his collection of *aggadot*,[53] but the protagonist of his tale is nameless. Since Nissim of Kairouan is slightly earlier than

---

[51] See M. Hengel, *Rabbinische Legende und frühpharisäische Geschichte: Schimeon b. Schetach und die achtzig Hexen von Askalon = Abhandlung der Heidelberger Akkademie der Wissenschaft philisophisch-historische Klasse* (Heidelberg 1984), 16–26. A clearly fictional story about 70 women executed in Rome for preparing poison is told by *Livy* (8.18).

[52] On the common belief in the ancient world that midwives could prolong birth pangs by magic see: J. Preuss, *Biblical and Talmudic Medicine*, translation F. Rosner (New York 1978), 37.

[53] Published by M. Gaster, *The Exampla of the Rabbis* (New York 1924), no. 412.

Rashi, we may assume that they both used the same tradition. Because the woman is nameless in R. Nissim, we may assume that the name in Rashi is a secondary insertion. In any case, whatever the historical status of this story, Yohani is yet another example of a woman dealing with matters which fell in the field of women's expertise anyway – midwifery – and perhaps men interpreted her abilities as magical because they simply did not understand them.

Another story which may be relevant here involves the woman who came to hear R. Meir in his study-house. R. Meir says: "Any woman who knows how to cure a sore eye by charm, come forth and charm for me" (*ySot.* 1.4, 16d). R. Meir seems to assume that various kinds of charms were known only to women. The woman in the story does not know any charms, and R. Meir is the one who shows her what to do. We can assume, therefore, that the link between woman and sorcery arose out of their experience in childbirth, healing, the preparation of potions and medicines, and even lamentation at the grave – all of which occupations were foreign to men and seemed to them perilously close to the invocation of evil forces. Actual witches we do not meet at all in this period.

Conclusion

In this book I have surveyed many aspects of the life of the Jewish woman in Palestine during the Hellenistic-Roman period as they emerge in the various sources that have survived. Since the sources are of diverse backgrounds and serve different, often conflicting purposes, a great variety of opinions could be found in them in many matters, sometimes even within the same source. It was thus possible to see that the attitude of the sources to women is not at all uniform and does not yield a one-dimensional, unambiguous set of laws. Nevertheless, two general tendencies do stand out in the sources.

a. All sources surviving from the Second Temple period were written by groups who maintained very high moral standards and viewed licentiousness as one of the most serious threats to those standards. Since all sources were written by men, the only remedies suggested for widespread licentiousness applied to women, who represented the temptation that drew men away from the straight and narrow moral path. Moreover, all sources describe the same ideal picture of society: women provide what is asked of them, be it producing legal heirs, doing housework, remaining faithful to their husbands, avoiding contact with other men unrelated to them or using their beauty to make their husbands' lives more pleasant. Women who deviate from this perfect behavior are described by all the sources as wicked. Men's ideal behavior is similar: men should avoid contact with women who are not their wives, and they should engage in sexual relations primarily to produce offspring.

b. These social norms were anchored in law, as it is laid out in *halakhic* literature. Yet here we are able to make a clear distinction between the law of the pietists and the more pragmatic *tannaitic*-Pharisaic law. The laws of the pietist circles resemble the requirements for an ideal society, and thus make severe demands, such as a man's strict obligation to avoid all sexual relations with his wife except for those explicitly intended for procreation (and even the number of these occasions was curtailed); or the proscription of polygamy or divorce; or the demand of the widow not to remarry. By contrast, the *tannaitic*-Pharisaic *halakhah* takes into consideration both real conditions which depart from the ideal picture of society, and human nature, which is much more complicated than that of the ideal member of society. The requirements of the *tannaim*-Pharisees are less severe than those of the pietists, despite the similarity in their world-views. For example, *tannaitic*-Pharisaic law permits frequent sexual relations, even when procreation is clearly not a desired result; it also permits polygamy and divorce, and recommends that every effort be made to find the widow another husband. Further, the *halakhah* of the earlier generations of Pharisees is different from and more stringent than that of the later *tannaitic* generations. For example, while strict adherence to levirate marriage was commonplace during the Second Temple period, after the Destruction the *tannaim* recommended the more lenient practice of *halitzah*. The differences in approach between Pharisees and pietists can be explained by the fact that the pietist circles of the Second Temple period were basically elitist societies with voluntary membership, and they designed their stricter laws for their own members. Rabbinic literature, by contrast, presumes to set down laws which are the same for everyone and apply to all Jews; "A decree cannot be made for the people unless most of the people can endure it" (*bBB* 60b). We may assume that, like R. Yose, who performed the commandment of levirate marriage "in the manner of the pietists (חסידין)," the framers of the Pharisaic *halakhah* also tried to adhere strictly to the requirements of the law in a way which approached the behavior of the pietists.

Yet we may ask whether the lenient *tannaitic*-Pharisaic *halakhah* was in fact equal for every person, and whether Jewish society of the Second Temple period did in fact follow it. Reality turns out to be different from the legislated ideal. The *tannaitic halakhah*, which by comparison to the *halakhah* of more extreme groups seems more pragmatic, nonetheless itself represents an extreme. For example, the rabbis would have us believe that all women of the Second Temple period followed the Pharisaic rulings regarding *niddah*, although the sources provide evidence that this was not really so: many groups, such as the Sadducees, did not follow the Pharisees in this matter. The rabbis also disqualified women as witnesses but the judicial system in Palestine of that period did not operate to any extent according to the Pharisees and in fact often needed testimony from women. Again, the sources give the impression that after the destruction of the Temple, the rabbinic courts had the power to force a husband to meet the conditions of his wife's *ketubbah* but marriage contracts written by Jews in Greek reveal that sometimes Jews preferred to rely on the more powerful imperial courts for their enforcement. Thus the condition in some marriage contracts obligating the husband to maintain his wife according to Greek custom indicates that the rabbinic law was not followed in all areas. The *tannaitic halakhah* specifies that the parents were the ones who married off their children, but this law was not always practiced, and we even hear of one institution whose function was to arrange for unmarried men and women to meet each other (*bTaan* 31a). Some Jews even practiced a sort of marriage in which the couple lived together without a marriage contract or any other formality of that sort. How can we explain this discrepancy? Or in other words: why did the majority of the population allow itself even greater liberties than those afforded by the relatively more lenient *tannaitic*-Pharisaic legal system? The answer to this question should, in my opinion, be divided into two parts: the first pertains to the character of Jewish society in the period under discussion, while the second pertains to the sociological character of the Pharisees and their *tannaitic* successors.

1. The Heterogeneity of Jewish Society in Palestine

In the Second Temple period Jewish society was highly heterogeneous. Different groups lived by different versions of Jewish law. *Tannaitic halakhah* was not fully adhered to in that period, both because it was not yet fully developed, part of it being written after the destruction of the Temple, and because only a particular group attempted to live by it before the Destruction. After the Destruction, adherence to *tannaitic halakhah* did not become more widespread, despite the disappearance of many other competing groups. It is also clear that not the Pharisees but the Sadducees ran the Temple while it stood, and the judicial system which operated from the Temple was more Sadducean than Pharisaic; yet at the same time there were additional judicial systems, such as gentile authorities to which Jews could turn, or special courts of the Jewish royal houses, which seem to have functioned according to a different system of law and procedure. The Pharisaic *halakhah* itself was not monolithic but characterized by different currents such as the Schools of Shammai and Hillel. Furthermore, although compared to the *halakhah* of extreme pietists such as the Dead Sea Sect Pharisaic *halakhah* gives the impression of being lenient, there were even more options available to a Jew at the time. For example, the only Sadduccean law known to us which pertains to women, dealing with a daughter's ability to inherit, is more lenient than the Pharisaic law on the same matter. Yet the Sadducean *halakhah* was designed for aristocrats, and thus most portions of the population, called in *tannaitic* literature *am ha-aretz*, who did not follow Pharisaic *halakhah*, would have been even less inclined to follow the Sadducees. Rabbinic literature itself acknowledges that so far as ritual purity was concerned, these parts of the population did not follow the Pharisaic laws. It is obvious that some of the customs pertaining to women which differ from the Pharisaic-*tannaitic halakhah* are connected to the traditions of these lower classes of people called *am ha-aretz*.

2. Social Class and Tannaitic Literature

In contrast to the heterogeneity of Jewish society, the authors of *tannaitic* literature and of most of the other surviving sources like Josephus and *Ben Sira* belonged to the upper-middle and aristocratic classes. This is revealed in a certain uniformity of approach among all the sources to the social problems involving women, which in turn explains various phenomena which we have encountered in this work, such as the fact that only a man of means could have separate women's quarters in his house. Thus the requirement that men and women be kept separate comes from social circles whose members had the means to put this into practice. Likewise, only a social class whose women could hire wet-nurses in order to save themselves the trouble and possible deterioration of the body would determine that nursing was neither an obligation nor a religious duty. Only families worried about preserving their own property would place great importance on the family backgrounds of the husbands for their daughters, and in fact would make every effort to ensure that the husbands came from related families or families of similar social position. Poor families, by comparison, would have preferred to marry up into wealthier classes. Yet as we have seen, laws made by only these upper social classes were not always appropriate for the lower classes: "A decree cannot be made for the people unless most of the people can endure it" (*bBB* 60b).

Bibliography

Aderet, A., "The Story in *Sefer Ha-Aggadah* B," *Alei-Siah* 4–5 (1978), 122–9 [Hebrew].

Adler, Rachel, "The Jew Who Wasn't There: *Halacha* and the Jewish Woman," *Davka* 1 (1971), 6–11.

– *"Tumah* and *Taharah*: Ends and Beginnings," in *The Jewish Woman: New Perspectives*, ed. Elizabeth Koltun (New York 1976), 63–71.

– "A Mother in Israel: Aspects of the Mother-Role in Jewish Myth," in *Beyond Androcentrism = Aids for the Study of Religion* VI, ed. Rita M. Gross (Missoula MO 1977), 237–55.

– "The Virgin in the Brothel and other Anomalies: Character and Context in the Legend of Beruriah," *Tikkun* 3/6 (1988), 28–32; 102–5.

Aiken, Lisa, *To Be a Jewish Woman* (Northvale NJ 1992).

Allegro, J. M., "The Wiles of the Wicked Woman: A Sapiental Work from Qumran's Fourth Cave," *Palestine Exploration Quarterly* 96 (1964), 53–5.

Alon, G., *Jews, Judaism and the Classical World* (Jerusalem 1977).

Andersen, F. I., "2 (Slavonic Apocalypse of) *Enoch*," in *The Old Testament Pseudepigrapha*, ed. J. H. Charlesworth (Garden City NY 1985), 91–221.

Anderson, G., "Celibacy or Consummation in the Garden? Reflections on Early Jewish and Christian Interpretations of the Garden of Eden," *Harvard Theological Review* 82 (1989), 121–48.

Appleman, S., *The Jewish Woman in Judaism* (Hicksville NY 1979).

Aptowitzer, V., "Asenath the Wife of Joseph: A *Haggadic* Literary-Historical Study," *Hebrew Union College Annual* 1 [1924], 239–306.

– "Spuren des Matriarchats in jüdischen Schrifttum," *Hebrew Union College Annual* 4 (1927), 207–40; *ibid.* 5 (1928), 261–97.

Archer, Léone J., "The Role of Jewish Women in the Religion, Ritual and Cult of Greco-Roman Palestine," in *Images of Women in Antiquity*, edd. Averil Cameron and Amélie Kuhrt (Detroit 1985), 273–87.

– "The 'Evil Woman' in *Apocryphal* and *Pseudepigraphical* Writings," *Proceedings of the Ninth World Congress of Jewish Studies*, Div. A (Jerusalem 1986), 239–46.

– *Her Price is Beyond Rubies: The Jewish Woman in Graeco-Roman Palestine = Journal for the Study of the Old Testament Supplement Series*, LX (Sheffield 1990).

– "'In Thy Blood Live': Gender and Ritual in the Judeo-Christian Tradition," *Through the Devil's Gateway: Women, Religion and Taboo*, ed. Alison Joseph (London 1990), 22–49.

Assaf, S., "Appointment of Women as Guardians," *Hamishpat Haivri* 2 (1927), 75–81 [Hebrew].

Avigad, N., "A Hebrew Ossuary Inscription," *Bulletin of the Israel Exploration Society* 25 (1961), 143 [Hebrew].

– *Beth She'arim: Report on Excavations During 1953–1958* III (New Brunswick NJ 1976).

Bacher, W., *Agada der Tannaiten* (Strassbourg 1890).

– "Ein polemischer Ausspruch Jose b. Chalfthas," *Monatsschrift für Geschichte und Wissenschaft des Judentums* 42 (1895), 505–7.

Baer, R. A., *Philo's Use of the Categories Male and Female* (Leiden 1970).

Bagatti, P. B. and J. T. Milik, *Gli Scavi del Dominus Flevit =Pubblicazioni dello Studium Biblicum Franciscanum* XIII (Jerusalem 1958).

Bailey, J. L., "Josephus' Portrayal of the Matriarchs," in *Josephus, Judaism and Christianity*, edd. L. H. Feldman and G. Hata (Detroit 1987), 154–79.

Bammel, E., "*Markus* 10 11f. und das jüdische Eherecht," *Zeitschrift für Neutestamentliche Wissenschaft* 61 (1970), 95–101.

Barag, D. and D. Flusser, "The Ossuary of Yehohanah Granddaughter of the High-Priest Theophilus," *Israel Exploration Journal* 36 (1986), 39–44.

Barker, W. P., *Women and the Liberator* (Old Tappan NJ 1972).

Baron, S., *A Social and Religious History of the Jews* (New York, 1952).

Baskin, Judith R., "The Separation of Women in Rabbinic Judaism," *Women, Religion and Social Change*, edd. Yvonne Y. Haddad and Elison B. Findly (Albany 1985), 3–18.

– "Rabbinic Reflections on the Barren Wife," *Harvard Theological Review* 89 (1989), 101–14.

– ed., *Jewish Women in Historical Perspective* (Detroit 1991).

Baumgarten, J. M., *Studies in Qumran Law* (Leiden 1977).

– "*4Q$_{502}$*, Marriage or Golden Age Ritual?" *Journal of Jewish Studies* 34 (1983), 125–35.

Belkin, S., "Levirate and Agnate Marriage in Rabbinic and Cognate Literature," *Jewish Quarterly Review* 60 (1969–70), 275–329.

Ben Chorin, S., *Mutter Mirjam: Maria in jüdischer Sicht* (München 1982).

Berkovitz, E., *Jewish Women in Time and Torah* (Hoboken NJ 1990).

Berman, D., "The Status of Women in *Halakhic* Judaism," *Tradition* 14/2 (1973), 5–28.

Biale, D., *Eros and the Jews: From Biblical Israel to Contemporary America* (New York 1992).

Biale, Rachel,*Women and the Jewish Law: An Exploration of Women's Issues in Halakhic Sources* (New York 1984).

– "Women and Jewish Law," *Encyclopaedia Judaica Yearbook* (Jerusalem 1986–7), 16–28.

Bin-Gorion, I., *The Paths of Legends: An Introduction to Folktales* (Jerusalem 1970) [Hebrew].

Bode, E. L., *The First Easter Morning: The Gospel Account of the Women's Visit to the Tomb of Jesus = Analecta Biblica* XLV (Rome 1970).

Böhl, F., "Die Matronenfragen im *Midrasch*," *Frankfurter judaistische Beiträge* 3 (1975), 29–64.

Boucher, Madeleine, "Some Unexplored Parallels to *1 Cor* 11,11–2 and *Gal* 3,28. The NT on the Role of Women," *Catholic Biblical Quarterly* 31 (1969), 50–8.

Boulding, Elise, *The Underside of History: A View of Women through Time* (Boulder CO 1976).

Boyarin, D., *Carnal Israel: Reading Sex in Talmudic Culture* (Berkeley 1993).

Bremen, R. van, "Women and Wealth," in *Images of Women in Antiquity*, edd. Averil Cameron and Amélie Kuhrt (Detroit 1985), 223–42.

Brodsky, Alyn, *The Kings Depart* (New York 1974).

Bronner, Leila, "Biblical Prophetesses through Rabbinic Lenses," *Judaism* 40 (1991), 171–83.

Brooten, Bernadette J., "Junia ... Outstanding Among the Apostles (Romans 16:7)," in *Women Priests: A Catholic Commentary on the Vatican Declaration*, edd. L. J. and Arlene Swidler (New York 1977), 141–4.

– "Konnten Frauen im alten Judentum die Scheidung betreiben? Überlegung zu *Mk* 10, 11–12 und *1Kor* 7, 10–11," *Evangelische Theologie* 42 (1982), 65–80.

– *Women Leaders in the Ancient Synagogue: Inscriptional Evidence and Background Issues = Brown Judaic Studies* XXXVI (Chico CA 1982).

– "Zur Debatte über das Scheidungsrecht der jüdischen Frau," *Evangelische Theologie* 43 (1983), 466–78.
– "Early Christian Women and their Cultural Context: Issues of Method in Historical Reconstruction," in *Feminist Perspectives on Biblical Scholarship*, ed. Adela Yarbro Collins (Chico CA 1985), 65–91.
– "Paul's Views on the Nature of Women and Female Homoeroticism," in *Immaculate and Powerful: The Female in Sacred Image and Social Reality*, edd. Clarissa W. Atkinson, Constance H. Buchanan and Margaret R. Miles (Boston 1985), 61–87.
– "Paul and the Law: How Complete was the Departure?" *The Princeton Seminary Bulletin Supplementary Issue* 1 (1990), 71–89.
Brown, Cheryl Anne, *No Longer Be Silent: First Century Jewish Portraits of Biblical Women* (Louisville, KY 1992).
Brown, P., *The Body and Society: Men Women and Sexual Renunciation in Early Christianity* (New York 1988).
Büchler, A.,"Die Straffe der Ehebrecher in der nachexilischen Zeit," *Monatsschrift für Geschichte und Wissenschaft des Judentums* 55 (1911), 196–219.
– "The Induction of the Bride and the Bridegroom into the חופה in the First and Second Centuries in Palestine," *Livre d'hommage à la mémoire du Dr. Samuel Poznanski (1864–1921)* (Warsaw 1927), 83–97.
– "Family Purity and Family Impurity in Jerusalem before the Year 70 C.E.," *Studies in Jewish History = Jews College Publications* n.s. 1 (London 1956), 64–98.
Burgman, H., "'The Wicked Woman': Der Makkabäer Simon?" *Revue de Qumrân* 8 (1974), 323–59.
Cady-Stanton, Elizabeth, *The Woman's Bible* (New York 1895).
Cameron, Averil, "'Neither Male nor Female'," *Greece and Rome* 27 (1980), 60–8.
Camp, Claudia V., "Understanding a Patriarchy: Women in Second Century Jerusalem through the Eyes of Ben Sira," in *"Women Like This'": New Perspectives on Jewish Women in the Greco-Roman Period*, ed. Amy-Jill Levine (Atlanta 1991), 1–40.
Carlisle, T. J., *Beginning with Mary: Women of the Gospel in Portraits* (Grand Rapids 1986).
Carmody, Denise L., "Judaism," in *Women in World Religions*, ed. A. Sharma (Albany 1987), 183–206.
Charles, R. H., *The Apocrphya and Pseudepigrapha of the Old Testament* (Oxford 1913).
Charlesworth, J. H., *The Old Testament Pseudepigrapha* (Garden City NY 1985).
Cline-Horowitz, Maryanne, "The Image of God in Man: Is Woman Included?" *Harvard Theological Review* 72 (1979), 175–206.
Cohen, J., "'Be Fertile and Increase, Fill the Earth and Master It': The Medieval Career of a Biblical Text* (Ithaca NY 1989).
Cohen, Naomi G., "The Personal Name 'Miriam' and its Latin and Greek Transliterations," *Leshonenu* 38 (1974), 170–80 [Hebrew].
– "The Theological Stratum of the Martha b. Boethus Tradition: An Explication of the Text in *Gittin* 56a," *Harvard Theological Review* 69 (1976), 187–95.
Cohen, S. J. D., "The Women in the Synagogues of Antiquity," *Conservative Judaism* 34/2 (1980–1), 23–9.
– "From the Bible to *Talmud*: The Prohibition of Intermarriage," *Hebrew Annual Review* 7 (1983), 23–39.
– "The Origin of the Matrilineal Principle in Rabbinic Law," *Association of Jewish Studies Review* 10 (1985), 19–53.
– "Menstruants and the Sacred in Judaism and Christianity," in *Women's History and Ancient History*, ed. Sarah B. Pomeroy (London, NC 1991), 271–99.
Cole, Susan G., "Could Greek Women Read and Write?" in *Reflections of Women in Antiquity*, ed. Helen P. Foley (New York 1981), 219–45.

Corrington, Gail P., "The Milk of Salvation: Redemption by the Mother in Late Antiquity and Early Christianity," *Harvard Theological Review* 82 (1989), 393–420.

Cotton, Hannah M. and J. Geiger, *Masada II: The Latin and Greek Documents* (Jerusalem 1989).

Cotton, Hannah M., "The Guardianship of Jesus son of Babatha: Roman and Local Law in the Province of Arabia," *Journal of Roman Studies* 83 (1993), 94–108.

Crook, J. A., *Law and Life of Rome 90 BC-AD 219* (New York 1967).

Danby, H., *The Mishnah* (Oxford 1933).

D'Angelo, Mary-Rose, "Women Partners in the New Testament," *Journal of Feminist Studies in Religion* 6 (1990) 65–86.

Daube, D., "Jesus and the Samaritan Woman: The Meaning of συγχράομαι," *Journal of Biblical Literature* 69 (1950), 137–47.

– *The Duty of Procreation* (Edinburgh 1977).

– "Johanan ben Broqua and Women's Rights," in *Jewish Tradition in the Diaspora: Studies in Memory of Prof. Walter F. Fischel*, ed. M. M. Caspi (Berkeley 1981), 55–60.

– *Ancient Jewish Law. Three Inaugural Lectures* (Leiden 1981).

Daum, Annette, "Blaming the Jews for the Death of the Goddess," *Lilith* 7 (1980), 12–3.

Davis, S., *The Revolt of the Widows: The Social World of the Apocryphal Acts* (Carbondale 1980).

Destro, Adriana, *The Law of Jealousy: Anthropology of Sotah = Brown Judaic Studies CLXXXI* (Atlanta 1989).

Deutsch, I., *Die Regirungszeit der judäischen Königin Salome Alexandra und die Wirksamkeit des Rabbi Simon ben Schetach* (Magdeburg 1901).

Efron, J., *Studies on the Hasmonean Period* (Leiden 1987).

– "The Deed of Simeon ben Shatah in Ascalon," in A. Kasher, *Jews and Hellenistic Cities in Eretz Israel* (Tübingen 1990), 318–41.

Elbaum, J., "Models of Storytelling and Speech in Stories about the Sages," *Proceedings of the Seventh World Congress of Jewish Studies 1977* Div. 3 (Jerusalem 1981), 70–7 [Hebrew].

Elliot, J. K., "Anna's Age (*Luke* 2:36–37)," *Novum Testamentum* 30 (1988), 100–2.

Engels, D., "The Problem of Female Infanticide in the Greco-Roman World," *Classical Philology* 75 (1980), 112–20.

Epstein, L. M., *The Jewish Marriage Contract: A Study in the Status of Women in Jewish Law* (New York 1927).

– *Marriage Laws in the Bible and Talmud* (Cambridge MA 1942).

– *Sex Laws and Customs in Judaism* (New York 1948).

Ewald, H., *History of Israel* V (London 1880).

Faxon, Alicia C., *Women and Jesus* (Philadelphia 1973).

Falk, Z., "The Inheritance of the Daughter and Widow in the Bible and *Talmud*," *Tarbiz* 23 (1952), 9–15 [Hebrew].

– *A Wife's Divorce Action in Jewish Law* (Jerusalem 1973) [Hebrew].

– *Introduction to the Jewish Laws of he Second Commonwealth* (Leiden 1978).

Feldman, D. M., "Woman's Role and Jewish Law," *Conservative Judaism* 26/4 (1972), 29–39.

– *Marital Relations, Birth Control and Abortion in Jewish Law* (New York 1974).

Feldman, L. H., "Josephus' Portrait of Deborah," *Hellenica et Judaica: Hommage à Valentin Nikiprowetzky*, edd. A. Caquot, M. Hadas-Lebel and J. Riand (Paris 1986), 115–28.

Field, Faye, *Women Who Encountered Jesus* (Nashville 1982).

Figueras, P., *Decorated Jewish Ossuaries* (Leiden 1983).

Fink, Greta, *Great Jewish Women: Profiles of Courageous Women from the Maccabean Period to the Present* (New York 1978).

Finkelstein, L., *Akiba: Scholar, Saint and Martyr* (New York 1936).

Fitzmayer, J. A., "Divorce among First Century Palestinian Jews," *Eretz-Israel* 14 (1978), *103–*10.

Flesher, P. V. M., *Oxen, Women or Citizens? Slaves in the System of the Mishnah = Brown Judaic Studies* CXLIII (Atlanta 1988).

– "Are Women Property in the System of the Mishnah?" in *From Ancient Israel to Modern Judaism: Intellect in Quest of Understanding: Essays in Honor of Marvin Fox* I = *Brown Judaic Studies* CLIX, edd. J. Neusner, E. Frerichs and N. S. Sarna (Atlanta 1989), 219–31.

Flusser D., rev. of Grintz, *Sefer Yehudith* in *Kirjath Sepher* 33 (1958), 273–4 [Hebrew].

Ford, Josephine M., "Levirate Marriage in St. Paul (*1 Cor.* VII)," *New Testament Studies* 10 (1963–4), 361–5.

Fraenkel, Y., "Paranomasia in *Aggadic* Narratives," *Studies in Hebrew Narrative Art = Scripta Hiersolymitana* 27, edd. J. Heinemann and S. Werses (Jerusalem 1978), 28–35.

Frankel, Z., "Zur Geschichte der jüdischen Religionsgespräche," *Monatsschrift für Geschichte und Wissenschaft des Judentums* 4 (1855), 161–81.

Friedmann, M., "Mitwirkung von Frauen beim Gottesdienste," *Hebrew Union College Annual* 8–9 (1931–2), 511–23.

Friedman, M. A., *Jewish Marriage in Palestine* (Tel Aviv 1979).

– *Jewish Polygyny in the Middle Ages* (Tel Aviv 1986), [Hebrew].

Friedman, T., "The Shifting Role of Women From Bible to Talmud," *Judaism* 36 (1987), 479–87.

Fuks, A., "Markus Julius Alexander: On the History of the Family of Philo the Alexandrian," *Zion* 13–4 (1948–9), 10–7 [Hebrew].

Gafni, I. M., "The Conversion of the Adiabene Kings in the Light of Talmudic Literature," *Niv Hamidrashia* (Tel Aviv 1971), 208–9 [Hebrew].

– "The Institution of Marriage in Rabbinic Times," in *The Jewish Family: Metaphor and Memory*, ed. D. Kraemer (Oxford 1989), 13–29.

Gaster, M., The *Exampla of the Rabbis* (New York 1924).

Gazov-Ginzburg, A. M., "Double Meaning in a Qumran Work (The Wiles of a Wicked Woman)," *Revue de Qumrân* 6 (1967), 279–85.

Geller, M. J., "New Sources for the Origins of the Rabbinic Ketubah," *Hebrew Union College Annual* 49 (1978), 227–45.

Gera, D., "The Reliability of the Tobiad History," in *Greece and Rome in Eretz-Israel*, edd. A. Kasher, G. Fuks and U. Rappaport (Jerusalem 1989), 68–84.

Gershonzon, Rosalie and E. Slomovic, "A Second Century Jewish-Gnostic Debate: Rabbi Jose ben Halafta and the Matrona," *Journal for the Study of Judaism* 16 (1985), 1–41.

Gilat, Y., "'If you are taken captive, I will ransom you and take you back as my wife'," *Bar-Ilan* 13 (1976), 58–72 [Hebrew].

Golden, M., "Demography and the Exposure of Girls at Athens," *Phoenix* 35 (1981), 316–31.

Goldfeld, Ann, "Women as Sources of *Torah* in the Rabbinic Tradition," in *The Jewish Woman: New Perspectives*, ed. Elizabeth Koltun (New York 1976), 257–71.

Goldin, J., "Toward a Profile of the *Tanna* Aqiba ben Joseph," *Journal of the American Oriental Society* 96 (1976), 38–56.

– "The First Pair (Yose ben Yoezer and Yose ben Yohanan) or the House of the Pharisee," *Association of Jewish Studies Review* 5 (1980), 41–62.

Gomme, A. W., "The Position of Women in Athens in the Fifth and Fourth Centuries," *Classical Philology* 20 (1925), 1–25.

Goodblatt, D., "The Beruriah Traditions," *Journal of Jewish Studies* 26 (1975), 68–85.

Goren, S., "Women in Positive Commandments Dependent upon Time," *Mahanaim* 98 (1965), 10–6 [Hebrew].

Goshen-Gottstein, A., "The Tzitzit Commandment, the Harlot and the Homily," *Rabbinic Thought: Proceedings of the First Conference,* edd. M. Hirshman and T. Gronner (Haifa 1989), 45–58 [Hebrew].

Greenberg, Blu, "Will There be Orthodox Women Rabbis?" *Judaism* 33 (1984), 23–33.

– "Female Sexuality and Bodily Functions in the Jewish Tradition," in *Women, Religion and Sexuality,* ed. Jeanne Becher (Philadelphia 1990), 1–44.

Grossman, Susan, "Women and the Jerusalem Temple," in Susan Grossman and Rivka Haut, edd., *Daughters of the King: Women in the Synagogue* (New York 1992) 15–36.

Gulak, A., "Deed of Betrothal and Oral Stipulations in *Talmudic* Law," *Tarbiz* 3 (1932), 361–76 [Hebrew].

Guttentag, Marcia and P. F. Secord, *Too Many Women? The Sex Ratio Question* (Beverly Hills 1985).

Guttmann, J. M., "Acquisition of Women According to the Bible and *Talmud,*" *Yediot ha-Machon le-Madaei Yahaduth* 1 (1925), 25–39 [Hebrew].

Haas, N., "Anthropological Observations on the Skeletal Remains from Givat Hamivtar," *Israel Exploration Journal* 20 (1970), 38–59.

Haas, P. J., ed., *Recovering the Role of Women: Power and Authority in Rabbinic Jewish Society* (Atlanta 1992).

Hachlili, Rachel, "The Goliath Family in Jericho: Funerary Inscriptions from a First Century A.D. Jewish Monumental Tomb," *Bulletin of the American Schools for Oriental Research* 235 (1979), 31–65.

Halevi, A. A., *The World of the Aggadah* (Tel Aviv 1972) [Hebrew].

Hallet, Judith P., *Fathers and Daughters in Roman Society: Women and the Elite Family* (Princeton 1984).

Harnack, A. von –, *The Mission and Expansion of Christianity in the First Three Centuries* (New York 1908).

Harvey, Z. W., "The Pupil, the Harlot and the Fringe Benefits," *Prooftexts* 6 (1983), 259–64.

Hauptman, Judith, "Women's Liberation in the *Talmudic* Period: An Assessment," *Conservative Judaism* 26/4 (1971–2), 22–8.

– "Images of Women in the *Talmud,*" in *Religion and Sexism: Images of Women in the Jewish and Christian Traditions,* ed. Rosemary R. Ruether (New York 1974), 184–212.

Hecker, A., *A Short History of Women's Rights* (New York 1914).

Hengel, M., "Maria Magdalena und die Frauen als Zeugen," *Abraham Unser Vater: Festschrift für Otto Michel = Arbeiten zur Geschichte des Spätjudentums und Urchristentums* (Leiden 1963), 243–56.

– *Rabbinische Legende und frühpharisäische Geschichte: Schimeon b. Schetach und die achtzig Hexen von Askalon = Abhandlung der Heidelberger Akkademie der Wissenschaft philosophisch-historische Klasse* (Heidelberg 1984).

Henry, Sondra and Emily Taitz, *Written Out of History: Our Jewish Foremothers* (Fresh Meadows NY 1983).

Herr, M. D., "The Historical Significance of the Dialogues between Jewish Sages and Roman Dignitaries," in *Studies in Aggadah and Folk-Literature = Scripta Hierosolymitana* XXII, edd. D. Noy and J. Heinemann (Jerusalem 1971), 123–50.

– "The Socio-Economic Status of Marriage According to the *Halakhah,*" *The Families of the House of Israel = Proceedings of the Conference on Jewish Thought* XVIII (Jerusalem 1984), 37–46 [Hebrew].

Heschel, Susannah, "Anti-Judaism in Christian Feminist Theology," *Tikkun* 5/3 (1990), 25–8, 92–5.

Hirschfeld, Y., *Dwelling Houses in Roman and Byzantine Palestine* (Jerusalem 1987) [Hebrew].

Hitzig, F., *Geschichte des Volkes Israel* II (Leipzig 1869).

Holst, R., "The One Anointing of Jesus: Another Application of the Form-Critical Method," *Journal of Biblical Literature* 95 (1976), 435–46.

Hooker, M. D., "Authority on her Head: Examination of *1 Cor.* XI 10," *New Testament Studies* 10 (1963–4), 410–6.

Hopkins, K. M., "The Age of Roman Girls at Marriage," *Population Studies* 18 (1964–5) 309–27.

– "Contraception in the Roman Empire," *Comparative Studies in Society and History* 8 (1965) 124–51.

– "Brother-Sister Marriage in Roman Egypt," *Comparative Studies in Society and History* 22 (1980), 303–54.

Horsely, H. R., *New Documents Illustrating Early Christianity 1979* (Alexandra Australia 1987).

Horst, P. W. van der, "Images of Women in the *Testament of Job*," in *Studies on the Testament of Job*, edd. A. Knibb and P. W. van der Horst (Cambridge 1989), 93–116.

– "Portraits of Biblical Women in Pseudo-Philo's *Liber Antiquitatum*," *Journal for the Study of the Pseudepigrapha* 5 (1989), 29–46.

– "Seven Months Children in Jewish and Christian Literature from Antiquity," *Essays on the Jewish World of Early Christianity = NOTA* XIV(Göttingen 1990), 233–47.

Hübner, H., "Zölibat in Qumran?" *New Testament Studies* 17 (1970), 153–67.

Hurwitz, S. Y., "R. Eliezer ben Hyrcanus and the Education of Women," *Hashahar* 11 (1884), 437–41 [Hebrew].

– "Maimonides and the Laws of Matrimony in Israel," *Hashahar* 11 (1884), 659–66; 12 (1885), 577–80 [Hebrew].

– "R. Aqiba and the Laws of Matrimony in Israel," *Hashahar* 12 (1885), 377–84, 423–33 [Hebrew].

– *The Hebrew Woman and the Jewess: The Status and Condition of Women in Israel in Family and Society during the Biblical and Talmudic Periods* (Berdichev 1891) [Hebrew].

Hutton, R. R., "Cush the Benjaminite and *Psalm Midrash*," *Hebrew Annual Review* 10 (1986), 127–30.

Hyman, A., *Biographies of Tannaim and Amoraim* (London 1910).

Hyman, Paula E., "The Other Half: Women in the Jewish Tradition," *Conservative Judaism* 26/4 (1972), 14–21.

Ide, A. F., *The Teachings of Jesus on Women* (Dallas 1984).

Ilan, Tal, "The Names of the Hasmoneans in the Second Temple Period," *Eretz-Israel* 19 (1987), 238–41 [Hebrew].

– "Notes on the Distribution of Women's Names in Palestine in the Second Temple and Mishnaic Period," *Journal of Jewish Studies* 40 (1989), 186–200.

– "'Man Born of Woman ...' (*Job* 14.1): The Phenomenon of Men Bearing Metronymes at the Time of Jesus," *Novum Testamentum* 34 (1992), 23–45.

– "Julia Crispina, Daughter of Berenicianus, A Herodian Princess in the Babatha Archive: A Case Study in Historical Identification," *Jewish Quarterly Review* 82 (1992), 361–81.

– "New Ossuary Inscriptions from Jerusalem," *Scripta Classica Israelica* 11 (1992), 149–59.

– "Queen Salamzion Alexandra and Judas Aristobulus I's Wife: Did Jannaeus Alexander Contract Levirate Marriage?" *Journal for the Study of Judaism* 24 (1993), 181–90.

– "Premarital Cohabitation in Ancient Judea: The Evidence of the Babatha Archive and the *Mishnah*," *Harvard Theological Review* 86 (1993), 247–64.

Isaksson, A., *Marriage and Ministry in the New Temple: A Study with Special References to Mt. 19:13–22 and 1Cor. 11:3–16. = Acta Seminarii Neotestamentica Upsaliensis* XXIV (Lund 1965).

Izraeli, Dafna, "Status of Women in Israel," *Encyclopedia Judaica Yearbook* (Jerusalem 1986–7), 37–52.

Jastrow, M., *Dictionary of the Targumim, the Talmud Babli and Yerushalmi and the Midrashic Literature* (New York 1950).

Jeremias, J., *Jerusalem zur Zeit Jesu* (Leipzig 1923) = *Jerusalem in the Time of Jesus* (Philadelphia 1969).

Jochnowitz, G., "...Who Made Me a Women," *Commentary* 71/4 (1981), 63–4.

Jordan, Ruth, *Berenice* (London 1974).

Jost, I. M., *Geschichte der Israeliten* I (Berlin 1820).

Kagan, Zipporah, "The Loyal Wife in the Folkloristic Story," *Mahanaim* 98 (1965), 132–43 [Hebrew].

Kahana, A., *The External Books of the Bible* (Jerusalem 1947) [Hebrew].

Kartanger, M., "Spuren und Reste des Matriarchats in Judentum," *Zeitschrift für Religions- und Geistesgeschichte* 29 (1977), 134–51.

Katz, J., *Halakah and Kabbalah Studies in the History of Jewish Religion, its Various Faces and Social Relevance* (Jerusalem 1984), 127–30 [Hebrew].

Katzoff, R., "*P. Yadin* 19: A Gift after Death from the Judaean Desert," *Proceedings of the Tenth World Congress of Jewish Studies* Div. C/1 (Jerusalem 1990), 1–8 [Hebrew].

Kayserling, M., *Die jüdischen Frauen in der Geschichte, Literatur und Kunst* (Leipzig 1879).

Kee, H. C., "The Socio-Religious Setting and Aims of *Joseph and Asenath*," *Society of Biblical Literature Seminar Papers* 10 (1976), 183–92.

Keuls, Eva C., *The Reign of the Phallus: Sexual Politics in Ancient Athens* (New York 1985).

Kittel, G., "Das Konnubium mit den Nicht-Juden im antiken Judentum," *Forschung zur Judenfrage* 2 (1937), 30–62.

Klausner, J., "Judah Aristobulus and Jannaeus Alexander," *The World History of the Jewish People* VI = *The Hellenistic Age*, ed. A. Schalit (New Brunswick NJ 1972), 222–41.

Klein, Birgit, *Die Stellung der Frau in Judentum: Rabbinische Initiative oder Legitimation? Demonstriert am Beispiel des jüdischen Vormundschaftrechts* (MA thesis, Hochschule für jüdische Studien, Heidelberg 1991).

Klein, S., "Hebräische Ortsnamen bei Josephus," *Monatsschrift für Geschichte und Wissenschaft des Judentums* 59 (1915), 156–69.

Kloner, A., "A Burial-Cave of the Second Temple Period at Giv'at Hamivtar, Jerusalem," in *Jerusalem in the Second Temple Period: Abraham Schalit Memorial Volume*, edd. A. Oppenheimer, U. Rappaport and M. Stern (Jerusalem 1980), 198–211 [Hebrew].

Kochavi, M., "The Burial Caves of Ramat Rahel 1962 Season," in *Excavations at Ramat Rahel Seasons 1961 and 1962*, ed. Y. Aharoni (Rome 1963), 65–83.

Kohut, A., *Aruch Completum* (Berlin 1926) [Hebrew].

Kokkinos, N., "Which Salome did Aristobulus Marry?" *Palestine Exploration Quarterly* 118 (1986), 33–50.

Koltun Elizabeth, ed. *The Jewish Woman* (New York 1976).

Kraemer, D., "Images of Childhood and Adolescence in *Talmudic* Literature," in *The Jewish Family: Metaphor and Memory*, ed. D. Kraemer (Oxford 1989), 65–80.

Kraemer, Ross S., "The Conversion of Women to Ascetic Forms of Christianity," *Signs: Journal of Women in Culture and Society* 6 (1980), 298–307.

– Review of Elisabeth Schüssler-Fiorenza, *In Memory of Her: A Feminist Theological Reconstruction of Christian Origins* (New York 1983), *Religious Studies Review* 11 (1985), 6–9.

– "Hellenistic Jewish Women: the Epigraphical Evidence," *Society of Biblical Literature Seminar Papers* 25 (1986), 183–200.

- "Non-Literary Evidence for Jewish Women in Rome and Egypt," *Helios* 13 (1987), 85–101.
- "Monastic Jewish Women in Greco-Roman Egypt: Philo Judaeos on the Therapeutrides," *Signs: Journal of Women in Culture and Society* 14 (1989), 342–59.
- On the Meaning of the Term 'Jew' in Greco-Roman Inscriptions," *Harvard Theological Review* 82 (1989), 35–53.
- *Her Share of the Blessings: Women's Religion among the Pagans, Jews and Christians in the Greco-Roman World* (Oxford 1992).

Krauss, S., "Die Ehe zwischen Onkel und Nichte," *Studies in Jewish Literature Issued in Honor of Prof. Kaufman Kohler* (Berlin 1913), 165–75.
- "The Jewish Rite of Covering the Head," *Hebrew Union College Annual* 19 (1945–6), 154–62.

Lacks, Roslyn, *Women and Judaism: Myth, History and Struggle* (New York 1980).

Lauterbach, J. Z., "Responsum on Question, Shall Women be Ordained Rabbis?" *Central Conference of American Rabbis Year Book* 32 (1922), 156–62.

Leipoldt, J., *Jesu Verhältnis zu Griechen und Juden* (Leipzig 1941).

Lerner, M. B., "Inquiries into the Meaning of Various Titles and Designations: 1. Abba," *Studies in Judaica = Teuda* IV, ed. M. A. Friedman and M. Gil (Tel Aviv 1986), 93–113 [Hebrew].

Levine, I. L., "The Zealots at the End of the Second Temple Period as a Historiographical Problem," *Cathedra* 6 (1976), 39–48 [Hebrew].
- "The Political Struggle between Pharisees and Sadducees in the Hasmonean Period," in *Jerusalem in the Second Temple Period: Abraham Schalit Memorial Volume*, edd. A. Oppenheimer, U. Rappaport and M. Stern (Jerusalem 1980), 70–7 [Hebrew].

Levy, J., *Wörterbuch über die Talmudim und Midraschim* III (Berlin 1924).

Levy, Y., "When a Woman Emits Semen," *Koroth* 5 (1970–2), 716–7. [Hebrew].

Lewis, N., *The Documents from the Bar Kokhba Period from the Cave of Letters II: Greek Papyri* (Jerusalem 1989).
- with R. Katzoff and J. C. Greenfield, *"Papyrus Yadin 18,"* *Israel Exploration Journal* 37 (1987), 229–250.

Licht, C., *Ten Legends of the Sages in Rabbinic Literature* (Hoboken, NJ 1991).

Licht, J., "The Wiles of the Wicked Woman," in *Bible and Jewish History: Studies in Bible and Jewish History Dedicated to the Memory of Jacob Liver*, ed. B. Uffenheimer (Tel Aviv 1971), 289–96 [Hebrew].
- "The Book of *Judith* as a Work of Literature," in *Baruch Kurzweil Memorial Volume* edd. M. Z. Kaddari, A. Saltman and M. Schwarcz (Ramat Gan 1975), 169–83 [Hebrew].

Lieberman, S., *Greek in Jewish Palestine* (New York 1942).
- "Quotations in Light of Their Sources," in *Studies in Memory of Moses Shorr*, edd. L. Ginzberg and A Weiss (New York 1944), 183–8 [Hebrew].
- *Tosefta kifeshuta* (New York 1955–88).

Lillie, W., "Salome or Herodias?" *Expository Times* 65 (1953–4), 251.

Loewe, R., *The Position of Jewish Women in Judaism* (London 1966).

Lowy, S., "The Extent of Jewish Polygamy in *Talmudic* Times," *Journal of Jewish Studies* 9 (1958), 115–38.

MacArthur, H. K., "Jesus Son of Mary," *Novum Testamentum* 15 (1973), 38–58.
- "Celibacy in Judaism at the Time of Christian Beginnings," *Andrews University Seminary Studies* 25 (1987), 163–81.

McCaul, A., The *Old Paths* (London 1837).

Mace, D., *The Hebrew Marriage: A Sociological Study* (New York 1953).

Mach, M., "Are There Jewish Elements in the Protoevangelium Jacobi?" *Proceedings of the Ninth World Congress of Jewish Studies*, Div. A (Jerusalem 1986), 215–22.

McKeating, H., "Jesus ben Sira's Attitude to Women," *Expository Times* 85 (1973–4), 85–7.

MacNamara, Jo Ann, "Sexual Equality and the Cult of Virginity in Early Christian Thought," *Feminist Studies* 3 (1976), 145–58.

– "Wives and Widows in Early Christian Thought," *International Journal of Women's Studies* 2 (1979), 575–92.

Macurdy, Grace H., *Hellenistic Queens* (Baltimore 1932).

– "Iotape," *Journal of Roman Studies* 26 (1936), 40–2.

– *Vassal-Queens and Some Contemporary Women in the Roman Empire* (Baltimore 1937).

Marcus, R., *Josephus with an English Translation* = *Loeb Classical Library* (Cambridge MA 1958).

Margulies, A., *The Wicked in the Bible Who are Righteous in Talmud and Midrash* (London 1949) [Hebrew].

Massey, Lesley F., *Women and the New Testament* (Jefferson, NC 1989).

Mayer, G., *Die jüdische Frau in der hellenistisch-römischen Antike* (Stuttgart 1987).

Meachem, Tirzah Z., *Mishnah Tractate Niddah with Introduction: A Critical Edition with Notes on Variants, Commentary, Redaction and Chapters in Legal History and Realia* (Ph.D. diss. The Hebrew University of Jerusalem, 1989) [Hebrew].

Meeks, W., "The Image of the Androgyne: Some Uses of a Symbol in Earliest Christianity," *History of Religions* 13 (1973–4), 165–208.

Meir, Ofra, "The Wedding in Kings' Parables (in the *Aggadah*)," *Studies in Marriage Customs* = *Folklore Research Center Studies* IV, edd. D. Noy and I. Ben-Ami (Jerusalem 1974) 9–52 (Hebrew).

– "The Story as a Hermeneutic Device," *Association of Jewish Studies Review* 7–8 (1982–3), 243–56.

Meiselman, M., *Jewish Women in Jewish Law* (New York 1978).

Merino, J. Luis Diez, "'Maria' en la onomastica Aramea Judia intertestamental (s. II a.C. - s. II d.C.)," *Scripta de Maria* 6 (1983), 29–37.

Miller, S., *Studies in the History and Traditions of Sepphoris* (Leiden 1984).

Milik, J. T., "Le travail d'édition des manuscrits du Désert de Juda," *Volume du congres Strasbourg 1956* = *Supplements to Vetus Testamentum* IV (Leiden 1956), 17–26.

Millhaven, Anni L., *13 Valiant Women Challenging the Church* (Mystic CT 1987).

Modersohn, E., *Die Frauen des Neuen Testaments* (Stuttgart 1982).

Moltmann-Wendel, Elisabeth, *The Women Around Jesus* (New York 1982).

Monceaux, P., "Épigraphique chrétienne d'Afrique," *Revue Archeologique* 4/3 (1904).

Moore, R. D., "Personification of the Seduction of Evil: *The Wiles of the Wicked Woman*," *Revue de Qumrân* 10 (1981), 505–19.

Naveh, J., "The Ossuary Inscriptions from Giv'at ha-Mivtar," *Israel Exploration Journal* 20 (1970) 33–7.

– *On Mosaic and Stone: Aramaic and Hebrew Inscriptions from Ancient Synagogues* (Jerusalem 1978) [Hebrew].

– with S. Shaked, *Amulets and Magic Bowls: Aramaic Incantations in Late Antiquity* (Jerusalem 1987).

Neeman, P., "Inheritance of the Daughter in *Torah* and *Halakhah*," *Bet Miqra* 47 (1971), 476–89 [Hebrew].

Negev, A., "Inscriptions Hébraiques, Grecques et Latines de Césarée Maritime," *Revue Biblique* 78 (1971), 247–63.

Neuberger, Julia, "Women in Judaism: The Fact and the Fiction," in *Women's Religious Experience: Cross-Cultural Perspectives*, ed. Pat Holden (London 1983), 132–42.

Neuman, E., *The Great Mother* (Princeton 1955).

Neusner, J., *A History of the Mishnaic Law of Women* V (Leiden 1980).

Ortner, Sherry B., "Is Female to Male as Nature is to Culture?" in *Women, Culture and Society*, edd. Michelle Z. Rosaldo and Louise Lamphere (Stanford CA 1974), 67–87.

Pagels, Elaine H., "Paul and Women: A Response to a Recent Discussion," *Journal of the American Academy of Religion* 42 (1974), 538–49.

Parvey, Constance, "The Theology and Leadership of Women in the New Testament," in *Religion and Sexism: Images of Women in the Jewish and Christian Traditions*, ed. Rosemary R. Ruether (New York 1974), 117–49.

Patai, R., *The Hebrew Goddess* (New York 1967).

– "*Jus Primae Noctis*," in *Studies in Marriage Customs = Folklore Research Center Studies* IV, edd. I. Ben-Ami and D. Noy (Jerusalem 1974), 177–80.

Pervo, R. I., "*Joseph and Asenath* and the Greek Novel," *Society of Biblical Literature Seminar Papers* 10 (1976), 171–81.

Peuch, E. "Inscriptions funéraires Palestiniennes: tombeau de Jason et ossuaires," *Revue Biblique* 90 (1983), 481–533.

Phipps, W. E., *Was Jesus Married?* (New York 1970).

– "Is Paul's Attitude toward Sexual Relations Contained in *1 Cor.* 7.1?" *New Testament Studies* 28 (1982), 125–31.

Piatteli, Daniella, "The Marriage Contract and Bill of Divorce in Ancient Hebrew Law," *Jewish Law Annual* 4 (1981), 66–78.

Plaskow, Judith, "Blaming the Jews for Inventing Patriarchy," *Lilith* 7 (1980), 11–2.

– *Standing Again at Sinai: Judaism from a Feminist Perspective* (San Francisco 1990).

Polotzki, Y., "The Greek Documents from the 'Cave of the Letters'," *Bulletin of the Israel Exploration Society* 26 (1962), 237–41[Hebrew].

Pomeroy, Sarah B., *Goddesses, Whores, Wives and Slaves: Women in Classical Antiquity* (New York 1975).

– "τεχνιχαὶ χαὶ μουσιχαί: The Education of Women in the Fourth Century and the Hellenistic Period," *American Journal of Ancient History* 2 (1977), 51–68.

– *Women in Hellenistic Egypt from Alexander to Cleopatra* (New York 1984).

– "Infanticide in Hellenistic Greece," in *Images of Women in Antiquity*, edd. Averil Cameron and Amélie Kuhrt (Detroit 1985), 207–22.

Portefaix, Lilian, *Sisters Rejoice: Paul's Letter to the Philippians and Luke-Acts as Seen by First Century Philippian Women = Coniectanea Biblica: New Testament Series* XX (Stockholm 1988).

Preuss, J., *Biblische und Talmudische Medizin* (Berlin 1911), =*Biblical and Talmudic Medicine*, translation F. Rosner (New York 1978).

Prusak, B., "Women, Seductive Siren and Source of Sin? *Pseudepigraphical* Myth and Christian Origin," in *Religion and Sexism: Images of Women in the Jewish and Christian Traditions*, ed. Rosemary R. Ruether, (New York 1974), 89–116.

Quere, France, *Les Femmes de l' Evangile* (Paris 1982).

Rabello, A. M., "*Hausgericht* in the House of Herod the Great?" in *Jerusalem in the Second Temple Period: Abraham Schalit Memorial Volume*, edd. A. Oppenheimer, U. Rappaport and M. Stern (Jerusalem 1980), 119–35 [Hebrew].

– "Divorce of Jews in the Roman Empire," *The Jewish Law Annual* 4 (1981), 79–102.

Rahamani, L. Y., "Jewish Rock-Cut Tombs in Jerusalem," *Atiqot* 3 (1961), 93–120.

– *The Decoration on the Jewish Ossuaries as Representations of Jerusalem Tombs* (Ph.D. Dissertation, Jerusalem 1977).

Reifenberg, A., *Ancient Hebrew Arts* (New York 1950).

Reinach, T., "Le mari de Salomé et les monnaies de Nicopolis d'Arménie," *Revue Études Ancien* 16 (1914), 133–57.

Reines, C. W., "'King and not Queen'," *Sinai* 67 (1970), 327–8 [Hebrew].

– "Beauty in the Bible and the Talmud," *Judaism* 24 (1974), 100–7.

Reinhartz, Adele., "From Narrative to History: The Resurrection of Mary and Martha," in *'Women Like This': New Perspectives on Jewish Women in the Greco-Roman World,* ed. Amy-Jill Levine (Atlanta 1991), 161–84.

Remy (Lazarus), Nahida (Ruth), *Das jüdische Weib* (Leipzig 1885) = *The Jewish Woman* (Cincinnati 1897).

Renan, E., *Histoire du peuple d'Israël* V (Paris 1893).

Richardson, H. N., "Some Notes on *1QSa*," *Journal of Biblical Literature* 76 (1957), 108–22.

Roth-Gerson, Leah, *The Greek Inscriptions from the Synagogues in Eretz Israel* (Jerusalem 1987) [Hebrew].

Ruether, Rosemary R., ed. *Religion and Sexism: Images of Women in the Jewish and Christian Traditions* (New York 1974).

Ryder-Smith, C., *The Biblical Doctrine of Womanhood in its Historical Evolution* (London 1923).

Safrai, Hannah, "Women and the Ancient Synagogue," in *Daughters of the King: Women in the Synagogue*, edd. Susan Grossman and Rivka Haut (New York 1992), 39–49.

Safrai, S., "Was there a Women's Gallery in the Synagogue of Antiquity?" *Tarbiz* 32 (1963), 329–38 [Hebrew].

– "Women Learned in *Torah* in the *Mishnaic* and *Talmudic* Period," *Mahanaim* 98 (1965), 58–9 [Hebrew].

– "Tales of the Sages in the Palestinian Tradition and the *Babylonian Talmud*," in *Studies in Aggadah and Folk-Literature* = *Scripta Hierosolymitana* XXII, edd. J. Heinemann and D. Noy (Jerusalem 1971), 209–32.

– "Education and the Study of *Torah*," in *The Jewish People in the First Century* II = *Compendia Rerum Iudaicarum ad Novum Testamentum Section One,* edd. S. Safrai and M. Stern (Assen 1976), 945–70.

– "Home and Family," in *The Jewish People in the First Century* II = *Compendia Rerum Iudaicarum ad Novum Testamentum Section One*, edd. S. Safrai and M. Stern (Assen 1976), 728–92.

Saldarini, A. J., *The Fathers According to Rabbi Nathan B* (Leiden 1975).

Saller, R. P., "Men's Age at Marriage and its Consequences in the Roman Family," *Classical Philology* 82 (1987) 21–34.

Sancini-Weerdenburg, Heleen, "Exit Atossa: Images of Women in Greek Historiography on Persia," in *Images of Women in Antiquity*, edd. Averil Cameron and Amélie Kuhrt (Detroit 1985), 20–33.

Sanders, E. P., *Judaism: Practice and Belief: 63 BCE-66 CE* (Philadelphia 1992).

Schaberg, Jane, *The Illegitimacy of Jesus: A Feminist Theological Interpretation* (New York 1990).

Schalit, A., "The Date and Place of the Story about the Three Bodyguards of the King in the *Apocryphal Book of Ezra*," *Bulletin of the Israel Exploration Society* 13 (1947), 119–28 [Hebrew].

– *König Herodes: Der Mann und sein Werk* (Berlin 1969).

– "Evidence of an Aramaic Source in Josephus' *Antiquities of the Jews*," *Annual of the Swedish Theological institute* 4 (1975), 171–81.

Schechter, S., "Women in Temple and Synagogue," *Studies in Judaism: First Series* (Philadelphia 1915), 313–25.

Schiffman, L. H., *The Halakhah at Qumran* (Leiden 1975).

– *Sectarian Law in the Dead Sea Scrolls: Courts, Testimony and the Penal Code* = *Brown Judaic Studies* XXXIII (Chico, CA 1983).

– "The Conversion of the Royal House of Adiabene in Josephus and Rabbinic Sources," in *Josephus, Judaism and Christianity*, edd. L. H. Feldman and G. Hata (Detroit 1987), 293–312.

– "Laws Pertaining to Women in the Temple Scroll," in *The Dead Sea Scrolls: Forty Years of Research* , edd. Devorah Dimant and U. Rappaport (Leiden 1992), 210–28.

Schottroff, Luise, "Women as Followers of Jesus in New Testament Times: Exercise in Socio-Historical Exegesis of the Bible," in *The Bible and Liberation, Political and Social Hermeneutics*, ed. N. K. Gottwald (Maryknoll NY 1983), 418–27.

Schuller, Eileen, "Women of the Exodus in Biblical Retelling in the Second Temple," in *Gender and Difference in Israel*, ed. Peggy L. Day (Minneapolis 1989), 178–94.

Schüssler-Fiorenza, Elisabeth, *In Memory of Her: A Feminist Theological Reconstruction of Christian Origins* (New York 1983).

– "A Feminist Critical Interpretation for Liberation: Martha and Mary: *Luke* 10:38–42," *Religion and Intellectual Life* 3 (1985), 21–36.

Schürer, E., *Geschichte des jüdischen Volkes im Zeitalter Jesu Christi* (Leipzig 1903).

Schwabe, M. "Notes on the Column Inscription from Ashkelon," *Tarbiz* 13 (1952), 66–7 [Hebrew].

– with B. Lifshitz, *Beth She'arim* II (Jerusalem 1974).

Schwartz, D. R., "KATA TOYTON TON KAIPON: Josephus' Source on Agrippa II," *Jewish Quarterly Review* 72 (1981–2), 241–68.

– *Agrippa I: The Last King of Judaea* (Tübingen 1990).

Schwarzbaum, H., "International Folklore Motifs in Joseph Ibn Zabara's 'Sepher Sha'shu'im'," in *Studies in Aggadah = Folklore Research Center Studies* VIII, edd. I. Ben-Ami and J. Dan (Jerusalem 1983), 55–80.

Schweizer, E., "Scheidungsrecht der jüdischen Frau? Weibliche Jünger Jesu?" *Evangelische Theologie* 42 (1982), 294–300.

Scroggs, R., "Paul and the Eschatological Woman," *Journal of the American Academy of Religion* 40 (1972), 283–303.

Segal, J. B., "The Jewish Attitude Towards Women," *Journal of Jewish Studies* 30 (1979), 121–37.

Segal, M. Z., "Notes on the History of the YHD sect (Based on *CD*)," *Tarbiz* 22 (1951), 136–52 [Hebrew].

– *The Complete Book of Ben Sira* (Jerusalem 1972) [Hebrew].

Seltman, C., *Women in Antiquity* (London 1956).

Selvidge, Marla L., *Daughters of Jerusalem* (Scottdale PA 1987).

Sergio, Lisa, *Jesus and Woman* (McLean, VA 1975).

Shalvi, Alice, "Introduction," *Encyclopedia Judaica Yearbook* (Jerusalem 1986–7), 12–5.

Shaw, B. D., "The Age of Roman Girls at Marriage," *Journal of Roman Studies* 77 (1987), 30–46.

Shenhar, Alisa, "On the Popularity of the Legend of Beruriah Wife of Rabbi Meir," in *Folklore Research Center Studies* III, ed. I. Ben-Ami (Jerusalem 1973), 223–7 [Hebrew].

Sievers, J., "The Role of Women in the Hasmonean Dynasty," *Josephus, the Bible and History*, edd. L.H. Feldman and G. Hata (Detroit 1989), 132–46.

Sigal, P., "Elements of Male Chauvinism in Classical *Halakhah*," *Judaism* 24 (1975), 226–44.

Sly, Dorothy, *Philo's Perception of Women = Brown Judaic Studies* CCIX (Atlanta 1990).

Smallwood, E. Mary, *The Jews Under Roman Rule: From Pompey to Diocletian: A Study in Political Relations* ² (Leiden 1981).

Smith, E. W. Jr., "Joseph Material in *Joseph and Asenath* and Josephus Relating to the *Testament of Joseph*," in *Studies on the Testament of Joseph = Society of Biblical Literature Septuagint and Cognate Studies* V, ed. G. W. Nickelsberg Jr., (Missoula, MO 1975), 133–7.

Smith, Patricia, "The Human Skeletal Remains from the Abba Cave," *Israel Exploration Journal* 27 (1977), 121–4.

– with Rachel Hachlili, "The Genealogy of the Goliath Family," *Bulletin of the American Schools for Oriental Research* 235 (1979), 67–70.

Speyr, Adrienne von-, *Three Women and the Lord* (San Francisco 1986).

Stagg, Evelyn and F. *Women in the World of Jesus* (Philadelphia 1978).

Stephens, Shirley, *A New Testament View of Women* (Nashville 1980).

Stendahl, K., *The Bible and the Role of Women* (Philadelphia 1966).

Stern, G., "Women in the Bible and the *Aggadah,*" *Hashiloah* 28 (1913), 51–7 [Hebrew].

Stern, M., "The Political Background of the Wars of Alexander Jannai," *Tarbiz* 33 (1964), 325–36 [Hebrew].

– "Aspects of Jewish Society: The Priesthood and Other Classes," in *The Jewish People in the First Century* II = *Compendia Rerum Iudaicarum ad Novum Testamentum Section One,* edd. S. Safrai and M. Stern (Assen 1976), 561–630.

– "Maccabees, Books of the *Maccabees,*" *Encyclopedia Biblica* V (Jerusalem 1978), 287–92 [Hebrew].

– *Greek and Latin Authors on Jews and Judaism* (Jerusalem 1976–84).

Sukenik, E. L., "An Ancient Jewish Cave Near the Highway Jerusalem-Nablus," *Bulletin of the Israel Exploration Society* 1 (1933–4), 7–9 [Hebrew].

– "Jewish Burial-Caves in the Vicinity of the Kidron Valley," *Kedem* 2 (1945), 23–31 [Hebrew].

Swidler, L. J., *Women in Judaism: The Status of Women in Formative Judaism* (Metuchen NJ 1976).

– "Beruriah: Her World Became Law," *Lilith* 3 (1977), 9–12.

– *Biblical Affirmations of Women* (Philadelphia 1979).

Tcherikover, V., "Palestine in Light of the Zenon Papyri," *Tarbiz* 4 (1933), 231–3; 238–41; *ibid.* 5 (1934), 42–3 [Hebrew].

– *Hellenistic Civilization and the Jews,* translation S. Applebaum (New York 1970).

Torrey, C. C., *The Apocryphal Literature* (New Haven 1945).

Trenchard, W. C., *Ben Sira's View on Women: A Literary Analysis = Brown Judaic Studies* XXXVIII (Chico CA 1982).

Urbach, E. E., "*Halakhot* Regarding Slavery as a Source for the Social History of the Second Temple and the *Talmudic* Period," *Zion* 25 (1960), 141–89 [Hebrew].

Valler, Shulamit, *Women and Womanhood in the Stories of the Babylonian Talmud* (Tel Aviv 1993) [Hebrew].

Vanderkam, J. C., ed., *'No One Spoke Ill of Her': Essays on Judith* (Atlanta 1992).

Vaux, R. de, J. T. Milik and P. Benoit, *Les grottes de Muraba'ât = Discoveries in the Judaean Desert* II: (Oxford 1961).

Vermes, G., "Sectarian Matrimonial *Halakhah* in the Damascus Role," *Journal of Jewish Studies* 25 (1974), 197–202.

Visotzky, B. L., "Most Tender and Fairest of Women: A Study in the Transmission of *Aggada,*" *Harvard Theological Review* 76 (1983), 403–18.

Wacholder, B. Z., *Nicolaus of Damascus = University of California Publications in History* LXXV (Berkeley and Los Angeles 1962).

Wahlberg, Rachel C., *Jesus and the Freed Woman* (New York 1978).

Walker, Susan, "Women and Housing in Classical Greece: The Archaeological Evidence," in *Images of Women in Antiquity,* edd. Averil Cameron and Amélie Kuhrt (Detroit 1985), 81–91.

Walker, W. O., "*1 Corinthians* 11:2–16 and Paul's View Regarding Women," *Journal of Biblical Literature* 94 (1975), 94–110.

Wasserstein, A., "A Marriage Contract from the Province of Arabia Nova: Notes on *Papyrus Yadin* 18," *Jewish Quarterly Review* 80 (1989–90), 105–30.

Watley W. D., and Suzan D. J. Cook, *Preaching in Two Voices: Sermons on the Women in Jesus' Life* (Valley Forge, PA 1992).

Weder, H., "Perspective der Frauen," *Evangelische Theologie* 43 (1983), 175–8.

Wegner, Judith R., "The Images of Women in Philo," *Society of Biblical Literature Seminar Papers* 16 (1982), 551–63.

– *Chattel or Person: The Status of Women in the Mishnah* (Oxford 1988).

– "Philo's Portrayal of Women: Hebraic or Hellenic?" in *'Women Like This': New Perspectives on Jewish Women in the Greco-Roman Period*, ed. Amy-Jill Levine (Atlanta 1991), 41–66.

Weiss, D. H., "The Use of קנה in Connection with Marriage," *Harvard Theological Review* 57 (1964), 244–8.

Weiss-Rosemarine, Trude, *Jewish Women Through the Ages* (New York 1940).

Weissman, Deborah R., "Education of Jewish Women," *Encyclopedia Judaica Yearbook* (Jerusalem 1986–7), 29–36.

Wellhausen, J., *Israelitische und jüdische Geschichte*[7] (Berlin 1914).

Wiedemann, T., *Greek and Roman Slavery* (Baltimore 1981).

Wire, Antoinette C., *The Corinthian Women Prophets: A Reconstruction through Paul's Rhetoric* (Minneapolis 1990).

Witherington B., III, "Rites and Rights for Women: *Galatians* 3.28," *New Testament Studies* 27 (1980–81), 599–600.

– *Women in the Ministry of Jesus* (Cambridge 1984).

– *Women in the Earliest Church* (Cambridge 1988).

Wolff, H. J., "Römisches Provinzialrecht in der Provinz Arabia (Rechtspolitik als Instrument der Beherschung)," *Aufstieg und Niedergang der Römische Welt* II.13 (Berlin 1980), 763–806.

Yadin, Y., "Expedition D," *Bulletin of the Israel Exploration Society* 25 (1961), 49–64 [Hebrew].

– "Expedition D: 'Cave of the Letters'," *Bulletin of the Israel Exploration Society* 26 (1962), 204–36 [Hebrew].

– *Bar Kokhba: Rediscovery of the Legendary Hero of the Second Jewish Revolt against Rome* (London 1971).

– "L'attitude Essénienne envers la polygamie et le divorce," *Revue Biblique* 79 (1972), 98–9.

– *The Temple Scroll* (Jerusalem 1983).

– with J. Naveh, *Masada I: The Aramaic and Hebrew Ostraca* (Jerusalem 1989).

Yaron, R., *Gifts in Contemplation of Death in Jewish and Roman Law* (Oxford 1960).

Zeitlin, S., "Queen Salome and King Jannaeus Alexander," *Jewish Quarterly Review* 51 (1960–1), 1–33.

Zimmerman, D., *Eight Love Stories from the Talmud* (Tel Aviv 1981) [Hebrew].

Zirndorf, H., *Some Jewish Women* (Philadelphia 1892).

Zucrow, S., *Women, Slaves and the Ignorant in Rabbinic Literature* (Boston 1932).

Zunz, Y. L., *Die gottesdienstlichen Vorträge der Juden* (Berlin 1832).

Zyl, A. H. van, *The Moabites.* = *Praetoria Oriental Series* III (Leiden 1960).

Index of Sources

Early Christian Sources

Proto-Evangelium Jacobi

Ignatius

Origen

Ad Africanus

Apocrypha and Pseudepigrapha

Index of Names

Index of Subjects